MW00808068

'Based on careful reading of a ɪ   ell
as many fascinating photograpɪ   ly
written biography of the psychiɑ   ne
life of a remarkable man. The stᴏ.., ...ᴄ.., ᴄ...ᴏᴄᴜᴜᴄᴜ ...ᴏ a ᴜᴜᴄᴜ...u..ɴg social,
political, medical, and cultural context, one that includes politics, war, religion,
and a psychoanalytic world that has been too-often forgotten. This biography will
be of interest to a wide range of readers, including medical historians, psychiatrists,
and anyone interested in one fascinating person's journey from pre-revolutionary
Russia to the twentieth-century United States.'
                    — *Joel Howell, MD, PhD, Elizabeth Farrand Professor of the History of*
                                        Medicine at the University of Michigan

'There are powerful myths about daughters in search of fathers. This biography
equals them. With lucidity, intensity, and vivid words the author Dr. Caroline
Zilboorg sets out, 60 years after his passing, to find and better know her father, the
psychoanalyst Dr. Gregory Zilboorg. Her search yields a generous gift to readers.
Gregory Zilboorg was an extraordinarily brilliant man with a personal history
extending from service in the ill-fated Menshevik government of revolutionary
Russia to an exceptional American career as a psychiatrist, medical historian, and
spellbinding public speaker. To tell his life is also to tell much of the history, not
without conflicts, of Freudian analysis in America. Caroline Zilboorg engages us
as her companions in a most fruitful search for identity.'
                    — *Roger Lipsey, author of* Make Peace Before the Sun Goes Down:
                        The Long Encounter of Thomas Merton and His Abbot, James Fox

'How does a poor Russian Jew become a revolutionary socialist, an orthodox
Freudian, and a devout Catholic, in that order? Read Caroline Zilboorg's
biography of her father Gregory and find out! In addition to providing illuminating
commentaries on the evolution of his work in the history of psychiatry, and the
social issues that animated Gregory Zilboorg as a public intellectual, Caroline
Zilboorg shows a keen and sensitive grasp of the vagaries of Jewish family life in
Czarist Russia, the vicissitudes and horrors of the Russian Revolution, the anguish
of immigrants adapting to America, and the sheer nastiness of psychoanalytic
politics. This is a searching, sympathetic, and richly embroidered biography
of a courageous, creative, generous, yet much-misunderstood man. It is "must
reading" for anyone interested in the history of psychiatry, psychoanalysis, and
the Jewish-American immigrant experience.'
                    — *Daniel Burston, Founding Scholar, British Psychoanalytic Council;*
                        author of Psychoanalysis, Politics and the Postmodern University *and*
                            The Wing of Madness: The Life and Work of R.D. Laing

The Life of Gregory Zilboorg, 1940–1959

The Life of Gregory Zilboorg, 1940–1959: Mind, Medicine, and Man is the second volume of a meticulously researched two-part biography of the Russian-American psychoanalyst Gregory Zilboorg and chronicles the impact of the Second World War on his work and thinking as well as his divorce, remarriage, and conversion to Catholicism.

With extensive references to Zilboorg's writing and politics, this book demonstrates the significance of his contributions to the fields of psychiatry and psychoanalysis in the context of his tumultuous intellectual, personal, and spiritual life. In his late work, he would argue, controversially, that there was no incompatibility between psychoanalysis and religion.

Grounded in a wealth of primary source material and impressive research, this book completes the compelling biography of a major figure in psychoanalysis. It will be of interest to general readers as well as scholars across a range of disciplines, particularly the history of psychoanalysis and religion.

Caroline Zilboorg is a life member of Clare Hall, Cambridge University, and a scholar of the British Psychoanalytic Council. Her books include *Richard Aldington and H.D.: Their Lives in Letters*, *The Masks of Mary Renault: A Literary Biography*, and the biographical novel *Transgressions*. She lives in Brittany, France, where she continues to write.

The History of Psychoanalysis Series

Series Editors

Professor Brett Kahr and Professor Peter L. Rudnytsky

This series seeks to present outstanding new books that illuminate any aspect of the history of psychoanalysis from its earliest days to the present, and to reintroduce classic texts to contemporary readers.

Other titles in the series:

For further information about this series please visit www.routledge.com/ The-History-of-Psychoanalysis-Series/book-series/KARNHIPSY

The Life of Gregory Zilboorg, 1940–1959

Mind, Medicine, and Man

Caroline Zilboorg

Routledge
Taylor & Francis Group

LONDON AND NEW YORK

First published 2022
by Routledge
2 Park Square, Milton Park, Abingdon, Oxon OX14 4RN

and by Routledge
605 Third Avenue, New York, NY 10158

Routledge is an imprint of the Taylor & Francis Group, an informa business

© 2022 Caroline Zilboorg

British Library Cataloguing-in-Publication Data
A catalogue record for this book is available from the British Library

Library of Congress Cataloging-in-Publication Data
A catalog record for this book has been requested

ISBN: 978-1-032-04215-2 (hbk)
ISBN: 978-1-032-04217-6 (pbk)
ISBN: 978-1-003-19097-4 (ebk)

DOI: 10.4324/9781003190974

Typeset in Times New Roman
by Apex CoVantage, LLC

To my seven granddaughters:

Adriana Stone Nevin and Alessandra Nevin,
Gita Lovisa Brunn and Elva Roswitha Brunn,
and
Leyla Nevin, Lily Nevin, and Thalia Nevin

Contents

Acknowledgements

All correspondence between Gregory Zilboorg and his brother James Zilboorg and between Gregory Zilboorg and Eugenia Zilboorg is in the James and Eugenia Zilboorg Papers (JEZB) at the Beinecke Rare Book and Manuscript Library at Yale University. I am grateful to the late Olga Zilboorg Irvine (daughter of James and Eugenia Zilboorg) and to Peggy Schaeffer (daughter of Natalie Zilboorg Fiess and granddaughter of James and Eugenia Zilboorg) for permission to quote from these and other letters by James Zilboorg.

All correspondence between Gregory Zilboorg and George W. Henry is in the Gregory Zilboorg Papers (GZB) at the Beinecke Rare Book and Manuscript Library at Yale University.

All correspondence between Gregory Zilboorg and Père Noël Mailloux as well as letters and documents related to their relationship and to Mailloux's efforts on behalf of Gregory Zilboorg's conversion are among Mailloux's papers in Les Archives Provinciales Dominicaines, Montréal, Québec, Canada (APD), and are quoted by permission of the archive.

Correspondence and other documents related to the Zilboorg family currently in Peggy Schaeffer's possession will in time be deposited in JEZB and GZB.

Correspondence between Gregory Zilboorg and James Fox and between Gregory Zilboorg and Thomas Merton is in The Thomas Merton Center, Bellarmine University, Louisville, Kentucky, unless otherwise noted; Fox's letters are quoted by permission of Father Elias Dietz, Abbot of Our Lady of Gethsemani, Bardstown, Kentucky. Quotations from unpublished letters from Thomas Merton (copyright 2020 by the Trustees of the Thomas Merton Legacy Trust) and from Merton's essay 'The Neurotic Personality in Monastic Life' (copyright 1991 by the Trustees of the Thomas Merton Legacy Trust) are used by permission of the Trustees.

All correspondence between Gregory Zilboorg and Henry Sigerist and members of the Sigerist family and between Margaret Stone Zilboorg and Henry Sigerist and his assistants can be found in Marcel H. Bickel's edition of *Correspondence: Henry E. Sigerist – Gregory Zilboorg, 1931–1956*. I am grateful to the late Marcel Bickel for permission to quote from Sigerist's letters.

Correspondence and documents not attributed to an archive are in my possession.

Arianne Dar's interview with Margaret Stone Zilboorg is quoted by permission of Arianne Dar. My interview with Anna Zilboorg is quoted with her permission.

M.L. Cohn's minutes, comprising 752 pages numbered sequentially, of the four special meetings of the New York Psychoanalytic Society's board of directors held at the New York Psychoanalytic Institute, between 31 October and 21 December 1941, and related documents are in the Archives and Special Collections of the New York Psychoanalytic Society and Institute and are quoted by permission of the New York Psychoanalytic Society and Institute.

I am grateful to Serena Martucci di Scarfizzi for translations from Italian, to John Zilboorg for translations from Spanish, and to Miranda Machado for translations from Portuguese. All translations from French are my own.

As my parents' executor I quote freely from their interviews, correspondence, and writings published and unpublished. I quote from correspondence with me by permission of the individual authors.

All images, unless otherwise noted, are from family files. Most of the photographs were taken by Gregory or Margaret Stone Zilboorg. Henry Sigerist's photographs are reproduced with Marcel Bickel's permission. The group photograph of the Saint John's 1954 summer session and the photograph of Gregory Zilboorg with Thomas Merton in 1956 are reproduced by permission of Saint John's University Archives, Collegeville, Minnesota.

The second volume of this biography has drawn on both general and specific histories and on archival sources. The enormous number of surviving photographs and letters – testament to social, professional, and intellectual life before the ephemera of email and the Internet – has been an invaluable help. I am grateful to my parents for having preserved so much material still in my possession and to the Beinecke Library for its stewardship of material already donated to them. Many documents I draw upon are, unless otherwise noted, still in my possession at the time of writing, but I intend in due course to deposit all of this material at the Beinecke.

The following institutions and librarians contributed to this volume in significant ways:

A.A. Brill Library, the New York Psychoanalytic Society and Institute, Archives and Special Collections (Nellie L. Thompson, Curator)

American Journal of Psychiatry (Michael D. Roy, Editorial Director)

Archival Sound Labs, Cutting Corporation (Aaron Coe, Sound engineer)

Archives of American Art, Smithsonian Institution (Erin Kinhart, Archivist)

Les Archives Provinciales Dominicaines, Montréal, Québec, Canada (Père Rodrigue Guilmette, O.P., Archivist, and Isabel Bigras, Secretary)

Avery Architectural & Fine Arts Library, Columbia University (Nicole Richard, Drawings and Archives Assistant)

Bancroft Library, Berkeley, California (Dean Smith)

Bedford Historical Society (Evelyn H. Ryan, Executive Director, and Christina Rae, Assistant to the Historian)

Beinecke Rare Book and Manuscript Library, Yale University (Moira Fitzgerald, Head of Access Services; Elizabeth Frengel, Research Services Librarian; Melissa Barton, Curator of Drama and Prose; and Nancy Kuhl, Curator of Poetry, Yale Collection of American Literature)

Biblioteca Apostolica Vaticana (Dr. Rita Andreina)

Bibliothèque Sigmund Freud, Paris (Cécile Marcoux)

Bodleian Library, Oxford University Archives (Alice Millea, Archivist)

Butler Hospital Library (Ruthann Gildea, Director, Library Services)

Catholic University Archives, Catholic University of America (Shane McDonald, Archivist)

College of Saint Benedict, Saint John's University Archives (Peggy Roske, Archivist, and Elizabeth Knuth, Assistant Archivist)

Fordham University, Walsh Library (Patrice M. Kane, Head of Archives and Special Collections)

Friends Academy, Locust Valley (Karl Hoenzsch, Archivist)

Harry Ransom Center, The University of Texas at Austin (Rick Watson)

Houghton Library, Harvard University (Emily Walhout, Archivist)

Howard Gotlieb Archival Research Center, Boston University (Laura Rosso, Archivist)

Karl Stern Archive, Simon Silverman Phenomenology Center, Duquesne University (Jeffrey McCurry, Director)

Library of Congress, Washington, D.C. (Jennifer Brathovde and Patrick Kerwin, Archivists)

Lloyd George Sealy Library, John Jay College of Criminal Justice, City University of New York (Ellen H. Belcher, Special Collections Librarian)

New York Academy of Medicine (Arlene Shaner, Historical Collections Librarian)

New York Public Library, Archives, Manuscripts, and Rare Books (Tal Nadan, Reference Archivist)

Oakwood Friends School (Matthew A. Voorhees and Wendy Giangrasso, Alumni Archivists)

Rhode Island School of Design Archives (Douglas Doe, Associate Archivist)

Rhode Island School of Design Museum (Jan Howard, Curator)

Saint John's Abbey Archives (Brother David Klingeman, Archivist)

Syracuse University Libraries, Special Collections Research Center (Nora Ramsey, Reference Assistant)

Vassar Quarterly, Vassar College (Elizabeth L. Randolph, Director of Alumnae/i, Communications and Editor, and Josephine Lovejoy, Editorial Assistant)

The Vatican, Archivum Secretum Vaticanum (Dr. Marco Grilli, Segretario della Prefettura)

Westtown School (Mary Brooks, Archivist)

Wiley Online Publishers (Romalyn Castellano)

No biography is possible without the interest, help, and encouragement of acquaintances, colleagues, friends, and family. I am indebted to the following in more ways than they know: Tobias Abeloff, Ilonka Venier Alexander, Bert Babcock, Helen Beer, the late Marcel Bickel, Cassandra and Ian Bullock, Daniel Burston, Vitaly Charny, Andrea Marquit Clagget, Michael Copp, Arianne Dar, Richard Davies, Rachel Ertel, Andrew Farah, Cathy Cato Foster, Andrew Frayn, Dorothy Gallagher, the late Gerald Grob, Sharon Hecker, Ludger Hermanns, Joel Howell, the late Olga Zilboorg Irvine, Tatiana Irvine, Thomas Irvine, Brett Kahr, Michail Kalnitsky, Ingrid Kästner, Catriona Kelly, Gloria Levitas, the late Mitchel Levitas, Roger Lipsey, Miranda Machado, Serena Martucci di Scarfizzi, William Maynez, Catherine Zilboorg McMillan, Natan Meir, William Middleton, Mary Miles, Austin Nevin, Elodie Nevin, Tobias Nevin, Thomas Nevin, Abraham Nussbaum, James Oles, Darren Oldridge, Etta Fay Orkin, Michel Peterson, Wendy Pollard, Susan Quinn, Gregory Radick, Natasha Randall, Iona Sachse, Alejandro O. Saitcevsky, Patrick Samway, Max Saunders, Peggy Schaeffer, Emily Schlemowitz, Michael Schröter, Robert Schwartzwald, Margo Stone Shearon, Roger Smith, Jennifer Terry, Daniel Todes, Mary Vance, Leon Wash, Clifton Edward Watkins, Jr., Jared Wickware, Anna Zilboorg, John Zilboorg, and Matthew Zilboorg.

I am finally grateful to my father, the memory of whose hard work and high standards I have carried with me throughout my life.

Series editor's foreword

I shall never forget my utter delight when, at the tender age of 18 years, I stumbled, quite unexpectedly, upon a remarkably special book, while browsing the shelves of my university library.

As a young first-year undergraduate student of psychology, I hoped that I would learn all about the struggles of human beings and, moreover, about the ways in which doctors of the mind might offer assistance. Instead, I received copious instruction in neurobiology, statistical research, and cognitive science – all deeply absorbing and engaging topics of great relevance, but, alas, by no means illuminating of the true plight that each of us must face as we journey through the cycle of life.

Desperate to read something more foundational, I clutched Dr. Gregory Zilboorg's 1941 textbook, *A History of Medical Psychology*, written in collaboration with Dr. George W. Henry, with both curiosity and relish. Within minutes of reading through the introductory chapter, I found myself utterly gripped by the author's superbly written and carefully researched tome on the nature of madness across the centuries, which outlined the dramatic and often shocking ways in which physicians attempted to offer treatments.

After weeks and months of attending lectures, often delivered in a dry style, on the difference between the thalamus and the hypothalamus and, also, on how psychological statisticians distinguish between correlation and causation, I simply could not believe the sheer gripping quality of Dr. Zilboorg's prose and, of course, the breadth and depth of his scholarship.

Indeed, I became extremely impressed that this man could embrace the entire history of medicine from the Paleozoic era to the twentieth century with such thoroughness and clarity. And, as the chapters unfolded, I received a unique education in everything from tuberculosis in the Stone Age, to an examination of Aristotle's "psychological physiology" (Zilboorg and Henry, 1941, p. 56), to a study of the eighth-century Nestorian physicians who practised "a rather crude psychotherapy of intimidation and reproach" (Zilboorg and Henry, 1941, p. 120), to the creation of Spanish lunatic asylums in the fifteenth century, and so much more besides.

Zilboorg's broad coverage, underpinned by compelling detail, truly captivated me. And, in due course, I knew that I wished to become both a practitioner of psychoanalysis and, also, an historian of the subject, just like the author.

In the upcoming years, I plunged myself into the works of Zilboorg with unrelenting delight, and he soon became one of my intellectual heroes. I particularly admired his tremendous clinical contributions, especially in relation to the role of parental antagonism in the development of severe mental illness. As a young psychologist working in a backwater psychiatric hospital in the English countryside, I found Zilboorg's (1929, 1931a, 1932, 1941) early papers on the psychoses truly innovative and inspiring.

Zilboorg struck me as an authentic Renaissance man. Not only did he have the capacity to practise medicine, psychiatry, and psychoanalysis, but he boasted many other talents as well, and I soon came to learn about his impressive historical scholarship and his great literary capacities. He also proved himself a most adept translator and, somehow, he even found the time to transform a landmark German-language book, written by the psychoanalysts Dr. Franz Alexander and Dr. Hugo Staub (1929), into a highly readable English edition (Alexander and Staub, 1931; cf. Zilboorg, 1931b), thus illuminating the ways in which psychoanalysts can assist forensic patients who have committed crimes. Zilboorg himself would, in later years, also write about psychoanalytical criminology in a very illuminating manner (e.g., Zilboorg, 1954, 1956).

It saddened me that, some years later, while reading Susan Quinn's (1987) biography of the German-born psychoanalyst Dr. Karen Horney, I encountered a very different Zilboorg. As many readers will appreciate, Gregory Zilboorg, like Karen Horney, immigrated to New York City, and both of these physicians became prominent members of the New York Psychoanalytic Society. In her account, Quinn suggested, much to my chagrin, that Zilboorg, one of Horney's colleagues, had perpetrated many unethical acts, exploiting his psychoanalytical patients for financial gain.

Subsequent to the publication of this exposé by Susan Quinn, other individuals began to allege further transgressions on the part of Gregory Zilboorg. For instance, Katharine Weber, the granddaughter of one of Zilboorg's analysands, Broadway lyricist Kay Swift, claimed that Zilboorg had seduced this woman in the middle of psychoanalytical treatment. According to Katharine Weber, her grandmother confessed, ' "He was the only man with whom I ever had a sexual relationship to whom I was not physically attracted" ' (quoted in Peyser, 1993, p. 263).

Needless to say, these damning portraits of Zilboorg shocked me and challenged my state of admiration, indeed, idealisation, of this great figure in the history of psychoanalysis.

As the years unfolded, I found a way to retain my deep admiration of Zilboorg's scholarship while also appreciating that, back in the olden days, long before the formalisation of more rigorous psychoanalytical training and supervision programmes, many of the early Freudians also engaged in much boundary-breaking behaviour, and that, in consequence, one could forgive Zilboorg for his sins whilst also appreciating his sainthood.

Happily, Dr. Caroline Zilboorg, the daughter of this controversial psychoanalyst and, moreover, a distinguished literary and historical scholar in her own right, has generously devoted herself to a more detailed study of Gregory Zilboorg's life and work than anyone previously. And, after years of painstaking research, Caroline Zilboorg has produced a two-volume masterpiece.

While most children of famous people tend to write personalised, first-hand memoirs of their parents – consider, for instance, Martin Freud's (1957) classic, *Glory Reflected: Sigmund Freud – Man and Father*, based entirely on reminiscences – Caroline Zilboorg has approached this project as a serious academician, conducting oral history interviews, examining unpublished archival materials with microscopic attention, and surveying a wide range of sources of every shape and size. Indeed, Dr. Zilboorg has written her father's biography with such professionalism and with such objectivity, one would presume that an independent scholar, with *no* personal family ties, had actually constructed these impeccable tomes.

This incomparable study of the life and work of Gregory Zilboorg will, in my estimation, never be surpassed. Not only has Caroline Zilboorg studied all of the relevant published and unpublished data but, moreover, she has curated this information in the most thorough manner imaginable, never brushing over the areas of controversy. Instead, she engages with all the Zilboorgian "scandals" in a truly direct and frank manner. Moreover, she helps us to develop a compassion for her father who, as a refugee to the New World, had to endure innumerable struggles with great fortitude and forbearance.

In spite of the fact that Caroline Zilboorg has written a lengthy, heavily referenced, two-volume biography, this substantial project reads with such fluidity and grace that I simply could not put it down. As a result, I have now come to appreciate that the story of this Russian-born man, regarded by some as a genius and by others as a scoundrel, contains infinitely more nuance and subtlety than we could ever have imagined.

Having now studied the two-volume biography in detail, I have come to acquire a much deeper appreciation of the ways in which Gregory Zilboorg impacted upon his colleagues. Certainly, he evoked a lot of envy from his less talented fellow psychoanalysts, and that factor undoubtedly played a part in the narrative of some of the accusations against him. While maintaining scholarly neutrality, Caroline Zilboorg has, nevertheless, helped us to develop a fuller comprehension of some of the complex dynamics among the members of the New York Psychoanalytic Society in the midst of the Second World War.

Neither idealising nor denigratory, this extraordinary tome – meticulously researched and stunningly crafted – will help us to appreciate the true complexity of the human character. Indeed, as I immersed myself in the book, I became convinced that if Caroline Zilboorg had devoted herself to a career in clinical psychoanalysis, rather than to a more academic lifetime in scholarship, she would absolutely have had all the sensitivity of a great clinician who must recognise the strengths and the vulnerabilities, the brilliance and the madness, and all of the other complexities of being a human.

I thank Caroline Zilboorg warmly for sharing this important story in such an open-hearted and serious manner, helpfully questioning and reconfiguring many of the unsubstantiated myths and rumours. This two-volume biography of Gregory Zilboorg represents, in my estimation, not only a vital contribution to the historiography of psychoanalysis but, also, a wonderful model of how we make sense of the multifaceted, complex, and often contradictory nature of the human mind.

August 2021
Professor Brett Kahr

References

Alexander, Franz, and Staub, Hugo (1929). *Der Verbrecher und seine Richter: Ein psychoanalytischer Einblick in die Welt der Paragraphen*. Vienna: Internationaler Psychoanalytischer Verlag.

Alexander, Franz, and Staub, Hugo (1931). *The Criminal, the Judge, and the Public: A Psychological Analysis*. Gregory Zilboorg (Transl.). New York: Macmillan.

Freud, Martin (1957). *Glory Reflected: Sigmund Freud – Man and Father*. London: Angus and Robertson.

Peyser, Joan (1993). *The Memory of All That: The Life of George Gershwin*. New York: Simon & Schuster.

Quinn, Susan (1987). *A Mind of Her Own: The Life of Karen Horney*. New York: Summit Books/Simon & Schuster.

Zilboorg, Gregory (1929). The Dynamics of Schizophrenic Reactions Related to Pregnancy and Childbirth. *American Journal of Psychiatry, 8*, 733–766.

Zilboorg, Gregory (1931a). Depressive Reactions Related to Parenthood. *American Journal of Psychiatry, 10*, 927–962.

Zilboorg, Gregory (1931b) Translator's Note. In Franz Alexander and Hugo Staub. *The Criminal, the Judge, and the Public: A Psychological Analysis*. Gregory Zilboorg (Transl.), pp. v–x. New York: Macmillan Company.

Zilboorg, Gregory (1932). Sidelights on Parent-Child Antagonism. *American Journal of Orthopsychiatry, 2*, 35–42.

Zilboorg, Gregory (1941). Ambulatory Schizophrenias. *Psychiatry, 4*, 149–155.

Zilboorg, Gregory (1954). *The Psychology of the Criminal Act and Punishment*. New York: Harcourt, Brace & Company.

Zilboorg, Gregory (1956). The Contribution of Psycho-Analysis to Forensic Psychiatry. *International Journal of Psycho-Analysis, 37*, 318–324.

Zilboorg, Gregory, and George W. Henry (1941). *A History of Medical Psychology*. New York: W.W. Norton & Company.

Chapter 1

Confrontation
1940–1941

Throughout the war, Peg would be a constant point of reference for Gregory, an editor who corrected more than his spelling, who polished his vocabulary, pitched his register, and shaped his phrasing and thinking, an intelligent woman unfailingly affirming and nourishing his capacity to love. He, in turn, opened his heart: He told her he adored and admired and needed her, suggested presents she should choose that they would buy together – a fur jacket, a winter coat, gloves – and arranged for her to have a standard poodle puppy from Lillian Hellman's country kennel, King KoKo, a bundle of brown curls with a white star on his chest. The 'outstanding' marriage George imagined would remain outstanding, but as war on the one hand and psychoanalytic and personal politics on the other swept through Gregory's landscape in the 1940s, Peg was his confidante, the source of optimism and gaiety, both lodestar and anchor.[1]

For Gregory, however, the demands of daily life continued at least superficially as if they weren't lovers during a winter he found hectic and depressing. The international news was disturbing on all fronts. Nazi bombs fell on London while British soldiers killed Italians in North Africa and German and Italian troops attacked Yugoslavia and Greece. Gregory was determined to push on with his history despite the war and a crowded professional roster. As many of his wealthier patients became involved with war work that took them to Washington, London, and Jerusalem, he accepted cases he treated without charge: Polish and German refugees seeking official status came to him for evaluations for employment as industrial bakers or tailors, while doctors recently arrived from France sought his help in qualifying to practise in the United States. Although Gregory had always done a measure of *pro bono* consulting, he would soon find himself pressed financially as well as by the constraints of time. Asked to support everything from the Allies in general to a group to buy shoes for refugee children in England, he was obliged to refuse most requests as well as invitations to speak at dinners on relief and democracy and aid to Jews who wanted to leave Europe for Palestine or America. With both old and new patients scheduled for Christmas eve and the following week, he celebrated his 50th birthday quietly in the city before escaping to the country to see in the New Year with the family on the farm.[2]

DOI: 10.4324/9781003190974-1

Gregory had reluctantly accepted a particularly challenging patient just before the holidays. Sam Forsyth, a publicist employed by Ingersoll to boost *PM*, was a volatile alcoholic whom Gregory would treat for three months between 17 December 1940 and 18 February 1941. There were unavoidable gaps, including Christmas and New Year's as well as five days at the end of January when Gregory spent a week in hospital with pneumonia, but the unreliable patient was often drunk or hungover and frequently simply 'skipped' appointments. His treatment posed problems for Gregory from the start.[3]

While the narrative of Gregory's life in Russia is complicated by the paucity of extant documents, an account of what happened during and as a consequence of Forsyth's treatment is complicated by the enormous volume of surviving evidence that includes not only the patient's version as well as Gregory's but reports of what other psychoanalysts thought might or must have occurred and lawyers' interpretations of everyone's story. Further, all the stories, told and retold to various people under various circumstances at various times, were inevitably slightly different. A more reliable witness than Forsyth, Gregory's account seems the most convincing, but he naturally had a vested interest in defending himself from accusations of whatever validity. His being put in a defensive position at all was the result of personalities and agendas having less to do with the facts than with personal and professional politics of exactly the sort from which Gregory had tried to extricate himself when he had stepped back from the New York Psychoanalytic Society and Institute over the matter of the library and bookshop eight years earlier. The patient, an unstable man capable of unpredictable aggression who both admired and resented his doctor, would play a role as catalyst and pawn, while Gregory would struggle to defend everything he had ever done or hoped to achieve.

Gregory grew increasingly uncomfortable with the case. Recommended by Ingersoll, Forsyth had come to Gregory because of serious problems at work. His publicity consisted of spreading rumours and getting *PM* mentioned in gossip columns, a dicey strategy at best, and he seemed to have had little confidence in the paper or its management nor any understanding of or sympathy with Ingersoll's aims. Like Gregory, he was a Jewish immigrant from Russia, but there the similarities stopped. He had come to America as a boy, grown up in rough poverty, and risen in life through bravado and threats. His idea of fun was lots of alcohol and sex with prostitutes. In spite of his crudeness and lack of education, he evinced a degree of charm but was given to violent verbal and physical outbursts. He had tried to jump out a window of Ingersoll's office and had several times come to work with his hands bandaged after having been in fights. When he failed to appear for appointments, Gregory worried he might have committed suicide or attacked or killed one of the women with whom he had spent the night. It quickly also became clear that Forsyth wasn't always comprehensive with the truth or even clear about what the truth might be.[4]

Forsyth was terrified and tense during their first sessions and had been drinking. He would have 'partial fugues' even when sober but hungover. Characteristically,

Gregory began with a general consultation devoted to discovering why the patient had come and what he expected from treatment. When Forsyth soon told Ingersoll he didn't think he could continue because Gregory was charging $225 a week, his employer told him to discuss the fee with Gregory and mentioned it himself. When Forsyth failed to broach the matter, Gregory finally asked him why he had misrepresented the $25 a session, $125 a week, he was actually paying. The patient said he didn't know. With a limited capacity for reflection, Forsyth didn't seem like a good candidate for psychoanalysis. Interpreting his miscalculation as 'resistance', Gregory proceeded as a psychiatrist and avuncular advisor.[5]

While therapy played a significant part in Forsyth's life, Gregory had other patients and was typically occupied with an overwhelming number of activities. So busy he still hadn't managed a visit with Sigerist to discuss not only professional but likely personal matters, in early January 1941 Gregory agreed to join the editorial board of the *Journal of Criminal Psychopathology*, assuming yet another responsibility as he prepared for a series of six fortnightly lectures on the psychopathology of neuroses to begin in the middle of the month at the Philadelphia Psychoanalytic Institute.[6]

Gregory's illness forced him to rest for the week he spent in hospital at the end of January, but he also had family concerns on his mind. Nine-year-old Greg was having problems at school. Easily hurt and brought to tears, he felt other boys were ganging up on him, was offended by something his athletics coach had said. Aware that his son was 'seriously unhappy', having trouble socialising, and disorganised both at home and at school, Gregory nevertheless felt Greg had recently shown 'an increasingly sense of responsibility and Spartan manliness'. Rather than arranging a conference with his teacher, Gregory wrote to the head of the school. His distanced approach was more European than American, as was his sense that fortitude and a sense of responsibility would address his son's sensitivity and rebelliousness. Greg's struggles probably involved what today would be called attention deficit hyperactivity disorder complicated by dyslexia, but he was certainly not helped by a detached mother and an authoritarian father who, despite his love for his son, even when physically present was often distracted and impatient.[7]

Although still 'fagged out' at the beginning of February, Gregory was now actively involved in the life of the New York Psychoanalytic Society and Institute, where internecine tensions continued to fester. Brill had ceded the presidency to younger colleagues in 1936: Bert Lewin had served as president until 1939 when Lawrence Kubie took over, followed by the Hungarian-born Adolph Stern, one of Freud's analysands, from 1940 until 1942. Under Kubie, the primary focus of internal politics had become the organisation and content of the Institute's courses. Karen Horney, whose feminist rethinking of psychoanalysis threatened the established order and the Society's commitment to Freudian tenets, had gained the backing of some students and members who either sympathised with her thinking or felt that divergent views should have a more central place in the curriculum. While Kubie supported classically trained psychoanalysts, Horney along with

Clara Thomson formed an opposing faction. The child psychoanalyst David Levy attempted to intervene on Horney's behalf. Ostensibly an agent of truth and peace, Levy regularly interjected himself into confrontations that had nothing directly to do with him. Feeling that Levy ground 'his own little axes so implacably' that he didn't always know what he was up to, Kubie would call him 'the self-appointed F.B.I.', although the 'impugning of dishonesty' to those members with whom one disagreed had in fact become 'the besetting sin of the Society on all sides'.[8]

Matters remained unsettled and acrimonious throughout the 1940–1941 academic year, during which Gregory served as chair of the Educational Committee, whose members included the Institute's vice-president Lillian Powers as well as Kubie, Rado, Stern, and Fritz Wittels, an Austrian-born psychoanalyst passionately opposed to Horney's ideas. Gregory and Rado were responsible for teaching the core 'History of Psychoanalytic Literature', while other members of the Institute – a heady mix of personalities including Gregory and Rado but also Daniels, Gosselin, Horney, Kardiner, Kubie, Levy (from spring 1941 president of the American Psychoanalytic Association), Lewin, Thompson, Stern, and Wittels – were responsible for the other courses.

In early January Gregory and Stern met with four students representing those who had written to Gregory as chair of the Educational Committee to complain that some students were less likely to be admitted to the Society if trained by faculty members who held views 'not in accordance with libido theory'. According to Levy's notes on his interview with Harold Kelman, one of Horney's ardent supporters, Gregory, although purportedly sympathetic, had become 'livid' and used 'verbosity, jokes, dramatics, and cleverness' in a vain effort to persuade the students to specify instances or particular individuals who felt they had been intimidated or discriminated against.

The students may have had a point – those who did not embrace basic Freudian concepts such as the Oedipus complex were less likely to be welcomed into a society founded on the espousing of Freudian principles – but so did Gregory: How could he do something about a vague protest in which no individuals or facts were mentioned? With only rumours to go on, taking action on the students' behalf would have involved the Educational Committee's selection for censure or dismissal of particular faculty who the students went so far as to suggest might be 'dropped from the list of approved instructors' because of their non-traditional views.[9]

The Society's members inevitably took sides. In a supposedly unbiased search for empirical confirmation, Levy now inserted himself into the fray and proposed to the Educational Committee that he survey students to gather evidence. The Committee, which hoped that the meeting with Stern and Gregory had addressed even if it hadn't completely resolved concerns, had no interest in continuing to stir up dissent and rejected Levy's offer. Refusing to be slighted, he went ahead anyway and sent out a questionnaire to current and former students in mid-February.[10]

Gregory may have been intimidating in what he saw as his defence of himself, the Educational Committee, and the Society and Institute, but many of his colleagues sympathised with his point of view. Both within and outside the Society he had friends who were neither intimidated nor offended, and he was invariably highly principled, capable of great kindness when not in a posture of defence, and generous to a fault – qualities which had earned him admiration and abiding friendships even if they didn't make him a comfortable team player. At the Society he was backed by Kubie, Lewin, and Stern as well as the other members of the Educational Committee. Gregory counted among his friends by the early 1940s not only Sigerist, Abe Abeloff, Lewin, and Gosselin but the Catholic psychoanalyst Leo Bartemeier, one of the founders of the Detroit Psychoanalytic Society, and the psychiatrist James King Hall, the eminent director of the Westbrook Sanitorium in Richmond, Virginia – all of whom would offer Gregory significant support during the difficult months ahead.

With Forsyth, Gregory had worked hard to establish a rapport. Striving for common ground in an early session, he had drawn attention to Forsyth's wristwatch, indicated that he, too, was a fan of wristwatches and had a collection of Patek-Philippes and Vacheron Constantins, which he showed him. When Forsyth then offered Gregory his rather ordinary watch, he refused, pointing out that it didn't have the sort of cordovan strap he preferred. Forsyth promptly got the strap replaced and offered the watch to Gregory again – an offer Gregory felt unable to reject without violating the bond he was attempting to forge.[11]

A week or so later the subject of prizefights came up. Through others on *PM*'s staff, Gregory had been offered free tickets to boxing matches, such tickets being one of a journalist's regular perks, and Forsyth knew of his interest. Unsolicited, the patient gave Gregory a couple of free tickets, which he accepted in another effort to affirm commonality, feeling such a freebie was permissible. In discussing the fight, it came up afterwards that the seats had not been very good ones; such free tickets were seldom for the best seats. Forsyth apparently then decided to buy expensive tickets as a gift. When Gregory saw how good the tickets were, he asked Forsyth if he had paid for them. The patient lied and said he hadn't, but later telephoned to admit he had indeed purchased them. During their next session, Gregory offered to pay, but Forsyth refused reimbursement.[12]

Among Forsyth's clients was Philco, the pioneering electronics company, and in early February he described an expensive radio he could get 'wholesale'. Gregory didn't need another radio, but when the patient brought in a catalogue and pressed him to place an order, Gregory finally selected a reasonably priced model and expected Philco to bill him in due course. Forsyth would remember feeling pleased about giving Gregory the watch as he was feeling very fond of his doctor at that point. He felt guilty about lying to him about the tickets, however, and 'annoyed' about the radio.[13]

Since trouble at *PM* had brought Forsyth into therapy, they sometimes talked specifically about his role at the newspaper, and Gregory made what the patient felt were valuable practical suggestions. They also discussed more generally the job of public relations and how much a person should be paid for responsible and effective work. Forsyth was losing accounts because of his drinking and impulsive behaviour; Gregory wanted him to realise that one's income depended not only on 'luck and connections' but on hard work. Again in search of commonalities to focus and motivate the patient, he pointed out that he, too, had to work hard and worried about bills and taxes.[14]

By early February Forsyth felt dependent on Gregory, but also confused and conflicted, holding his doctor in high regard but identifying himself with him in ways that made him suspicious of him. The patient was as erratic in his payments for treatment as he was in attendance. On the morning of 13 February, Forsyth was so hungover or drunk that his session was pointless, and as he had done on 7 February, Gregory arranged an appointment later the same day without an additional charge. Before he left the office Forsyth paid $250 cash for ten appointments through 7 February. At the end of the afternoon a private messenger delivered to the office an envelope from Forsyth containing $1,000 in cash. When the patient came in for his session on Friday 14 February, Gregory found him 'blocked and inarticulate', unable to offer an explanation for the $1,000. Gregory told him he would let the sum stand as part of his future fees. Gregory's bookkeeper, who came in once a week, recorded Forsyth's $250 under 'Professional Fees', but neither she nor Gregory knew how to record the $1,000, so she entered it under 'Loans' as 'Cash from Gregory Zilboorg'. On Monday 18 February Forsyth was extremely distressed. He failed to appear for appointments scheduled after that date and would later confess having been 'in a very bad state'.[15]

When Forsyth or his secretary rang to cancel one appointment after another, it began to seem unlikely he would continue his therapy. Gregory decided not to bill him for the last week of treatment: He attended only one of the final ten scheduled appointments and Gregory calculated that the amount Forsyth owed would just about cover the cost of the wristwatch and prizefight tickets. He was still waiting for Philco's bill and had no idea what to do with the $1,000, but when Ingersoll told him Forsyth had gone to Florida with a friend, Gregory decided to deal with the matter by letter once he knew the patient had returned to New York. Gregory was probably somewhat disappointed in Forsyth's decision but also relieved by the departure of someone he hadn't much wanted to accept in the first place. Furthermore, he was used to unpredictability in his patients and to impulsive termination of therapy. Indeed, in late February another suicidal alcoholic, whom Gregory had hospitalised at Bloomingdale, tried to force him to stop treating him; when Gregory refused to reject him, the patient abruptly 'discharged' him. Gregory told the man's employer that sadly 'this is not unusual in such cases'.[16]

Gregory in any event had much else on his mind. In mid-February he finally managed to spend part of a weekend with Sigerist in Baltimore. Amid the cooking and photography and discussion of medical history, he probably finally told his friend something about his relationship with Peg. By this time, as their father's research assistant, she had met both Greg and Nancy, and was often in the office both early and late. Occasionally telling her parents she was staying with Mary-Alice, she spent the night with Gregory. They often went out for an early dinner, but sometimes ate whatever Della had left them or Gregory himself put together.

With a large repertoire of complicated dishes he enjoyed preparing when he had the time, he could certainly also cook kasha, knew how to make an omelette. Peg could toast toast. They would light a fire in the fireplace, listen to the record player, turn in early. Some of all this Gregory confided to Sigerist, the first person he would explicitly tell, even if by February the office staff certainly knew: Although one of the older secretaries disapproved and Della acknowledged nothing at all, Pauline was accepting while the bookkeeper, who was particularly fond of Gregory, was quite understanding.[17]

Not only visits with friends but correspondence and lectures in New York, Boston, Philadelphia, Washington, Detroit, and Chicago also claimed Gregory's attention. At the end of February Gregory addressed the New York Psychoanalytic Society on 'Psychology and Culture'. In early March he spoke at the Boston Psychoanalytic Society on 'The Sense of Reality', the same lecture he would deliver in Detroit and elsewhere during the spring, then spent the following day with his friend the Russian-born analyst Moses Ralph Kaufman, one of the founders and president of the Boston Society. Gregory responded in mid-March to a letter from Alexander, whom he addressed in friendly terms as 'Feri', in which the Hungarian had asked for help in finding a publisher for the proceedings of a symposium. Gregory told him his request was 'unfortunate' – he was so pressed he had not even had a 'chance for a good night's sleep of late'. He joked, 'Someone else will have to do it. I mean the negotiations – perhaps the sleep, too!' Gregory then discouraged Alexander from writing an introduction to *A Spectacle of a Man*, a superficial novel about psychoanalysis by Alvin L. Barach, a well-respected New York pulmonologist and former patient of Alexander's in Chicago whom Gregory and most of his New York colleagues regarded as a 'quack' analyst.[18]

March was indeed a typically full month. Gregory was apparently being completely truthful when he told Forsyth he was worried about taxes. Giving his life insurance policy as security, on 10 March Gregory took out a personal loan of $6,500 from the Guarantee Trust Company of New York. The following evening he spoke at the New York Neurological Society on 'Ambulatory Schizophrenias', evidently a tour de force. Two nights later he dined with literary friends: Doris Schneider Hatcher, an editor at Harcourt Brace, and her husband Harry Hatcher, advertising manager of the *New Yorker* but about to become an editor at the New York office of Oxford University Press. Gregory's schedule was as busy with social engagements as with professional responsibilities. He had squeezed in the visit with Sigerist after one of his lectures in Philadelphia, where he regularly dined with the organiser, the psychoanalyst Leroy M.A. Maeder, and with Oliver Spurgeon English, chair of the Department of Psychiatry at Temple University.[19]

Back in New York the politics at the New York Psychoanalytic Society continued to weigh upon him, as he hinted in a letter to J.K. Hall on his election to the presidency of the American Psychiatric Association. Gregory praised 'the spiritual leadership of the South', felt specifically that Hall was among those 'good people below the Mason and Dixon line' who had 'a far greater and deeper appreciation of the world tragedy of to-day than many around here who are confused, and whose allegiance to their own axes beclouds their judgment and mars the probity of their thought'. The axes that in Gregory's view were clouding the judgement and thought of his Society colleagues were being wielded by Horney and her supporters. In a letter to Gregory addressing the matter, Gosselin used language far more explicit and saltier: In his blunt opinion, Horney was 'a shit'. Since nothing could be gained 'by descending to her level & arguing about details', Gregory's official letter on behalf of the Educational Committee on 11 March, in which he responded to the students' petition, was a move in the right direction, while the petition itself could, in Gosselin's view, be 'an opening eventually to hoist the slut by her own petard'.[20]

Gregory's formal letter pointed out that the students were under the misapprehension that training at the Institute automatically conferred Society membership. Admitting that students 'trained one-sidedly are naturally at a disadvantage', Gregory nevertheless insisted that there was no evidence that students of 'liberal' psychoanalysts had greater difficulty gaining membership than those trained by more 'orthodox' analysts. In the Committee's view, he wrote, the crux of the problem was that the students wanted the Society to teach 'two types of psychoanalysis', while the Society was constitutionally committed to teaching 'psychoanalysis as it was founded by Freud'. Although the burden of response fell on the students, the real crux was not the students' desires but the teaching of more 'liberal' analysts who had fundamental arguments with Freudian ideas of personality development.[21]

Addressing the Society on behalf of the Educational Committee a fortnight later, Gregory reported on a meeting with Thompson earlier in March during which she had conceded the evidence she presented to substantiate allegations of intimidation was weak and inconclusive. Kubie submitted a 'supplementary report', placing responsibility for the increasingly bitter controversy pitting 'certain members of the Society against other members of the Society, against the Society itself, and against the Society's Educational Committee' on 'hostile and irresponsible members of the Society'. There was no doubt in anyone's mind that those hostile and irresponsible members were Karen Horney, Clara Thompson, and their supporters.[22]

The problem went beyond different views of psychoanalysis. Horney's conflict was about authority and her occasionally admirable, sometimes foolish, and generally antagonistic views towards structures not her own. As associate director of the Chicago Psychoanalytic Institute eight years earlier she had clashed with Alexander about personal as well as methodological and theoretical matters, and had rallied supporters, including Henry Stack Sullivan, Erich Fromm, and Lionel Blitzsten, who found Alexander's research careless as well as insufficiently informed by social and cultural factors. They also felt that, as the Institute's director, he allowed wealthy people without medical degrees excessive influence. It is unsurprising that Horney left Chicago after only two years; that she brought with her the same challenging attitudes and antipathies made her time at the contentious New York Psychoanalytic Society even more fraught.[23]

Gregory was likely relieved to be leaving New York at the end of March for ten days of lectures and meetings in the Midwest. He must have felt he had at least addressed the issues pending at the Society, while at the office he tried to wrap things up as best he could. Having just finished his translation of Paracelsus, he left it on his desk for Peg to type and put the manuscript of his history in his briefcase. He wrote Sigerist about plans for a commemorative volume to celebrate the centenary of the American Psychiatric Association in 1944, but there were also more immediate matters to clear up. Forsyth had evidently requested payment for the radio: He had paid for it himself and at some point in March decided that he should 'bill' Gregory for it. Having heard from Ingersoll that Forsyth had returned, Gregory sent him a cheque on 21 March with a gentle note in which he tried to calm a patient he knew was volatile and probably feeling guilty for having cancelled appointments. He told Forsyth how sorry he was that they hadn't had 'a good, frank talk' before Forsyth decided 'to break off the treatment' and added that perhaps he would now give him a ring so they could 'have a visit and also clear up certain practical details'. Signing the note 'With kindest regards, yours cordially', Gregory clearly hoped to assuage any negative feelings that the difficult sessions might have provoked in the patient while he also needed to know if Forsyth intended to resume therapy and, if not, to return the $1,000.[24]

Forsyth did indeed have mixed feelings, and by March was a very upset and confused man. He told several people that Gregory had taken advantage of him, had asked for gifts, and finally proposed that they go into business together, demanding $5,000 in advance for commercial advice. Forsyth had not understood exactly what was happening, but when Gregory accepted $1,000 in cash, Forsyth no longer had any faith in him. As the story started to spread, Forsyth did what his girlfriend's wealthy father insisted he do: He went to Chicago and consulted Alexander, who had been her analyst and who, they had heard, knew Gregory.

Taking Gregory's note with him as proof, Forsyth saw Alexander twice during a two-day visit. Surprised and distressed by the accusations, Alexander was torn. He felt some responsibility towards the patient – who, it seemed obvious to him, had a tendency 'to put another fellow in the wrong who established himself in a situation of trust towards him' – but he also felt an obligation towards 'the profession', which he saw as threatened by the behaviour of a 'brilliant' psychoanalyst who must be 'in a disturbed mind'. Alexander finally made two suggestions: Forsyth should ask for his money back and enter therapy with another analyst. Forsyth duly wrote to ask Gregory to return the $1,000 for 'services' he could not provide since Forsyth was no longer in treatment with him and showed the letter to Alexander, who approved its contents. For his part, having recently received the letter in which Gregory mentioned being so busy it was hard to get a good night's sleep, Alexander decided that his former analysand was likely suffering from acute 'external or internal stress' and felt that he had to do something, although he wanted to hear Gregory's side of the story first.[25]

Forsyth's letter arrived at the office in Gregory's absence. Acknowledging its receipt on 31 March, Peg forwarded it to Chicago, where Gregory received it in early April. With much else on his mind, however, he waited until his return to respond. As was his habit, he used the time on trains and in hotels to concentrate on his own writing. Away from the family, the office, and the Society, Gregory was able to focus on his history. He left New York on 28 March on an overnight train for Detroit, where he addressed the Detroit Psychoanalytic Society and saw Bartemeier and his family before going on the next day to Chicago, where he held a seminar at the Chicago Institute for Psychoanalysis and addressed the Chicago Psychoanalytic Society. On 31 March he left for Topeka, Kansas, to deliver a paper and work with his friend Karl Menninger at the Menninger Clinic, then returned to Chicago for the night on 5 April before taking another train back to New York.[26]

During his brief time in Chicago Gregory saw Alexander on several occasions, but only late in the evening after his presentation to the Psychoanalytic Society did the two men have a chance to speak together privately. Alexander invited Gregory back to his home, where they discussed a patient Alexander had referred to him as well as personal matters. Gregory probably mentioned to his former analyst not only the problems Horney was causing in New York but his own situation at home and relationship with Peg. Alexander suggested that Gregory re-enter analysis and Gregory agreed: The customary panacea was always a good recourse, but there was inevitably the matter of making time for it in addition to the issue of whom to consult given the current conflicts in psychoanalytic circles. Although they talked until three in the morning, Alexander didn't mention Forsyth's visit or his accusations.[27]

Soon after he returned to New York, Gregory answered the letter he understood as Forsyth's response to the note he had sent on 21 March. He explained that he had hoped Forsyth would resume therapy so he could have returned the money in person, but now that he clearly wasn't going to see Forsyth again, he enclosed a cheque for 'the thousand dollars which you were good enough to advance to me just before you stopped coming to me'. Thanking Forsyth for his 'prompt response', he concluded with his best wishes.[28]

This sincere and cordial letter is painfully ironic given Forsyth's meeting with Alexander and what had been happening in New York in Gregory's absence. Towards the end of March Nathan Levin, an accountant and friend of both Forsyth and David Levy, had told Levy that Forsyth had told him that Gregory had made a business proposition to him. Like Alexander, Levy had been shocked, but rather than speak to Gregory, he had decided to take the problem into his own hands and asked Levin to arrange a meeting with Forsyth so that he could 'verify' the story. Forsyth was reluctant to get further involved and, having demanded his money back, simply wanted to move on. When Levin pressed the issue, Forsyth told him – and Levin told Levy – that he had seen Alexander, who was now taking care of the matter.[29]

In utter ignorance, Gregory felt the challenges Forsyth posed were behind him. He dined with Marshall Field on 14 April to discuss funding for the volume he had mentioned to Sigerist, but he and Field were friends as well as colleagues and must have enjoyed a convivial evening. Gregory had missed the opening night of Hellman's anti-fascist play, *Watch on the Rhine*, but impressed with the script, had invested a substantial sum towards its production; he must have enjoyed attending a performance of the play that at the end of the month received the New York Drama Critics' award for the best American play of the season. Indeed, Gregory's schedule was as full as ever throughout the spring. He agreed to be interviewed in March for *I'm an American*, a radio programme touting the virtues of democracy and featuring prominent immigrant conductors, composers, actors, and opera singers as well as Albert Einstein and Thomas Mann, and spoke on 18 April in Washington on 'The Ways of the Unconscious', one of seven public lectures on a course entitled 'On the Frontiers of the Mind' sponsored by the Graduate School of the U.S. Department of Agriculture. Gregory declined, however, the philanthropist Maurice Wertheim's invitation to participate in a match at the Manhattan Chess Club in early May because even he couldn't be in two places at the same time; in early May he would be delivering papers and attending meetings in New Jersey and Virginia.[30]

At the New York Psychoanalytic Society where Horney and her cohort remained disgruntled, however, life was by no means convivial. Levy had submitted the results of his unsolicited survey on student intimidation, but both Kubie as president and Gregory in consultation with the Educational Committee wanted to deal with the root of problem. At a Society meeting on 29 April Gregory reported the Committee's position: Students should not begin their control analyses on the basis of theoretical and emotional orientations contrary to fundamental psychoanalytic principles. While the Committee supported 'free and unhampered discussion of all points of view', it was convinced that a thorough grounding in Freudian tenets was essential. Gregory then announced the Committee's decision to demote Horney from instructor (a category of training analysts in charge of their own courses and students) to lecturer (someone teaching on occasion in courses in which others were in charge). Levy twice questioned the Committee's unanimous decision, but its report was accepted by a majority vote. Horney, Thompson, and three other members immediately rose and walked out. Two days later, on 1 May, the five analysts jointly resigned. The New York Psychoanalytic Society and Institute was now free to turn its attention to the next crisis.[31]

The relief Gregory may have felt when he left New York for the Midwest in March must have paled in comparison to the relief he certainly felt with the Horney controversy behind him as he set off for a joint meeting of the American Psychoanalytic and American Psychiatric Associations in Richmond. Exactly what happened during the conference merits close attention because of its dramatic repercussions, and as with all controversies, there would be various accounts.

J.K. Hall had kindly invited Gregory to stay at his home and he had happily accepted, but Hall had even more kindly offered him the use of his suite at the Jefferson Hotel where the conference was taking place. Gregory arrived after 11:00 pm on Saturday 3 May and, rather than disturb Hall at that late hour, went directly to the suite for the night. On Sunday afternoon Gregory would remember exchanging a few words with Alexander in one of the hotel's public spaces. A few moments later another analyst came up and told him, ' "I don't want you to be foolish; don't think that Alex is your friend." ' When Gregory asked 'Why?' he said, ' "I don't know, but he and Levy and Kardiner have been sitting there and talking, and every little while I heard 'Zilboorg'. Their faces don't look good." '[32]

Gregory was not immediately disturbed, however, for he had much else on his mind. On Monday morning 5 May he chaired the inaugural meeting of the Committee on the History of Psychiatry. The group's first tasks were planning the centennial meeting of the Association in Philadelphia in 1944 and preparing a history of American psychiatry. Gregory was excited about the prospect and gratified to have been chosen as chair.

He couldn't play chess in New York at the same time as he launched the committee in Richmond, but he did do his best to be in two different places at once. As soon as this meeting concluded, he flew to Atlantic City for a symposium on Paracelsus organised by Sigerist under the auspices of the American Association for the History of Medicine. Gregory spoke on 'The Place of Paracelsus in the History of Psychiatry', a celebration of the project on which he and Sigerist had been working for months. The pharmacologist Chauncey Leake thought all of the addresses were 'brilliant' and the symposium itself 'splendid'. After a collegial dinner that continued well into the evening, Gregory finally returned to Richmond on Tuesday morning 6 May having had only four hours sleep.[33]

He was in Hall's suite taking a shower when Alexander rang and invited him to Levy's room. Gregory suggested the two men join him instead. Travel-worn and with his hair still damp, Gregory was unprepared for the confrontation that followed. Alexander, who en route to Richmond had seen Forsyth in New York and heard from him about Levy's interest, had reflected for six weeks and finally decided on a course of action with Levy and Kardiner, who was willing to advise but wanted no part in challenging anyone directly. Alexander began what turned into a highly charged two-and-a-half-hour conversation by again discussing the patient he had referred to Gregory, setting up what would initially seem a consultation on a particular case, before bringing up the reason for the interview. Forsyth had told him 'the whole story': Gregory had asked the patient for gifts and accepted them; he had made a business proposition and asked the patient to pay him $5,000 in cash. Convinced by Forsyth's consistency, Alexander had decided his account must be true.

Shocked, Gregory tried to explain the circumstances and his own reasoning as well as Forsyth's behaviour. Alexander countered Gregory's interpretation of the patient's psychology, while Levy grew impatient with analysis he saw as beside the point. Eventually Alexander, without naming Kardiner, told Gregory what the three men had agreed: Gregory should resign from all official positions in psychoanalytic and psychiatric societies and stop teaching or presenting papers. While he might continue to practise, he should enter further analysis and consider going into another profession. When Gregory asked, certainly not without irony, if he could continue to serve as editor of *Psychoanalytic Quarterly*, they reluctantly agreed, but the important thing, they insisted, was that he 'should not be before the public eye'. Having concluded that Gregory was guilty of gross professional misconduct, the three men had decided on behalf of psychoanalysis that the best thing to do was to limit his influence and visibility.

Even had such an odd punishment been appropriate, it would have been difficult to enforce. Gregory had by the 1940s attained unsolicited renown even beyond psychiatric and psychoanalytic circles. He had recently been one of 14 alluring men featured in 'Why Do Women Fall For – ?', a chirpy two-page spread in *Harper's Bazaar*. Among the others were Franklin Roosevelt, Ernest Hemingway, Ezio Pinza (the Italian 'glamour boy of the opera'), and actors Jean Gabin, Charles Boyer, Rex Harrison, Jimmy Stewart, and Errol Flynn, the 'Nimble Knight' of Hollywood. Such company suggests the celebrity Gregory had unwittingly achieved, the degree to which he – along with film stars, a politician, a writer, an athlete (the Austrian skier Hans Hauser), an American bandleader (Leighton Noble), and an Argentine playboy (Arturo Ramos) – was noticed not only by psychiatrists and psychoanalysts but by readers of glossy fashion magazines and the general public. Limiting his visibility was essentially beyond his control and certainly beyond the control of irritated colleagues.[34]

Gregory was deeply shaken by the encounter. Facing the president of the American Psychoanalytic Association and his own analyst, he felt 'castrated': They were accusing and judging him, threatening to deprive him of all he had struggled to achieve professionally. Under attack, he accepted he had erred in his treatment of the patient, but would feel he had offered explanations for his reasoning that should have excused any misjudgements. Convinced of his guilt, however, Alexander and Levy would think Gregory had admitted the truth of Forsyth's accusations.

Exactly what was said, conceded, and admitted is not so much lost in the mists of time as it was remembered and interpreted differently by each of the three men in Hall's suite on that birthday Peg shared with Freud. Alexander would recall the spirit of the conversation as 'extremely friendly', although he appreciated that Gregory was 'naturally very emotional'. Levy would be convinced that, despite prevarication, Gregory had ultimately confessed to deeds of moral turpitude and confirmed his culpability by accepting the terms of punishment. According to Alexander, Gregory acknowledged what Forsyth had reported by nodding while he had agreed to their terms by declaring with abject sincerity, 'I will do whatever you suggest, because I know that you, Alec, you are friendly, and Levy is not hostile.' According to Gregory, however, when he declared that Alexander was friendly and denied Levy's hostility, he was being sarcastic. He would above all insist that he never 'confessed' to anything, although what he apparently did do in his horrified state of shock was accept the terms.[35]

Always an emotional man more likely to fly off the handle than bewail his fate, more likely to push on than give up, Gregory was probably for the only time in his life completely devastated. He knew he needed help and sought out a colleague, a man he would only refer to as 'the dean of American psychoanalysts', who invited him to his room. There, between sobs, Gregory told him what had happened, that he had been confronted and had finally given in 'for no reason' out of what he saw as mortifying cowardice. The older analyst put his arm around him and said, '"Don't you think they are trying to kill you? Go home and defend yourself. What is the matter with you? Can't you fight?"' Gregory must have been heartened, but controlling his feelings and determining a course of action would take time. Still upset, early that evening he decided to consult Kubie, a colleague of his own generation. The two had always been collegial, although Gregory had never confided in Kubie, but he was now desperate. He recounted the essential details, telling Kubie a patient had complained and mentioning the watch, the fight tickets, and the sum of $1,000. Gregory seemed to Kubie to be in a nearly beaten frame of mind, completely crushed by the episode, floundering under the emotional impact, and eager to know what Kubie thought he should do. Alarmed by the confrontation as well as by the emotional state of a man he respected, Kubie wisely advised Gregory to consult other members of the New York Psychoanalytic Society and to discuss the situation with a lawyer.[36]

Gregory didn't introduce a round-table discussion held that evening nor would he appear as a discussant of Levy's paper the following day, but with time he grew calmer and more focused. Whether part of a plan to celebrate her 23rd birthday or something hastily arranged because he needed her, Peg joined Gregory in Richmond before 8 May. She was a stabilising force, and on Friday morning, 9 May, Gregory spoke as scheduled on 'The Psychology of Revolt, Obedience and Panic'. He had typically left the writing of his paper until the last minute, but when the last minute arrived, he was too distracted for formal composition on a topic now so ironically appropriate. Peg likely helped him to regain a measure of composure, but at the lectern where he had always been at his most confident, he spoke ex tempore from notes.[37]

The conference would continue until Sunday, but Gregory and Peg returned to New York on Friday afternoon. They probably spent at least part of the weekend together, and it is nice to think that at some point there was champagne, but Gregory had a full schedule ahead of him before the summer he needed to devote to finishing his history, and he wanted to consult his attorney. In addition to seeing patients, as the academic year drew to a close he also had duties at the New York Psychoanalytic Society, where he as well as Levy were among the candidates for the chair of the Educational Committee in an election slated for 20 May. Levy soon reported to Alexander what he considered evidence of the violation of the 'pledge' they had extracted: Gregory's presentation in Richmond, his continued membership of the Educational Committee, and his name on the ballot. Alexander indicated that as far as he was concerned the problem was now a matter for the Society. Apparently without reluctance, Levy took on the challenge.[38]

Gregory and Levy and their respective lawyers quickly set wheels in motion. For his part, Gregory grew increasingly uneasy as gossip about events in Richmond quickly spread throughout the Society. There was some respite in mid-May when he and Sigerist spent a weekend together cooking and taking photographs on the farm. In the long talks the two men treasured, Gregory told his friend that he had been accused and was now preparing to defend himself, that underneath the normal life he continued to lead, he was deeply shaken. It was impossible not to read the newspapers and listen to the radio, and he and Sigerist would have also discussed the war, the surrender of Yugoslavia and Greece at the end of April, and the strange flight of Rudolph Hess, Hitler's deputy, to Scotland in May. Daily reports from Europe reminded Gregory of the time and space that separated him from the culture that defined him, from music and art and thinking and colleagues still on the other side of the Atlantic in countries he could not visit, news that insisted on matters more disturbing if not more personally pressing than psycho-analytic politics in New York.[39]

Over lunch on 20 May with Bert Lewin and Adolph Stern, now chairman of the board of directors of the New York Psychoanalytic Society, Gregory confided that he was having 'a very painful time', under terrific pressure not only due to the accusations but because he couldn't understand Alexander's behaviour. Lewin, Gregory would remember, said he had always found Alexander's attitude towards Gregory 'abnormal', but neither Lewin nor Stern offered an explanation nor did either man suggest a clear way forward.[40]

As the sunshine on that warm afternoon gave way to thunder and finally rain, the Society at their evening meeting announced the results of the vote for chair of the Educational Committee. Neither Levy nor Gregory was elected. Levy was surely disappointed, but Gregory was probably neither very disappointed nor surprised – continuing in office wasn't particularly significant in the grander scheme of things. More important to him emotionally was a letter from Manfred Bleuler in Switzerland. Having finally been passed by the U.S. censors, it had taken two months to arrive but reminded Gregory that despite world turmoil his European colleagues were still alive and working. He must also have been gratified to learn a few days later of his election to the Executive Committee of the New York Society for Medical History and continued to hope for a calm summer during which he could focus on finishing the book.[41]

Likely on his lawyers' advice, Gregory wrote nearly identical letters to Levy and Alexander on 26 May. Reminding them that they had 'repeated' to him 'accu-sations of unprofessional conduct' reputedly made by one of his former patients, he told them he felt 'an unjustice' was being done to him and flatly denied 'any improprieties'. Levy was incensed. Convinced Gregory had completely misrep-resented what had occurred in Richmond, he pressed Forsyth, now in treatment with Lewin, to lodge a formal complaint with the New York Psychoanalytic Soci-ety. Forsyth reluctantly agreed to meet with Levy, their mutual friend Levin, and Levy's lawyer Henry Gale on 3 June. With Gale's help, he then wrote a 12-page statement describing his experience but insisted he didn't consider his statement a complaint. Levy and Alexander edited Forsyth's statement by blotting out mate-rial they felt was irrelevant, and on 18 June Levy submitted it to the board with a letter asking them to act on it.[42]

Gregory was aware trouble was brewing, heard that Forsyth had signed something, that Levy intended to take the matter up with the board. When Gregory asked Lewin for support, he reluctantly refused because he was treating Forsyth but assured his friend that in his opinion everything would 'blow over'; addressing him warmly as 'Grisha', he told him he had more friends than he realised. Gregory would need those friends but began now to count on the friends he was already aware of. He wrote Mo Kaufman in the middle of June that what he understood as the 'aftermath' of the political struggles at the New York Society was 'unsavory and frightful'. Gregory was under no illusions: The tensions in the Society had degenerated into a predicament in which he was apparently going to bear the major burden and the situation was starting to appear 'extremely serious'. Unwilling or unable to share in correspondence the depth of his distress or the specifics of the 'aftermath', Gregory told Kaufman he hoped they could have a long talk soon; indeed, he confessed he felt 'the need of it'.[43]

With Ray and the children away for the summer in Pound Ridge, he had the gas and electricity turned off in the family apartment and moved into his office where he plunged defensively into writing. Peg put in longer hours than usual, present as his amanuensis and typist, his loving companion and encouraging confidante. 'Head over heels' in his book, he also turned to Bartemeier and Sigerist for support. On a Saturday in mid-June Peg accompanied Gregory to rural Pennsylvania where he addressed the League for Industrial Democracy on 'Force and Submissiveness in the Social Changes of To-Day', then drove Peg home and collected Bess and Leo Bartemeier, who had just finished a lecture at Bronxville's Sarah Lawrence College, and drove them to the farm for what remained of the weekend. He was cutting it close, spending not only weekday evenings with Peg but portions of his weekends as well. He would soon be cutting it even closer: The following Saturday morning he and Peg left New York for lunch with Sigerist in Baltimore, then Gregory drove her back to Bronxville once more before heading to his family in Pound Ridge on Saturday night.[44]

At least apparent rectitude as well as true moral correctness and attention to detail were certainly on Gregory's mind. He refused point blank, for example, to be interviewed in June for a lengthy 'personality sketch' for *Life* magazine. Quoting at length from the 'Principles of Professional Conduct of the Medical Society of the State of New York', Gregory pointed out that, while the reporter was free to write what he wanted, it behoved doctors for the sake of their patients to maintain a low profile and avoid anything that might be construed as advertising. Citing 'reasons guiding our professional conduct', he similarly refused to help the editor of *Current Biography*, although he was quick to correct a draft of the entry she intended to publish. He criticised the accompanying picture as 'not entirely me but a poor suggestion of what I might be', but explicitly requested she delete the remark that he charged his patients '$75 an hour', an untruth he thought could only be based on 'none too benevolent gossip'. Insisting he had never in his life received such a fee, he wrote that even if offered such a payment, he would refuse, because 'no doctor's hour is worth $75.00'.[45]

Technical correctness in his history, meanwhile, was a matter of careful research and meticulous attention to language, critical matters in the overarching volume he had first imagined 15 years earlier. Even as his publisher's August 1 deadline approached, he was still trying to verify facts. In late June Peg wrote the librarian at Catholic University of America to ask about Weyer's status in the *Index Librorum Prohibitorum*, in which his book on witches was listed shortly after publication in 1563. Gregory wanted to know if it was still on the list in 1590. In July he wrote Harold C. Gardiner, editor of the Jesuit magazine *America*, to check the veracity of a document by 'Scobardi' about Mesmer and mesmerism. Gregory suspected his account was flawed and that Scobardi wasn't even a Jesuit. Gardiner confirmed his suspicions. But as Gregory strove to write a history that would be erudite and eloquent as well as accurate and accessible, verifying facts would be the simplest of his problems.[46]

Despite Gregory's urging, one thing after another had delayed Henry's completion of his section. He had visited the farm to discuss the project in the spring of 1940 and shown Gregory drafts of chapters that were rambling and inaccurate. Gregory persuaded him to omit passages on sexual intercourse, religion, and neurasthenia, but a revision didn't materialise and exactly what could be cut and what would stay remained vague. In January 1941 Henry had wanted to discuss the matter further and, given his obligations at Brooklea Sanitorium, imagined a sociable visit to Pound Ridge with his family, but informed Gregory that Eleanor was just 'emerging from a mild depression' and didn't feel up to appearing in public. At the end of March, Henry repeated that his wife was still 'slowly emerging from a mild depressive condition' and not yet up to social engagements, but by the spring of 1941, Gregory wasn't interested in a family get-together; he wanted his collaborator to buckle down and complete the required work.[47]

In early April, Henry submitted an over-long, scarcely altered version with marginal notes indicating possible revisions and omissions. Barely holding his temper in check, Gregory informed him he needed two chapters totalling 80 pages typed on regular not legal-sized paper. Henry shouldn't expect him to revise the chapters at this point since he had his hands full 'rewriting the thousand-odd typewritten pages' of his own. Very simply, Henry needed to complete a substantial revision with a coherent chronological narrative by June 1. Given his experience of Henry's limitations, Gregory suggested his own secretaries would retype, edit, and index whatever Henry finally produced. Not without irony, he told his inept collaborator he was sorry to have to hurry him but was sure he appreciated the situation.[48]

On 6 June Henry finally sent Gregory his ostensibly revised chapters but was still having difficulty following directions. The section on psychiatric education, for instance, was in his view already so condensed he had decided to leave it 'just as it was'. Gregory himself now struggled to get Henry's section into shape.

Henry's description of psychiatric education was indeed so brief he wasn't certain he could include it at all. What Henry had written about occupational therapy would also need to be omitted as the topic was so large Gregory felt it would require a separate book. He also deleted Henry's account of 'ancient civilizations' because it was 'too fragmentary to be conclusive' and Gregory had already dealt with this material at greater length elsewhere in the book. It was not only content, however, that presented problems. Henry's footnotes were 'too casual': In some cases a work's title or publication date was omitted and there was no uniformity, so 'the scientific value of the notes as references for others' was lost. Gregory diplomatically invited Henry to come into the office to 'take a look at the way we are doing it here' and reminded him the publisher required they follow the *Chicago Manual of Style*.[49]

Henry may have come into Gregory's office for yet another discussion about what remained to be done, but in the end Gregory and Peg took responsibility for the necessary revisions. When the galleys arrived at the end of August, Gregory tactfully asked if Henry wanted Gregory's secretaries to read and correct his two chapters since 'they have retyped them and know the text well'. In the end he sent Henry a duplicate anyway but informed him he needn't make corrections. When the page proofs arrived a month later, Peg took care of indexing while another secretary sent Henry his version as a courtesy, but he wasn't required nor did anyone expect him to do anything at all.[50]

Unsurprisingly, Kaufman would find Gregory 'awfully tired' when he visited the farm for the talk Gregory had longed for. Determined to submit the book to Norton on time, Gregory had spent July working tremendously hard even by his own standards, often writing 'through the nights', then working all day on revisions alongside his office staff. On several occasions both he and his secretaries 'had to take benzedrine' in order 'to keep on going without plainly collapsing'. When he finally came up for air in August, he had to apologise to Sigerist for delaying the volume on Paracelsus: His translation and accompanying essay simply could not be carefully gone over and typed until the history was finished. The first weeks of August were then devoted to completing his work on Paracelsus, but by the middle of the month he finally felt able to take a much-needed break.[51]

Leaving his secretaries in New York and his family in Pound Ridge, Gregory drove north on his own for a peaceful weekend with Sigerist, who had rented a cottage for the summer in Bolton's Landing in upstate New York. As always, there was a great deal for the two to talk about: The Committee on the History of Psychiatry was preparing to start its work and Gregory wanted his friend's involvement in that, while with so much of Europe in turmoil, both men were interested in promoting collaboration in South America. Indeed, Gregory was now planning a trip to Brazil in mid-September, a matter of liaising with colleagues and delivering several lectures in Rio di Janeiro as well as getting the rest he could only achieve by getting away. Gregory would have at least mentioned to Sigerist his hopes for a future with Peg, a bittersweet matter that necessarily depended on his leaving Ray and the children, something he was for myriad reasons loathe to do. Peg wouldn't be going with him to Brazil, but escaping family tensions probably played into his decision to take this autumn trip; instead, Abe Abeloff would go along as a fellow medical man and sympathetic companion. Over the weekend Gregory certainly also shared with Sigerist his distaste for the pending brouhaha at the New York Psychoanalytic Society, a matter with no sweetness in it that would be inevitably bitter.

In late July Gregory had received a formal notice, accompanied by a copy of Forsyth's statement, from Philip Lehrman, the Society's secretary, announcing a special meeting of the board of directors on 8 October 1941. The purpose of the meeting was to respond to Forsyth's 'complaint', which Levy had transmitted to the board. Deep in work on his history, Gregory had little emotional energy for countering accusations but contacted his lawyers to discuss an appropriate response. In the thick of proofreading galleys in early September, he finally wrote to Lehrman objecting to the special meeting itself and requesting further particulars. He also asked that any confrontation be postponed until after his return from Brazil in late October.[52]

Gregory would need to finish reading the proofs of Paracelsus before sailing on 13 September, but he managed to spend time with Peg after long days at the office and likely took her with him when, through *PM*, he got prizefight tickets for 'excellent' seats in early September, for which he duly paid by cheque. He certainly needed the outlet of displaced aggression, and Gregory had much hanging over him in addition to the special meeting. On the personal front, he found himself in a classic quandary: Increasingly frustrated with his wife, he nevertheless felt obligated to stay in the marriage because of his love for his children and concern for their welfare. From time to time he tried to broach matters with Ray, but she was unwilling to discuss his unhappiness and he was aware of her dependence on him. Divorce from an emotional, practical, and legal perspective seemed an impossibility even as both he and Peg continued to hope for a life together. While they worked alongside one another during the week and snatched special evenings and rare nights, weekends apart in their separate homes were becoming more and more difficult. With her conventional family in suburban Bronxville, where her father was now bedridden after a second stroke, Peg was acutely conscious of the limitations the affair placed on her social life and could not help imagining her lover with his wife and children. Gregory, for his part, struggled with domestic tensions as well as with his own psychological incapacity to bring about change. Short-tempered in the best of times, he punctuated his notes to Peg with occasionally defensive but generally abject apologies for his behaviour and his moods. Fridays were especially hard, while Mondays too often consisted of 'kiss and make up business', but a year into their affair, Gregory could see no way forward.[53]

Reports from Europe also upset him. The war had taken a particularly poignant turn with the Nazis' invasion of Russia at the end of June, and Gregory followed events on the Eastern Front with mixed emotions. While he hoped this move would bring about 'the end of Hitler', the invasion also revived upsetting memories of his experiences of German soldiers in Kiev in 1918. By the end of August, the Nazis had encircled the city in what would be a decisive and destructive victory, and Gregory's feelings were both realistic and resigned. News of the bombing of Kiev's Duma, of panzers rolling down the broad swathe of Khreshchatyk Street and ruined bridges over the Dnieper, was disturbing but completely predictable. After all, he wrote Sigerist, 'this is war and wars cannot go on, particularly nowadays, without frightful destruction', yet at the same time he couldn't help but wonder if either of them would live long enough to see this particular war end.[54]

Gregory's mood was not leavened by second thoughts about his history. He remained in many ways an emotional and pessimistic Russian, not exactly 'bent on destruction', as he had humorously quipped when discussing suicide in Washington three years earlier, but certainly not the 'cheerful' American to whom he had juxtaposed the stereotypical Russian. He confessed to Sigerist that the more he thought about his book, the more disappointed and unhappy he felt. He wondered if he shouldn't have first written 'a six-volume history of medical psychology and then prepared a one volume abridged edition for that part of posterity whose intellectual stomachs are delicate and need to be spoon-fed.' Despite the years of research during which he had put his heart and mind into imagining the history he wanted to write, he now felt he had produced 'something immature'.[55]

On 8 September the Germans attacked Leningrad, a siege that would last 900 days, and Gregory's heart was heavy as he prepared to leave New York. Nearly overwhelmed by feelings of futility, he told Sigerist that he would rather be on the outskirts of the city where in 1917 he had fought General Khabalov's Cossacks alongside the workers of the Obuchow and Putilov plants. If the boat to Brazil were torpedoed, he would drown ignominiously without having fired a shot. He was not entirely joking when he told his friend that should the boat go down, Sigerist and 'Miss Stone' would attend to the few posthumous notes and his sense of uselessness would be corroborated by the little left behind. His spiritual exhaustion included regret and frustration, self-doubt and righteous anger: 'The bloody vistas which reign over the horizon of our generation' appeared to him 'more as indictment than threat' while 'the smallness of all those who are content to remain vociferous onlookers' nauseated him. He would be taking work to Rio in an effort to satisfy himself that he would at least be doing something, a 'sort of a pale edition of remaining with one's boots on to the last'. Although he probably also confided these feelings to Peg, Gregory was nowhere near so open with other friends as with Sigerist; he merely told Kubie truthfully and succinctly he was off to Brazil to get 'a badly needed rest'.[56]

Gregory's Brazilian visa photo, August 1941

Travelling first class with Abe on the elegant *S.S. Brazil*, Gregory regained his composure and made the most of his time on board. He ate well, slept late, read and wrote in the ship's library, and mingled with people strolling on the lido deck and drinking cocktails in the bar. He made a point of getting to know interesting Brazilians and arranged a champagne dinner to include his new acquaintances.

By the time the ship docked in Rio Gregory was once more ready to rise to whatever occasions presented themselves. He had arranged meetings with the minister of education and the Brazilian minister of foreign affairs at the Itamaraty Palace, and soon after his arrival began a series of lectures at the Foreign Ministry, the National Academy of Medicine, and Brazilian-American Cultural

Union. Addressing packed halls in French with fluency, nuance, and aplomb, he was as much a hit with cultured Brazilians as he had been when last lecturing in French on the subject of the Russian revolution to Dutch, Belgian, and shipboard audiences over two decades earlier. The history of psychiatry was his primary topic, but his asides were as interesting as his subject. Discussing 'The Role of Psychiatry in Modern Civilization', he told his listeners that science does not pretend to know everything; rather, he quoted Montaigne, 'science is the ignorance which knows itself'. In contrast, he posited, 'Nazism is the ignorance which denies itself', observing wryly that such an attitude was 'the reason for the current Reich's aversion to psychiatry'. Insisting he was hopeful about the future not only for psychiatry but also for the world generally, Gregory deplored the 'massacre' of the individual – the carnage of war that destroyed the physical human being but also the mass media that annihilated the human spirit by levelling opinions and standardising ideas.

Local newspapers celebrated him as 'one of the most respected neuro-psychiatrists of North America' and 'President' of the American Psychiatric Association's Committee on the History of Psychiatry, and summarised his wide-ranging talks to responsive audiences who frequently interrupted with enthusiastic applause. His presentations were subtle, 'literate', and diplomatic (he praised 'the peace of which the American peoples are still the custodians'), while he examined 'erroneous notions' (the mediaeval idea that mental illnesses involved spiritual sickness) and paradoxes (if the soul is immortal, it couldn't fall ill) as well as the impact of Kraepelin, Bleuler, and Freud on twentieth-century psychiatry. In short, Gregory's success was characterised by ironic wit as well as 'great erudition and brilliance'. Abe must have enjoyed being along for the ride, entertained by the warm reception and happy to join his old friend for a quiet whisky at the end of long days of sightseeing, receptions, and public performances.[57]

Gregory returned to the United States on 20 October with calling cards and menus, theatre programmes and newspaper clippings. Restored by having been well and truly away, he soon felt well and truly back. As arranged with his publisher just before his departure, copies of the nearly 600-page *History of Medical Psychology*, hot off the press, had been sent during his absence to over 50 friends, colleagues, and acquaintances. He was welcomed by Ray and the children at home, where nothing had changed, while in his office his own copies of the book awaited him along with Peg, who had sorely missed him, and an avalanche of letters and reviews lauding his achievement. Within days Gregory sent out additional autographed copies to nearly everyone he could think of who might have been interested in the book which had taken so many years to research and write and which had consumed so much of his attention since his first years at Bloomingdale.

The responses were overwhelmingly positive, and the most insightful must have pleased Gregory no end. V.C. Branham, editor of the *Journal of Criminal Psychopathology*, wrote that no one else in the field of psychiatry in America could have handled the subject as well as Gregory, whose 'immense reading and understanding' he found readily apparent in the wealth of historical allusions and scope. He found the book more than a history: 'it is essentially a philosophy for those of us who have chosen this particular type of work for their life effort.' The philanthropist Frank Altschul was particularly impressed with the book's erudition and scholarship. Bartemeier praised Gregory as an excellent teacher as well as a generous friend and called the volume original, 'a great landmark in the history of our science'. Like many others, Clarence O. Cheney, medical director of the Westchester Division of New York Hospital, noted the time and effort that had obviously gone into the book. Isador H. Coriat, one of the founders of the Boston Psychoanalytic Society, congratulated Gregory on 'the best history of psychiatry', not a mere collection of disconnected biographical sketches but a brilliant and convincing study of the cultural and social forces behind psychiatric achievements. Kubie found the impressive book 'magnificent'. Long an admirer of Gregory's use of language both in speaking and in writing, the psychiatrist Clinton Preston McCord was particularly impressed with Gregory's faultless diction and graceful mastery of English. Adolph Meyer found the book 'fascinating'. Merrill Moore, the poet and medical director of the Washington Hospital for the Treatment and Prevention of Alcoholism, commended the book in an effusive review: 'Nobody in America writes with more fluency than Gregory Zilboorg'; the book, which brought to America 'the best of the European tradition', avoided 'psychoanalytic bias', having been written from a 'philosophic and humanitarian point of view' anchored in 'broad human contacts and vast learning'. Father Thomas Verner Moore, head of the Department of Psychology and Psychiatry at Catholic University of America, congratulated Gregory on a 'great book'. Indeed, praise came in from medical colleagues in psychoanalysis and psychiatry (including Portia Bell Hume), from leaders of the Catholic Church and of Jewish organisations (such as the Rabbi of Union Temple of Brooklyn, Sidney S. Tedesche), from former patients (among them Marshall Field and Beatrice Kaufman), and from leading academic figures (for instance the historian of science George Sarton). Brill found Gregory's book a 'very important work' that thoroughly covered the history of medical psychology in ways both scholarly and informative. The *New Yorker* would find the book remarkably coherent and readable, 'learned but not too opaque for the general reader' and 'lit by original observation'.[58]

Gregory could at last be deservedly proud of what his years of thought and research had produced. The modern reader can object that throughout the book 'man' is used for human beings and 'he' is used in ways no enlightened editor would now allow. Readers today may also criticise the book for not venturing far beyond a history of white European men, though advances by Western women are mentioned, particularly in accounts of events in America in the nineteenth and twentieth centuries. But Gregory was attempting something admirably grand and synthetic, a history to illustrate 'the search for human experience as the source for the understanding of man', a quest he felt 'started vaguely and obscurely around the eleventh century and was clearly defined by the thirteenth century' and reached its peak 'in the psychoanalytic study of man' which he believed was 'the true successor of the sixteenth-century humanism minus the latter's cultivation of Greco-Roman erudition'. The book is not academic history of the sort scholars write today, but it is facile to dismiss its unintentional errors and even the shape of the project as an example of Whig history, an account which merely portrays the past as an inevitable and positive progression towards a better, more enlightened world, of which (in a history of medical psychology by a Freudian psychiatrist in 1941) psychoanalysis was the apotheosis.[59]

What Gregory thought he was doing, what he was trying to do, is best described by him in 'Medical History as a Force in Medical Functioning':

> The history of medicine, in the true sense of the words, is not the history of medical discoveries only; nor is it, of course, the accumulation of the biographies of great medical personalities. All these things are only a part of the history of medicine.... The history of medicine is really a complex synthesis of man's life through the ages, in sickness and in health, in peace and in war, in living and in dying – man as a patient whose suffering is to be alleviated, man as a poor wretch who cannot pay for his health and who pays for life with disease, man as a victim of the carelessness of the community as a whole, man as a part of the community which looks after the health of the great and the small. In other words, the history of medicine involves the history of the economic, social, intellectual, and cultural life of man. It is also the history of the doctor's functions as a healer and a research worker, as a student who studies without pay and who, while economically dependent on the patient, must yet remain independent, in some transcendental way, of all economic motives – which is, of course, impossible. It is also the history of the doctor's sense of responsibility toward the underprivileged and the social derelicts. In short, it is the history of the doctor as a social phenomenon and as a plain human being with all his frailties and his prejudices – economic, social, racial. It is the history of the cultural atmosphere in which medicine has bathed, or has been stifled, or has lived throughout the ages.

Gregory was an idealist throughout his life, but he wasn't blind to the realities of reality. He was an optimist, a revolutionary, hopeful always that the world could become a better place than the one he saw around him. He was also always concerned with the individual and saw the history of medicine as 'a living history of our culture in its human manifestations' because the individual's needs are inevitably 'in the center of the picture'. This makes history important in ways other elements of medicine cannot be, although these other elements have their own significance. 'Pure technology', he felt, 'stresses means, efficiency, and a number of other things' which treat people more or less impersonally. 'Pure economics' is also impersonal in being statistical. But 'the physician's job ultimately concerns the individual in relation to himself, to his community, to his culture, to the economic structure of the society in which he lives'. The history of medicine is thus moral: 'it makes the physician more aware of his cultural function and social responsibilities'.[60]

In the autumn Gregory was intensely aware of his moral and social responsibilities as a historian, a doctor, and an individual – and of his limitations. News of the war's progress had followed him to Brazil and back. On 19 September the Nazis took Kiev; two weeks later, they began their advance north to Moscow; on 16 October, they took Odessa in the south. Shortly after he returned, the Germans captured Kharkov in eastern Ukraine, and on 30 October they reached Sevastopol on the Black Sea. As Gregory resumed his New York life, he followed events on the Eastern Front with a heavy heart. The cities and towns that fell to the Nazis he knew from his childhood and youth, from his medical and legal studies and lecture tours for the provisional government; each news report recalled his travels as far as Baku with Sokolov and on his own, the workers' soviets eager for information, the crowded trains on lines now used by Hitler's soldiers, the theatres in Moscow where Nazi officers would soon fill the best boxes, the streets of Leningrad that had been his Saint Petersburg, his Petrograd, where as the autumn advanced, snow began to fall. He remembered the Neva freezing, the cold winters, and the breadlines.

Amid the correspondence waiting for him on his return was a stunning letter from Lehrman detailing the further particulars Gregory had requested: The special meeting, rescheduled for 31 October, would be an 'investigation and hearing', for the board of directors regarded Forsyth's statement 'as constituting a statement of charges'. Although no one claimed Gregory had violated any specific rule or regulation of the Society, he was accused of

> the commission of acts which may unfavorably affect the character of the psychoanalytic movement or the interests and reputation of the Society or of its members, and hence of conduct which the Board and the Society may regard as unprofessional.[61]

Notes

1 GZ to MSZ, nd.
2 GZ to HES, 16 December 1940; Mildred Chernov to GZ, 13, 24 December 1940; GZ to Leo Bartemeier, 6 January 1941, and to Beatrice Rapoport, 18 February 1941; 'Record of Mr. F.'s Visits and Payments'; GZ to James Warburg, 28 May 1941, all GZB.
3 'Record of Mr. F.'s Visits and Payments', GZB, and GZ, NYPSB, 28 November 1941, 268, 279–280. For reasons of confidentially I am not using the patient's real name, which was originally distinctively Jewish but changed by the patient to an Anglo-American name similar to Sam Forsyth.
4 GZ, NYPSB, 28 November 1941, 255–256, 260, 279–280; Forsyth, NYPSB, 31 October 1941, 61; Virginia Schoales, NYPSB, 12 December 1941, 493; 'Creating a New Kind of Paper Is an Adventure in Journalism: *PM*', *Click: The National Picture Monthly*, August 1940, 15.

5 GZ, NYPSB, 28 November 1941, 255–256, 260, 262; Forsyth, NYPSB, 31 October 1941, 47.
6 GZ to HES, 6 January 1941; GZ to V.C. Branham, 9 January 1941, and to Paul Holmer, 4 February 1941, GZB.
7 GZ to Helen Parkhurst, 29 January 1941, GZB.
8 GZ to Raymond Gosselin, 4 February 1941, GZB; Lawrence Kubie to John M. Murray, 25 September 1941, and to David Levy, 3 April 1941, 17 November 1939, DL, Box 8, Folder 33.
9 Harold Kelman and Emeline Place Hayward to GZ, 9 January 1941, and David Levy, Kelman interview, 8 February 1941, DL, Box 8, Folder 33.
10 David Levy to Lawrence Kubie, 31 March 1941, and Kubie to Levy, 3 April 1941, DL, Box 8, Folder 33.
11 Forsyth, NYPSB, 31 October 1941, 50; GZ, NYPSB, 28 November 1941, 282–283.
12 Forsyth, NYPSB, 31 October 1941, 53; GZ, NYPSB, 28 November 1941, 284–288.
13 Forsyth, NYPSB, 31 October 1941, 53, 54–55, 73; GZ, NYPSB, 28 November 1941, 290–291.
14 Forsyth, NYPSB, 31 October 1941, 57–68; GZ, NYPSB, 28 November 1941, 292–295.
15 Forsyth, NYPSB, 31 October 1941, 73, 81; GZ, NYPSB, 28 November 1941, 296–300; 'Record of Mr. F.'s Visits and Payments', GZB.
16 GZ, NYPSB, 28 November 1941, 304; GZ to Eugene Black, 17 February 1941, GZB.
17 GZ to HES, 4 February 1941; HES to GZ, 7, 19 February 1941; MSZ, Dar interview; GZ to MSZ, nd.
18 Moses Ralph Kaufman to GZ, 8 February 1941, GZB; Franz Alexander to GZ, 25 February 1941, and GZ to Alexander, 14 March 1941, NYPSB, 28 November 1941, 314–315.
19 Joseph V. LeRoy to GZ, 10 March 1941; Raymond Gosselin to GZ, 12 March 1941; GZ to Harry Hatcher, 14 March 1941; Oliver Spurgeon English to GZ, 3 March 1941, all GZB.
20 GZ to J.K. Hall, 6 March 1941, and Raymond Gosselin to GZ, 12 March 1941, GZB.
21 GZ to student representatives, 11 March 1941, quoted in Quinn, 343–344.
22 Reports by GZ and Lawrence Kubie, NYPS minutes, 25 March 1941, NYPSI.
23 Quinn, 271–274.
24 GZ to HES, 27, 31 March 1941; Forsyth, NYPSB, 31 October 1941, 55; GZ to Sam Forsyth, 21 March 1941, DL, Box 8, Folder 36.
25 NYPSB, 31 October 1941: Forsyth, 88, 89, 90, 92; Alexander, 108, 110, 111.
26 MSZ to Sam Forsyth, DL, Box 8, Folder 36; GZ to Leo Bartemeier, 25 March, 14 April 1941, and Bartemeier to GZ, 8, 9 April 1941, GZB; GZ, NYPSB, 28 November 1941, 308–309.
27 Alexander, NYPSB, 31 October 1941, 103, 113, 114.
28 GZ to Sam Forsyth, 10 April 1941, DL, Box 8, Folder 36.
29 Levy, NYPSB, 31 October 1941, 137, 138, and 28 November 1941, 187.
30 GZ to William C. Menninger, 15 April 1941; Max Hellman to GZ, with monthly cheques, June–December 1941; Maurice Wertheim to GZ, 18 April 1941; GZ to Paul Kaufman, 25 February 1941, all GZB.
31 GZ to Lawrence Kubie, 16 April 1941, GZB; Kubie to David Levy, 28 March 1941, and Levy to Kubie, 31 March 1941, DL, Box 8, Folder 33; Educational Committee minutes, 7 April 1941, and NYPS minutes, 29 April 1941, NYPSI.
32 J.K. Hall to GZ, 19, 25 April 1941, James King Hall Papers, Southern Historical Collection, Manuscripts Department, Wilson Library, University of North Carolina, Chapel Hill; GZ, NYPSB, 28 November 1941, 318–319.
33 GZ, introduction to 'The Diseases', 127–134; Leake to HES, 18 September 1941, in Bickel, ed., Correspondence: HES – Chauncey D. Leake; GZ, NYPSB, 28 November 1941, 319.

34 'Why Do Women Fall for – ?', *Harper's Bazaar*, 15 March 1941, 32–33.
35 GZ, NYPSB, 28 November 1941, 313, 319–320, 321–322, 323, 328, 329; Levy, NYPSB, 31 October 1941, 139, 140, 141, 146, 153, and NYPSB, 28 November 1941, 177; Alexander, NYPSB, 31 October 1941, 105, 106, 108, 117, 119, 122, 123, 126, 127, 128, 130.
36 GZ, NYPSB, 28 November 1941, 330; Lawrence Kubie, NYPSB, 12 December 1941, 455.
37 GZ to Roscoe W. Hall, 14 May 1941, and to Austin Davies, 30 October 1941, GZB.
38 GZ to Roscoe W. Hall, 14 May 1941, GZB; NYPSB, 31 October 1941: Levy, 177, 209; Alexander, 129, 134.
39 HES to GZ, 6 March 1941; GZ to HES, 11 March, 21 April 1941; GZ, NYPSB, 12 December 1941, 419.
40 GZ, NYPSB, 12 December 1941, 419, 420.
41 NYPS minutes, 20 May 1941, NYPSI; GZ to Manfred Bleuler, 20 May 1941, and Albert Deutsch to GZ, 25 May 1941, GZB.
42 GZ to David Levy and Franz Alexander, 26 May 1941, NYPSB, 31 October 1941, 154, 161; Levy to GZ, NYPSB, 31 October 1941, 160; Joseph Walker, NYPSB, 31 October 1941, 5.
43 Bertram Lewin, NYPSB, 12 December 1941, 422; GZ to Moses Ralph Kaufman, 12 June 1941, GZB.
44 GZ's secretary to Consolidated Edison, 6 June 1941, GZB; GZ to HES, 5, 19 June 1941; GZ to Leo Bartemeier, 5 June 1941, GZB; HES to GZ, 6 June 1941.
45 Noel Fairchild Busch to GZ, 12 June 1941; GZ to Busch, 17 June 1941; GZ to Maxine Block, 10 September 1941, all GZB.
46 MSZ to librarian, 23 June 1941; GZ to Harold C. Gardiner, 8, 15 July 1941; Gardiner to GZ, 14 July 1941, all GZB.
47 GZ to GWH, 22 April, 30 July 1940; GWH to GZ, 23 April, 4 August 1940, 18 January, 30 March 1941.
48 GZ to GWH, 10, 11 April 1941.
49 GWH to GZ, 6 June 1941; GZ to GWH, 2 July 1941.
50 Telegram, GZ to GWH, 27 August 1941; GZ's secretary to GWH, 22 September 1941.
51 Moses Ralph Kaufman to GZ, 3 November 1941, and GZ to Lawrence Kubie, 10 September 1941, GZB; GZ to HES, 15 July, 8 August 1941.
52 Philip Lehrman to GZ, 22 July 1941, and GZ to Lehrman, 5 September 1941, NYPSB, 31 October 1941, Exhibits 1 and 2.
53 GZ's secretary to Robert Brumby, 4 September 1941, GZB; GZ to MSZ, nd.
54 GZ to HES, 24 June, 25 August 1941.
55 GZ to HES, 25 August 1941.
56 GZ to HES, 8 September 1941; GZ to Lawrence Kubie, 10 September 1941, GZB.
57 GZ to HES, 8 August 1941.
58 GZ from V.C. Branham, 30 October 1941; from Frank Altschul, 29 October 1941; from Leo Bartemeier, 3 November 1941; from Clarence O. Cheney, 7 November 1941; from Isador H. Coriat, 19 November 1941; from Lawrence Kubie, 30 October 1941; from Clinton Preston McCord, 20 November 1941; from Adolph Meyer, 28 October 1941; from Merrill Moore, 28 October 1941; from Thomas Verner Moore, 29 October 1941; 'Excerpts from letters about HMP' and 'Excerpts from reviews of HMP', all GZB.
59 GZ, 'The Changing Concept', 446.
60 GZ, 'Medical History', 6–7, 8.
61 Philip Lehrman to GZ, 18 September 1941, NYPSB, 31 October 1941, 5–6.

Chapter 2

'I do not consider myself up for charges'

1941–1942[1]

The special meeting began at 8:00 pm on 31 October 1941 and quickly took shape as an investigation, a hearing, and a criminal trial. In addition to the ten members of the Society's board of directors, chaired by Adolph Stern, those present included Chester Rohrlich, the board's lawyer; Sam Forsyth with his lawyers, Leo Gottlieb and Joseph Schrieber; David Levy and Franz Alexander with their lawyers, Murray C. Bernays and Henry Gale; and Gregory with his lawyers, Joseph Walker and Roswell C. May. Also in attendance were Nathan Levin, apparently to provide moral and corroborative support to Levy and Forsyth, and M.L. Cohn, a stenographer and notary public, who recorded the minutes verbatim. Various evidence would be submitted as numbered 'exhibits', and the lawyers would call witnesses, who were asked to swear to tell the whole truth, then questioned primarily by lawyers but also by board members. The witnesses in turn would be repeatedly interrupted and asked to clarify particular statements 'for the record'. Long before midnight it would become clear to everyone that trying to investigate and charge Gregory with anything nefarious would be much more complicated and difficult than anyone – except perhaps Gregory himself – had foreseen or even imagined.

The meeting opened, however, with Walker's objections. First, he argued, the board had no authority to hold a hearing on 'charges' because no formal complaint or accusation had been made. Second, he objected to the meeting as an 'investigation and hearing', as legally the two were separate functions. He contended that the roles of prosecutor and judge couldn't be combined; his client's rights would be different in each situation and were thus about to be violated. The board had put Gregory 'in the impossible position of being asked to cooperate with it, but also in effect advised that his cooperation might be the basis of a decision of the Board recommending disciplinary action'. Third, Walker argued the board had no power to recommend or take disciplinary action in response to the commission of an act unfavourable to the character of psychoanalysis or to the Society's or its members' reputations because the Society had 'failed to promulgate any code of conduct or set of standards indicating what act or acts might unfavorably affect the character of the psychoanalytic movement or the interests or reputation of the Society or its members.' Fourth, Gregory had not been told exactly what act or acts the board regarded as reflecting unfavourably on either the profession or the

DOI: 10.4324/9781003190974-2

Society and its members. Fifth, Walker moved to dismiss the purported complaint or statement of charges because it didn't show acts that reflected unfavourably on psychoanalysis or the Society or its members and hence didn't constitute unprofessional conduct. Sixth and finally, his client denied 'the accuracy of the account of his relations with Mr. Forsyth as set forth in the documents transmitted by Dr. Levy to the Board'. Everyone in the room except Gregory and his lawyers must suddenly have realised they were in for more than they had bargained for. The board promptly adjourned to consider the objections.[2]

When the meeting resumed, Gottlieb, obviously uneasy about the apparent gravity of what his client was undertaking, pointed out that Forsyth did not wish to be a 'complainant' and hadn't made any 'charges'. Walker then moved to dismiss the proceedings, emphasising the seriousness of what the board was doing if it went ahead:

> we are dealing with a matter that involves a fellow member of the profession, his professional standing, his standing in the community, and his livelihood…. You are undertaking to embark on a proceeding to establish a precedent entirely contrary to the letters which were written and entirely contrary to the powers concerning discipline in your New York Psychoanalytic Society.

Rohrlich then pressed Levy's lawyer to know if his client was willing to think of himself as having made charges, but Bernays wouldn't allow that Levy was the complainant. Levy's position, he insisted, was 'the complaint if any is within the facts themselves'. The board then took another break to consider their predicament.[3]

On returning, the board declared its determination to proceed. Once again Walker emphasised objections: Without a complainant or charges, the meeting was continuing as 'a group of gentlemen', each represented by an attorney, no one of whom was willing 'to bear the burden on his shoulders of becoming a complainant', while the ten board members were personally assuming the simultaneous roles of prosecutor, judge, district attorney, and jury. When Forsyth was called as the first witness, Gregory and his lawyers left the meeting, which continued without them.[4]

In response to legal questions, Forsyth waived his right to confidentiality and declared Gregory might later disclose all that had transpired between them. He then recounted his experience, elaborating on the points in the formal statement written with the help of Levy's lawyer in May. He confirmed his early miscalculation of the treatment's cost before alleging that Gregory had asked him for 'several things', among them a watch, prizefight tickets, a radio, and a 'glass tank' for developing film. When questioned, he clarified, qualified, and explained. He had actually 'offered' Gregory his watch, had been very happy to give his therapist a present early in his treatment at a time he was beginning to feel quite fond of him. He next admitted he had lied about the tickets, first telling Gregory he hadn't paid for them, then confessing he had. He added gratuitously that he had never been reimbursed before moving on to the matter of the radio, for which Gregory had in due course written a cheque because Forsyth had 'billed' him. He alleged Gregory had asked him if he could get him at a reduced rate some special glass tanks for developing photographs, but he had done nothing about it. Prompted by the board, he agreed that, towards the end of the therapy, he was less happy, beginning to feel imposed upon and annoyed. Finally he alleged that in February Gregory had proposed helping him look after his business interests at a cost of $5,000 a year. When questioned, he admitted being confused; the proposal had occurred eight months earlier; he had 'rehashed' the incident 'ten thousand times and probably tried to forget a part of it'. Dependent on his therapist and emotionally attached, Forsyth had at first figured the business proposition might be 'a test of some kind', then wondered if he might be 'suffering from complete hallucinations'. He had given Gregory $1,000 to see if he would accept it. Soon after he was not only confused but extremely conflicted and felt he could not continue in therapy. Having discussed the situation with several people including his girlfriend, matters seemed clearer to him. Feeling Gregory had taken advantage of him, he went along at his girlfriend's father's insistence to consult Alexander: He wanted him to follow up and he wanted his money back – 'not $990 or $995' but every single penny.[5]

Forsyth's testimony was followed by lengthy testimony from Alexander, who had made a special trip to New York in order to attend, and then from Levy. The board turned its attention to what had occurred in Richmond in May. Alexander explained his decision to discuss the matter with Levy and to involve him in the confrontation. The two had met several times 'in order to decide a plan of action'. Levy reported that a third colleague, who didn't want his name mentioned, had heard the story from another source, and the three of them had met together. As Alexander and Levy delineated what they expected to ask Gregory to do if he couldn't incontestably refute the story that 'was getting around', this colleague refused to go along. Convinced of their wisdom, however, Alexander and Levy concluded that in 'the best interest of everybody concerned, [the] psychoanalytic movement's interest, future patients' interest', Gregory should reduce his professional profile and seek further analysis. Alexander went further: Believing Gregory had made a business proposition to Forsyth, he thought 'he might better take up this publicity work' instead of psychoanalysis; he 'should not appear, after this whole thing, representing psychoanalysis'. While they didn't stipulate that Gregory 'change his profession', they thought 'he might himself come to such a conclusion', and insisted he 'withdraw from being so much in the public eye' and specifically refuse to hold 'any offices'. Levy got on his high horse to justify his actions:

I took it upon my shoulders as a member of this profession to run down a story that I thought was, in the first place, if true, a complete exploitation of the patient, and in the second place, completely opposed to psychotherapy and to the standards of the profession to which I belong.

After six and a half hours of testimony and legalistic questioning, the meeting finally ended at 2:30 a.m. on 1 November 1941.[6]

In the days that followed, rumours abounded within and outside the Society, but the board wasn't prepared to dismiss the 'charges' or to recommend possible consequences to the Society's membership for a vote. Since there was no complainant, Gregory's position continued to be that there were in fact no charges and no case. Walker and May on Gregory's behalf and Rohrlich for the board as well as Gottlieb and Schrieber for Forsyth and Bernays and Gale for Levy and Alexander scrutinised the minutes and pressed Forsyth, Levy, and Alexander to refuse or assume the position of complainant. Gregory naturally wanted everyone to refuse, while board members had mixed feelings about pursing the issue; Alexander and particularly Levy wanted Forsyth to assume the responsibility of the aggrieved. Alexander was unwilling to assume the position; he wasn't a member of the Society and felt the matter was New York's business. Having recovered his $1,000, Forsyth had cooperated reluctantly at Levin's urging and by November wanted no more to do with anyone or anything connected with psychoanalysis. That left Levy, who definitely wanted to press ahead and finally agreed *faut de mieux* that he would be the complainant. There is no record of the board's feelings, but they, like Gregory, would probably have been relieved had Levy refused, allowing them formally to drop the matter. Gregory wasn't pleased either, but neither was he surprised. When a second special meeting was scheduled for the end of November, Gregory spent some of his energy planning a strategy, but he had many other responsibilities and a great deal else also on his mind.

Gregory had been back from Brazil for less than two weeks and there was much to bolster his spirits and distract him from the Society's machinations. Congratulatory letters in the response to his history continued to arrive; his patient roster, which included Lillian Hellman and Ralph Ingersoll, was full, and he had personal correspondence to catch up on. When Hall welcomed him home as 'My dear Gregory', he responded with filial devotion:

> A word from you always brings cheer into my heart and relights a faith in man which at times flickers but feebly amidst the many cruelties of man to man which we are called upon to witness. James was bitter in his epistle and when he admonished us that 'Faith without work is dead' he must have known what hypocrisy, bigotry and cruelty of man was.

Gregory appreciated Hall's affection and kindness, and assured him of his loyalty and abiding regard: 'after all true love can never be repaid but with love'. Neither man mentioned the war – a subject on both their minds in the context of which professional quarrels paled – nor the controversy, but Hall was aware of the special meeting; his note implicitly offered Gregory his support and Gregory was deeply grateful.[7]

Despite his personal troubles, Gregory maintained a perspective that encompassed life's larger issues. When Raymond de Saussure failed by a small margin the diagnosis and gynaecology sections of the New York State Medical Board exams, Gregory asked for a review so that Saussure could 'join our medical fraternity at the earliest possible time'. Similarly, Gregory didn't hesitate when he received a pathetic request for a loan of $50 from Henry Denlinger, a former lecturer on the Chautauqua Circuit now retired from teaching at Connecticut Agricultural College. Grateful to those who had supported him during his early days in America, Gregory sent the sum Denlinger had humbled himself to ask for, insisting with typical eloquence, understanding, and generosity that his 'preference' was that Denlinger shouldn't feel obligated to reimburse him 'unless and until circumstances warrant'.[8]

Some of the matters that claimed Gregory's attention gave him unalloyed pleasure – he looked forward to photographing the painter Leon Kroll for an art journal – while others were simply business, although Gregory never restrained the trenchant humour that survived no matter what pressures were put upon him. Brooks Brothers was the recipient of his wit in the middle of November:

> Please note that your letter of October 4 which I am inclosing misspells my name as well as my address. The blue knickers which were returned to you proved to be too small. I am sorry that despite the measurements taken they were made for a smaller boy.

Whether the underpants were intended for ten-year-old Greg – which seems unlikely – or for Gregory himself is lost to biography.[9]

Both methodical and centrifugal, Gregory had committee meetings to plan and ideas for future projects he wanted to share with Sigerist. He managed a weekend in the country, where on 22 November he chaired the first meeting of the Committee on the History of Psychiatry, while back in the city, he sent Ludvig Aubert, the Norwegian minister in Buenos Aires, a copy of his history, various medicines, and a bottle of brandy. In the midst of this flurry of professional activity and gestures of thanks to his South American colleagues, Gregory took time to commiserate with Field, who was being widely mocked in tabloids as a dabbling 'fat cat', a 'do-gooder', a 'silk-hat' publisher whose wealth, playboy youth, and psychoanalysis supposedly called into question not only the sincerity but the moral validity of his support of progressive causes, which now included not only *PM* but a newspaper of his own, the *Chicago Sun*, whose first issue would appear in December. The cynical columnist Jack Alexander pilloried Field in the *Saturday Evening Post*, belittling his achievements and trivialising Gregory as 'a minor darling of Manhattan's intellectual cocktail set', a 'soul doctor' who flitted 'in the background with the evanescent quality of a Cheshire cat', a 'devil' incarnate, a mesmerising 'Svengali'. Even Gregory's physical appearance was disparaged as suspiciously un-American, pretentious, and unwholesome: His hairstyle was one 'affected by concert pianists of the nineteenth century'; his dark eyes, whose 'effect' was 'heightened by thick-lens glasses', were 'upsetting'. Jack Alexander was a particularly malicious bully, but his snide vitriol was typical of the treatment Gregory regularly received in the popular press. By 1941, however, Gregory was somewhat inured to such aspersions and told Field philosophically, 'The noble gentlemen who attack you and make me out an Americanized-Russo-Luciferian power from the beyond are bound sooner or later to get stuck in the quagmire they are creating.'[10]

With such an attitude, Gregory seemed well prepared to face Levy and the board, and he had the encouragement of loyal and sympathetic colleagues. Emeline Hayward, a fellow analyst at the New York Society, had made a point of finding out what she could. With negative comments about him appearing in both the New York and Chicago newspapers, she proposed a quiet counter-campaign to inform the membership 'what a frame-up the whole thing is'. By mid-November she had spoken to several board members, some of whom hadn't yet made up their minds. She reported that Samuel Atkin felt he had heard only one side of the story, most of which didn't seem to involve 'facts'. In his opinion Gregory should stop standing on legalities and testify in his own defence. Atkin agreed with Hayward that the source of the gossip in the papers was probably the same, the purpose being to set Gregory's colleagues against him, and encouraged Hayward to speak with other Society members so that if the matter came to a vote of the entire membership (as it would if the board decided on censure), they wouldn't be prejudiced against him. Grateful to Hayward, Gregory was nevertheless reluctant to 'campaign'. He deplored 'the terrible situation which was created by a member of the Society', but much as he appreciated the support of those who favoured him 'out of a sense of justice', he felt his friends would help him most if they took the position that he was being 'victimized by malice and slander'.[11]

The second special meeting convened on the evening of 28 November 1941. All ten board members were present, as well as Levy and Gregory and their lawyers. Alexander was invited but didn't attend because of commitments in Chicago. Forsyth had also been invited but had done as much as he wanted to do; he was not only through with psychoanalysis, he was through with special meetings. With Levy as 'the complainant and the presenter of the alleged charges', Gregory agreed to attend the second meeting on condition that the board not assume a multiple juridical role or depart from fundamental principles of fairness or its constitutional powers. Determined to see the matter through on his own terms, he also reserved the right to question the authority and position of the board and requested that he not be interrupted during his presentation of his case, although he was willing to be cross-examined afterwards.[12]

Gregory's lawyers began by questioning Levy. They made the significant point that when Levy sent Forsyth's edited statement to the board in June, he didn't mention that in late May Gregory had written to him and to Alexander denying Forsyth's story and any impropriety. In deciding how to proceed, the board thus had Levy's statement of Gregory's admission but not his denial. Levy explained that as far he was concerned Gregory had admitted his guilt in Richmond, so he and Alexander had had no other course but 'to take his denial as an untruth' and insisted what they had done was 'fair'. Pushed to explain how keeping Gregory from active participation in professional associations was calculated to prevent his demonstrating again what Levy had characterised as 'bad faith' towards a patient, Levy indicated he had wanted to avoid a confrontation with the board and thought such a step would be 'corrective': It would not only make Gregory's name less prominent but would serve as 'a reminder to him and as well a warning'.[13]

When Gregory was called to give his version of events, he stipulated he would 'affirm' rather than swear to tell the truth, taking charge of what would follow while reminding his audience of his status as a Quaker, for whom integrity was essential. Having insisted on complete liberty to tell the story as he wished, Gregory finally began. His presentation of his case immediately transformed the atmosphere from one of a criminal trial to that of a dramatic performance. The examination and cross-examination during both of the special meetings up to now seem to have been designed to reduce the detailed evidence to points which could ultimately be affirmed or denied. Once Gregory took the floor, a story materialised that was substantially different in quality and substance from anything that had gone before. Using humour, sarcasm, irony, wit, and all the powers of his sharp intelligence, he presented a colourful and eloquent narrative designed to move and convince.

He started *in medias res*:

> You realize, of course, ladies and gentlemen, in telling my story I am fully aware of what developed heretofore, from the fact that I read the record of the testimony and listened to the cross-examination. Therefore, in telling my story I shall naturally be unable to refrain from knitting all the ends together.

Whether there was laughter at this point isn't recorded. Gregory continued:

> In the first place, I want to be very certain of one fact, that as a member of the Society and as a recent member of this very same board, I talk as doctor to doctor and as analyst to analyst and do not consider at all my opinions, unfair or otherwise, expressed by lawyers, and this includes my lawyer. I hope they will not interfere with me. I do not like lawyers, and this includes my lawyer, too. They are here merely to be tolerated and as guides accepted in legal form.

Rohrlich interrupted to say they accepted 'that definition'; Gregory retorted, 'That is not a definition; it is a statement of attitude.' He continued:

> I also want it to be perfectly clear that in talking to doctors and in spite of the fact that in the testimony reference was made to laymen and ladies in this room, the ladies in this room are my colleagues and doctors, not to be

differentiated from other doctors. I am talking only for the benefit of other doctors and not laymen.

Gregory's characteristic concern for linguistic precision as well as his dramatic flair contributed to the persuasiveness of his defence and his credibility.[14]

Gregory held his audience in suspense as he started to focus on the substance of the allegations: 'There is one mistake in the record. I mean there is one simple mistake.' Forsyth had told the board he consulted Gregory in September 1940. Obviously, Gregory pointed out, 'that is a slip'. Rohrlich interrupted, 'That was intended to be December, I am sure.' Gregory acceded with a curt and eloquent 'Yes' and didn't develop his suggestion that Forsyth was an undependable witness; the word 'slip' was certainly sufficient to convey his implication to his sophisticated audience.

Then Gregory plunged into the fray:

> Since a great deal of stress on what we call facts – or what some call facts – is made, I want to state from the outset, ladies and gentlemen, that there was a watch, which is still in my possession, a wrist watch. There were three sets of prize fight tickets that I did use. There was a radio, for which I paid. There were a thousand dollars, which I returned. There was no suggestion as to an arrangement for $5,000 for what was termed here non-therapeutic services.

He continued theatrically,

> If you are satisfied with the statement of so-called gifts, I have nothing else to add. If this is what is wanted from me, that is all I have to say. I am at the disposal and order of the Board.[15]

Of course the board wasn't satisfied and Gregory had a good deal more to say. When Adolph Stern urged him to 'go right on', he did. He prefaced his account of his experience with Forsyth by making a fine ethical point: It was appropriate that Forsyth was absent since, even though the patient had waived his right to confidentiality, he would not have felt free to discuss his case 'because there are certain aspects in every case which are obvious to the doctor but are not discussed with a patient at any time.' Gregory finally began.[16]

Because of the case's difficulty, Gregory told the board he did not begin anything like treatment at first or even make a formal 'anamnesis' (case history). His careful use of highly precise and technical words was clearly intended to convey his insight and medical sophistication. He told his audience that it quickly became evident to him that the patient was suicidal; there was also 'a perfectly definite homicidal drive which appeared in the form of impulsive seemingly unmotivated relentless hostility'. The confrontation with Levy and Alexander and now with the board were implicit evidence that Gregory was right, but he now addressed the issue of gossip and the nasty rumours in newspapers. He had begun to hear stories about himself from various sources: He was about to be kicked out of the Society because he had raped a patient; he was up on charges before the American Medical Association and would soon be tried; the father of a young virgin was going to sue him. He declared, 'Well, I have no virgin in analysis; I doubt whether anyone has a virgin in analysis nowadays.'[17]

Gregory resumed his defence by focusing on various statements Forsyth had made. Forsyth had testified he had told Gregory of his concern and mistake about the cost of treatment; Gregory insisted,

> It is not true. One of the outstanding characteristics of this patient is actually to tell enough of the facts that it should not appear wrong, and refrain from telling enough of the facts so that it should be ultimately untrue.

Gregory added he never used the words 'resistance' or 'free association' with his patients – words Forsyth had used in his testimony – thus implying he had been prompted. Gregory insisted that in both therapeutic psychiatry and psychoanalysis he never used 'technical terms of which people make hors d'oeuvres before dinner when psychoanalysis is discussed'. He prided himself on using 'plain English to explain plain human business'. Strategically apologising for what he warned his listeners would be explicit and shocking frankness in mentioning outright untruths and murder, he reiterated a fine point: 'I do not accuse a man of being a criminal or call him a liar'; rather, his own statements were 'clinical observations, which are not prompted by a desire to blacken a person's name because I am up for charges'. Gregory teased his listeners: 'I do not consider myself up for charges. What I consider myself you will know at the end of my testimony.'[18]

Gregory next returned to one of his main points: Forsyth 'was not under analysis'. As an example of the impossibility of analysing him, Gregory cited two occasions when he saw him twice in one day because during the first session Forsyth was 'too sick, too drunk, too disoriented, to do any work with'. Gregory countered the accusation that he advised Forsyth about how to do his job or asked him to share his suggestions with Ingersoll. Forsyth's publicity idea for *PM* was 'legs' – that is, to spice up the paper with gossip and sexual innuendo.' Gregory had suggested to Forsyth that his inability to function at *PM* lay in the fact that he did not grasp the paper's policies. Forsyth's claim that Gregory wanted him to transmit ideas to the editor was patently 'foolish'.[19]

Gregory then focused on the allegations concerning gifts. Confiding that watches had 'a profound psychological meaning' for him, he explained that in finally accepting Forsyth's watch he had been trying to confirm a shared interest in timepieces, to encourage the patient's identification rather than competition with him, and insisted he told Forsyth that in due course he would pay him for it. Gregory went on to talk about the prizefight tickets. Just as he had confided his fondness for watches, he now declared in good storytelling fashion that he liked prizefights: 'That is my sublimation of my murderous instinct.' This confidence was something of a joke, of course – an in-joke among psychoanalysts. Gregory declared he had accepted the tickets because he was convinced Forsyth's impulse to give him something was very strong and had felt that if he refused anything, 'there was the possibility of a suicidal impulse breaking through'. Gregory understood this was a matter of judgement and humbly volunteered that he wasn't infallible; he did what he thought he ought to do 'to prevent the patient from possible calamity'. He had, however, informed Forsyth that in time, as in the case of the watch, he would reimburse him for the tickets, too. Photography was another shared interest, but Gregory flatly denied asking for a glass tank which, given that film had to be developed in complete darkness, was in his opinion an absurdity. Finally Gregory moved on to the subject of the radio. He had refused to accept a radio as a gift because it was not part of his encouraging a common interest, something that could provoke therapeutic discussion. When Forsyth persisted and presented the catalogue, Gregory felt the patient would interpret his refusal as an imputation of inferiority, so he agreed to order an inexpensive radio if Philco billed him for it directly.[20]

As for the business proposition, Gregory flatly denied any desire to do business with the patient but shared with the board his opinion of how Forsyth might have gotten this idea. The patient's drinking, unrealistic views, and tendency to sabotage his own success were contributing to his financial losses. Gregory had suggested seeing him twice a day, explaining that even if the additional sessions cost Forsyth $5,000 a year, the potential therapeutic improvement could prevent him from losing accounts and making poor business decisions, so the extra sessions would be worth the cost. Gregory believed 'the idea of becoming a partner originated in the patient's mind' during the last week of treatment, and 'he was unable to talk because he could not say it.' Forsyth had given him the $1,000 'as an unconscious, impulsive, spontaneous way to homosexual ejaculation'. During their final session, Gregory reported, Forsyth had broken into tears. When Gregory had asked him why, Forsyth had said, ' "I don't know, but I have a feeling that I am in love, that I love you." ' Gregory interpreted the patient's discontinuation of therapy as homosexual panic and flight.[21]

Having responded to Forsyth's account of his therapy, Gregory turned his attention to Alexander's testimony, but first raised the ethical issue of whether an analyst should testify against a former patient. Levy had contended this was acceptable if the analyst didn't betray confidences. Gregory called Levy's conclusion foolish; whatever Alexander said was inevitably based on his knowledge of Gregory's psychology. As his analyst, Alexander couldn't help but use his knowledge of Gregory's unconscious. Walker at this point called a recess so the board could consider excluding Alexander's testimony.[22]

The board decided, however, that Alexander's testimony was in this case acceptable, so Gregory continued: Alexander had reprehensibly failed to mention Forsyth during the many hours he and Gregory had spent together in Chicago in March and had misinterpreted the letter in which Gregory had joked about having so much work that someone else would need to sleep for him. In Gregory's view Alexander wanted to report to Forsyth's girlfriend's wealthy father that he had 'done something'; he wanted to appear responsible and ethical to some-one in a position to support his institute financially. As for what had followed in Richmond, Gregory confided that while he had no cowardice at all when on his feet talking, he was 'a physical coward', frightened when 'face to face with a hold-up'. Reiterating his point about the analyst's power over an analysand, he addressed the board very personally: 'You know if Freud got up and faced you' – here he named three of the analysts on the board – 'and told you that he is going to stand up and accuse you and castrate you and deprive you of your livelihood and achievement that you have obtained in your profession, you would get fright-ened.' In Richmond he had 'accepted the conditions', but 'confessed nothing' and 'denied everything'.[23]

By the time Gregory finished, everyone was exhausted. When Bernays men-tioned a future meeting, Lehrman interrupted, 'If there will be one.' Perhaps con-vinced by Gregory's testimony, he seemed to feel that the matter might end there. Indeed, everyone present was ready to halt the investigation at least for the time being. Given how late the first special meeting had lasted, the second had begun half an hour earlier, but to no avail. The second meeting concluded at 3:00 am on 29 November.[24]

However difficult the situation, Gregory had said what he wanted as he wanted and must have felt he had acquitted himself well. While he waited to see what the board would decide, colleagues and friends continued to support him both directly and indirectly in public and in private. Describing the author of *A His-tory of Medical Psychology* as 'a dynamic figure ... with an insatiable curiosity about practically everything and a wide range of knowledge', the social historian Albert Deutsch, now on the staff of *PM*, concluded his review with an affection-ate and timely jibe, pointing out that, like many Russians, Gregory was 'a flu-ent conversationalist, with a penchant for hogging the floor'. There were floors, however, that he couldn't hog, and he was well aware of the constraints on his fluent conversation. He wouldn't, for example, publicly defend either Field or himself from the scurrilous things Jack Alexander had written, as he told Aus-tin Davies, executive assistant of the American Psychiatric Association. Noting that Gregory had been called a 'Svengali', Davies had kidded him: Although he couldn't say for sure if this were true, he did know that Gregory's handling of the recent history committee meeting was 'very masterful'. Gregory explained the article was

> one of those attacks on Marshall Field by his competitors who don't like a newcomer in the newspaper fold. Not being able to say anything bad about this good man, they accuse me of having cured him of his neuroses. To them it is a crime. Of course, they would have preferred him to remain a playboy.

Gregory concluded, 'There was and is no way of stopping this idiotic attack. It is unfortunate that a doctor under these circumstances cannot do anything but take it lying down without talking back.' Gregory would, however, take the floor once more, for the board soon announced a third special meeting as they wanted to examine a further 'witness'.[25]

Some of Gregory's attention went into consultation with his lawyers, but he refused to devote all his energy to the pettiness of contentious psychoanalysts and wrangling attorneys. He couldn't have avoided following news of the war closely. The attack on Leningrad continued despite the winter while German panzers reached the outskirts of Moscow as temperatures plummeted during the largest blizzard of the year. The papers also reported on battles in regions less emotively important to Gregory: British forces were struggling near Tobruk while the Japanese invasion of China was continuing into Siam and Burma. However distant Bangkok and Rangoon might seem, Gregory was a sophisticated observer of war and had no trouble remembering the Russo-Japanese conflict of his youth, knew that old and new orders were connected the world over.

He was thus appalled but unsurprised by the bombing of Pearl Harbor on 7 December and by Roosevelt's moving declaration of war the following day as the dominos began to fall. Thanking Field on behalf of the Committee on the History of Psychiatry for his cheque for $3,500 to support the publication of the history planned for the American Psychiatric Association's centenary, Gregory reflected on the 'expected clouds over the horizon of our country'. While they didn't dim his convictions and hopes, they nevertheless made him shudder. 'The fall of man to the level of brutality, to primitive sadism', he told Field, 'awakens one to a sense of duty which both frightens and inspires. Those of us who are too old to fight with arms in their hands are particularly aware of the duty these days impose on them.' Field had served in France during the First World War while Gregory had treated soldiers and taken his place at the political heart of the revolution, but over two decades on, the realms in which these two men could 'do their duty' had shifted. Although no one could predict what would be left of values 'in the wake of victory', Gregory now wondered whether 'a true army of scholars and research workers in the field of the humanities' could 'put their supreme effort and last breath into study and preservation of those values which are so easily lost in the atmosphere of smoke and blood'. Reminding Field of a newspaper editor's responsibility to guide public opinion and the public conscience, Gregory told him that if he were humble enough to pray, he would pray for Field ardently. In times of war, spiritual values and prayer, like the war itself, weighed heavily on Gregory's mind.[26]

In such an atmosphere, the third meeting of the board on 12 December seemed poignantly petty and irrelevant, a waste of time and effort to little purpose. Having started the process, however, there seemed no way out but to see it through to whatever shabby conclusion it was heading for. All ten board members were present as well as Gregory and Levy, their lawyers, and three 'witnesses' – Bert Lewin (with his lawyer Davidson Sommers), called by the board, and Lawrence Kubie and Ralph Ingersoll's assistant Virginia Schoales, both called by Gregory.

Lewin had worked with Forsyth between early May and mid-September, and the board wanted to compare his experience with Gregory's. The purpose of the questions Rohrlich and the board posed to him seems to have been to discover whether Forsyth was a dependable person whose story could be believed. Lewin began by recounting the curious circumstances under which he had accepted the patient. Alexander had telephoned him twice, instructing him to keep his work with the patient a secret, especially from Gregory. Alexander had mentioned the gifts, implying they had been 'forced' on Gregory, an impression Lewin's work with the patient confirmed. Alexander had indicated, however, that Gregory's suggestion of a business arrangement had led to the termination of therapy. Under these circumstances Lewin had begun psychoanalysis with Forsyth, but had found the work difficult. The patient had been erratic in attendance and mood, sometimes 'very, very depressed' and at other times 'keyed-up', ecstatic. The analysis was further complicated, Lewin confessed, by the 'disorientation' in his own mind 'as to what was going on', while he felt that Levy's request for a statement had increased Forsyth's 'resistances'. In Lewin's opinion, Forsyth bore no malice towards Gregory and in fact had 'quite a sense of guilt' towards him.[27]

Although Forsyth had written a letter indicating that Lewin should feel free to say anything he wished, Lewin felt compelled to be discreet. When Lehrman tried to get around Lewin's reluctance by asking him about the trustworthiness of a hypothetical patient who behaved as Forsyth had, breaking appointments and not giving 'his original, correct name', he made little progress, and Smiley Blanton finally interrupted in frustration, telling his colleague he didn't care about straw men; he wanted to know about Forsyth. Sparks flew again when Blanton pressed Lewin to give 'a valence' to the alleged business deal as a reason for Forsyth's decision to stop treatment with Gregory in February. Blanton also wanted a number, with ten as 'the base line', that would measure the impact of Levy's request for a statement on Forsyth's resistance and asked specifically which factor had the greater influence in making the patient stop therapy first with Gregory and then with Lewin: the $1,000 'transaction' or the interviews with Levy and Alexander. Lewin refused to answer and finally recommended wryly that Blanton read Lancelot Hogben's *Mathematics for the Million: How to Master the Magic of Numbers*. Gregory was not alone in feeling that the proceedings had descended to the level of the ridiculous.[28]

Gregory had his own turn, however, to question Lewin, who felt that he had been manipulated by Alexander and Levy. When asked, Lewin now repeated that he hadn't known what was going on and reemphasised that Forsyth had been 'annoyed' by what Alexander and Levy had asked of him. Gregory's questions were often loaded. He asked Lewin if he remembered saying over their lunch with Stern that Alexander's attitude towards Gregory was 'abnormal', Lewin said he didn't recall the exact details of the conversation. Gregory quickly retorted, 'I do', a remark immediately jumped on by Bernays and Rohrlich. Lewin did, however, remember Gregory's saying Forsyth might not come to the first special meeting, but not what Gregory claimed as his response: 'Forsyth double-crossed you, and he will double cross them, too.' Having cleverly gotten this statement into the record, Gregory was happy to move on, but Rohrlich intervened: Gregory should not 'misunderstand' that testimony could not be interjected into cross-examination. Gregory quipped, 'Don't misunderstand me. I am in the best spirit of compliance.' Corrected later for transgressing again, Gregory contended with apparent humility that he was still learning to be a cross-examiner. Needless to say, he knew exactly what he doing and he continued to do it. In the end, Lewin turned out to be as much a witness in Gregory's favour as a neutral witness capable of clarifying matters for the board.[29]

But after Gregory was through with his 'cross-examination', matters were far from clarified. Kubie next took the stand and explained he had agreed to testify after hearing about the first special meeting from Gregory, who subsequently shared the minutes of that meeting with him. In the wings as a prospective witness on Gregory's behalf, he had been present during the second meeting. Before he began during the third meeting, however, Bernays objected, stating that whatever Gregory may have told him was 'hearsay'. Walker immediately objected to the objection. When the board decided that it would determine after listening to Kubie's testimony whether it was relevant or should be struck from the record, Walker stated that he would 'reserve the right to object' to Bernays's 'right to object'. On another point of order, a series of interchanges among lawyers ensued, during which Rohrlich revealed he had evidently forgotten that Levy had assumed the position of complainant. Now 'in the dark as to what these proceedings are about', Blanton admitted he didn't know why Kubie was appearing at all. Blanton may have been only momentarily lost, but his comment reflects the increasingly confused focus of the entire investigation. This confusion may well have been part of Gregory's strategy.[30]

As Kubie began his testimony, he conveniently morphed into a morally scrupulous 'expert witness' rather than merely a witness for the defence. As well as being an impartial colleague who had come to know Gregory in various professional contexts, Kubie was a close friend of Lewin's and the two had discussed the therapeutic challenges Forsyth had posed, including the difficulties caused by Alexander and Levy's intervention. Kubie had additionally followed events from the time Gregory had sought his advice in Richmond. While Kubie felt a loyalty to Lewin, he also felt a responsibility towards the Society and the particular analysts involved. He had finally decided he would do 'the greater harm' by not speaking out in specific detail and testified that Forsyth, who had risen out of 'gangsterdom' in Chicago's stockyards, was capable of extreme aggression and sometimes went into 'alcoholic rages'. He once got into a nightclub brawl, assaulted someone he knew and then a complete stranger. The next day, during a session with Lewin, he had been in a severe panic, unclear whether he might have killed someone. That he was likely trying to hide dreadful things he had done in the past made the analysis extremely difficult, while being 'thrown into the vortex of this controversy … gave scope to all the pathological hostilities which were part of his make-up'. Kubie finally saw Forsyth as more psychopathic than neurotic, a diagnosis closer to Gregory's than to Lewin's, and asserted Gregory might conceivably have been justified in accepting Forsyth's gifts. Having portrayed Forsyth as unreliable and his treatment fraught with difficulties, Kubie implied that the patient's assertions were not to be trusted while confirming the possibility that Gregory's professional judgement had been sound.[31]

It was nearly midnight when Virginia Schoales, Gregory's last witness, took the stand. She had known Forsyth since May 1940, six months before he entered therapy, and Gregory hoped her impressions of his character and behaviour would sway the board in his favour. Schoales stated that Forsyth had initially succeeded in furnishing promotional ideas and arranging free radio publicity for the paper, but by early December 1940 he was drinking a great deal and had become unpredictable and unreliable. She told the board about his bandaged hands and attempt to jump out Ingersoll's office window. Confiding in Schoales he told her he often could not explain his bizarre behaviour even to himself and that his therapy was making him very unhappy; he couldn't stand discovering so many horrible things about himself. When he finally produced a long-delayed promotional plan at the end of February, Ingersoll hadn't liked it and had threatened to fire him. At first Forsyth had taken this calmly, but had rung up the next day and claimed *PM* was obligated to pay him $5,000 at the severance of his contract. Forsyth later admitted to Schoales that this claim was 'fantastic'.

Focusing at last on the matter at hand, Schoales testified that Forsyth constantly gave people presents, so she had been dubious when he told her Gregory had asked him for gifts as well as for $5,000 for fees having to do with business. Over the summer Forsyth had recounted a confused story about what happened in Richmond and contended Gregory had in the end threatened to sue Levy and Alexander for libel. Reasoning that it was up to him to defend the two analysts, he had agreed to make a statement at Levy's lawyer's request, but when Forsyth heard there was going to be a special meeting, he was upset, felt taken advantage of, and didn't want anything more to do with the entire thing. In search of a true picture of Forsyth, Lehrman asked Schoales if she recognised his 'characteristics' from Lewin's testimony, but even as the late hour grew later Bernays had the energy to object. Schoales herself, however, retorted snippily that Lewin didn't know Forsyth as well as she did. On that sour yet inconclusive note, the meeting finally adjourned at 1:00 am on Saturday 13 December 1941.[32]

The lights on the huge Christmas tree in Rockefeller Center were lit that weekend, but although the holiday would be festive for the children, the war as well as the board's special meetings continued to hang over Gregory. He rang Kubie soon after the third meeting to thank him for testifying on his behalf, then followed up with a letter of gratitude, telling him that his testimony, which had been very helpful, had also been 'an act of true courage and loyalty to psychoanalysis'. Conscious that his personal troubles were 'minor as compared with the whole structure of psychoanalysis and its future', Gregory bluntly admitted he knew that Kubie had never liked him and that his emotional loyalty was to Lewin, so he was doubly grateful:

> To overcome this affective allegiance of many years standing and to follow the principles of truth and public service under the circumstances must have

been ... very difficult. In these days, particularly when so many persons, peoples, professions, groups and classes are found wanting in courage and ability to make personal sacrifices, it is truly inspiring to find a few who stand up without fear.

Revealing his characteristic awareness of the larger picture, Gregory's letter is moving in its elegant language, measured feeling, and awkwardly brutal honesty. Gregory had assumed his witnesses would be the end of the matter, but the controversy was no mere three-act drama; more was to come. While correcting his method of cross-examination, Rohrlich had informed him he would have further opportunity to testify. Whatever frustration and fury Gregory felt as his reputation continued to be assailed, he tried to keep the matter in perspective, referred to it to merely as 'the jam' he was in, and held his temper as he prepared for what he hoped would be the final meeting now scheduled for 19 December. He just had time to pass on his prizefight tickets for that evening to the journalist Bob Brumby at *PM* and to read a letter from Alexander, a copy of which had been sent to each member of the board and to Levy's lawyer, who had shared it with Walker, who had in turn shared it with his client at what must have seemed the 11th hour.[33]

On the evening of the day Hitler declared himself commander-in-chief of the German army, the fourth special meeting began with various legal arguments about Alexander's letter. He had urged the board to decide against Gregory for a variety of reasons, but because the letter was an expression of opinion, Walker contended that it was inadmissible by a man whose only role in the proceeding was as a witness to testify to conversations with Gregory and Forsyth. Nevertheless, with both Alexander and Levy present in the room, the board – at least some of whose members now apparently viewed the matter as a controversy 'between Dr. Alexander, Dr. Levy and Dr. Zilboorg' – decided to hear Gregory's response, pitting him uncomfortably against his former analyst.[34]

Gregory rose to the occasion and spoke at uninterrupted length, repeating much he had already said as he attacked the specific points in Alexander's letter. Alexander had characterised Gregory's November testimony as the 'irrational accusations of a desperate man', a description Gregory quickly refuted explicitly and implicitly in his logical but impassioned dismantling of his former analyst's assertions. Questioning Alexander's right as a psychoanalyst and human being to consider a story true because it 'impressed' him as true, Gregory reiterated his earlier assertion that Alexander and Levy had decided he was culpable long before they arrived in Richmond. Alexander had formed his opinion 'on the basis of what I knew of Gregory's psychology because I was his analyst'. Gregory repeated that testimony based on intimate psychoanalytic experience was not only a violation of trust but of professional ethics.

Unable to suppress his anger, Gregory rapidly became discursive but no less persuasive as he developed one argument after another in his own defence. He attempted to explain Alexander's behaviour: His former analyst, who had reasons to feel aggressive towards him, considered him doomed and had wanted to appear as his saviour. That Gregory had not raised the matter 'spontaneously' in

Chicago indicated to Alexander that he was guilty, but Gregory countered that he didn't bring it up because he had been totally unsuspecting. Alexander's letter once again accused him of asking Forsyth to pay 'for practical aid in his business as well as for therapeutic aid'. Gregory pleaded with his fellow analysts:

> This is a lie on the part of the patient, and I must repeat time and time again, that when I say that the patient tells an untruth, when I say that the patient shows murderous drives, I don't want it to appear to be that I am a desperate, irrational man trying to blacken a person's name. I am speaking in clinical terms that you all use and understand.

He stated yet again that he had never suggested a business partnership with the patient for which he would be paid $5,000 in advance: 'This point, unfortunately, cannot be proven by Alexander, no matter how impressionable he is, nor can it be proven by me, no matter how mathematical I am.'

Praising Alexander as 'one of our leading analysts', playing Marc Antony to Alexander's Caesar, Gregory finally accused him of hubris: Alexander had made up his mind about Forsyth's story after two hours with him and, on that basis, wanted to cancel Gregory's version based on 30 hours of psychiatric work. 'Freud', Gregory contended, 'would not have dared to assume so much.' Alexander wanted 'to eunuchize' Gregory professionally because he hated 'to see a son rise one hair above his father'. In Richmond, Gregory repeated, 'There was no gentlemen's agreement. There was heated talk. I got frightened. I confessed nothing; and I gave in.'[35]

It is hard to believe that such a crescendo could give way to humdrum legalistic cross-examination, but that was at least what the board and its lawyer attempted. With Gregory on the stand as well as on the spot, however, humdrum clarification would not be forthcoming. The questions that followed covered three topics: Gregory's behaviour in Richmond, his therapy with Forsyth, and his relationship with Alexander. While the cross-examination produced a great deal of repetition as the same territory was reviewed over and over, Gregory addressed points of particular interest to individual members of the board with impressive patience, occasional irritation, and frequent wit. On the subject of the confrontation in May, for example, Gregory repeated that he had been 'stunned' when Alexander and Levy had levelled their accusations despite his awareness that among analysts 'mutual and reciprocal plotting and political moves against one another is almost the rule'. When Leonard Blumgart asked how it was possible for him to have been 'both stunned and at the same time extraordinarily clever', Gregory retorted that he may have been upset, but he had not been confused; he had been 'emotionally' stunned, but he had at no time lost his 'intellectual capacity'. As to his being extraordinarily clever, 'It is a matter of your opinion.'[36]

On the subject of Forsyth, Rohrlich wanted Gregory to reconcile his description of Forsyth as a man with a substantial income but also very impressed with his own rather inexpensive watch. Gregory responded that the 'cheap watch' was gold and Forsyth was 'what might be called a Broadway guy' whose clothes were 'sometimes very loud'; 'being impressed by a watch', Gregory explained scathingly, was 'a matter of aesthetics'. About paying Forsyth, Gregory insisted it was his judgement that when the patient through his gifts created an opportunity to put himself at Gregory's level, he didn't want 'to cancel this by an immediate compensation, which makes it a transaction, and it is nothing'. Rohrlich then focused on the receipt and recording of Forsyth's $1,000. Asked what he had done with the money when it was delivered to him, Gregory said he had kept it in his pocket in the original envelope. When his bookkeeper came in the next day, he had simply given it to her, but had only discovered she had put the sum under 'Loans' for want of a better category after he was asked to come to the special meetings. In fact, he told the board, he never looked into his books, a statement that may have surprised Rohrlich but which was undoubtedly true. About paying Forsyth later, Gregory explained he would have paid him 'in the regular course of events' had he returned for treatment; when Gregory had written Forsyth that he would like him to come in to adjust some practical matters, Gregory had thought that either he would return the $1,000 in person or Forsyth would resume treatment.[37]

Each member of the board then had the opportunity to ask questions about his handling of the case. Gregory admitted that by the end of the third week it had become clear to him that Forsyth could not be analysed, in part because of his alcoholism, but when Lehrman asked if he felt that his therapeutic efforts had been futile, Gregory acknowledged that even if they had not achieved very much, 'in relation to the patient' he had 'absolutely no sense of guilt, except, perhaps, the natural professional narcissistic feeling, "Damn it, here something went wrong." ' When Phyllis Greenacre followed up, Gregory confessed that while 'a number of things suggest themselves' that he might have done 'otherwise', he suspected that had he done things differently, another method would also have failed. He concluded with only slight exasperation:

> I do not consider myself infallible, but in so far as handling this case, when I was handling it, this was my judgment and opinion, and if there were any mistakes, to which I neither confess nor reject the possibility, I consider I was doing the right thing with the patient in this way at this time.

When Isra Broadwin finally asked if he would treat another patient like Forsyth in the same way, Gregory could only respond sardonically: he would 'keep away with a thousand-foot pole' and 'send him to Levy.'[38]

Such comparatively composed, measured, and occasionally witty reflection disappeared, however, when the questioning turned to Gregory's relationship with Alexander. Gregory confided that in relation to his former analyst he had 'an unconscious sense of guilt'; there were reasons that made him dislike and fear him. When questioned about specifics, Gregory was cagey: His antipathy went back approximately three years because he didn't like being 'used'. Various board members then pushed him to explain why Alexander would want to attack him, and Gregory struggled at some length to account for his former analyst's behaviour: While Levy and Alexander saw themselves as crusaders for psychoanalysis, Gregory alleged it was typical of Alexander to be unable to do it 'without getting somebody to help him', although in Gregory's opinion the protection of psychoanalysis was 'a secondary motivation'. He repeated his hypothesis that perhaps Alexander had decided to do something forceful about Forsyth's story in order to pacify a prospective donor. However tenuous or persuasive Gregory's theory, the board must have realised Gregory's analysis of his former analyst's psychology was really beside any point that, as the hour grew later, anyone wanted to make. It was after midnight and there was still someone else waiting in the wings to be heard.[39]

Karl Menninger, current president of the American Psychoanalytic Association, had decided it was his duty to intervene in a matter he felt had gotten grossly out of hand. Having waited patiently for four and a half hours, he was now tired as well as exasperated, but began what he had come to say in relative calm, declaring that he hadn't come to defend or attack anyone. Conceding the board's earnest and honest efforts, he felt they were nevertheless 'forgetting something' which as president of the Association he felt obligated to remind them of: Gregory was accused of having behaved in such a way as to hurt psychoanalysis, but 'nothing could hurt psychoanalysis like the prolongation of this inquiry and the creation of the criticism it is causing'. He was appalled that the investigation had become 'lawyers' business' when it should be only 'our business as physicians', and pleaded with the board to let him speak with Gregory, Levy, and Alexander in private to settle the matter then and there with 'the damn lawyers out of the room'. Increasingly passionate, Menninger tried to draw the board's attention to the larger context: Time, energy and money were being wasted on the confrontation while the nation was at war; what they were doing was 'unfair' to themselves as well as to Alexander, Levy, and Gregory; it was even 'unpatriotic'. When Menninger went still further and referred to the investigation as a 'silly performance', however, Blanton interrupted, 'Charges are brought before us and we have to sift the charges.' Menninger barely held his temper: 'You can sift the charges as long as you like, but there is nothing in God's world that compels you to take any action.' Doggedly refusing to let the matter drop, Carl Binger countered that the board saw pursuing the case as the Society's 'duty', while Stern, begrudgingly acknowledging Menninger's good intentions, went so far as to reprimand him for having gone about his mission 'the wrong way'.[40]

As soon as Menninger left the room, Rohrlich volunteered that his words were ungermane, so the dutiful board members voted they should be stricken from the record. Following a good deal of procedural back-and-forth, the board next decided to dismiss a witness on Gregory's behalf (whose testimony they considered hearsay) and, with the stenographer conking out, they deferred Gregory's cross-examination. The fourth special meeting finally ended at 2:00 am on Saturday morning 20 December 1941.[41]

There would be little time for Gregory to thank much less console Menninger for his bootless effort or even to do more than catch up on sleep before the fifth special meeting convened exactly 36 hours later at 2:00 pm on Sunday afternoon. Testimony from Forsyth, Levy, Alexander, and Gregory and from various others on Gregory's behalf and for the board had all been heard and recorded. Everyone except Gregory had been cross-examined by lawyers as well as board members, and board members had already had their opportunity to ask Gregory any questions they wanted. The final cross-examination, which Gregory had anticipated since it had been threatened during the third meeting eight days earlier, would consume nearly the entire four hours of the final meeting and would be led by Levy's lawyer Murray Bernays.

After a lengthy discussion among the lawyers about the purpose of the cross-examination – Gregory's treatment of Forsyth being the crucial issue and his relationship with Levy at best a tangential matter – Bernays went for the jugular. He began by asking Gregory to confirm his 'position': that Forsyth was 'a person without substantial credibility' but that he himself was 'worthy of belief'. The other lawyers immediately understood the classic tack Bernays was taking, but he then stated for the benefit of the board that he was 'embarking on a line of examination going directly to Dr. Zilboorg's credibility'. In short, Bernays wanted to demonstrate that Gregory's testimony was untrustworthy because he was a liar who had misrepresented himself and his achievements and lied to the board, a deeply and essentially mendacious person unqualified to practise medicine.[42]

Walker and Rohrlich were uneasy with this line of questioning, and much of what followed that Sunday afternoon was uncomfortable for everyone except perhaps Bernays and Levy. Lawyers as well as psychoanalysts continued to argue about parameters while Gregory refused to answer questions from Bernays pertaining to Forsyth, insisting as he had from the start that he would only speak to his medical colleagues about matters concerning psychology. Bernays, however, had no intention of asking Gregory about his treatment of Forsyth and started on the apparently trivial subject of what Gregory had said about 'glass tanks'. Gregory confirmed his earlier testimony: Film needed to be developed in the dark and there was 'no such thing as a glass developing tank'. Bernays then read from *Making a Photograph* by Ansell Adams, who stated, 'Developing, fixing and washing tanks for cut films should be of glass, hard rubber, or non-corrosive metal.' Gregory tried to explain the difference between the shallow trays he used in his amateur laboratory on the farm and deeper tanks such as those Adams described, insisting that he had not lied. Bernays pressed the issue, but Binger interrupted: Gregory's 'credibility' did not 'come into the question at all'; Blanton immediately concurred.[43]

Bernays was more than willing to move on. He next cited biographical data from the 1941 edition of the *Biographical Directory of Fellows and Members of the American Psychiatric Association* and presented a photostatic copy listing Gregory's medical qualifications: an MD in 1916 from the Psycho-Neurological Institute in Petrograd and an MD in 1926 from Columbia

University. Once Gregory had confirmed the qualifications, Bernays wanted to know what other 'degrees' he had. Gregory rapidly realised where Bernays was going and responded that he didn't think he held any other degrees; he had passed exams, but he had no 'diplomas'. Rohrlich tried to get Bernays to focus on Gregory's credibility in facts and circumstances related to the matter at hand rather than on the issue of his 'general truthfulness', but Bernays insisted that Gregory's truthfulness about 'the matters which are on trial here' should be 'tested by whether or not he makes misrepresentations to his colleagues and to the public in other matters'. Bernays wanted to offer 'unimpeachable documentary evidence' to show that 'this man is not worthy to be believed by this Board'; he was justified, he contended, because Gregory had indicated the board would finally have to decide on the matter based on whether it believed him or Forsyth, Alexander, and Levy. Bernays then read from a copy of Gregory's Columbia University transcript, indicating the basis of admission as 'MD 1917' and 'LLD 1914'. After citing another transcript indicating the basis of admission as 'Pre-Medical and additional degrees, LLD, University of Kiev 1914; MD and PhD Psycho-Neurological Institute of Petrograd 1917', Bernays finally submitted 'a sworn statement bearing the signature of Gregory Zilboorg ... purporting to certify that he completed an examination in Latin at a Gimnasium in Kiev in 1913'.[44]

What followed was a humiliating invasion of Gregory's privacy as Bernays badgered him with questions about his Russian education. Bernays attempted to show that Gregory couldn't have passed a Latin exam in 1913 and received a law degree only a year later and couldn't have received an LLD from both the University of Kiev and the Psycho-Neurological Institute. To conclude, Bernays submitted a letter written to him 'by an expert in Russian law' along with photostatic copies of officially translated documents about the study of law in Russia in an effort to prove that Gregory's statements about exams and diplomas and degrees were 'untrue because they could not have been true'.[45]

Gregory was at last rattled. He called some questions 'stupid' and others 'foolish', telling the board that if the cross-examination did not focus on 'the case', he would leave, because 'these documents, they present absolutely nothing'. He begged his colleagues not to allow 'all of the gossip and all the suspicions about me in America' to be 'ventilated here', yet when Lehrman felt compelled to ask if Bernays were aware of the difficulties Jews had in Russia, Stern declared the interruption out of order and urged Bernays to move on. Approaching the end of his tether, Russian syntax began to influence Gregory's still eloquent English. Feeling he was being 'left under a cloud' as Levy's lawyer pushed ahead, Gregory informed him, 'I answered Mr Rohrlich this question' and 'This I don't remember'; he didn't tell Forsyth or his bookkeeper, who was 'attending to the purse strings', what was 'in my own secret thought' and didn't want 'to answer twice to one question'. However exasperated, he wanted to go on record as stating that 'in reporting everything that Alexander and Levy told me, under oath, I don't mean to say that I inadvertently photographically, as it were, repeated by heart everything'. When Bernays then asked him why Alexander insisted on imposing conditions, Gregory responded, 'I am not searching his reasons.'[46]

Gregory didn't grow calmer when Walker tried to help him out, posing questions that forced him to make public for the board a history that was personal and painful. Gregory insisted he 'did not lie a thing about these documents'; his medical 'degree' had been the result of a special wartime dispensation, but 'from the legalistic point of view', he possessed 'no degrees whatsoever' except for his American medical degree; he had discussed his education at length when applying for admission to Columbia, whose professors had decided his experiences were commensurate with various American equivalents. Prompted by Walker, Gregory patiently described his education in Russia, his completion of his legal studies in Kiev, and his medical studies at the Psycho-Neurological Institute, the system of exams, the challenges he had faced as a Jew in terms of eligibility, and even the right to live in Petrograd.[47]

The questions that followed from individual board members revealed their ignorance, persistence, and insensitivity. Blumgart asked Gregory if he had done 'a certain amount of work at the University of Kiev'. Gregory responded, 'Not a certain amount; full work.' Blumgart posited that 'due to certain circumstances', the legal authorities hadn't given him 'a legal certificate or degree or acknowledgement of the work'. Gregory denied this was the situation and tried to explain. Blumgart then asked if mobilisation in 1914 was the reason Gregory had 'no documentary proof' of his degree in law. Gregory held his temper and told his colleague he had 'no documentary proof on account of many other things'. Perhaps intending to do Gregory a favour by allowing him to explain the difficulties faced by Russian Jews, Lehrman even questioned Gregory about his status at primary school, wanting to know if as a Jew he had been permitted to attend 'as a registered student'. When Greenacre had difficulty believing he had been admitted to Columbia 'without any documentary evidence', Gregory became haughty: He had never concealed anything; he had been 'treated with absolute credibility' by all those colleagues who considered him a future colleague. When pressed to know if he had any 'documentary proof' at all of his medical qualifications from the Psycho-Neurological Institute, Gregory reached the end of his patience: 'I have no documentary proof as to anything, or even as to when I was born.... The situation is perfectly clear, and I would prefer that you don't all benefit by this situation and pry into my private life.'

To refute Gregory's testimony Bernays finally wanted to call in an expert in Russian law to testify on the matter of degrees. Walker protested that any 'prolongation' of the situation' would be 'very, very difficult', and indeed everyone, except perhaps Bernays, was eager to bring testimony to an end. The board resolved that it did not need to hear further witnesses, but Bernays pressed the issue until Rohrlich offered him on Levy's behalf and Walker on Gregory's the option of submitting memoranda for the board to consider during their deliberations. The fifth and last of the special meetings finally finished at 6:00 pm on Sunday evening, 20 December 1941.[48]

The first Christmas of the war was a strange holiday. Much was as it had always been, despite the sense that it would not remain so. On New York's Fifth Avenue shops were filled with commodities that would soon be rationed or unavailable. Winston Churchill spent Christmas with Roosevelt in Washington, confirming America's support of the Allies, and as military conscription loomed, it would for many be the last occasion for a long time for families to spend time together. Ingersoll enlisted in the United States Army just before the end of the year, leaving Shadow, his Labrador, with Gregory on indefinite loan, a Christmas present for the children but also a reminder of his absence. Gregory himself spent the holiday in the city, missing Peg in the moments he spent at home and, except for Christmas and New Year's Day, attending to pressing matters at the office where Peg worked close by at her desk. There was a great deal for Gregory to try to catch up on while the cloud continued to hang over his head.

He was still angry, of course, but felt he had done his best and was convinced, as he had told the board, that the situation was a 'conspiracy' made up of 'three different lines'. Forsyth was the first, and Gregory considered him a 'very sick man' who was 'very dangerous to himself and others', although Gregory would not feel his former patient was 'guilty' no matter how much Forsyth might harm him. Alexander was the second, and Gregory saw him as 'a very sick man' who was 'guilty of a murderous assault on his son', whose attack he found unforgivable. The third 'line' was Levy, whom Gregory considered 'honest' but 'frequently confused', a man who – as Levy had repeatedly demonstrated to the New York Psychoanalytic Society – thought he had a duty he was compelled to perform, yet was too often 'thoroughly misled'.[49]

Gregory had talks to prepare that, given his circumstances, were particularly ironic. On 23 December he spoke at the Hotel Peter Stuyvesant on 'How Men Fight: A Psychological Approach', a speech about soldiers in wartime but peculiarly personal in its emphasis on the psychology of self-defence and attack. At Emeline Hayward's request, he had agreed to address the Women's City Club in January on 'The True Meaning of Punishment', a subject that must have resonated uncomfortably as he waited for the board's decision. Much on his mind, however, had nothing to do with the New York Psychoanalytic Society. The war, now that America was involved, seemed an urgent matter about which he wanted to do what he could. The situation in Russia had a particular claim on his heart, and he planned to speak on behalf of Russian War Relief early in the new year. With so many public commitments and Ray's limited understanding of the war and the special meetings, he longed simply for privacy and peace. He missed Sigerist and longed 'to get together' at leisure to 'chat, drink, eat, and chat again' with the friend who over the years had become for him a 'source of inexhaustible enthusiasm and serenity'. Although it often involved cancelling appointments with patients and making clandestine arrangements, he stole moments alone with Peg.[50]

As the year drew to a close, Gregory struggled to put the season as well as the ethical questions at the investigation's forefront in a wider and meaningful historical and psychological context. More general and broadly spiritual concerns were inevitably on his mind as he celebrated the holiday that was also his 51st birthday, while his personal and practical difficulties included his professional reputation but also the conflict posed by his loyalty to his wife and children on one hand and his love for Peg on the other, a head-on collision in the making. While the board deliberated, he thought about morality and responsibility, about belief in anything as well as Christianity as a response to the world's problems and those of the individuals in it.

While reluctant to discuss the pending judgement, when colleagues continued to express their support both obliquely and directly, Gregory responded in kind. He had discussed the ordeal with Sigerist when the two dined together during a brief visit to Philadelphia in mid-December, but when he wrote to wish him a happy new year, he mentioned neither the investigation nor any of the other weighty matters on his mind. In contrast, he confided to Hall that he found this first Christmas of the war 'really sad'. Reflecting on life's incongruities, Gregory affirmed that faith was indeed a good thing, 'yet realities keep on jarring us so badly that one contemplates the Sermon on the Mount with a longing which is almost more a sense of melancholy loss than a hope.'[51]

Such longing did little, however, to mitigate Gregory's bitterness about recent events. When he shared with Peg his letter to Robert Palmer Knight, chief of psychotherapy at the Menninger Clinic, she couldn't refrain from editing. The original was, she told him in a note, 'you fighting bitterly against everyone who has hurt you in the past fifteen years … nothing but vindictiveness levelled at the world'; although Horney, Alexander, and Levy railed against him, he shouldn't descend to their level. From her perspective, his position was strong and he was in 'a crucial spot': Psychoanalysis was 'shaking', but 'decent even thinkers' like Knight 'are going to take hold of it and do something', as she was convinced good men always did, yet such men needed 'the counsel and active help of the quick, clever, keen men with a spark of genius'. That sort of wisdom and aid Gregory could give 'beautifully', not as 'a bitter winner' in a trivial feud, but as someone who had developed 'a tempered judgment' and come to realise 'the pitfalls of petty bickerings'. Only Peg could have chastened Gregory like this, could have been so optimistic and affirmative: 'You *can* think in this way – I have watched you do it and love you for it. It will be terribly hard for you to do it in psychoanalysis, but you can.' In response, Gregory scribbled a note of his own at the bottom of hers, the letter thanking Knight for his support having been produced at his desk and delivered in person to Peg at her desk in the next room, the edited version with her note having been returned by hand to him still at his desk on the other side of the door: 'Yes, darling, you are right, so right! I love you for this and so many, many things.' Touchingly, having taken Peg's words to heart, he now sought her approval: Did she think the letter 'as corrected' was 'alright'?

From his crucial spot in his strong position, Gregory sent the joint effort to Knight. He told him that among those who had 'found it possible to assure me of their friendship and loyalty you and Karl [Menninger] were the most straightforward and sincere, and I was deeply moved.' Echoing his letter to Hall and still in search of a context within which he could make meaningful sense of experiences that had consumed the better part of the year, Gregory was more specific:

> This business is dirty and very inhuman. It looks as if it will be finally resolved without much further damage, but it is so painful to lose faith in those whose duty it is to remain decent. Alexander proved to be a perfidious, small man. Levy – smaller and as perfidious. A pity. I gave no quarter and I think I won – as far as the immediate, formal issue is concerned – but analysis was hit badly.[52]

Gregory, with Peg's help, tempered his judgement and tried to rise above the petty bickering, but Levy and his lawyers did not. Although Rohrlich had written Bernays and Gale before the fourth special meeting that further information about education in Russia was unnecessary, and although the board had made clear at the end of the fifth meeting they didn't want additional testimony from an 'expert' on Russian law, Levy's lawyers nevertheless decided, likely at their client's urging, to pursue the matter in order to challenge Gregory's 'studies and degrees'. In a letter to the board on Christmas eve, Bernays and Gale summarised an affidavit by a 'fully qualified' authority, contending that Gregory's 'claims' represented 'legal impossibilities' because the Psycho-Neurological Institute couldn't have granted a medical degree prior to 1918, indeed it had had 'no right to grant degrees of any kind'. Further, according to the expert, no 'special rule of the government' in wartime would have allowed the Institute to qualify doctors because its curriculum was insufficient and its admission requirements substandard – that is, it had been 'a school of mixed character', an institute that had accepted Jews and female students who didn't have the qualifications necessary for university matriculation.

Levy's lawyers followed up with a long memorandum, a digest of what in their view had transpired during all five special meetings, drawing attention to differences in the various versions of what had happened during Forsyth's treatment and in Richmond. Their position was that Gregory was lying to defend himself while Forsyth, Levy, and Alexander were unbiased and telling the truth. In their opinion, Gregory had fact and logic against him at every turn; the board was obligated to consider if Gregory had told the truth about anything.[53]

Just as Levy had conducted his survey on student intimidation against the express wishes of the Educational Committee and just as Bernays and Gale had gone ahead with the qualified authority despite the board's stated lack of interest, Levy could not resist adding to his lawyers' memorandum his 'Personal Statement and Some Psychological Observations Concerning Dr. Zilboorg's Testimony'. Resentful and jealous, unable to let go or move on, Levy was incensed that Gregory had used 'dramatic talent, emotional appeal and psychological persuasion' while the same 'latitude', he contended, hadn't been given to him or Alexander. Specifically, Levy resented having been cast in the role of a liar and a perjurer, 'an accomplice in a nefarious plot to destroy an innocent man', and alleged he and Alexander had been 'besmirched'. He then pilloried Gregory, accusing him of pleading for the board's sympathy and understanding; in fact, Levy wrote, he had 50 examples in his notes but would cite only a few. Gregory had 'revealed his showmanship to the highest degree', playing 'fast and loose' with his audience and going into unnecessary detail 'to display his knowledge of watches and photography'; Gregory had tried to show 'how ethical he was' but had made 'unnecessary revelations from his analyses'. According to Levy, Gregory had used 'cajolery', complimenting the board's attorney and representing board members as colleagues who alone could understand his situation. Gregory had sometimes 'sobbed and pleaded'; at other times, he had been 'sarcastic and vituperative', using 'all the methods of the theatre ... to stir the emotions of his audience and distract their attention from the issue': his dastardly 'exploitation' of Forsyth. Angry and indignant, Levy had clearly had no editor to plead for tempered judgement and the better part of valour.[54]

Walker and May in their turn wrote a memorandum on Gregory's behalf in which they calmly, succinctly, and eloquently laid out their case in seven numbered points. They argued in the first three that the board did not have power to discipline in this case. First, the Society's constitution only authorised 'discipline' in the case of an act that 'unfavourably affects the character of the psychoanalytic movement'; the Society promoted, advanced, and protected doctrine 'rather than policing activities of members in their daily practice'. Second, the Society couldn't discipline Gregory because there was no law, statute, code, or standard which he had specifically violated; unless and until the Society formulated the standards of conduct it considered the standard of Freud and his pupils, the Society couldn't legally discipline a member for conduct that a particular board of directors or the membership of the Society *pro tem* might consider contrary to their respective precepts. Walker and May's third point was the one Gregory had made at the very first meeting: The Society was without power to discipline because he did not analyse Forsyth.

With their fourth point, the lawyers shifted focus, asserting that even if the board had the power to discipline Gregory, he should be cleared of the alleged charges. The issue was Forsyth vs Zilboorg; Levy and Alexander were irrelevant. The patient was 'inconsistent and mendacious', while Gregory had acted 'conscientiously and in good faith' and 'in accordance with his professional lights'. Indeed, the board and the Society had a duty to vindicate Gregory, who had been subjected to 'malicious persecution', rather than to penalise him for 'essaying a difficult case'.

With their fifth point, Walker and May took a different tack: The 'hearing' had not been fair for several reasons. First was the matter of who had brought 'the charges'. Forsyth didn't himself submit a complaint to the Society and had said he wasn't the complainant; Levy had finally volunteered to assume the role. Second, the board had ended up both prosecuting and judging, which was patently unfair. Third, the entire matter of Gregory's education in Russia was inadmissible and 'extremely prejudicial to a fair decision'. The lawyers' sixth point followed from the fifth: Alexander's testimony should be stricken from the record because he had 'violated the confidential relation' of analyst and patient. The lawyers' seventh and final point was that Gregory's alleged 'confession' in Richmond 'should be given no weight.' Levy and Alexander had taken it upon themselves to pass judgement and propose a punishment, then in order to protect themselves, they had obtained a statement from Forsyth, 'forwarded it to the Society and pressed its allegations'. The lawyers characterised the two men as hostile to Gregory for personal and political reasons; both had acted with 'witting or unwitting biases'. In sum, it wasn't Forsyth's story that had made this matter a *cause célèbre* but 'the atmosphere' created when Levy and Alexander got behind it and pushed it. The simple question was if the board was going to destroy 'an eminent member of this Society' because of the story of an ex-patient, 'a sick, unfortunate man whose untruthfulness is self-confessed, is established by his own conflicting statements and by documentary evidence and is part and parcel of the pattern of his disease'. Gregory couldn't have done better had he written the memorandum himself; indeed, perhaps he had done or at least made a substantial contribution.[55]

There would be no immediate decision by the board over the holiday. They would in the end deliberate well into 1942, their options being to exonerate or to take the matter to the full membership for a vote with a recommendation to reprimand, suspend, or expel. Meanwhile, Gregory displaced his 'murderous instincts' by attending a few prizefights, his preferred 'mode for channelling off a great deal of insecurity and aggression'. In early January he even managed to get ringside tickets for the much-touted Joe Louis–Buddy Baer match at Madison Square Garden. Gregory didn't, however, have much chance to exercise displacement during the dramatically brief fight – Louis knocked his opponent out just before the end of the first round. Louis enlisted in the army the following day, declaring for the waiting newsreel cameras that, having left the ring, he was now eager to fight the 'Japs', but Gregory couldn't displace any violent tendencies he might have had through physical combat with Hirohito's forces. He would simply need to summon his patience and trust in Peg's mitigating good sense and generosity of spirit.

At the end of February, Lehrman as the Society's secretary notified Gregory, Levy, and Alexander of the board's recommendation. By a vote of seven to three they had decided the membership should reprimand Gregory. The majority (Adolph Stern, Lillian Powers, Phyllis Greenacre, John A. Millet, Carl A.L. Binger, Smiley Blanton, and Leonard Blumgart) believed he had 'failed to offer a consistent or satisfactory explanation for his behavior, especially for his acceptance and retention for two months of the $1,000 from the patient'. They found his testimony 'frequently inconclusive and lacking in simple directness and candor', and regretted that he chose 'to attack those who testified against him, rather than frankly to meet the testimony itself'. They attributed his 'injudicious acts' to 'unconscious motivations', but blamed him for shirking his 'responsibility to employ a technique not susceptible of misinterpretation' and concluded his 'acts were such as to reflect unfavorably the character of the psychoanalytic movement and the interests and reputation of this Society and of its members.' The minority (Samuel Atkin, Isra Broadwin, and Philip Lehrman), noting 'the patient's own testimony that he was alcoholic, depressed and suicidal, the fact of his unreliability in keeping appointments in business, and with his physicians, and other character testimony bearing on his dubious credibility', had been 'impressed with the patient's untrustworthiness'. They asserted that had Alexander really had Gregory's 'welfare at heart', he should have spoken to him 'under more propitious circumstances than he did in Richmond'. Levy had been 'naïve' and Alexander irresponsible in deciding to believe the patient after only two interviews. Atkin, Broadwin, and Lehrman finally found 'no proof of dishonesty or any other unprofessional conduct'. At least now Gregory knew where he stood.[30]

At a special meeting of the Society on 3 March Blanton put forward a resolution that Gregory be reprimanded for his behaviour. Before the vote was taken, Gregory was invited to address his peers. Summarising his lawyers' 30-page memorandum with all the drama and eloquence of which he was capable, he spoke as he had always done when at the dais; put at the mercy of his audience, he rose above the occasion, held his listeners in thrall. Ratcheting up the suspense, Kubie then took the podium and moved that the membership take no action on the resolution due to the highly political nature of the investigation and because the board's failure to determine 'the facts', whatever they might have been, made it impossible to share evidence on the basis of which the membership might fairly vote. Acknowledging there had been 'electioneering' on 'both sides' and that many members had determined to vote against or in favour of 'the accused' before the meeting, Kubie also proposed that the entire 'matter' be expunged from the Society's records. The board, however, wanted blood, and members were eager to register their opinion. Given the 'temper of the meeting', Kubie diplomatically withdrew his motions. A secret ballot was finally taken on the board's recommendation, and out of 56 votes cast, one was blank, 16 were in favour, and 39 were against. The motion was declared lost, and *viva voce* the membership extended to Gregory a vote of sympathy.[57]

The aftermath would resonate down the decades. In a reprise of Horney's high dudgeon, Levy immediately submitted a letter of resignation to Lehrman, attributing his decision to an inability 'to stomach the recent action of your Society in connection with the disciplinary proceedings against Dr. Zilboorg'. Gregory and Levy, whose speciality was child psychology, would seldom cross paths in the future. Their interests, patients, and research had little in common, and with other disaffected colleagues (among them Carl Binger, George Daniels, John Millet, and Sandor Rado), Levy would quickly go on to found a rival group to the New York Psychoanalytic Society: The Association for Psychoanalytic and Psychosomatic Medicine. In due course this association would become the Psychoanalytic Clinic for Training and Research based in the Department of Psychiatry at Columbia University. Gregory, however, would remain a member in good standing of the New York Psychoanalytic Society for the rest of his life, and when he had concerns about his own children or those of his patients, he would consult Margaret

Mahler, the Hungarian-born analyst who would replace Levy at the Society as an instructor.[58]

Despite feeling vindicated on ethical grounds, Gregory was well aware of the politics involved in what had happened. He could on occasion joke about divisions and divisiveness within psychoanalysis, but only in general terms, and given his experiences, such jocularity was inevitably barbed. In 1956 he would write,

> Psychotherapy is today in a state of disarray, almost exactly as it was two hundred years ago. The difference between today and two hundred years ago seems to be merely this: two hundred years ago we did a lot of things without knowing what we were doing; today we do things and keep screaming from the house-tops that each of us knows exactly what he is doing, and that the other does not.

Writing generously in the late 1950s about the neo-Freudian analyst Erich Fromm who, lacking a medical degree, was ineligible to join not only the New York Psychoanalytic Society but the American Psychoanalytic Association, Gregory acknowledged,

> It is an open secret ... that psychoanalysis, like any other *organized* movement, is bound to pay a heavy tribute to the art of politics, to the struggle for power, to egocentric sensitivities, and to promotional drives. In doing so psychoanalysis may or may not gain ground as a movement, but it is bound to find some of its scientific progress rather frayed at times, and to leave a portion of its best men on the sidelines.

Gregory would always argue for the individual, the person ironically forgotten or at least insufficiently central to the issue at hand – be it a matter of politics, law, or psychoanalysis – but here he might as well have been making a point about his own situation in the New York Psychoanalytic Society in 1941–1942.[59]

In his particular case, Gregory would harbour resentment against his analyst for the rest of his life. In 1955 he would write of Alexander's early work and refer to him as the man who first noticed possible discrepancies in Freud's use of various terms for the superego, before adding that since 1930 his interests had sadly 'run to other things'. Noting that Alexander was inclined to believe that the ego ideal belongs to the ego rather than to the superego, Gregory concluded rather snidely that Alexander then 'dropped the matter, which is not a very good thing to do with ego ideals, but that is what he did.' A paragraph later Gregory twisted the knife again: 'It is perhaps of more than passing interest', he told his readers, that he had been Alexander's pupil 'in his Berlin days, not his Chicago days'.[60]

In his correspondence Gregory would mention the confrontation only obliquely and in passing. Six days after the vote, he informed Sigerist that the 'dirty business' was over. Gregory couldn't help feeling as pleased as he was relieved and added with a measure of pride that the Society had 'voted almost four to one' in his favour. The degree to which the confrontation had weighed heavily on Gregory for the past ten months is only evident in Sigerist's prompt reply. Delighted at the news, he told Gregory that, as far as he was concerned, the outcome had never been in doubt, although he recognised 'what a worry' it had been.[61]

Notes

1 GZ, NYPSB, 28 November 1941, 269.
2 Joseph Walker, NYPSB, 31 October 1941, 9, 11, 12.
3 Leo Gottlieb, Joseph Walker, Murray C. Bernays, NYPSB, 31 October 1941, 21–22, 23–24, 25.
4 Joseph Walker, NYPSB, 31 October 1941, 31, 32.
5 Forsyth, NYPSB, 31 October 1941, 47, 50, 55, 68, 73, 80, 81, 86.
6 Alexander and Levy, NYPSB, 31 October 1941, 118, 119, 138, 139, 143.
7 J.K. Hall to GZ, 5 November 1941; GZ to Hall, 7 November 1941, both GZB.
8 GZ to R.I. Hamilton, 26 November 1941; Henry K. Denlinger to GZ, 4 November 1941; GZ to Denlinger, 18 November 1941, all GZB.
9 Leon Kroll to GZ, 6 November 1941; GZ to Brooks Brothers, 17 November 1941, both GZB.
10 GZ to HES, 17 November 1941; GZ to Rolf Christensen, 19 November 1941, GZB; Jack Alexander, passim; GZ to Marshall Field, 17 November 1941, GZB.
11 Emeline Place Hayward to GZ, early November, 11 or 12 November, mid-November 1941, and GZ to Hayward, 18 November 1941, all GZB.
12 Joseph Walker to Chester Rohrlich, 21 November 1941, NYPSB, 28 November 1941, 166.
13 Levy, NYPSB, 28 November 1941, 215–216, 222–223, 229.
14 GZ, NYPSB, 28 November 1941, 250–251.
15 GZ, NYPSB, 28 November 1941, 251–252.
16 GZ, NYPSB, 28 November 1941, 255.
17 GZ, NYPSB, 28 November 1941, 260, 281, 282.
18 GZ, NYPSB, 28 November 1941, 263, 269.
19 GZ, NYPSB, 28 November 1941, 269, 273, 292.
20 GZ, NYPSB, 28 November 1941, 281, 282, 283, 284, 286, 287, 288–289, 291.
21 GZ, NYPSB, 28 November 1941, 275–276, 278, 295, 302, 303.
22 GZ, NYPSB, 28 November 1941, 309.
23 GZ, NYPSB, 28 November 1941, 309, 310–311, 323.
24 Murray C. Bernays and Philip Lehrman, NYPSB, 28 November 1941, 339.
25 Albert Deutsch, 60; Austin Davies to GZ, 4 December 1941, and GZ to Davies, 8 December 1941, GZB.
26 Marshall Field to GZ, 9 December 1941, and GZ to Field, 11 December 1941, GZB.
27 Bertram Lewin, NYPSB, 12 December 1941, 361, 373, 374, 386, 393, 404, 405, 408, 412.
28 Philip Lehrman, Smiley Blanton, and Bertram Lewin, NYPSB, 12 December 1941, 400, 402, 411.
29 NYPSB, 12 December 1941: Bertram Lewin, 414, 420, 423; GZ, 420, 423, 436; Chester Rohrlich, 436.
30 NYPSB, 12 December 1941: Joseph Walker, 449; Smiley Blanton, 451.
31 Lawrence Kubie, NYPSB, 12 December 1941, 457, 459, 463, 464, 465, 468, 472.
32 Virginia Schoales, NYPSB, 12 December 1941, 493, 494, 496, 497, 498, 499, 502, 503, 508, 512.

33 Chester Rohrlich, NYPSB, 12 December 1941, 436; GZ to Lawrence Kubie, 17 December 1941, and GZ's secretary to Robert Brumby, 19 December 1941, GZB; Franz Alexander to NYPS Board of Directors, 16 December 1941, Exhibit 27, NYPSB.
34 NYPSB, 19 December 1941: Joseph Walker, 518–519, and Carl Binger, 515.
35 GZ, NYPSB, 19 December 1941, 523, 524–525, 526, 528, 530, 531, 535, 540.
36 NYPSB, 19 December 1941: GZ, 562, 577; Leonard Blumgart, 577.
37 Chester Rohrlich, NYPSB, 19 December 1941, 553; GZ, 553–554, 557–558, 561.
38 NYPSB, 19 December 1941: GZ, 567, 568, 575, 587, 603; Phillip Lehrman, 567; Phyllis Greenacre, 586; Isra Tobias Broadwin, 602–603.
39 GZ, NYPSB, 19 December 1941, 590, 598, 599, 611.
40 NYPSB, 19 December 1941: Karl Menninger, 613–618, passim; Smiley Blanton, 618; Carl Binger, 621; Adolph Stern, 623, 624.
41 Chester Rohrlich, NYPSB, 19 December 1941, 625.
42 Murray C. Bernays, NYPSB, 21 December 1941, 649, 641.
43 NYPSB, 21 December 1941: Murray C. Bernays, 661–662; GZ, 662, 663, 664; Carl Binger and Smiley Blanton, 665.
44 Murray C. Bernays, NYPSB, 21 December 1941, 667, 668, 670, 676; GZ, 667, 669; Exhibits 28, 29, and 30, NYPSB.
45 NYPSB, 21 December 1941: Murray C. Bernays, 679–680, 686, 688; Chester Rohrlich, 688, 689; Exhibit 31, NYPSB.
46 NYPSB, 21 December 1941: GZ, 690, 691, 708, 719, 720, 723, 725, 727; Philip Lehrman, Adolph Stern, 691.
47 GZ, NYPSB, 21 December 1941, 731, 732, 733–735.
48 NYPSB, 21 December 1941: GZ, 738, 739, 740, 742; Carl Blumgart, 738, 739; Philip Lehrman, 744; Phyllis Greenacre, 742; Murray C. Bernays, 746; Joseph Walker, 747; Chester Rohrlich, 749.
49 GZ, NYPSB, 19 December 1941, 553, 554.
50 GZ to Emeline Hayward, 19 November 1941, GZB; GZ to HES, 29 December 1941.
51 GZ to HES, 29 December 1941; GZ to J.K. Hall, 29 December 1941, GZB.
52 Notes between GZ and MSZ; GZ to Robert Palmer Knight, 30 December 1941, GZB.
53 Ernst, Gale, Bernays and Falk to NYPS Board of Directors, 24 December 1942; Murray C. Bernays and Henry Gale, 'Analysis of the Proof', 48, 49–50, both NYPSI.
54 David Levy, 'Personal Statement', 52, 54, 55, 64, 65, 66, 67, NYPSI.
55 Joseph Walker and Roswell May, 'Memorandum', 2, 4, 6, 9, 10, 11, 14, 16, 17, 18, 20, 24, 26, 29, 30, NYPSI.
56 Murray C. Bernays to David Levy, 20 February 1942; copies of majority and minority reports by members, NYPS Board of Directors, all DL, Box 8, Folder 36.
57 NYPS minutes, 3 March 1942, NYPSI; Lawrence Kubie, 'Statement' and Kubie to David Levy, 4 March 1942, both DL, Box 8, Folder 36.
58 David Levy to Philip Lehrman, 20 March 1942, DL, Box 8 Folder 33; George E. Daniels, 2–3.
59 GZ, 'Rediscovery', 108, and review, 'Bypaths', 40.
60 GZ, 'Derivation', 113, 114.
61 GZ to HES, 9 March 1941; HES to GZ, 11 March 1942.

Chapter 3

Mind, medicine, man
1942–1943

The 'dirty business' had caused Gregory a great deal of personal and professional distress, but he was never without perspective. His relationship with Peg was more important to him than his relationship with his former analyst and his New York colleagues, and while waiting for the board to vote, he even told her that he finally didn't really care what the Society did because as 'a good and inspired team' the two of them would 'overcome any obstacle and weather any storm'. Although he didn't yet see a path out of his marriage, it was clear to him that things couldn't go on as they were; he thought about the psychology as well as the practicalities involved for everyone concerned and tried to imagine a future different from the fraught and fragile status quo. He also recognised that Peg was suffering from the constraints of the relationship. Because of it she didn't socialise with most of her Bronxville and Vassar friends, didn't confide in anyone except her brothers and Mary-Alice, and she certainly couldn't mention their love to either of her parents: Her mother couldn't be expected to understand or sympathise, while her bedridden father was increasingly past understanding, one small stroke having followed another since Peg had admitted to the head of the Baltimore school that he wasn't well.[1]

Financial issues paled in comparison to the problems posed by love, but Gregory's lawyers' bill was a hefty $5,000. He would pay it, but a bit of uncomfortable belt-tightening would necessarily follow for the man who didn't keep track of money and preferred in general simply not to think about it. The war was also a constant concern, and in addition to activity for Russian Relief, lectures, articles, and work for the American Psychiatric Association centenary, he had started another book – not the diluted version of his *History of Medical Psychology* for readers with delicate intellectual stomachs he had mentioned to Sigerist but an explanation of psychoanalysis for the general reader.[2]

Gregory had begun *Mind, Medicine, and Man* in the autumn of 1941. His new book would draw on material and ideas that for various reasons did not end up in *A History of Medical Psychology*, and it would focus on Freud, his thinking and relevance in the twentieth century, not on the history of psychiatry in general but on psychoanalysis itself. While *Mind, Medicine, and Man* would be dedicated to Greg and Nancy, Gregory would write it with Peg as both his editor and his

DOI: 10.4324/9781003190974-3

interested general reader. The book would thus have a coherence impossible when working with a challenging collaborator like George Henry. The history had in addition been the product of over 15 interrupted years of research and thinking and had involved reworking material in *The Medical Man and the Witch* and the introduction to his translation of Paracelsus as well as lectures and articles dating as far back as Gregory's historical work at Bloomingdale before his analytic studies in Berlin. In contrast, he would finish *Mind, Medicine, and Man* with its contemporary focus in less than 15 months. The book would inevitably reflect Gregory's personality, his sense of historical and cultural context, his awareness of figures from Hippocrates to Hitler, Newton to Nietzsche, and Petrarch to Picasso; it would complement his history by bringing the account up to the present and allowing him to address issues currently on his mind: psychology and sociology (especially in the chapter 'Civilization and the Social Sciences'), psychiatry and law (explicitly in 'Crime and Judgment'), even psychoanalysis and faith (in 'Psyche, Soul, and Religion'). The book would integrate many of the ideas Gregory had been exploring from the time of *The Passing of the Old Order in Europe* while completing what his history had set out to do – and although he could not have been conscious of it in 1942, the book would also define the agenda for all of the writing that still lay ahead of him.

Yet he could not – even had he wished – devote his entire attention to matters so intellectual and even abstract. Fera had kept him abreast of family life in Mexico. The news usually consisted of trivialities and familiar complaints: Anna had a pain in her side, was out of breath, needed rest; Nadia was home from university for the holidays; Basia had taken over the household cooking. In January 1942, however, Fera reported that Moses was seriously ill, and for the first time in over a year Gregory wrote James, taking a measured medical approach that was both objective and solicitous. From Fera's fragmentary description of his symptoms, Gregory believed that an enlarged prostate was impeding their father's bladder functions. This, Gregory explained, 'is a condition commonly found in old men. It is an annoying, painful and, of course, dangerous condition. The only way out is an operation.' In straightforward, simple, unemotional sentences Gregory attempted to bridge the awkwardness between the brothers, telling James kindly that 'since this condition occurs in old people and since the operation is a serious one, it is very difficult to decide what to do: there is always the danger of not surviving the operation.' Gregory finally revealed his real concern: He wanted to help, to learn their father's 'actual condition' from his doctor, and stressed that 'it is very important to alleviate father's condition as effectively as it is possible under the circumstances.' Gregory was really quite upset: 'I shall appreciate more than I can tell your writing me about the whole situation.'

James replied in an appalling letter encapsulating all Gregory objected to in his family. What had happened was apparently the result not only of old age but of neglect and selfishness on everyone's part. As James rationalised, his egocentric narrow-mindedness must have repelled his brother who was genuinely concerned for their father's well-being. James reported that he had just 'deposited the old man in the hospital'. Admitting 'some guilt of negligence', he pointed out that he didn't see the family very often, and since Moses was never in anyone's good graces, the family hadn't paid attention to complaints of frequent urination and discomfort. Basia, in spite of her nurse's training, had been too embarrassed to take their father to a physician and left the matter to James, who had dithered: The urologist his 'medical friends' recommended was reputedly authoritarian and expensive, then Anna and Basia felt hospitalisation would make Moses even grumpier and he didn't want to go. James and Eugenia had argued with them for a couple of weeks, but James had resisted everyone's plea 'to write to Gregory' for medical advice, emotional support, or financial help: James told him bitterly he had feared receiving 'another tirade'. Only when Moses became incontinent did his second son finally take the initiative. The brusque specialist was treating Moses for uremic poisoning and a bladder infection, but according to James he was one of the greatest urologists on the continent and too busy to communicate directly with Gregory. Basia was at their father's bedside and Moses, now catheterised, was moaning a good deal, but James insisted this was probably 'more from habit than from serious pain'.

Gregory responded with admirable restraint. Irritated that the family had waited so long to seek treatment for an incapacitated old man, he emphasised that his 'considerable pain' was 'very real'. Gregory was peeved that his brother was reluctant to put him in touch with the urologist, noting that 'even the most bearish doctors do not refuse a colleague the courtesy of a report'. He then pleaded with James not to be foolish about 'tirades', pointing out it was 'unwise and rather unrealistic to permit one's own resentment to intrude into matters of this kind'. Gregory may have appeared detached, but he was disturbed that his father was seriously ill and regretted he wouldn't 'see him now for a brief moment before he goes'. Reassuring his brother that death was the usual 'story' in such cases and that James had no reason to reproach himself, Gregory knew what his brother was up against: 'The diagnostic wisdom of Mother and the diagnostic sloppiness of our older sister are certainly to be questioned and should at no time be heeded.'

By early February, however, Moses was responding to treatment. He had obviously been frightened of dying and would remain in hospital for several more weeks, but James couldn't resist telling Gregory that as their father's physical condition improved, his disposition became worse. Moses complained James didn't spend enough time with him and that Gregory didn't care. James, who likely didn't visit often or stay long, urged his brother to write Moses directly: 'With the least friendly gesture on our part he becomes so proud of his sons.' James concluded, 'In addition, send him a check.'

Gregory quickly sent a letter to his father with notes from Greg and Nancy as well as a cheque. Both the letter and funds were timely as Moses had surgery towards the end of the month and another cheque was necessary. As he recuperated, however, he became less cranky and insisted to the degree he was able on resuming his normal life. James generously acknowledged,

> Sentimental though our parents be, no doubt they did for us in childhood – in illness and in health – all they could do without consideration as to

either reward or necessarily hope that we would develop into shining stars for them,

but he now complained about their father's efforts to assert his autonomy. He told Gregory that Moses

still clings to his perverse obsession as to bowel movements. This seems an old habit of his, to go six times daily. In the hospital this is very trying for those who have to take care of him, and even the doctor does not seem to be able to talk him out of it.

Calling on his reserves, Gregory only urged James to check his 'unnecessary petulance in the midst of a very human situation'.

After eight weeks in hospital Moses finally returned home at the end of March. Weak and having lost nearly 30 pounds, he was once more, James reported, 'cheerful enough'. Gregory and James continued to correspond about their father's health and related family matters, but the intense exchange of letters provoked by Moses's illness would moderate as both men focused on their separate lives. Gregory no longer sought a confident in James, and James would never be comfortable with the star who was his successful older brother.[3]

Moses, Anna, Olga, Basia, and Nadia, in the hospital garden in Mexico, March 1942

Typically, there was much that claimed Gregory's attention. Perhaps in part because of his reflections on finitude, priorities, and purpose provoked by his father's frailty, Gregory had begun to think even more seriously about spiritual matters. References in his letters and professional writing reveal his close reading of the Bible, while the rhythms of his prose offer evidence of his attention to the King James Version, the translation Peg grew up with and admired throughout her life. Gregory had occasionally accompanied Peg to Anglican services, but was unmoved by sermons on neighbourly kindness while the liturgy that comforted her in its familiarity and affirmation of continuity failed to offer him either clarity or consolation. She would have pointed out to him that the even the spelling of the word 'hymns' was a reflection of who she was – the final three letters were her initials; as a little girl discovering how to read, she had understood the word as a personal greeting: 'Hi, MNS'.

Gregory would have been amused by her precocity, but he wasn't drawn to the Episcopalian community, didn't find in the priest or among the congregation the substantial reflection that would engage not only the psyche but the soul. The spiritual – not simply social and moral obligation, but a relationship to the transcendental – had by the spring of 1942 assumed a personal urgency that pervaded his work. It would be no accident that *Mind, Medicine, and Man* would culminate in 'Psyche, Soul, and Religion'. Following chapters on what human beings didn't know or misunderstood, on history and Freud and those who deviated from him, on aggression in ordinary life and in war, and on crime and social response, it was now logical and necessary for Gregory to address the issue of the soul and the matter of faith. In 'Theories and Practice' he would analyse what he saw as the errors of Jung and Adler, and in the book's final chapter he would philosophically differentiate soul from psyche, but how Gregory's theoretical understanding of religion would play out in practice in his own life remained unsettled.

Work on *Mind, Medicine, and Man* vied for attention with the projects planned for the centenary of the American Psychiatric Association. With fellow editors J.K. Hall and Henry Alden Bunker, his colleague at the New York Psychoanalytic Society, Gregory was working with two editorial boards – one of psychiatrists and psychoanalysts, the other of historians of medicine – on *One Hundred Years of American Psychiatry*. This substantial book with an introduction by Hall would include Gregory's chapter on 'Legal Aspects of Psychiatry' as well as contributions by distinguished colleagues: Richard H. Shryock, professor of history at the University of Pennsylvania ('The Beginnings: From Colonial Days to the Foundation of the American Psychiatric Association'); Henry Sigerist ('Psychiatry in Europe at the Middle of the Nineteenth Century'); Winfred Overholser ('The Founding and the Founders of the Association'); Samuel W. Hamilton, an authority on institutions for the mentally ill ('The History of American Mental Hospitals'); John C. Whitehorn, professor of psychiatry at Johns Hopkins ('A Century of Psychiatric Research in America'); Henry Alden Bunker ('American Psychiatric Literature during the Past One Hundred Years' and 'American Psychiatry as a Specialty'); William Malamud, director of clinical psychiatry at Worchester

State Hospital in Massachusetts ('The History of Psychiatric Therapies'); Albert Deutsch ('The History of Mental Hygiene', 'Military Psychiatry: The Civil War, 1861–1865', and 'Military Psychiatry: World War II, 1941–1943'); Edward A. Strecker, consultant to Roosevelt's secretary of war ('Military Psychiatry: World War I, 1917–1918'); the Benedictine monk Thomas Verner Moore, professor of psychiatry at Catholic University of America in Washington, D.C. ('A Century of Psychology in Its Relationship to American Psychiatry'); and Harvard anthropologist Clyde Kluckhohn ('The Influence of Psychiatry on Anthropology in America during the Past One Hundred Years').

Galvanising his colleagues, Gregory would be a driving force not only in the routine tasks of chairing meetings and editing text but in organising several special events. There would, of course, be a commemorative gathering at the 1944 meeting of the American Psychiatric Association, but two years in advance of the celebration, Gregory came up with the idea of an emblem to appear on the cover of the book and be reproduced as a bronze medallion. To publicise the project, he went into high gear once more as the director of the *corps de ballet* and, in consultation with his friend and country neighbour the painter and lithographer Leon Kroll, decided on a competition. The elegant two-page announcement reflected Gregory's convictions about art and medicine – indeed, it isn't difficult to read it as a personal statement of convictions, his view of history and his own life, a revealing reflection of his sense of himself and his aspirations in the spring of 1942.

Affirming scientific and artistic cultural values under assault by war, Gregory was obviously the unacknowledged author of the 'Explanatory Folder', which began by insisting on the individual artist's independence: 'The announcement of the competition leaves the artist his full creative initiative'. Despite masculine pronouns and the generic 'man', the document made an effort at inclusivity: While 'pondering the drawing he or she would conceive for the occasion of the centenary' the artist was invited 'to consider the steadfast continuity of the [American Psychiatric] Association, its national, North American, and international scope as well as its sustained effort to keep the psychiatric profession a united scientific body'. The author in inimitable phrasing offered the competitors a bit of background: 'the "insane" is but a sick man – sick in all his humanness and human in all his sickness', while the Association's founders were not merely doctors but 'men of spiritual stature and wide cultural horizons'. Gregory's sketch reflected the principles of his calling and highlighted figures he had come to admire, among them Benjamin Rush, who founded the society that became the Association, and Isaac Ray, 'the Oliver Wendal Holmes of American psychiatry'. Nevertheless, he pointed out, the judges (Kroll, the sculptor Paul Manship, and the architect Eric Gugler) preferred not to have portraits as the emblem because of the Association's 'corporate work' which no one person could represent. Gregory went on to describe American psychiatric history, the training schools for doctors and specialised nurses 'both men and women', as well as institutions for treating patients. Psychiatry was, Gregory pointed out, 'a medical specialty, a scientific discipline, humane in purpose, educational in endeavor, conscious of its medical, social and cultural role', active in hospitals, clinics, courts, prisons, laboratories, universities, and schools. Like Gregory, the Association's 'horizons grew with its knowledge, its scope with its duties, its enlightenment with its social consciousness.'

Gregory saw his role in lofty terms, demanding a great deal of himself as he followed in the tradition he described, but he also identified himself with the artist invited to represent the Association. He urged the competitors

> to contemplate this general background, the trends and the humanitarian and cultural hue of psychiatry, and to tell it to us in his way, in a manner of a whole or of an outstanding part, by the way of the imagery which is his language.

This, too, was the task Gregory set for himself as a doctor, psychoanalyst, historian, writer, and human being with a particular calling. It was as well as the task he set for himself in photography, in the images which were his visual language and which focused on people, on portraits. With the individual's limits on his mind, Gregory also encouraged the competitors to consider that

> the span of one hundred years for a professional organization of this nature is but a brief moment; it is not a terminal of rest but a sign post marking an indeterminate distance ahead. It is not the settledness of settled age, but the verve and faith of the coming of age.[4]

The 'Explanatory Folder' is an extraordinary document suggesting in impersonal terms the issues weighing upon Gregory during the war years. Having weathered the confrontation with the New York Psychoanalytic Society, he increasingly saw his own life in personal (rather than professional) and spiritual (rather than merely historical) terms. What pressed upon him as his frail father walked out in the Mexican sun, as Abe entered the Army Medical Corps, as Peg's brother Lou prepared for Officer Candidate School, and as her good friend Mary-Alice enlisted in the Women's Army Corps, was the fragility and brevity of life, his own limits and limitations, transience and perpetuity.

Gregory was 51 in the spring of 1942; Peg was, at nearly 24, less than half his age. Only marriage to the man she loved would make the children she wanted possible, and he wanted a second chance – or perhaps, thinking back to Sonya and his own fractured familial relations, even a third chance – at family. Spending several nights a week at the office with Peg and weekends in the country occasionally with the children but without Ray, he was slowly withdrawing from conventional married life while attempting to create an alternative. Sigerist remained one of the few friends whom Gregory and Peg visited as a couple, and he now invited his research assistant Genevieve Miller, a young woman of Peg's age, to the meals he arranged. Trips to Baltimore became romantic escapes: Gregory and Peg would take a ferry from lower Manhattan to Jersey City, then a train south along the Eastern Seaboard; away from New York, they were briefly free from social constrictions and subterfuges, simply lovers en route.[5]

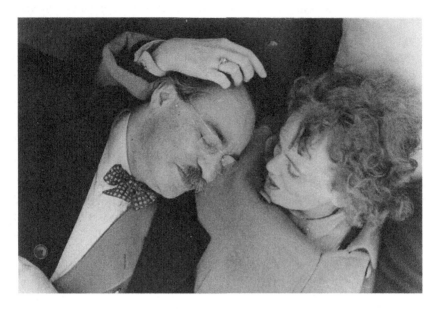

Gregory and Peg, together on a boat, 1942

Gregory made sure that the contest received considerable attention. He persuaded New York's Waldorf-Astoria Hotel to host an exhibition of the drawings in April, an event followed at the end of the month by a show at the Providence Museum of Art. Finally, at the annual meeting of the American Psychiatric Association in Boston in May, the members selected the sculptor Wheeler Williams as the winner. His elegant image depicts hands from above removing a head covering from a female figure in semi-profile who gazes out in wonder beyond the emblem's circle.[6]

Needless to say, the centenary wasn't the only professional matter on Gregory's mind. In late April he addressed the annual meeting of the American League to Abolish Capital Punishment followed by a lecture to the Beaumont Medical Club in New Haven on 'Humanism in Medicine and Psychiatry'. In early May Peg accompanied him to Atlantic City for the annual meeting of the American Society for the History of Medicine. In Boston, after the emblem's selection, he had addressed the Association on 'Psychiatry as a Social Science'. He told Sigerist April alone had been 'one of the busiest months imaginable', but when he finally closed the office for a fortnight in early July, he inevitably worked rather than rested.[7]

Amid work on lectures and articles as well as on *Mind, Medicine, and Man*, Gregory reviewed two books for *Psychoanalytic Quarterly*: the Capuchin friar Alphonsus Bonnar's *The Catholic Doctor* and Thomas Verner Moore's *Cognitive*

Psychology. Placing their writing in context, Gregory argued, 'the time will come when good and courageous Catholics will study psychoanalysis seriously ... and will find nothing in clinical psychoanalysis that would contradict their religious faith.' Traditional thinkers like Bonnar, Gregory contended, engaged in 'pseudo-philosophical argumentation' in order to reject the empirical findings of psycho-analysis because of their attitude towards the problems of determinism and free will, but 'official Catholicism' finally objected to Freud 'because he was an unbe-liever' and not because the Church had 'verified the facts discovered and found them false'. Later editorial work on *One Hundred Years of American Psychiatry* would encourage a friendship with Moore, and *Mind, Medicine, and Man* would give Gregory ample opportunity to address the thorny matters of determinism and free will as well as guilt and absolution. Indeed, he was now reading contempo-rary Catholic authors with their particular reservations about psychoanalysis, but his approach was philosophical and moral rather than religious. He remained, however nominally, still a member of the Society of Friends. When explaining to James his decision to forego a summer holiday, Gregory comfortably quoted his old Quaker colleague Jesse Holmes: He would just have 'to keep on keeping on'.[8]

In the country where Ray and the children spent most of the summer, family life went on as it had done, but Gregory was less and less content. The work that took him away from the city involved consultation about a patient at the Mayo Clinic in Minnesota. He stopped en route there and back in Chicago, where he lunched with a colleague and missed Peg, went to Marshall Field's department store and remembered a trip when they had gone shopping together. Away from her, he felt disconnected, while a 'midwestern state of mind' meant the radio featured poultry and hog prices 'with greater frequency and emphasis than war news', which was reduced to a few words about the Russian front. He felt restless and low-spirited, a fugitive from his work, 'suspended in the nowhere doing nothing'. In short, calling Peg 'darling' and 'dear', he told her how important to him she was, that he loved her and simply didn't feel at all right without her; what he wanted was to return to New York and have her there to meet him.

Peg must have missed him in turn, but she wasn't in the city that week. Having arrived safely at the home of a Vassar friend in North Carolina, she informed her mother that her return train would arrive late; she would spend the night in the New York, but after work the following day, she would hurry home 'as early as the Bluebeard on 75th Street will allow'. In fact, Gregory planned to return from the farm early in the evening so that they could be together to 'talk and love and talk and love'. Ray, who surely suspected Gregory was romantically involved with his research assistant, refused to confront how much Peg meant to her husband, but Gregory was no Bluebeard, despite the ruse Peg maintained of an exploitative employer demanding overtime from an obedient secretary. During the summer Gregory and Peg would manage a week together at Harry and Doris Hatcher's country house in Pennsylvania, but being with friends, they hadn't been really alone, and in their own ways they were keeping on keeping on, in a holding pat-tern, preserving appearances even though their hearts were pledged.[9]

Moses, however, could not keep on keeping on and underwent prostate surgery early in July. A month later he took pride in getting in and out of bed by himself, but James reported that he remained 'pretty weak' before adding gratuitously, 'So is the rest of the family, for that matter, with their limited resources.' Fera spent the summer in Mexico, and while James acknowledged that her 'usual good sense' served the family well, the 'hospital atmosphere' in their parents' apartment tried everyone's patience; Basia was 'in shreds' from the strain. Fera's departure at the end of August upset Moses, who became suddenly worse. James described the sad details: In 'a peculiar state of apathy', he was struggling with coordination and speech; unable to hold a spoon or fork straight, he seemed to understand what was said to him, but couldn't find the right words to reply. Despite the surgery, he had not regained control of his bladder and had developed bad headaches. James, who was beginning to have sympathy for Basia, decided to call in a 'famous' Spanish neurologist, the 'head of a very important psychiatric clinic in Mexico'.[10]

Fera spoke with Gregory as soon as she returned to New York. James was chronically offended by Gregory's impatience with Basia and their mother, whose complaints and pettiness James did little to counter and too often shared. Gregory immediately wrote apologetically, telling his brother that he was truly pained that James was so easily affronted when what Gregory wished was to see all human beings 'more tolerant, less sensitive to small things, and more responsive to actual human problems'. Given their personal history, he suggested it would be easier if James considered the two of them as strangers who needed to 'be polite and overlook one another's singularities' and who could then attend to the business at hand 'with dispassionate civility and simple directness'. Offering no reproaches or advice, Gregory nevertheless revealed his disappointment that he hadn't been consulted because he was, after all, 'a son who happens to be a physician'. Unable to offer yet more financial help, he could at least have communicated with Moses's doctor as an informed colleague.

Gregory then shifted to calm, medical analysis: He had observed during his last visit premonitory signs of cerebral arteriosclerosis; Moses's incontinence was probably due not so much to his bladder condition as to a mild stroke, while 'His tendency to cry, his deep changes of mood, mild states of absence, the thing which appears to the uninitiated outsider as mild mental confusion' were 'due to various tiny but potent brain injuries which are typical of certain older people'. Gregory finally came down to brass tacks: 'he will not be with us for very long, for one does not recover from these things', and ought to be looked after as 'an invalid, a very old man who is about to die'. Gregory's primary concern was that Moses be treated with 'care, understanding, quiet, composure, tolerance, considerateness, patience' rather than with the 'volatility, irascibility, tense self-assertive "I told you so" and peremptory smallness of mind' that Fera had reported and Gregory had known since childhood.

Both realistic and philosophical, Gregory didn't feel an individual death was 'a tragedy'; he wasn't horrified by it and felt little sympathy for those who didn't treat it with 'dignity and poise and humble yet proud surrender to that which is but the natural end of all things, preordained and forever established and happily not reversible'. Moses was to his eldest son an individual who had lived his life on his own terms:

> He could have been killed in any of the pogroms or during the revolution. He survived and came to Mexico. There he founded the first [Ashkenazi] Jewish Synagogue and the first [Ashkenazi] Jewish consecrated burial grounds in which he and his brethren wished to have their remains rest.

Gregory saw in such a life 'a bit of melancholy poetry' as well as 'humble justice and spiritual consolation', and pleaded with James to intercede, if possible 'to move him to some quiet place, where the sun would beat in his window and where a good simple person could attend to his few needs and just keep him physically clean'. The current situation was intolerable, an offense to their father's dignity; Gregory found it disgusting 'to hear complaints of how hard this or that one works'. He insisted eloquently,

> No superhuman efforts are required. He cannot be rejuvenated; he cannot be saved, but he should be made to feel no one around him carries on with that manner of ostentatious tragedy which is offensive to the living and sacrilegious to the dying.

While Gregory felt that for years the family had only been a family nominally and that not much could be done to change the present state of affairs, he was compelled to share a heartfelt understanding that went far beyond his medical observations: 'what we call the end is not the end at all, but a tenuous flicker of something purely eternal.'[11]

James went ahead with a neurological consultation anyway and defended his limited understanding of the medical situation by declaring snippily that he was 'only an engineer'. Unable to understand his brother's feelings, James told Gregory he shouldn't be miffed not to have been consulted because the specialist hadn't been expensive. Gregory's evaluation of the situation had, of course, nothing to do with money, and most of his moving letter had been an eloquent appeal for pragmatic kindness. Prickly and finally mean, James attributed what he saw as Gregory's judgements to professional strain with which, James declared, he could hardly help him.[12]

Gregory refused to engage with James on such petty terms and did his best to comfort his brother as Moses declined. By October, disoriented and frustrated, their father needed to be restrained from trying to leave his bed; he was no longer able to read and convinced that his eldest son was nearby. With gentle kindness, Gregory told James that he should guard against interpreting Moses's reactions in terms of normal reactions:

> When Father mentions me, it is most probably a sort of automatic reverberation of past impressions and thoughts which are not integrated with his

present at all.… His emotional reactions at present are rather fragmentary and it will be easier on your own feelings if you bear this in mind and you don't take all his expressions literally.

The situation was particularly difficult, he pointed out, when the stroke victim was one's father and when the son didn't understand the medical details. Even for a psychiatrist, Gregory admitted, it was painful to see a personality disintegrate and act 'like a cracked phonograph record which reproduces fragments only. These fragments still mean to us the whole song, but it is no more a whole song on the record.'[13]

Gregory had to offer a good deal of succour in the autumn of 1942. Everyone involved with Russian Relief was upset by the war on the Eastern Front. In Leningrad the German siege continued as another winter loomed, while in Stalingrad, a city strategically between the Black and Caspian Seas, Nazi forces mounted a new offensive; reports of aerial bombardment and house-to-house fighting made daily headlines in the New York papers. The effects of cerebral haemorrhage also implicated Gregory closer to home as Peg's father's health declined. Like Moses in Mexico, by October Louis had lost the ability to speak, and with Lou and George in the army, the burden of care fell on Louise, who continued to sleep, although not well, in the same bed as her now incontinent husband. Sensing the family was losing perspective and convinced that very sick people belonged in hospital, Gregory now referred to Louise and Louis simply as 'mother' and 'father', and in a touchingly intimate emotional displacement, he urged Peg in early October not to 'let father die in this atmosphere of oppressive lack of true organized care'. Reflecting that difficult autumn on the complex role of the physician as the conveyor of humanitarian and cultural values, he insisted a doctor was called to heal impartially and not to judge, to restore the value of individual and communal life:

This task is medical in spirit and in practice, inalienable from the doctor in war as well as in peace. It is a task the responsibility for which is imposed on the physician by the very tragedy of human life.

Gregory could counsel his brother against ostentatious tragedy, against bewailing that their father was dying, but he was well aware there was something inestimably sad in the fact that life inevitably ended.[14]

Louis Stone died at home in Bronxville on 29 October 1942, and three days later, on 1 November, Moses Zilboorg died in Mexico City. James wrote to Gregory the next day and asked him to share the letter with Fera, who he hoped would forgive him for not writing her directly. James was typically both melodramatic and pathetically defensive, telling his brother that 'after an agony of nearly eighteen hours' their 'old man finally gave up the struggle' and breathed 'his last breath'. Despite Gregory's advice, the family had done everything they could to keep Moses alive, hoping for a miracle. Wondering if he and Gregory were living up to the standards Moses had set for himself, James saw their father's death as 'the first crack in our family', and asked, 'Which next? Or, does it make any difference?' before concluding rather glibly, 'The women folk are pretty well down, of course.'[15]

More upset than they had anticipated, Gregory and Peg shared the experience of grief. What they were going through, Gregory explained, was 'natural, inevitable and inexorable'; they were doing the necessary psychological 'work of mourning' while continuing as if nothing had happened. In the deep, inner recesses of their minds and hearts primeval and mysterious things were going on, and all they could do, he told her kindly, was 'not bow or crumple down under the pressure of the work within which is going on and which we don't know and don't understand even if we do know a little bit.'

With James, Gregory was equally perceptive but more reserved, while the biblical language he chose is less psychoanalytic and suggests the solace he and Peg also sought in Christian understanding. He admitted feeling melancholy, unable to do much as he followed their father's demise from a distance, but simultaneously certain he could have done little to alleviate anyone's feelings had he been present. He pointed out that people in general don't know how to make peace with death, while 'people of the order of Mother and our sister know not the greatness of death any more than the depth of life'. He understood his brother's emotions but couldn't fully share them, for he felt that the mystery of death was 'beyond our ken, to combat it beyond our sinew'. His own experiences had additionally shaped his psychology:

> Those of us, physicians and public men, who sat behind the barricades or in the trenches are not very impressed with death. There is the natural anxiety about one's life coming to an end, but this has nothing to do with the actual facts of life and death. It is like the natural, silent and anxious gasp when one reaches a great height. This does not prevent one from climbing high mountains or buildings.

He told his brother wisely, 'All these things just happen and happen they will like a sunset or a sunrise – and no feelings or such barbarities as solemn funerals will ever propitiate the straight, calm and inexorable rhythm of coming and going.' In the larger context of war, he saw Moses's death as 'the most natural and simple thing', and concluded philosophically:

> The world as it stands just now does not offer much opportunity or reason for grief about death. For is it not by death that the world is living today? And is it not by death that it is trying to save its life? This is just how it is and shall be.[16]

The year bumped along to its end. If grief brought Gregory and Peg even closer, he remained unable to broach with Ray the idea of leaving his marriage, couldn't imagine how the children would cope with the break-up or how he could settle things in a way that would protect them. Separation would also involve money, and his family depended on him. If he left the household physically, he would still need to be present economically, and he worried about managing that. Even if money was, in Ray's case, all he wanted to offer, he was determined to keep the children in his life, felt it was essential for their physical and emotional well-being that he continue to be a presence in theirs.

Gregory's many notes to Peg attest to the psychological and practical predicament. He was a passionate and deeply reflective man, expressive in all his moods, volatile, and easily moved not only to anger but to tears and joy. His situation at home was stressful, and the notes additionally offer a vivid glimpse of family dynamics. As Gregory's marriage made him increasingly unhappy, he and Peg wrote about the problem; they talked it through face to face, alternatively distressed and heartened, and arrived at a number of psychological insights, but nothing externally changed.

The matter nearly reached a crisis in late November. A deadly fire at the Cocoanut Grove nightclub in Boston, an event that made headlines, was to Ray a greater calamity than the scuppering of the French fleet at Toulon, a strategic necessity as the Nazis moved south to extend their occupation throughout Vichy. Even 'the dog urinating out of turn' was to Ray 'a severer blow than the ups and downs of the war'. Gregory confessed a wish he was nearly unable bring himself to admit: that Ray, who so often seemed ill, might 'dye soon'. His misspelling of 'die', which he apparently didn't notice, suggests how unutterable he found this idea, but he recognised it as a stunning death wish 'so plain that even the worry as to funeral expenses and cold calculations about funeral arrangements' passed through his mind as well as the impact on the children, who were 'good' and 'simple' in their natural love for their mother, so he felt a sense of guilt towards them while he found her 'disgruntled, sharp, tactless' and consistently 'flat'. The language he used was anguished: Ray fed his death wishes; his heart brimmed with the 'pain and sorrow' of his 'impotence to solve this problem actively, decently'. He must have intimated that he was considering a life apart, but his wife was unwilling to budge or change or even admit a problem existed. Gregory would tell Peg that Ray 'solves nothing and wants nothing to be solved'; she simply wanted to continue 'boring me and breaking me without wishing to admit that she is breaking me'. All he wanted was to flee the confrontation, to hold Peg in his arms, to talk to her, love her, and have faith.

On a Friday morning in early December the apartment brimmed with tension. Young Greg was doing less and less well academically and socially, while Nancy was excelling at school but today had a sore throat and would stay home. Shadow, Ingersoll's Labrador who had replaced poor Bobo, had produced a healthy litter in late November. Gregory wanted solitude and peace, time to work, and time with Peg; Ray wanted to know his weekend plans. He recreated the scene. Announcing at breakfast that he would be going to the country, Ray asked only, 'When?' Gregory: 'I don't know. Tonight.' Ray: 'Before dinner?' Gregory: 'Perhaps.' Ray: 'Where will you eat?' Gregory: 'I'll see.' At that juncture he thought how good it would be to spend the evening with Peg and imagined staying overnight at the office only to realise what 'a mess' there would be if some emergency occurred and Ray phoned him in the country. He briefly envisaged an evening working alone in Pound Ridge, then thought of offering Peg his car to take to Bronxville so she could later join him, then revised his fantasy: He shouldn't ask her to change her plans to suit his whims; although she would come, he would only be creating another 'mess'. When Ray suggested taking Greg along, his heart fell; he told his wife the boy 'might run about too much alone' and he couldn't cook for him, while realising that if Greg stayed in New York, Peg might come after all. All these thoughts and feelings as he prepared to go to work that morning were difficult 'gyrations'. At the desk in his treatment room as he wrote to Peg at her desk on the other side of the door, he paused to ring Nancy: He wondered how she was and was concerned about the puppies. Ray answered the telephone: 'When are you going to the country?' Gregory: 'I don't know yet. Probably directly from the office.' Ray: 'Around five?' Gregory: 'I don't know yet. I will let you know at three pm.' Ray: 'Alright, let me know.' Gregory felt hounded, depressed by the vacuity of their conversations, stymied.

There were lighter moments. He wrote to Peg, 'I am missing you and missing you and can't rid myself of the awareness that you are in my debt. You owe me quite a number of xxx which I want back.' A postscript appended to another note continued in the same vein: 'I love you so much I want to weep ... Is it not G.D. Russian?' When Schwester, the Pound Ridge farmer, threatened to quit, Gregory bristled. He told Peg, 'If I could milk cows even a little bit – or if I could have you with me all the time and for good, we both would have figured out how to milk and to hell with Schwester'. Gregory recognised he was upset about managing the farm in part because he was feeling 'burdened and hopelessly stifled' by his home life at the same time that he had a deep need for Peg and felt he was failing her. 'Forgive me, dear', he wrote, 'You are very, very direct and I love you and I like your fur coat.'

Despite minor confrontations, the tensions took their toll. The deep sense of alienation that paralysed Gregory at home left him seething. When Ray argued with him about attending a colloquium, his presence somehow rendering him 'ridiculous' and provoking gossip, her 'attack' seemed to him 'cheap'. In his view she insisted on what was 'external, banal, foolish, boring' while refusing to recognise much less understand what he saw as the larger issues. Powerless to command his love, she wanted to control at least the external elements of his life, where he went and what he did, while apparently his 'scientific, intel- lectual, spiritual and emotional' life was unimportant or invisible to her. He felt he had become to Ray merely 'a piece of property', while what he sought as he tried to find a way forward was 'a friendly mutual respect' that would allow them to consider the children's welfare. In a posture of accusation, she insisted on his being something he had never been; he, in turn, felt 'chained' and unable to liberate himself. Having found reasoning with Ray impossible, he nevertheless didn't feel capable of simply walking out. Greg was now 11 and Nancy was nine; had they been a little older, he told Peg, he could have talked to them, protected them from the crippling pain he was certain his leaving Ray would cause.

Gregory was also aware that the clock was ticking, that Peg was, as he put it, 'growing to full greatness of womanhood', a painful process he also found 'good and fruitful'. In 'full growth', however, she might well leave him. He told her there was no reason for her to be afraid, for he understood that when she came to the point of having to leave, he would need to let her go. Over and over he declared his love and devotion, but also told her repeatedly that he felt alone and burdened and did not see any light. As 1942 drew to a close he confessed he was reaching a nadir: He often didn't even feel like working.

For her part, Peg was aware of the predicament but wasn't yet ready to desert him or free herself, couldn't imagine a future without him, and didn't know what to do except hang on and literally pray. She was in many ways quite a conventional woman; in desperate moments she left the office and went to church to pray as her parents had taught her to do. At one point Gregory told her he hoped she had prayed for the strength to leave him since, because of his 'spiritual or circumstantial bankruptcy', he couldn't give her all he wanted and she deserved. Peg in her turn was frank with him: If there were any hope at all of their living together 'freely and fully', she wouldn't leave; she didn't pray to be 'delivered', she insisted, but only to understand herself. By the end of the year prayer as well as hope were important elements in their struggle for the free and full life they both continued to imagine.

Gregory and Fera came to terms with their father's death as did Peg with life without her father, but James had a harder emotional time and turned to his brother. Ever the kind doctor, Gregory rose to the occasion, all the water under the bridge well under. He wrote James that difficulty sleeping and thoughts about death were 'a natural and almost universal reaction'; even if subjectively one might not perceive any anxiety, such thoughts were a form of what he explained technically as *Die Trauerarbeit*, a 'death anxiety' that 'works itself through'. For his brother's depleting insomnia he recommended Seconal, the best in his opinion of the medicinal remedies because as soon as one woke it was 'excreted out of the body' with 'the first urination'. Although offended 'when small things' were presented as 'the center of the Universe', Gregory reassured his brother that he should never hesitate to ask him for 'an opinion, advice, favor, or help'. As for his own health, two days before Christmas and his 52nd birthday, he told James sincerely,

> I feel well, I feel younger than when I was thirty, rather vigorous and active physically and mentally, unable to catch up with the millions of things to be done, and I am watching not without anxiety my second world war and hope that life will go on.[17]

Gregory's sense of well-being and joy as well as the hope he mentioned to James were anchored in his relationship with Peg, although he revealed nothing of the difficulties it posed nor even Peg's significance in his life. With Sigerist he had been more open, and the two friends enthusiastically planned to cook a Russian meal for Peg and Genevieve in Gregory's office. When Sigerist had to beg off at the last minute because of professional commitments, Gregory was disappointed and understanding. He, too, found it impossible to put aside research, writing, and speaking commitments. If civilisation had already given up the bulk of its cultural values, he told Sigerist, before the war ended a great many more would fall by the wayside:

> As mere social beings we might feel guilty because we are not in the fighting line, but as social beings who have a little historical perspective we cannot help but feel that ours is the duty to salvage and work at the few cultural values which we are fortunate enough to have in our hands.

Musing that his view might be rooted in a sort of megalomania, he nevertheless insisted, 'we are realistic when we think that as direct or indirect cannon fodder we are really of not much significance and that our job is the work which we are doing as best as we can.' Characteristically tempering such seriousness with bonhomie, Gregory urged his friend to promise that when the Russians retook Rostov-on-Don, they would drop whatever they were doing and celebrate together.[18]

Soviet troops pushed the Germans back in February, but the long-anticipated dinner had to be postponed yet again as Gregory became involved in a court case he found deeply disturbing. In this instance he was not the defendant but an expert witness on behalf of a 14-year-old boy accused of first-degree murder. Gregory's recent confrontation with the New York Psychoanalytic Society had made him acutely aware of the perils of legal questioning, but a psychiatrist on the witness stand confronted specific professional and legal problems. Like anyone else, the psychiatrist had to 'submit to attacks made on him as a person, attacks challenging his personal integrity and casting aspersions and shadows or various adumbrations on his character', but although the discrediting of the expert witness was a recognised courtroom tradition, Gregory found such treatment of a doctor and specifically a psychiatrist morally unjustifiable,

> a trick sanctified by habit and based on the assumption that the expert is a hired man and therefore, like any hired man, has sold himself to the highest bidder, who pays more in either money or prestige for services rendered.

For Gregory, a doctor had

> a moral duty in the courtroom as much as in the hospital ward. He must remain a doctor even in the performance of his highest civic duties; he cannot and should not become an amateur lawyer who by means of various legalistic devices which 'his side' offers him pushes the wheels of legal justice in one or another direction.

In order to circumvent taking sides, Gregory thought no psychiatrist should 'testify for any side except the court', because psychiatry itself as a medical discipline was otherwise manipulated, discredited, praised, or sneered at. In his view the individual psychiatrist as well as psychiatry as an organised discipline needed to take responsibility for stopping such degradation of their work. Psychiatrists were further undermined in court because they were asked to accept 'the psychological terminology which the law adopted some three hundred years ago' – that of legal sanity or insanity. These thoughts had been percolating for a long time: As a psychiatrist, he would ultimately need to leave the law to the lawyer; personally he had moral and ethical feelings about the case, but in court he would have to deal 'only with questions of health and disease'.

During a difficult week in West Virginia Gregory interviewed the boy several times and diagnosed him as schizophrenic. Gregory's eloquent testimony contributed to saving the defendant from the gallows, he told Sigerist, but the experience upset him. He expounded his position concisely in a later essay. Frequently perceived as 'the defender of the indefensible', the psychiatrist testifying in a criminal case had a solemn and often painful task

> for he who has been trained to heal and to save lives may at some time be forced by circumstances either to contribute to a man's being convicted and sentenced to death, or to stand up and fight with all the power of his service to scientific truth for a poor derelict against whom the law and public opinion are both aroused and uncompromising.

Given Gregory's view of the moral dimensions of these challenges, it is unsurprising that the penultimate chapter of *Mind, Medicine, and Man* would be 'Crime and Judgment'.[19]

Although a convivial Russian dinner finally took place at Gregory's office in March, Sigerist found his friend 'worn out'. In a letter to his brother Gregory attributed his exhaustion to the war, which made life 'uncertain', and glossed over his worries by insisting he was occasionally able to relax; the family was well; the children were growing; despite 'War, revolution, murders – life just goes on.' He was concerned, however, about his finances. In a postscript in Russian he admitted rather cryptically, 'Things are growing increasingly difficult' and asked James if 75 rather than the customary $100 would now be enough for their mother. Never one to pry, James reluctantly agreed to the reduction, though he couldn't refrain from adding that 'for this month she hopes that you have already sent the allowance as before'.[20]

Moral issues continued to occupy Gregory's thoughts, and among contemporary Catholic thinkers he had begun to read the work of the French philosopher Jacques Maritain. A convert from Protestantism married to a Russian Jew who had also become a Catholic, Maritain and his wife, both trained scientists as well as philosophers, worked together for international human rights and liberal ideas. Maritain specifically championed the work of the Dominican Thomas Aquinas, whose *Summa Theologica* dealt not only with strictly religious matters but with ethics and the law. By 1943, Gregory was also reading Aquinas.

There were few people with whom Gregory could share his spiritual and theological concerns. His ethical thinking is evident in his writing on psychiatry and the law, in his discussions of the physician's obligations as well as in his understanding of history, but theology and the specific matter of faith transcended professional interests. He wouldn't talk about personal spiritual matters with Ray or other members of his family, although he naturally confided in Peg, yet intelligent as she was, she was not an intellectual; throughout her life she was a more dutiful than reflective believer. Intellectually as well as politically and morally Gregory and Sigerist were on the same page, but Gregory would be unable to share his interest in theology with his more practical and worldly friend. Neither was an admirer of Stalin, yet both Gregory and Sigerist, whose *Socialized Medicine in the Soviet Union* had received a great deal of positive as well as negative attention on its publication in 1937, were convinced that only socialised medicine could offer equal treatment for all; because of their broad humanitarianism as well as their first-hand knowledge of Russia, the two men shared a concern about the effect of the war on the Russian people. Gregory would thus feel able to mention to Sigerist Maritain's resignation from a Pan-Europe organisation: The philosopher had taken his decision not only because he rejected identification with reactionary Catholics but because he felt that 'No organization which does not include Soviet Russia as a full equal is really liberal'. Gregory was confident Sigerist would sympathise with such clever reasoning, but Maritain's religious beliefs and Thomist philosophy remained beyond the boundaries of their friendship.[21]

Intellectual conviviality, cooking, photography, good food, and good humour remained at the core of the rare moments Gregory and Sigerist managed to spend together, and such happy times were a welcome diversion from intense and complicated daily life in New York. For two days in April Gregory and Peg made up a jolly foursome with Sigerist and Genevieve in Baltimore. Sigerist had responsibilities at Johns Hopkins, but Gregory assured him that he and Peg would be happy in the university library while Sigerist was busy or they might even go to the movies; he had not, he admitted, seen one for almost a year. Gregory particularly appreciated the wide-ranging discussions with his old friend, 'the refreshing comfort of just talking and laughing without pressure'. Sigerist in his turn would tell Peg the entire visit was simply 'great fun' and jokingly hoped he and Genevieve and Gregory had convinced her of 'the superiority of the Soviet system as well as of the beauties of Mexico and recent progress in dentistry'. With his thanks for 'the very good time', Gregory sent both Sigerist and Genevieve several rolls of special film, which Sigerist told him they would enjoy experimenting with together. While earlier encounters had involved sending Ray and Emmy off to the theatre or the garden while Gregory and Sigerist worked in the dark room or talked late into the night, the friendship between the two men now clearly included both young women.[22]

Gregory and Peg went on from Baltimore to a professional meeting in Washington before returning to New York, where on 13 April he addressed a combined meeting of the New York Neurological Society and the New York Academy of Medicine on 'Psychosomatic Medicine: A Historical Perspective', but the spring's big event was the publication of *Mind, Medicine, and Man*. Copies had been sent to potential reviewers, colleagues, and friends in advance of the official publication on Freud's and Peg's birthday on 6 May. On the day itself Sigerist joined Gregory and Peg for a celebratory dinner at Peking House, Gregory's favourite Chinese restaurant. There was much to be merry about as the food was delicious and the book was already being well received.[23]

Indeed, the praise from far and wide was almost without exception fulsome. Gregory's friend and colleague Win Overholser thought the book 'should be read by every intelligent person who is interested in himself and the rest of the human race'. Similarly impressed, the German novelist Thomas Mann told John Woodburn, Gregory's editor at Harcourt, Brace, that the book's 'enlightening tendency and capacity make it worthy of widest circulation.' Reviews and notices appeared in specialist journals (including the *Bulletin of the Medical Library Association* and the *Journal of Criminal Psychopathology*), as well as in newspapers (from the *Boston Globe* to the *Los Angeles Times*) and in magazines for sophisticated readers (such as the *New Yorker* and the *Saturday Review of Literature*) and for particular audiences (such as *Parents' Magazine*). The Book of the Month Club would choose *Mind, Medicine, and Man* as one of its featured books for July 1943.[24]

The publisher's publicity emphasised the book's wide appeal and timeliness, and many reviewers agreed. The influential international journalist Raymond Gram Swing declared *Mind, Medicine, and Man* was 'devoid of arrant dogmatism'; 'Pervaded by the scientific spirit', it would enlighten anyone who sought to learn 'what contribution can be expected from the pioneering of Freud.' Clyde Kluckhohn claimed the book was 'one of the finest yet most provocative, one of the broadest and yet soundest treatments of some of the critical problems of our age'. Other readers were more precise. The social worker Leah Feder recommended that all case workers have a copy on their shelves 'not only for reference on specific subjects but also for general reading'. The linguist S.I. Hayakawa was especially impressed with the author's arguments for the significance of language and recommended the book as 'required reading for teachers, preachers, scholars and other exponents of the verbal arts – including book reviewers'.[25]

The most negative review came from the German-American psychiatrist Frederic Wertham, who, despite a nod to Gregory's 'fluent presentation and learnedness', was sharply critical of his 'attitude toward social phenomena'. Wertham ground his own axe, as reviewers tend to do, arguing for a quicker and more egalitarian form of therapy than Freudian analysis and contending that 'Rome burns while New Yorkers psychoanalyze each other.' Such crankiness, however, provoked a carefully argued letter from the social worker Marguerite Pohek, a student of Otto Rank's, who found Wertham's review a flagrant misreading of *Mind, Medicine, and Man* and 'a masterpiece of pettish chicanery'.[26]

Many readers singled out individual chapters. Arthur Ruggles, the president of the American Psychiatric Association, described Gregory in his foreword to the book as a visionary 'pathfinder', mentioning specifically 'Civilization and the Social Sciences' (an examination of the 'clear pattern of social and anthropological forces' upon people and their behaviour) and 'Crime and Judgment' (the chapter Ruggles enjoyed most, an illustration of 'the author's wide reading and understanding of medical jurisprudence over the ages'). Calling *Mind, Medicine, and Man* 'a comprehensive and scholarly work in which logic is applied to many controversial aspects of psychobiology', Edwin R. Eisler, a charter member of the Chicago Psychoanalytic Society, found 'Civilization and the Social Sciences' an exceptionally clear account of 'the relationship between cultural anthropology, modern sociological concepts and psychoanalysis'. He also praised the author for pointing out in his final chapter 'a methodological error – that of applying psychoanalytic hypotheses and findings to the problem of values'. Eisler was especially impressed, however, that 'throughout the book the author manifests a true humility before the immensity of the forces involved in every manifestation of mental life.' Other readers were also moved by Gregory's humble attitude towards his material. The Swiss-born psychoanalyst Paul Friedman, who had worked with Gregory on the Committee on Suicide, admired the 'modesty and caution' with which the author set forth original thinking and ideas. Calling 'Crime and Judgment' 'a masterpiece', Friedman drew attention to Gregory's 'arresting clarity' in pointing out that 'all punishment is based on revenge which society vents on the criminal'. Friedman reserved special praise, however, for the book's final chapter: Gregory had 'most eloquently demonstrated' that it was possible to reconcile religion and psychoanalysis 'inasmuch as there has never existed any real antagonism between religion and psychoanalysis except in the minds of certain groups of people'.[27]

Some reviewers, however, were surprised and perplexed by 'Psyche, Soul, and Religion', in which Gregory contended that while psychoanalysis challenged many aspects of ecclesiastical form and ritual, it didn't and couldn't challenge fundamental faith or religious feeling. Referring to Gregory as an outstanding psychoanalyst of his generation, 'a serious student' of Freud and 'a good teacher', Brill reviewed the book for the *New York Times* within ten days of publication. He thought it 'very interesting and informative' and 'well worth reading', but had serious reservations about the concluding chapter, which he felt made 'much ado about very little'. While the psychologist Samuel B. Kutash liked the book, he was similarly puzzled. Praising Gregory as 'a capable and learned medical historian' and pointing out that *Mind, Medicine, and Man* offered 'insight, inspiration and erudition' for the 'criminal psychopathologist, the lawyer, social worker, medical man and psychologist' as well as the general reader, Kutash saw no conflict at all between religion and psychoanalysis and thought the final chapter should have been omitted.[28]

Other, more sensitive reviewers – among them Jews, Protestants, and especially Catholics for whom faith and religious practice were matters of significance – found the final chapter of *Mind, Medicine, and Man* subtle, persuasive, and important. Walter Millis, a staff writer for the *New York Herald Tribune*, described Gregory as 'thoughtfully aware of the larger issues of our civilization', interested 'not only in explaining his medical specialty, but in bringing it into its just relation with the fields of sociology, law, philosophy and religion'. For Millis, 'Psyche, Soul, and Religion' offered a 'brilliant' analysis and seemed a fitting conclusion to 'this singularly illuminating study on a subject of critical importance to our times'. Karl Menninger also found the final chapter particularly noteworthy: Gregory had argued that, instead of being antithetical, psychoanalysis and religion were two aspects of the same thing and tended, if properly understood, to support each other. Both endeavoured to make people happier and better. They used different techniques, based on different assumptions, were represented by different 'personnel', and had some apparent theoretical differences, but they had more in common than in opposition.[29]

In large measure because of its final chapter *Mind, Medicine, and Man* would receive a good deal of attention from Catholic readers. As the anonymous reviewer in *Loyola Educational Digest* discovered, 'Psyche, Soul, and Religion' was an impassioned plea for mutual understanding between psychoanalysis and religion. Analysing Freud and explaining psychoanalysis, Gregory argued that Freud's atheism and opposition to religion were the result of his lack of philosophical training and his preoccupation with the individual; Freud was irreligious, but it didn't follow that his theories were necessarily irreligious. Gregory then tackled a number of contentious issues head on – not only the existence of the soul but the apparent problems of guilt, absolution, and free will. Asserting that despite Freud's personal views, 'as a scientist' he did not contradict 'the fundamental principles of the descriptive, philosophical psychology of St. Thomas, Gregory posited a natural schema consonant with Thomistic tradition: 'body-psychic apparatus-soul'. As for guilt, confession (as a conscious and ritual act of repentance), and absolution, Gregory claimed, 'Psychoanalysis is not confession, nor is it like confession' and the psychoanalyst cannot absolve or relieve the patient of guilt. Rather, learning through psychoanalysis to differentiate fantasy from reality and infantile from adult impulses, the patient is relieved 'from feeling guilty about things of which he is not guilty at all, and he continues to feel guilty about those things of which one usually does and should feel guilty'. Further, Gregory argued that true (as opposed to neurotic) religious faith couldn't be touched by psychoanalysis. Finally, psychoanalysis only seemed to be in conflict with 'the postulate of free will'. Gregory explained, 'Psychological determinism can be as acceptable as physiochemical determinism' because 'the adjective "psychological" is used in the sense of the functioning of the psychic apparatus and not in the sense of "spiritual," of and pertaining to the soul.' That is, free will depends on 'free reason', and reason cannot be free unless a human being functions without the impediments which psychoanalysis terms 'neurosis': 'The deficiencies or malfunctions' of the psychic apparatus 'vitiate the free exercise of the will as much as do deficiencies and pathological changes of the brain.' The idea of agency, responsibility and reason – that is, free choice liberated from psychic illness – was, Gregory contended, inherent in psychoanalysis, which supports the idea of free will by its striving to liberate reason and will from the frailties biological and psychological imperfections impose. Indeed, because of an unshakable faith in human will and the human ability to choose freely when unfettered by disease, Freud would steadfastly claim that 'adulthood, love, and a free reason are a unit and the hope and goal of life.'[30]

In his review, Thomas Verner Moore asserted that Gregory had formulated 'the fundamentals of psychoanalysis anew in such a manner that neither as a philosophy nor as a technique would psychoanalysis be repugnant to the religious' – or specifically the Catholic – 'mind.' Even Freud's pansexuality shouldn't threaten the religious mind, Gregory suggested, for when Freud used the term 'sexual', he meant what Saint Thomas meant by '*sensualitas*'. Moore claimed Gregory argued 'like a good Catholic theologian' and praised him as 'an eminent psychiatrist' who had 'risen to this important concept of Thomistic philosophy.' Francis Cecil Sumner, chair of the Department of Psychology at Howard University, was even more perceptive. Drawing attention to Gregory's independent thinking in the book's last chapter, Sumner wrote that, in discussing religion, 'the author parts company with Freud by viewing it not as a compulsion-neurosis but as a triumph of the love-tendencies over the aggression-instincts.' Thus, 'The book as a whole is touching as a tribute and as a confession of faith on the part of an unsullied Freudian.' Friedman, too, understood *Mind, Medicine, and Man* as a personal and revealing text. In his review he concluded that Gregory went beyond explaining away the perceived conflict between psychoanalysis and religion; he had suggested that psychoanalysis could 'corroborate the tenets and lore of religion since both are based on the same principle – love'.[31]

Love as well as faith were very much at issue for Gregory in the spring of 1943, and readers in Catholic circles quickly became aware of his work. Having read *Mind, Medicine, and Man*, the Dominican monk Noël Mailloux made a point of introducing himself at a joint meeting of the American Psychoanalytic Association and the American Psychiatric Association held in Detroit in mid-May. Born in Canada on 25 December 1909, Mailloux had earned his first degree in philosophy at the Université de Montréal followed by a doctorate in philosophy at the Pontifical University of Saint Thomas Aquinas in Rome, then stayed on to study theology and joined the Dominican Order in 1937. On his return to Canada in 1938, he joined the faculty of philosophy at the Université de Montréal, and in 1942 founded the university's Institut de Psychologie, where he was now director. At the age of 33, Mailloux was nearly 20 years younger than Gregory, an able young man whose spiritual path had been apparently coherent and clear. That he was eager to learn more about psychoanalysis and was multilingual as well as widely read drew the two men into a relationship that would soon move beyond collegial acquaintance. That the two men shared a Christmas birthday would help to cement the bond.[32]

If matters of faith and love were an undercurrent in Gregory's professional and personal life in 1943, he typically also had much else on his conscious mind. May was a pivotal month in the war, and war rather than faith or love was a constant topic of conversation as its progress dominated the news. Axis troops in North Africa surrendered in the middle of the month, and the Allies turned their attention to bombing Sicily and Sardinia in preparation for an invasion of mainland Italy. In northern Europe British forces intensified their bombing of the Ruhr industrial valley, while as snow melted in Leningrad, the Russian population prepared to weather the second spring of the German siege. In Detroit Gregory presented several papers to various groups, and none of them had anything explicitly to do with *Mind, Medicine, and Man* or religion. He addressed members of the two associations on the broad topic of 'Present Trends in Psychoanalytic Theory and Practice' and a smaller group of colleagues on 'Historical Sidelights on the Problem of Delinquency', while his third paper, 'Fear of Death', was clearly prompted by the war. Back in New York, he addressed the Group Forum on the subject of his book at the end of the month, but the topic of war was again on his agenda when he spoke at the beginning of June to the Overseas Press Club of America on 'A Psychiatric Journey along the Axis'.

Gregory again took no real holiday over the summer. In New York he attended a preview of the film version of Hellman's *Watch on the Rhine*. Under Shumlin's direction and with a screenplay by Dashiell Hammett, the movie would receive several Academy Award nominations and Golden Globe awards. Such success by two of his patients certainly pleased Gregory as did the play, whose moral and political issues now seemed even more relevant. If Gregory attended such public occasions on his own or with Ray and spent weekends with his family on the farm, his life and Peg's were nevertheless in tandem, overlapping and parallel, connected even when physically apart. When Sigerist lectured at Sarah Lawrence College in Bronxville at the end of June, Peg invited him to join her and her mother and aunt for Saturday dinner. When Gregory's review of Richard M. Brickner's *Is Germany Incurable?* appeared in the *Bulletin of the History of Medicine* in July, it was immediately followed by Peg's review of Marie Beynon Ray's *Doctors of the Mind: The Story of Psychiatry*. Although the voice in this essay was her own, the perspective was Gregory's. Asking if a layman was capable of writing the history of a science he didn't understand, Peg unsurprisingly answered 'no'. Three years after having fallen in love with Gregory but still growing into 'the greatness of womanhood', Peg had taken on a great deal of his worldview as well as his hobbies and tastes. Despite a predilection for popular musicals, she had developed an interest in classical music and opera; she would never play chess well and wasn't artistic, but under his tutelage she had learned to use complicated cameras. Gregory in his turn would come to see Peg as his *Wunschmaid*, Brünnhilde to his Wotan.

Gregory took heart as Soviet troops struggled to push the Nazis westward, as Mussolini fell and British and American soldiers landed in Sicily. Throughout the summer he carried his papers from the office – where he continued to see the few patients who remained in the sultry city, to write notes to Peg and work at his desk – to the country, where he watched the children gambol on the lawn with the dogs, listened to the Metropolitan Opera broadcast on Saturday afternoons, and continued to work. *One Hundred Years of American Psychiatry* was coming along, but it involved a good deal of coordination, editing, and gathering together of bits and pieces. In July Gregory asked Sigerist if he could help him find copies of the signatures of all past presidents of the American Psychiatric Association; in August Gregory reported he had in hand some photographs and had begun going through the galleys, although he was still waiting for Sigerist's overdue chapter, which he wouldn't in fact receive until the very last possible minute in December. En route back to Baltimore at the end of August after a month in Bolton's Landing, Sigerist, who was as busy as Gregory, stopped off in Pound Ridge for a rushed but convivial dinner, then left behind in his haste a large bag of vegetables, a sample of the farm's plenty of which Gregory was so proud. Leaving behind the cows and pigs and melons and berries, Nancy and Greg, now 10 and nearly 12, went back to school at the beginning of September as Gregory's patients who had fled the city's summer heat returned to their Manhattan apartments and their regular round of appointments.[33]

Italy surrendered unconditionally on 8 September, but as British soldiers slaughtered Italians retreating from one Greek island after another, the Germans moved in. There was little to rejoice in even as the Soviets took Smolensk, a walled city on the Dnieper 600 kilometres north of Kiev where Gregory had never been. In early October the New York papers began to report the escape of thousands of Danish Jews to Sweden: Fishing boats in the dead of night had carried most of Denmark's Jewish population to safety in Malmo and Helsingborg and the little towns that dotted the western coast as far north as Gothenburg. Gregory admired Sweden, admired the Danes who had enabled the exodus, but what about the rest of European Jewry? He imagined the psychological toll on those in the midst of what was clearly a holocaust whose dimensions he could not fathom. What were Americans doing? And what of Florence and Siena and Rome, where the Nazis were now in charge, where young Mailloux had lived and studied, where Gregory had enjoyed lavish meals with Eddie and Bettina Warburg in that long-ago summer of 1934? And what was Pius XII doing now in the Vatican? Gregory couldn't answer any of these questions any more than he did other than keep on keeping on at home and at work and on behalf of Russian Relief and with Peg. His impotence frustrated him, but he took pleasure in the occasional experiences that brought him joy (Nancy's sunny attention, Greg's moments of calm, his barber's jokes, a pastrami sandwich or strong whisky with a colleague, a stolen night with Peg) and he worked harder on *One Hundred Years* and on the numerous other professional tasks that commanded his immediate attention.

Distractions were not always welcome. Gregory didn't need Sigerist to draw his attention to the long article on Field that appeared in *Life Magazine* in October. A photograph of Gregory as well as several of Field accompanied Francis Sill Wickware's snide and snappy article. Sigerist would exclaim, 'What publicity!', but Gregory didn't want such popular attention and most of what Wickware wrote was unpalatable. Entitled "Marshall Field III: He Tries to Atone for His Many Millions by Good Works and Profitless Journalism', the article was filled with gossip: It suggested that analysis with Gregory was responsible for Field's divorce from his second wife as well as his support ('to the tune of some $50,000') for the Committee for the Study of Suicide. Wickware cited Ingersoll as another of Gregory's patients and repeated, albeit as 'wildly embroidered by the press', the insinuation that Gregory had used his psychoanalytic influence to persuade Field to back *PM* at a time when his analysis had put him in a state of 'beatific dizziness'. Although Gregory was credited with Field's 'conversion to good works', with rendering Field happy and his life 'useful', Wickware was clearly suspicious of psychoanalysis and doubted Field's sincerity and generosity, calling the *Chicago Sun*, which Field took over in late 1941, a 'schizophrenic newspaper', and concluding with apparent relief that at least Field 'no longer required the services of Dr. Gregory Zilboorg'.[34]

Gregory was, however, used to scurrilous gossip and knew the best policy was not to take notice of things one preferred others not to have said or written. The end of the year was devoted to yet more work on *One Hundred Years* and to yet more work in general as the war continued its worrying destruction. In late November Roosevelt and Churchill met with Chiang Kai-shek in Cairo, then with Stalin in Tehran in an effort to agree on Allied strategy and plan for a post-war world. In Russia the Soviet effort to push the Germans back from the Dnieper had finally reached Kiev, where bombs from both sides fell on the landmarks still standing after two years of Nazi occupation. Further north in the snow falling outside of Leningrad German troops dug in for another Russian winter as the city's residents continued to resist and starve.

Gregory recognised he was working too hard; he always worked too hard, but he was apparently working especially hard now as if to compensate for the war's wide-scale destruction and his frustration with his inability to leave his marriage and with Ray's unwillingness to engage in the process of letting him go. He confessed to Sigerist that he had reached 'the point of saturation' and, on the evidence of his own 'physical and mental state', realised 'how hard it is to keep on pulling and pulling'. He concluded that both of them had to 'cut down on a number of things' if they were to continue to work well, yet every day he found 'more things which must be done, rather than fewer'. Gregory proposed a weekend on the farm in early December: 'We will walk in the woods and cook our food and sleep.' But Sigerist was also too busy, and once more a much-needed and vividly imagined escape was put aside, deferred, relegated to fantasy.[35]

Gregory spent Christmas of 1943 preparing *One Hundred Years* for the press and reflecting not only on the war, the history of psychiatry, and the state of psychoanalysis, but on the problems of faith and love. Franklin Day had taken issue with 'Psyche, Soul, and Religion' in an essay submitted to *Psychoanalytic Quarterly*, and Gregory took advantage of his editorial prerogative to write a response to appear alongside the article. Day contended that the reconciliation Gregory had suggested between psychoanalysis and Catholic theologians was impossible. Gregory pointed out that he had not urged psychoanalysis to reconcile itself to religion but had attempted to explain to 'serious and devout theological thinkers' that there was nothing unacceptable in psychoanalysis. Day's problem, Gregory insisted, was that, like many people, he failed to understand that psychoanalysis and religion were afraid of one another. What theological thinkers needed, as he had argued in *Mind, Medicine, and Man*, was a factual understanding of the psychic apparatus and the science of psychoanalysis; what psychoanalysis needed was an 'emotional understanding' of religion. Following Freud, Day had erred in believing that 'reason alone' would allow psychoanalysis to dismiss religious belief and practice as ritualistic, narcissistic, unhealthy, and immature as well as unscientific. Rather, Gregory wrote, psychoanalysts would understand religion better if they focused on 'the psychocultural function' of religion as 'one of man's fundamental ways of living and of meeting life'. Gregory confessed to feeling 'disconsolate' in his 'somewhat isolated position', but he nevertheless looked forward to the day when 'true emotional understanding' would prevail. However carefully measured this professional response to a professional matter, Gregory must also have been aware that only emotional understanding in personal as well as religious matters would enable him to bring about the changes in his own life that he continued to hope for.[36]

Notes

1 Notes, GZ to MSZ.
2 Note, GZ to MSZ; GZ to HES, 25 August 1941.
3 GZ to JZ, 19 January, 2 February, 2 March 1942; JZ to GZ, 27 January, 4, 13, 23 February, 1, 15 March 1942.
4 'Explanatory Folder'.
5 GZ to 'Très Saint-Père', 31 January 1953, APD; GZ to HES, 29 June 1944; JZ to GZ, 20 April 1942.
6 GZ to HES, 3 April 1942; GZ to Leon Krull, 13 April, 7 May 1942, Archives of American Art, Smithsonian Institution.
7 GZ, 'Some Primitive Trends', 'Humanism', 'Psychiatry as a Social Science'; GZ to HES, 3 April, 3 July 1942.
8 GZ, review, '*The Catholic Doctor* ... and *Cognitive Psychology*', 419, 420; GZ to JZ, 23 July 1942.
9 GZ to MSZ, 9 July 1942; notes, GZ to MSZ; MSZ to Louise Stone and Margaret Norton, nd.
10 JZ to GZ, 16 July, 12, 24 August, 7 September 1942.
11 GZ to JZ, 8 September 1942.
12 JZ to GZ, 21 September 1942.
13 GZ to JZ, 9 October 1942.
14 Notes, GZ to MSZ; GZ, 'The Doctor', 534.

15 JZ to GZ, 2 November 1942.
16 Note, GZ to MSZ; GZ to JZ, 16 November 1942.
17 JZ to GZ, 15 December 1942; GZ to JZ, 23 December 1942.
18 GZ to HES, 31 December 1942.
19 GZ to HES, 24 February 1943; GZ to JZ, 15 March 1943; GZ, 'Murder', passim, and 'The Role', 196, 197.
20 HES to GZ, 11 March 1943; GZ to JZ, 15 March 1943; JZ to GZ, 3 April 1943.
21 GZ to HES, 25 March 1943.
22 GZ to HES, 25 March, 2, 14 April 1943; HES to GZ, 21 April 1943; HES to MSZ, 26 April 1943.
23 GZ, 'Psychosomatic Medicine', 3–6; HES to GZ, 13 May 1943.
24 Overholser, 275; Thomas Mann to John Woodburn, nd.
25 Harcourt, Brace publicity; Feder, 394; Hayakawa, 61.
26 Wertham, 708; carbon, Marguerite Pohek to New Republic, 31 May 1943; excerpt in 'From the New Republic Mail Bag', New Republic, 5 July 1945, np.
27 Arthur Ruggles, 'Foreword' to MMM, v, vi; Eisler, 175; Paul Friedman, 567, 570.
28 Brill, 12; Kutash, 201, 202, 203.
29 Millis, 6; Menninger, 536.
30 Review, Loyola Educational Digest, vol. XIX, October 1943, 8–9; GZ, MMM, 320, 328, 329, 330, 333, 334.
31 Moore, 285, 286, 288; Sumner, 134.
32 NM to Donald Pleshette, 23 August 1976, APD.
33 GZ to HES, 15 July, 10 August, 5 October 1943.
34 HES to GZ, 18 October 1943; Wickware, 106, 112, 114, 118.
35 GZ to HES, 26 November 1943; HES to GZ, 28 November 1943.
36 Day, 84–92; GZ, 'A Response', 94, 100.

Chapter 4

War and peace
1944–1946

The Russian snow would finally defeat the Germans before the Nazi soldiers defeated the people of Leningrad. By the end of January 1944 Soviet forces had pushed the retreating German army over 100 kilometres west of the devastated city. As if in celebration, Gregory sent Sigerist from his farm 'a noble victual' – a suckling pig, which his friend took great joy in preparing (stuffed with barley and sausage) and serving (with sauerkraut and potatoes) to Johns Hopkins colleagues: Owsei Temkin; the historian of Greek medicine Ludwig Edelstein; his secretary Hope Trebing; and, of course, Genevieve. Everyone toasted Gregory in gratitude. The merry Sunday lunch would have continued into the evening had Sigerist not been compelled to leave for Canada, where he had agreed to give 18 lectures during an exhausting ten days. For his part, Gregory couldn't attend because of everything that held him in New York: Peg, his patients, his family, his writing, lectures he had long ago agreed to give, and involvement with causes related to the war, including a benefit he was organising for the American Soviet Medical Society. *One Hundred Years of American Psychiatry* was at last in press, but Gregory was also in charge of the centenary celebration planned for mid-May. 'I am so rushed of late that I find it a bit too much even for me', he told Sigerist in March. Ever the master of the *corps de ballet*, however, Gregory had decided that, on top of all else he was juggling, the celebration required a performance, and he had begun to write a play.[1]

There was in Gregory's life a great deal of joy as well as work and frustration. He was by turns hopeful and depressed about his personal life, but he had little by little begun to do something about it. He had by the spring of 1944 made clear to Ray his desire to leave their marriage. She surely realised her husband was involved with the woman she considered merely a secretary, but Ray failed to understand the reasons for his frustration, the depth of his unhappiness, or the seriousness of his intentions. Stymied by her lack of comprehension, her refusal to consider divorce, and his concern for the children, Gregory's talks with Peg had finally enabled him to take a practical look at his finances. The facts were stark: He was supporting his family extremely comfortably and his country home required a good portion of his income; he also had expenses right and left that he couldn't curtail such as taxes and rent on his office. If he got a divorce, he

DOI: 10.4324/9781003190974-4

would need to pay for it not only emotionally but in lawyers' fees and alimony. He explained in a note to Peg:

> You see, darling, I lived now for years without truly loving and being loved and I just was disorderly and financially reckless as if this was an adequate outlet. It was not, of course. Now I have you. You have me.

Gregory's notes to Peg are replete with such psychological reflection. On the subject of hurting one another, he insisted he was not a vindictive person and couldn't imagine feeling vengeful towards her, but

> When I feel pressed and harassed and held as if by ropes and unable to find a single moment of relaxation, I also feel as if I don't belong to myself at all, as if everybody owns me and everybody wants to assert his ownership.

Preferring to such beleaguered unhappiness 'not to be alive at all', he told her, 'I am living on a very small margin of safety and the edges are very sore, painful.' Having gradually accepted the idea of selling the farm, he confessed, 'I think my frequent states of low spirit even when other things seemed to be going alright, were due to the burden of the farm and to the pain in connection with the need to part with it.' He now began to think concretely about the future: 'I want to save some tools and the photographic equipment – the latter I would sell (some of it) without regret. The lathe I would sell in the hope of getting a better one after the war.' The property had, however, enormous symbolic and emotional as well as practical value: 'I know that in selling my farm I am depriving my children of the only thing they felt was home.' He imagined vaguely buying another 'smaller, simpler' place 'somewhere' after the war, and asked Peg, as he so often did with touching desperation, to help him think the matter through both logically and emotionally; 'only you', he declared, 'can help me in this'. He repeatedly told her how much he loved and needed her, how much he depended on her; over and over, rephrased with anguish and affirmation in note after note, he told her, 'You are the only hope and the only sense of living I have.'

Gregory was not, however, other than the man he had always been. He still wasn't good with money – in one sweet note late in 1943 he had written, 'Darling, Darling, I am rather embarrassed.' He had given the children something for Christmas shopping, had gone out to restaurants twice with friends over the weekend and paid each time, had not bought anything for himself but found he had only a couple of dollars in his pocket on Monday morning and no idea where the rest had gone. Having spent a night with Peg at the office, he could be with her the charming, kind, and relaxed man he so often longed to be; 'half dreamy', he recreated the scene: 'You in your slippers – loose dress – no typewriter, I also loungy. Talk, music, quiet, love and you and I and peace and Shadow and Ko-Ko at our feet.' Yet even when Peg and Gregory felt upbeat, the situation remained discouraging and nothing appreciably changed. When Pauline complained about Gregory's frequent crankiness, his demands for 'this and that' at the office, Peg attributed his behaviour to tiredness and the various pressures he was under, insisting her love for him and his for her were 'wonderful' in spite of everything. Pauline retorted bitterly that Peg was a fool to go on.

In contrast to Peg's probable foolishness and almost imperturbable sunniness, Gregory frequently doubted himself and had little confidence he could create the future they dreamed of; self-flagellation dragged him into the depths of despair. If they were married, he told Peg, taking a vacation would be no problem, there would be no 'farm problem', but they weren't married, had no prospect of being and the fault lay, he wrote, entirely with him, with his 'incompetence in matters practical', with his 'inability to live right and do right in this world with people, land or cash'. If they were not together 'soon and for good', Gregory felt by the beginning of 1944 that it was 'undoubtedly too late' for him to learn to be and behave differently. Recognising 'the sacrifice' Peg was making in continuing to wait, he felt 'small, selfish, petty', resentful of his 'contemptible incapacity' to live up to what he felt she needed and deserved. 'As matters stand now', he confessed, 'there is not a square foot in the world where I feel at home and at ease', not in the family apartment – where one after another, because of the war and his own economic situation, the servants had left and not been replaced – 'not on the farm, not in the street, not even in the treatment room'. Everywhere and constantly, Gregory had a 'sense of uselessness and not belonging'; he felt he was drifting, without 'true direction or bearings'. He could only beg Peg's forgiveness for continuing to love her. Feeling hounded by silent or vocal reproaches of not being satisfactory to anybody, he became at times frantic, under 'tension, tension, tension', convinced that somebody was always dissatisfied with him, with what he did or didn't or couldn't do.

It didn't help that Greg and Nancy were aware of their father's unhappiness as well as his affection for Peg and sought opportunities just to be near him. One night, as he worked, 11-year-old Greg settled at his feet and played solitaire for over an hour, remarkably 'relaxed, serene, sweet and really good'. When Gregory left his desk at the end of one working day, his son, waiting in the office hallway, asked with childish simplicity, 'Where is Peg, Daddy?' In July 1943, as soon as Greg had arrived at camp to which, Miss Darroche having been dismissed, the children were now sent each summer, he had written his father an obligatory post card in astonishingly awkward handwriting, a mixture of pen and pencil, cursive and printing: 'Dear Pop: I have arrived safely Nothing to write about. Love Gregory P.S. Give my regards to Peg'. Although younger, Nancy had a sharper awareness of what was going on. She mentioned Peg's name only when she and her father were alone. Late one night she told him she had been thinking ' "bad things" ', confessed she had cried herself to sleep for two nights after he left for Brazil. In tears, she put her arms around him and begged, ' "Please, Daddy, promise me, never leave me when you go away for good." '

Gregory wrote to Peg in desperation: He couldn't stand it any longer; no one would lose if he were 'to disappear'; if he did, the man who had made a study of suicide simply hoped that Peg wouldn't hate him. Such desperation wasn't fleet-ing adolescent angst or dismissible Russian rhetoric; it was serious and 'frightful' anguish. Gregory was over and over again 'sad', filled with a 'sickening' loneli-ness that made him want 'to cry and cry'. He wrote of his own spiritual ruin, Peg's redeeming grace.[2]

The man who bared his soul to the woman he loved was nevertheless able to function professionally, and no mood was yet so low that Gregory hadn't been able to rally. By the spring of 1944, a corner seemed to have been turned, the way forward clearer or at least more hopeful. He evidently hadn't considered re-entering analysis, and despite his emotional distress, his problems were not primarily psychological. His difficulties were largely practical, and as he struggled to act, what he needed was spiritual solace and grace. Père Mailloux's entry into his life couldn't have been more timely.

Gregory's personal problems didn't figure in the correspondence with Mail-loux that began after they met in Detroit. The premise of their relationship was the priest's search for a deeper understanding of psychoanalysis and the two men's shared interest in Christian philosophy and particularly Thomas Aquinas. When Mailloux entered psychoanalysis in 1945, Gregory accepted the role of wise physician while Mailloux became both patient and postulant. The analy-sis took place during Mailloux's visits to New York and in Montreal, where he would invite Gregory to lecture. A new world of intellectual Catholics was opening up to Gregory at a particularly auspicious moment. In due course he would also analyse many of Mailloux's colleagues in Quebec, including the Spanish refugee Miguel Prados, the French-born psychologist and philosopher Théo Chentrier, and Mailloux's fellow Dominican Augustin Deslauriers. Such men as well as Mailloux himself would bring Gregory opportunities he hadn't even imagined.[3]

That world opened slowly, however, and the spring of 1944 was quickly filled with other commitments. In mid-April, having just discovered material on the problems of military psychiatry as seen by Soviet psychiatrists, Gregory changed the focus of an essay he was writing for Sigerist for the recently founded *American Review of Soviet Medicine*. Such was the pace of his work that Gregory promised the article would be ready within days. During the last week in April he addressed the New York Psychoanalytic Society on an entirely different topic, 'Affects, Per-sonal and Social'. A fortnight later he was in Providence, Rhode Island, for Butler Hospital's centenary celebration, where he spoke on 'Psychiatric Problems in the Wake of the War'. Without a book on the hob, Gregory's literary energies went into talks, reviews, and articles, and he took advantage of the freedom to examine whatever topics captured his attention.[4]

Gregory's spring was dominated, however, by preparations for the American Psychiatric Association's centennial in Philadelphia in mid-May. Peg and Sigerist joined him. The three dined together before the conference and, while Gregory attended meetings, Peg and Sigerist visited the city's art museum. Both of them, however, were in the audience for Gregory's delightful drama paying homage to major historical figures in American psychiatry, a performance that reminded everyone of his mastery of theatre.[5]

At once genuinely funny and modernist, the play toyed with the illusions suspended and broken in live drama, breaking the boundaries between audience and actors, between real and dramatic time, between the modern present and the historical past. The script was amusingly self-referential – the 'Radio Announcer' commented early on, 'Whew! What a script!' Set on an evening in Philadelphia after a day of meetings celebrating the centennial, the play featured a voice-over by the radio announcer-narrator and characters as diverse as Alfred E. Smith (New York's former governor and one-time presidential candidate) and the nineteenth-century social reformers Dorothea Dix and Isaac Ray. The cast also included two fictitious psychiatrists, Kimberly and Brandon, who were attending the centenary gathering and served as foils through whom Gregory poked fun at his colleagues and the conventions of psychiatry and professional meetings. The text was peppered with in-jokes, and the author satirised not only his contemporaries but himself. Thus at one point Brandon told Kimberly that he had just seen Gregory Zilboorg with other psychiatrists backstage. Their comical interchange revealed Gregory's awareness of how he appeared to others as well as his ability to make fun of both himself and others' perceptions of him:

KIMBERLY: What is Zilboorg doing here?
BRANDON: I don't know … He talks well, that guy – but he is always up to no good. *He* told us, you and me, that we are talking too much and should cut it short. He is a [damn] definite guy, all right.
KIMBERLY: I'm glad *you* talked to him.
BRANDON: I wish *you* had. What a temper!
KIMBERLY: Never mind – a temper is a swell thing. It gets you places – sometimes.

The play was also sweet and touching. Dix and Ray were treated generously, and Gregory captured their voices with elegance and precision. Ray agreed to address the audience with typical period charm, declaring, 'I don't believe I have anything to say to you', before continuing,

My good friends of one hundred years ago are among you in this hall. They are wiser than I am, as they have always been; it is [a] pardonable bit of sagacious strategy on their part that maneuvered me alone onto this stage.

With similarly old-fashioned eloquence Dix mentioned the 'men of courage and women of faith and fortitude' who shaped the field of psychiatry. Al Smith, meanwhile, spoke in contemporary colloquialisms of reforms that succeeded despite 'the grumbling of some sour pusses, dyed-in-the-wool standpatters'. The brash politician, describing his achievements in mental health, insisted state hospitals were never jails ('that jail stuff is pure bunk and baloney') before giving the lectern to Dix, who whispered 'New Yorkers never change.' Towards the end, Ray invited James King Hall and Arthur Ruggles to leave their seats in the audience and join the actors on stage. Dix closed the play with a tribute to military nurses, recalling her own experiences in the American Civil War while drawing the audience back to the current war, declaring hopefully that the women now serving with the military and the Red Cross in conflict zones would return 'with victory, peace and loving service'.[6]

Back in New York, Pauline held down the fort, assuring James that the cheques he was worried about had indeed been sent in both March and April. James, who had huffily broken off the correspondence with his brother in the summer of 1943, was again fretting that Gregory would fail to support the family in Mexico. Gregory followed up on his return from Philadelphia. He felt that once more his brother's anxiety was 'much ado about nothing'. Apparently James had told Basia the cheques had not arrived; Basia had immediately written Fera, who had telephoned the office. Gregory blew off steam:

> Why Basia should be initiated into something that concerns only you and me I do not know. Why she should write Fera I do not understand. Why such massive attacks of such little strategic importance I do not comprehend. Such are the ways of some funny people.

As the spring gave way to summer, Gregory simply refused to engage in such pettiness; he had much more important matters weighing on his mind and heart.[7]

With the invasion of France on 6 June 1944, it seemed clear to Americans that the war was moving in the direction of an end. Considerable battling lay ahead, but the indications were good that the Allies would win, that – whatever the aftermath might be – physical combat would soon be over, occupied territory would be liberated, peace would prevail, and a new post-war era would begin. As New York Mayor Fiorello La Guardia in Madison Square Garden echoed Roosevelt's prayers in his nationwide broadcast, Gregory must have sensed that his own struggle to liberate himself from his marriage in many ways paralleled the progress of the larger war on the world stage. Peace was the goal of both, and harsh decisions as well as courageous actions would inevitably be required, come what may, even by those frightened by physical force and pacifist on principle. When Sigerist tempted him with a meal at a new restaurant serving Chesapeake Bay crabs, Gregory didn't contain his enthusiasm or hesitate to draw on the war as a metaphor for his feelings. 'I am in a state of very acute conflict', he joked,

> I do want to accept your invitation and come to Baltimore, and so does Peg. Of course, there are a great many things that we would want to talk over, and those Chesapeake crabs are a point of major importance. That territory must be invaded, with mortars, tanks, by land, by air and by sea.

He wanted specifically to discuss the autumn programme for the first meeting of the Soviet-American Medical Society – there were 'practical and tactical details' to work out – but he was also simply 'sick and tired of working without fun' and confided that, for 'a moment' after the centenary festivities, he hadn't even had any fun in working because he had taken an emotional 'nosedive'.[8]

Having addressed the Medical Correction Association on 'Unconscious Factors in Crime' at the end of June, Gregory cleared his desk and set off with Peg in mid-July for the jolly weekend Sigerist had proposed. On their return, however, they sat back and took stock. Although unable to bring himself to walk out on his children, Gregory had been spending more and more nights at the office with Peg or on his own. Greg and Nancy were again at camp, but even before the summer he had broached his problem with Joe Walker and, on his legal advice, begun payments to Ray of $1,000 a month ($14,000 today). Discussing practical matters with Peg, Gregory agreed he would need to borrow from his life insurance policy to pay Walker what he still owed him, a hefty amount that included bills as far back as the confrontation with the New York Psychoanalytic Society. Gregory's old habit of simply working harder to increase his income was now impossible; he was working as hard as he could and there wasn't much more income he could generate. How he would pay a lawyer for handling a divorce remained an open question, while the generous monthly sums hadn't convinced Ray she would be well provided for if she changed her mind – and she hadn't changed her mind.[9]

Free to choose whatever topic he wished, Gregory must have taken a great deal of satisfaction in writing in the spring and summer of 1944 his extraordinary essay 'Masculine and Feminine: Some Biological and Cultural Aspects'. He was surely conscious that the subject had particular personal resonance as he struggled to leave one union and confirm another, as he grappled with his paternal relationship with a difficult son, whose general behaviour struck him as simultaneously childish and threatening, and with an adored daughter on the brink of at least physical maturity. Thinking not only about faith, family, and finances, Gregory was also taking a fresh look at psychoanalysis. His reflections certainly involved considering the tensions in the New York Psychoanalytic Society that had preceded the confrontation, and while he hadn't exactly concurred with Gosselin that Karen Horney was a 'shit', it was clear to him that Horney's ideas as well as the fact that she was a woman had figured in the reactions she provoked and her resignation from the Society. He typically addressed personal issues only obliquely. Just as 'Psyche, Soul, and Religion' had owed as much to Gregory's subjective experiences as to his reading of Aquinas, in rethinking libido theory – specifically the castration complex and penis envy – Gregory drew not only on his clinical observations, wide reading, and personal experience but on a particular text: *Pure Sociology: A Treatise on the Origin and Spontaneous Development of Society* by the nineteenth-century American sociologist Lester Frank Ward. Looking at the problem of masculinity and femininity from the point of view of science and history – especially biology and culture – Gregory argued once again that methodological errors had led psychoanalysis to struggle with theoretical problems it hadn't yet been able to solve. Despite the essay's modest subtitle – which indicated attention only to 'some' of the many particular 'aspects' of its weighty subject – Gregory set himself the enormous task of recasting psychoanalytic theory on the basis of biological, sociological, and anthropological evidence.

Given what Gregory was attempting as well as his astonishingly modern and feminist conclusions, this long essay merits a detailed summary as an expression of mature thinking at once courageously imaginative, sharply insightful, and rigorously scientific. Beginning with a broad historical sweep, Gregory pointed out that the First World War had challenged traditional views of conventional femininity as women took on many traditionally male jobs and took up social habits – such as smoking and drinking – previously reserved for men. Women's general appearance had also changed as they put aside corsets and bobbed their hair, exposing themselves to 'the gaze of the male in a manner of self-contained provocativeness, assured initiative, and almost complacent challenge' and questioning the 'Mid-Victorian cast of chastity, innocent prudery, coyness, and romantic passivity'. What Gregory saw as 'truly revolutionary' in the 1920s was the beginnings of women's 'psychological equality with man, individual initiative, executive ability, frank assertion of her right to choose a sexual partner'. While in the 1930s a woman's appearance reverted to more traditionally feminine 'norms' as skirts lengthened and hair again became ornate, 'the fundamental psychological change held and consolidated its newly conquered position'. Over 30 years before the feminist film critic Laura Mulvey would theorise 'the male gaze', Gregory here examined the idea of the performative masculine and feminine gaze not only in the cultural and specifically psychoanalytic ways that Mulvey explored but in the context of evolutionary and physiological biology.

Turning his attention to his own field, Gregory contended that psychoanalysis, although it had accepted female psychoanalysts as 'equal partners', had 'failed surprisingly to analyse this new shift in culture'. Reviewing recent contributions from Ernest Jones and other analysts on the subject of female psychosexual development, he singled out for particular praise the work of Helene Deutsch, which he found 'brilliant', and Horney, which he found bold and original, although 'intuitive'. Despite the importance and disquieting nature of the question of female libidinous development, however, 'no really new answers to the old questions had been found, and the old answers failed fully to meet the new and legitimate queries about female sexuality.' Indeed, even though such problems were 'specifically psychoanalytic', psychoanalysis had 'failed thus far to offer a truly satisfactory solution of or a comprehensive hypothesis regarding the problems of feminine sexuality and the so-called battle between the sexes'.[10]

In all fairness to psychoanalysis, sociology and biology as well as literature had struggled with the same problems. Citing Tolstoy, Ibsen, Shaw, and Zola, Gregory suggested, 'the whole struggle between the two age-long ideals of *la femme mère* and *la femme maîtresse*' had come 'to full expression without any possible solution of the riddle in sight'. Psychoanalysis seemed to accept that it is a man's world and women have a hard time of it; psychoanalysis had even apparently lent 'some support to the traditional attitude of modern civilization by pointing to the woman's organic, psychological, and cultural inadequacy'. While

Gregory defended Freud against accusations of misogyny by embittered critics, contending that his 'scientific life and leadership and his personal life would automatically exclude accusations of this sort', he explained that the 'suggestion that a woman is a castrated being ... and her business is to stay castrated and at home' is an 'old theme' that – however wrong – found 'its authoritative reverberation in the psychoanalytic theory of feminine sexuality'.

Gregory saw this theme's recurrence 'in the unconscious of both men and women, its constant repetition under various guises in the minds of the ancient Greeks and of others through the ages down to Auguste Compte and Schopenhauer' as 'a real psychological force, a need perhaps on the part of man to emphasize woman's castrated state, as well as a need on the part of woman to castrate man'. He posited that 'man is almost as deeply interested in proving the fact of woman's inferiority because of her being castrated as woman is constantly eager to protest against her sad lot.' In psychoanalytic terms, men expressed their superiority over and contempt for the 'weaker sex' by means of 'reaction formations': The mid-twentieth-century Western man tipped his hat; stood up when a woman entered the room; offered her his seat in a street car – in sum, he went to great lengths 'to express politely this superiority-contempt in relation to woman'. Gregory developed his insights by contrasting what he termed the 'Dominican misogyny' of the *Malleus Maleficarum* with 'the genuine adoration' of the Virgin Mary, an 'ideal of virginity and immaculate conception' he found of 'utmost significance'. He contended this ideal appeared 'wherever the hatred for woman is a dominant factor', but 'existing psychoanalytic hypotheses and theories do not sufficiently explain the nature and quality of this hostility, nor do they offer a comprehensive idea as to its origin and development.' Some theorists, such as Alfred Adler and Horney, had ended up rejecting all or part of Freud, but 'psychoanalysts in general' seemed to Gregory 'to founder on the invisible reefs of the problem' – in short, on the issue of libido development and organisation, psychoanalysis had demonstrated 'a certain refractoriness and perhaps inability to clear up the confusion as well as the scientific conflict'.

Gregory next turned his attention to women in the midst of the current war during which they had become 'assistants and participants' in 'the total war effort', roles calling into question women's 'so-called' physical and psychological 'passivity'. Terming this phenomenon the 'masculinization' of women simply reduced the problem of psychological femininity and masculinity to a matter of semantics, while even during the war, the birth rate had not fallen and women continued to become mothers. Contrasting the 'masculinization' of women in anti-fascist countries, where they were 'integrated', with the idea and practices of womanhood in fascist counties, where maternity was idealised, Gregory pointed out that one might logically but wrongly conclude that the Nazis had a psychologically healthy conception of a healthy woman, but every psychoanalyst would agree there was something missing and wrong in such a conclusion. He then offered a brilliant analysis of the nature of the argument over masculinity and femininity: 'One side is led to reassert with greater vigor the established hypotheses, while the other rejects them wholesale and turns towards a set of derivative phenomena called culture and chooses to consider them primary factors.'

Focusing on libido theory and on what he called 'feminine psychology', Gregory set himself the task of presenting a 'historicopsychological' and 'psychosociological' analysis of psychoanalytic thought on the essay's subject. He suggested the value-laden 'concept of the superiority of man in the psychoanalytic theory of sexual development' was responsible for what he kindly referred to as 'the general lack of clarity'. Most recent dissenters from psychoanalysis had 'stumbled when the implications of the theory of sex led to the theory of man's primary superiority'; the theory had activated a 'personal masculine narcissism', a 'hypertrophic masculinity' that went 'beyond biological and rational needs' to become 'antonymous, a part yet independent of and detrimental to the whole'. The 'battle of the sexes' had thus always been solved, Gregory argued, by man in favour of himself, and he had taught woman to accept this solution almost without questioning, while many theorists, immobilised by the argument of masculine superiority, incorrectly reduced it to culture, 'pure science', or 'pure biology'.

Offering various historical and cross-cultural examples of 'the social and psychological history of man's self-assertion', Gregory contended that patriarchy had existed since the beginning of history and everywhere: 'The whole history of humanity is pervaded by this attitude, whether expressed directly or in a more or less disguised form, in earnest or in fun, in civilized culture or statutory law, in superstition or religious belief.' Further, 'This antifeminist drive, while primarily expressed in terms of hostility toward women, is equally valid as an expression of man's conviction of his own superiority.' Such an 'androcentric point of view' is, however, unstable, threatened, always in need of assertion or defence, yet man feels he cannot fail, and 'if failure comes, it is just failure' or attributable to 'feminine influence'. Gregory considered such convictions 'the psychosociological heritage bequeathed to the generation which was called upon to create and to develop psychoanalytic theory'.

While some psychoanalysts had begun to examine androcentric bias, Gregory contended they had failed to pursue their investigations and Horney had made 'a methodological misstep'. By failing to look at its biological origin, the problem of masculinity and femininity appeared simply a cultural issue; even psychoanalysis could be put aside, for 'only the androcentric superstructure of culture', only 'masculine institutions' seemed important. Gregory generalised that the modern feminist woman 'in her very modernity' tended to mistake 'the structure for the function instead of the reverse' as 'androcentric, phallocentric bias' was rejected with 'the whole mass of empirical facts', leaving merely 'sociological speculations' repetitively asserting that 'only institutions shape one's mind.' Without a more scientific approach, Gregory pointed out that one is left with the naïve idea that human beings, male or female, are psychologically 'an exceptional product of life', living by the institutions they themselves have created and not by their 'biopsychological endowment'.

Agreeing, however, with Horney and with Freud, Gregory acknowledged that woman stands in relation to man as slave to master while both childbirth and breastfeeding seemed 'deeply and primordially connected in the biological and psychological development of woman'. Turning his attention to nineteenth-century research on sexuality that had occurred simultaneously and independently of Freud in entomology, botany, zoology, biology, anthropology, and sociology, Gregory synthesised the conclusions of the German zoologists Richard Hertwig and Ernst Haeckel, the American entomologist Leland Ossian Howard, and the French biologist Jean-Baptiste Lamarck: The male's role in reproduction was biologically secondary to the female's. In contrast to Sandor Ferenczi's belief in woman's fundamental castration tendency, Gregory proposed Ward's '*gynaeco-centric*' view of the female as 'primary, more essential for the preservation of the race of living things, and therefore superior'.

Gregory set out in 'Masculinity and Femininity' to incorporate such scientific observations into psychoanalytic theory. Ward had argued that the female's 'original power of choice' accounted for the natural section of the bigger, more colourful male in nature; 'biogenetically... the female originally reigned supreme'. Connecting male hostility towards women and fear of the female with a remote biological past in which the male was dispensable after fertilisation, Gregory asserted, 'Even aggressiveness and combativeness, which are traditionally considered the very essence of masculinity' must be reassessed psychoanalytically. According to Ward, the female had the prerogative of discrimination – males fight and she chooses the winner. In developed species, the male does nothing for the young and families; the mother cares for, feeds, and defends. The female of the species is thus the most dangerous to human beings: While males flee, she defends her young and fights for them. According to Ward, the male is actually rather cowardly. Ward hypothesised that – far earlier than what might be observable in Freud's 'primitive hoard' – the social order had been matriarchal: 'At a remote and very primitive gynecocentric period, there was only the mother to be tied to, to worship, or to hate. Her choice of the male was free and supreme and final.' Ward further believed that man's discovery of his paternity 'made him assert himself and perform the revolution of dethroning the woman from her high biological position of privilege and primitive maternal authority.' Gregory imagined that young females found maternal consolation in growing up to be like their strong mother, while 'the young male must have been a very sorry sight indeed: young, inexperienced in getting food for himself, and not strong enough yet to be the object of choice by the fastidious, self-assured woman.' Perhaps, Gregory posited, this dynamic was the root of clinically observed male hostility to women as well as 'woman-envy' and male maternal yearnings.

Gregory next went further and wondered if rape rather than patricide was 'the primordial deed' about which Freud wrote in *Totem and Taboo*, the subduing of the woman rather than a man's killing/overthrowing the father: 'The power with which the human male for the first time overwhelmed the human female marked the end of woman's biological security and ability to choose, of her right to be her own mistress and the mistress of her brood.' Gregory posited that such a 'primal rape' was 'an act devoid of any genital, object-libidinous strivings. It was a phallic, sadistic act.' The male didn't seek fatherhood but pregenital gratification; the primal deed was one of infantile hedonism, egotistic infantilism. Thus notions of Eve as the primal seducer were, Gregory theorised, merely a psychobiological 'projection into the woman of man's own guilt for his infantile hedonism'. Further, an economic '*motif*' was soon added to 'the narcissistic sexual *motif*, which inaugurated the subjection of woman', and human evolution became at once psychosexual and cultural. Gregory asserted, 'Neither man's nor woman's sexuality can be properly understood from the psychoanalytic point of view, unless these two main lines are properly evaluated.'

Working psychoanalytically from sociology, anthropology, and biology, Gregory warned against 'androcentric bias' in the idea popularly termed 'the survival of the fittest'. Arguing that 'man's unconscious physical sadism' led him 'to elevate his most primitive reactions to lofty heights of biosociological creative progress', Gregory offered examples from the work of the nineteenth-century Russian sociologist Paul von Lilienfeld, who presented the process of fertilisation as a race of sperm conquering the ovum. Gregory asserted that Ward's major ideas were 'easily translatable into psychoanalytic concepts'. Man's discovery that woman could not only be raped but made to serve him was simultaneously an economic development and evidence of man's sadistic impulses that further deprived women of choice: 'Once having sensed blood, as it were, man was quick to assert his mastery and take measures to secure and perpetuate it forever.' This exercise of power was a 'narcissistic anal pattern', an expression of the need to have and to hold, to possess and master, not love and protect. As woman was enslaved and became property, the male master extended his scope of influence; as his needs correspondingly increased, the desire to gratify those needs was enhanced. Through such mastery and conquest, his 'standard of living' gradually became 'the false measure' of culture.

Gregory posited that 'the development of the human family ought to be viewed' in light of this economic process. Quoting Augustine's mother, he noted that marriage was originally 'a contract of servitude' while 'the demands for pre-marital chastity and the consecration of virginity spring from the need to possess and not from the drive to love.' Even 'Matrilineal inheritance made the mother and children belong to one class, while the father belonged to another.' Thus father-daughter incest was acceptable long after brother-sister or son-mother was forbidden, yet 'it was not object-libidinous genital paternity' that prompted the man to seek to establish a family, but 'assurance and extension of the narcissistic gratification of his primitive sexual drives'. Turning traditional psychoanalytic thinking on its head, Gregory concluded that, since enslavement of the mother preceded murder of the father, phylogenetically as well as ontogenetically

> man arrives at object-libidinous paternity not in that direct way which many
> have become accustomed to imagine in psychoanalysis, but in a manner at

least as complex and circuitous if not more so than the one by which woman arrives at psychological maternity.

Gregory suggested that even Freud sensed the flaws in his oedipal theory when he introduced the concept of the preoedipal phase, but his androcentric bias nevertheless prevented him from considering the remote past preceding the cultures described in *Totem and Taboo*.

Gregory argued that, because of androcentric bias, psychoanalysis had thus far failed properly to access 'the phylogenetic roots of male hostility to women and the father's unconscious hostility against his children'. In fact, 'Man does not want the woman to be a mother, but a convenient sexual servant or instrument.' However, Gregory posited that the human male, who hated the woman-mother, must have envied her, too, because of the love and devotion she received from her children. The female attained felicity, serenity, and security in being loved: Man wanted these and could not get them through sexual prowess and physical force. Jealous, he also wanted to be a mother. Indeed, the power of the mother figure was recognised even before the male understood his paternity, his role in reproduction. Simultaneous womb envy and hatred, worship, and hostile identification help explain the many maternal deities as man moved from 'an ever-murderous, unconscious fertilizer' to 'a conscious master'.

Gregory analysed the nature of human paternity. Man achieved 'psychological fatherhood' out of 'a magic, compulsion-neurotic, hostile identification with the mother'. As a result, 'the sense of paternity is essentially a feminine attribute' acquired by the human male in 'his attempt to keep his mastery of the female more secure and less disquieting in the light of periodic demonstrations of female superiority by way of having children'. In psychoanalytic terms, Gregory posited that 'it is not penis-envy on the part of woman, but woman envy on the part of man, that is psychologically older and therefore more fundamental'. Fatherhood is thus a maternal trait, while the 'deep ambivalence towards the primordial mother and the first wife-slave ... sheds considerable light on ... the female castration complex.'

Moving towards his conclusion, Gregory argued that androcentric bias in psychoanalysis had confused understanding; even many female analysts had succumbed to androcentric thinking. He praised Jones for seeing Freud's methodological weaknesses while continuing to affirm libido theory, but with Horney clearly in mind, Gregory noted that others because of their own emotional biases had felt compelled to reject libido theory outright. In contrast, reverence for Freud had, in Gregory's opinion, often complicated issues and impeded the progress of scientific insight.

Gregory couldn't conclude his revision of psychoanalysis without looking beyond history and science at both Western folklore and the Christian tradition. After examining the psychological dynamics of the mythic man-hating Amazons, he reflected on 'the true psychological meaning' of the story of Eve and the image of the Holy Virgin. He presented the Old Testament account of Adam's fall as the projection of man's own strivings onto woman, while Mary in the New Testament represented in his view the reestablishment of the free and devout mother – with the Holy Spirit as father, the son of God was free, not the son of man and therefore not a slave. Gregory saw this perennial struggle – between the free woman and the man who envies her and wishes to deprive her of her primordial right – in myth, religion, philosophy, and sociology; its expression was logically also reflected in psychoanalytic thought. Freed from androcentric bias, psychoanalysis would be at once richer and more scientific, but much work remained to be done. If, as Gregory argued, penis envy followed primal rape, which had followed the worship of fecundity and motherhood, the whole question of so-called male activity and female passivity would have to be 'restudied' as well as the question of male and female narcissism. Hazarding that part of striving for equality may actually be 'a reassertion of the woman's original state of freedom', Gregory concluded that fundamental ideas of masculinity and femininity would also need scientific re-examination, as would the cultural changes which had led to modern Western culture and 'many of the traditional views on the psychology of striving for equality among the sexes'.[11]

Such radical insights anticipate modern feminist thinking from Simone de Beauvoir (whose *Second Sex* was published in France in 1949, five years after 'Masculine and Feminine') to American writers who focused on the experience of rape (Susan Brownmiller's *Against Our Will: Men, Women, and Rape* appeared in 1975 and Andrea Dworkin's *Intercourse* in 1987) to European philosophers including Jacques Lacan, Julia Kristeva, Luce Irigary, and Hèlène Cixous. Psychoanalysis, like other disciplines in which gender figures, is indeed still going through the process of restudying that Gregory advocated. Having said what he had to say about masculinity and femininity, he was by no means finished with the challenges gender posed for him as a professional psychoanalyst or as a husband and father in his own life – his own re-examination would continue – but he was ready to refocus his psychoanalytic as well as personal attention on those matters he had from his youth considered spiritual.

The summer drew to a close with hopefulness. By the end of August the Allies had secured most of France; in Italy American troops pushed the Germans north of Florence and took the Philippine island of Guam from the Japanese. In Pound Ridge Gregory began preparing lectures for students at Catholic University of America where, under the aegis of Thomas Verner Moore, he had been appointed associate professor of psychiatry. Starting in the autumn of 1944, Gregory would commute from New York to Washington once a week. The part-time post was not exactly the teaching and research position he had imagined as his calling at Bloomingdale, but it was an academic appointment in a university environment that suited him while his relationship with Moore quickly moved beyond collegial cooperation to a friendship in which the capable monk became both spiritual confidante and guide.[12]

The beginning of the academic year brought a number of other changes as well. Peg's family dynamics were shifting, increasing her uneasiness with a life defined by her conventional mother and aunt in the female household in Bronxville. She had always been more comfortable confiding in George than in Lou, but both brothers were now geographically distant. On his graduation with a degree in English from Yale, George had enrolled in Columbia's medical school, where he soon found he had neither an aptitude nor the discipline required for medicine. By the autumn he was a private in the U.S. army, training to administer electro-encephalograms at a Texas military clinic. Lou, recently promoted to captain and assigned to the Office of Strategic Services in Washington, would by October be working in military intelligence in London.

While Gregory shared his spiritual concerns with Moore, he had no one but Peg to confide in when it came to his marital problems. When James passed through New York in September on his way to deliver Natalie to Antioch College, Gregory revealed only his anxiety about his stressful professional life. The upshot of an evening together was agreement that Gregory could reduce Anna's monthly support. By October, however, James regretted his acquiescence. Fera explained the appalling situation she had witnessed during her summer visit to Mexico while James wrote to confess that it was now impossible for Anna to cover even bare expenses. Gregory responded immediately: He would, of course, increase his support to the previous level, but wondered why James hadn't raised the matter during their long conversation; his brother's insularity, cowardice, and failure to communicate, he wrote, made his own heart bleed with pity. Infuriated, James took no responsibility for having failed to inform his brother, pathetically blaming Gregory ('after your long peroration – four hours plus! – on your own financial straits and health concerns, you left me utterly disarmed and unable to ask you to help') and telling him not to bother responding. Gregory evidently took James at his word, provoking a two-year break in the correspondence and cutting himself off finally and permanently from the only family confidant he had ever sought.[13]

Even Sigerist was no longer available for those weekends during which Gregory was free to be with Peg and relax and talk about anything under the sun. With the war in Europe approaching some sort of resolution, Sigerist had gone to India for five months of fieldwork. In November Gregory would attend the first meeting of the American-Soviet Medical Society on his own, while throughout the autumn weekends became more and more difficult. In an anguished note in October, unhappy and afraid, he wrote Peg that – although her goodness and inspiration, her zest and strength made him feel alive as never before – the more they loved each other, the more he wanted to die because they were not striving to live 'the full gamut of life'. 'My week-ends', he continued, 'tear my heart out': 'my children love me and need me and cling to me', while Ray 'continues as she always has done to treat everything with a limited horizon, no vision, no understanding, no human sympathy'. He felt reduced to 'a piece of property' and resorted to 'endless artifices, a variety of devices for self-control, for civility, for evenness', but still felt vulnerable, 'threatened and exposed to intrusions and attacks'. The weekends were 'poisoned with uncertainty' until there was 'no dignity' at all, just a constant, chronic 'make-shiftness'.

Facing Peg's stalwart goodness and understanding, he felt ever smaller and more worthless. 'You are the very substance of my work', he wrote, 'You give me faith; you *are* my faith and my self-respect and my dignity – I borrow it from you without returning even a part of it.' He bewailed that circumstances made it impossible for him to be fully with her and was 'tormented by the slips' which he felt made him 'a bad father' – indeed, 'no father, no husband, no lover' except by 'the book-keeping columns of life, the official heartless ledger of living'. He was grateful for Peg's every kiss, caress, and smile, 'yet perturbed, frightened, hounded and haunted'; 'churned and ground' by artificiality; 'blind' and unable to see a way forward. Feeling weak, unfit and unworthy, without the knowledge and strength to find and carry out a solution, he praised Peg and pleaded with her: 'God bless you – pray for me –'.

As the leaves in Central Park turned and fell, Gregory became even more reliant on Peg and clearer in his own mind about what he would need to do to free himself from his depleted and depleting marriage. Lonely and desolate except when with her, he was horrified by how little time they spent together. Young Greg was increasingly difficult; life at home was altogether 'awful'. He finally saw he would have to 'put an end to it', because it 'just cannot go on any longer', and told Peg he hoped they would soon be 'together for good and to hell with selfish, foolish people – who torture themselves and others'.

While divorce wasn't common in mid-twentieth-century America and was generally frowned upon, it was accepted and understood in sophisticated circles. Edward VIII had married a twice-divorced American, an international scandal because of his royal status, yet the problems the marriage posed were primarily political. Several of Gregory's patients had gone through divorces – Jimmy Warburg and Marshall Field, for example, would each go through two – but although the emotional challenges of leaving a marriage were among the factors bringing such patients into analysis, Gregory had seen them through the psychic and practical difficulties relatively swiftly and easily. Close up and at a distance, Gregory had also seen colleagues go through divorces – Henry had divorced in 1926 and married again the following year; Horney had divorced in 1937; Menninger had divorced and married again in 1941. Children naturally complicated matters, and Gregory's situation was particularly difficult because his children were young, but his prolonged suffering had its source in his deeply emotional nature and his high ethical standards. What for other people might be primarily practical problems were for Gregory spiritual issues; difficulties others might resolve relatively rapidly were philosophical conundrums as well as moral dilemmas demanding principled solutions. For Gregory there was no morally clear path out of his marriage, but the emotional toll had become intolerable.

By late November he had resolved to leave his family come what may. He told Peg he had come to a point where he had to 'make some final step' and was 'ready to make it': 'I shall inform my wife that I am going to leave and live alone as of

January First.' Difficult as this decision was, however, it wouldn't free him to create a new life with Peg, and he was clear about the consequences:

> At the same time it is apparently in the cards that I will have to tell you that after January First, you ought to feel absolutely free to look for another job, which you will not have to take so seriously – I will not return to my so called home and I cannot just chain you to me while I am refused a divorce. So I must dare to meet my fate and will try to meet it with the best grace I have, or can – I love you –

Circumstances finally prevailed over reasoned decisions and tortured argument. During a December breakfast heated words were exchanged as Gregory prepared to leave for work, and his overweight son, who may have been drinking Coca-Cola rather than eating his cornflakes, balked over having to go to school. One can imagine unfinished homework on the table, Nancy quiet, Ray inured and silent. Picking up the coke bottle to emphasise a point, Gregory was a menacing figure, raising his voice in frustration at Greg, who surely shouted back. Nothing was resolved by the time Greg and Nancy trudged out the door, by the time Gregory, briefcase in hand, left soon after. Calmer by the time he reached his desk, he rang the Dalton School and left a message asking Nancy to join him for an early dinner at Peking House. There, alone with his 11-year-old daughter, he gently told her over the egg rolls and fried rice that he had left home for good. Explaining with paternal kindness and responding patiently to the questions she posed, he finally sent her back to the apartment to tell her mother. Nancy was unhappy although she couldn't have been surprised, nor was Greg, but when she dutifully informed Ray that her husband wasn't coming back, her mother's response was 'Nonsense'. Ray's refusal to acknowledge much less accept what had happened would continue to be an obstacle to the new life Gregory still hoped for, but he had at last walked out of his marriage.[14]

Gregory's decision may have appeared in the end arbitrary and impulsive to his wife and children, but in November Peg had written George that she expected to be able to send him 'an important message' very soon. Necessarily discreet about a very irregular situation, Gregory probably told Sigerist early in the new year – when his friend proposed meeting in New York in January, he concluded his letter, 'My love to you and Peg' – but the delicate circumstances meant that even as Peg began to buy the dishes and linen necessary to transform the professional apartment into a household where they hoped they might soon live together, she waited over a month to confide in George; telling Lou would come later, while informing Louise would be difficult even after Peg was sure of her brothers' support. Gregory's decision to leave Ray would change Peg's relationship with her family, and Peg's family would inevitably have an impact on the new life Gregory was trying to build.

George was delighted his sister was 'no longer under the heart-breaking strain of living two lives' and unfazed by her unconventionality, but he shared her worry about their mother's reaction. Peg felt she could go on 'for a year or longer' while waiting for the divorce, yet in such a state of suspension they could not plan, could not make a home or start a family of their own. George's response was encouraging but indicated the rocky road ahead: He knew she longed for children and hoped their mother realised that 'Grisha' was 'something besides a Russian' despite their father's 'doctrine of intolerance of anyone born outside America'. Peg also worried about Greg and Nancy. George already felt admiration and affection for Gregory; having met both children several times, he was less concerned than his sister: 13-year-old Greg seemed to him a bully capable of cruelty and lacking in humour, a troubled and troublesome boy who would be troubled in any case, while Nancy appeared a little pompous but 'intellectual', 'fascinating', and 'serious', an able girl who would weather the storm.[15]

In early February, Peg finally told Lou that Gregory had left Ray, but while he, too, was completely supportive of his sister, he was also his mother's confidante, and by late February, Peg had told Louise, who was predictably 'terribly upset and confused'. Letters sailed back and forth across the ocean to and from Lou in London. Louise blamed Gregory for a relationship that seemed to her 'ridiculous'. Distressed by her mother's persistent incomprehension, at the end of March Peg even discussed the problem with the rector of the family's Bronxville church. Louise remained distraught and perplexed throughout the spring. She liked Gregory, she told Lou, just not in the 'proposed role' of her daughter's beau, and felt there was something so wrong about the situation she could not see it as right. When Peg and Gregory dined in Bronxville in mid-April, however, she reported that everything was 'very nice and natural': both Peg and 'Dr. Z' (whom she couldn't bring herself to call 'Gregory' or 'Grisha') were 'very lovely' to her, so she simply ended up feeling 'truly sorry for two very nice people'. In many ways as conventional as Margo, Louise could only console herself with the hope that, despite everything that made Gregory in her eyes unsuitable, he and Peg would eventually be able to marry.[16]

Gregory was understandably even more impatient than Louise to resolve matters. When he visited Peg's family, Margo insisted he sleep in a room off the kitchen, a sort of demeaning banishment; he wrote Peg from his office that he saw his nights in Bronxville as 'merely a means of being not far from you when you are not close to me here'. He was tired of 'pain', naturally longed to have 'some fun' after so much turmoil, to live with her in a place of their own. In sum, he wrote, 'I hate to be without you and must be with you'. Always an emotional and expressive Russian, when he realised he wouldn't have the privilege of working in her suburban Victory Garden, he felt 'forlorn, unhappy, mad, angry', and declared, 'I want you to be with me and take care of me. I want to have a little home with you – be it a single room somewhere – where we are alone – by and for ourselves.'

James would hear of the separation from Ray, who mentioned rather casually in a letter to Eugenia in March that Gregory had left and the children were unhappy. James didn't write Gregory nor did Eugenia feel up to responding to Ray, being too upset at the idea of a failed marriage and busy with Russian Relief. Instead James turned again to Pauline. Unable to take 'home-wrecking' in his stride or to imagine Gregory's love for another woman, he wondered what kind of 'modus vivendi' had been established. In his view his brother was 'an utter fool' and 'headed for a smash'. Excusing himself for writing to Pauline about family matters even while effusing, James was also concerned that Gregory continue to pay their mother's allowance.[17]

As Gregory and Peg navigated their changed circumstances, he dealt with his usual round of patients and the various professional responsibilities he had more or less willingly agreed to take on. The trips to Washington were tiring, but he enjoyed the teaching and his colleagues. In late January he and Moore were called as expert witnesses for the defence in the Washington trial of Earl McFarland, a marine accused of having raped and murdered a young woman during a night out. If McFarland did indeed commit the crimes, Moore opined he should not be held responsible as he was suffering from 'malarial psychosis'. Gregory's judgement was that the accused had a mental illness 'of a schizophrenic nature' as a result of combat experiences. The prosecution called its own defence witnesses to testify to McFarland's sanity, among them two psychiatrists from St. Elizabeth's Hospital and two naval doctors specialising in neuropsychiatry and tropical diseases. The lawyers pitted the psychiatrists against each other in exactly the sort of legal process Gregory abhorred, yet he also detested the prospect of execution and perhaps particularly for a soldier suffering from the sort of post-traumatic stress he had observed as early as his experiences at the Russian front. Gregory must have felt a moral as well as professional obligation to testify. In the event, McFarland was convicted and sentenced to death by electrocution.[18]

In mid-February Gregory left New York for lectures in Montreal, an altogether more positive experience. Indeed, Gregory's week in Quebec was a revelation, and he wrote Peg with overflowing enthusiasm that he had 'talked and talked and talked with and to Dominican priests, professors of philosophy, psychiatrists, general physicians, journalists' as well as 'railway porters and redcaps, the latter all young and numerous'. He had stood at the podium of a large modern hall crowded with young male and female lay students in medicine, psychology, and social sciences, professors of the Faculty of Medicine 'mixed with the many brown cloaks of Franciscan monks, white Dominicans, brown and black, black and white sisters' – all taking notes. Having tempered his lectures with characteristic wit, he told Peg that it did his heart particular good 'to see them all roar with laughter'. He was also impressed by several individuals, some of whom he already knew, others to whom he was now introduced for the first time. Père Deslauriers had invited him to lunch with other Dominicans at the Institute of Medieval Studies, where Gregory had been thrilled to meet an Irish Dominican, Robert Edward Brennen, author of *Thomistic Psychology: A Philosophic Analysis of the Nature of Man*. A professor from McGill University – likely the German-born psychiatrist Karl Stern – spoke with Gregory privately on the recommendation of Jacques Maritain, who had apparently read *Mind, Medicine, and Man*. At this time Gregory probably also met Marie-Alain Couturier, the French Dominican who spent the war years in Montreal and New York. A champion of both modern art and ecumenism, Couturier was the editor, with the Alsatian Dominican Pie-Raymond Régamey ('Père Pie'), of *L'Art Sacré*. Gregory was above all impressed with 'Père Mailloux', with whom he developed an immediate bond, describing him to Peg as 'a delightful person', 'a true radical and kindest soul', 'a great scholar and a great heart'. Those Gregory met were equally impressed. In his *History of Psychology*, published later in the year, Brennan would call him 'one of the clearest thinkers in the fields of psychiatric literature'.[19]

Gregory had mentioned his Canadian lectures to Sigerist, just back from in India. Addressing him light-heartedly as 'Father Gregory', Sigerist wondered what order he was thinking of joining, then recommended the Greek Orthodox Church since it stood 'for socialism' while he saw the Catholic Church as 'the bastion of monopoly capitalism'. Gregory couldn't help bristling: 'Your letter is as soft as Cashmere but its impact as strong as the tusk of a Maharaja's elephant.' Defensive of his Catholic affiliations, he quickly retreated to a moral high ground, displacing his irritation: He had been asked to write an article for the *American Review of Soviet Medicine* on Vladimir A. Negovsky's 1943 monograph 'Some Physiopathologic Regularities in the Process of Dying and Resuscitation'. Having been translated by five different people, the work involved 'Five styles, five modes of inaccuracies, five ways of misunderstanding the original', and had been dropped in his lap unsolicited: 'All this is disquieting and discomforting and to this waste of energy and time is added the wasteful sense of silently controlling one's irritation and warding off an uncalled-for pressure.' He suspected the review's well-intentioned staff didn't have the time 'to read a book or think over a general problem', and confessed, 'even without claiming any indulgence because of some very severe weeks in my personal life … when I have no time to study or to think, I feel wilted and unable to do any work at all.'

He was once again feeling beleaguered and would in the end write nothing about the monograph, which he tellingly denominated 'Agony and Death'. He hadn't even delivered his report on suicide at the specified time, nor at the later date to which the delivery date was postponed, and still hadn't written a word. Completing the report, he pointed out defensively, was 'not a purely personal ambition': Over $100,000 had been entrusted to him and spent on research; he felt financially responsible to those who had put up the money as well as morally and scientifically to himself. He informed Sigerist, 'I just can't carry more of a load than I do. If this proves disappointing to my friends, I am sorry but I can't help it.' Gregory's petulance and exasperation suggest not only the weight of professional obligations but his growing attachment to Catholicism as well the persistent difficulties in his personal life.[20]

While Ray remained intransigent and Louise continued to be distressed, the spring was not without positive moments. After a goodwill mission to Russia and a month in London, Lillian Hellman was now back in analysis and giving enthusiastic interviews about her kind reception by the Soviet people. Gregory and Peg were entertained by her vivid impressions. Between trips to Washington, Gregory travelled to Chicago in March to address the Illinois Society for Mental Hygiene on 'The Psycho-Social Paradoxes of Returning from the War', where he reflected on his experiences in November 1918 in a particularly personal and charming after-dinner speech peppered with references to his wide reading. He seemed generally amusing rather than melancholy, as well as typically perceptive and learned. He mentioned among other figures Lincoln, Churchill, Lloyd George, Emerson, Thoreau, de Tocqueville, Clarence Darrow, Carlyle, William Ellery Channing, Harriet Beecher Stowe, William Lloyd Garrison, Margaret Mitchell, Dorothea Dix, Clara Barton, Margaret Fuller, and Nathaniel Hawthorne, his allusions for the most part remarkably American. Reflecting on his recent lectures in Montreal, he concluded, 'Ours is a civilization that spurns tradition and insists on pragmatic, mechanical routine, whereas the remedy in our civilization lies in restoring the continuity of the tradition, of humanism, and abolishing pragmatic, materialistic routine.' His point of view was consonant with his earliest social convictions and his psychoanalytic principles, but by placing his remarks in the context of his lectures in Quebec, it is clear that the Catholic humanist tradition was becoming an integral part of his frame of reference.[21]

President Roosevelt died shortly before the British liberated Bergen-Belsen in mid-April, while in Italy at the end of the month Mussolini's body was hung up for display in Milan's Piazzale Loreto. By the time reports of the concentration camps appeared in the New York papers, Harry S. Truman was installed in the president's White House office with a plaque on his desk that read, with homespun confidence, 'The buck stops here.' While the carnage in the Pacific would carry on into the summer, the Japanese began to withdraw from China, and on 7 May 1945 General Eisenhower accepted the Germans' unconditional surrender at Rheims in eastern France. New Yorkers celebrated with a ticker-tape parade. The war's aftermath had begun and American's spirits soared.

The end of the war in Europe did not, however, solve Gregory's immediate problems, although it did provide a kind of watershed, and he finally put the farm on the market. When Henry Sigerist passed through New York on a Saturday in late May, Gregory was unable to see him because it was Nancy's 12th birthday. Given the 'situation', he explained, he was particularly eager to spend the day with her – it had been 'literally months', since he had seen her or Greg for any length of time. With Henry, Gregory and Peg were now a couple: Peg joined him, he concluded, in sending Henry their love and hadn't given up hope of his coming to help them cook and consume a dinner in the office. As spring gave way to summer, the children went off to camp and Gregory arranged to sell the livestock – the pigs and chickens, the two bulls and the cows, including his beloved Sunshine. Even the country dogs would remain country dogs and were rehomed with a local farmer. As vestiges of the animals no longer part of his demesne, the city dogs were hugely important to him. KoKo divided his time between Bronxville and the office, where Shadow was a regular presence, and in an impulse towards the family they hoped one day to have, Gregory and Peg together acquired a gentle Kerry Blue they called Nora Shoebutton because of her bright dark eyes.[22]

The farm sold quickly. Tools and furniture were disposed of separately while much of the photographic equipment was stored. Gregory left most of the packing to Ray, who reported to James that now that her husband was no longer at home, she could be 'human' and do as she liked. Her letter was understandably bitter but also superficial, disjointed, and confused. She insisted the children seemed 'very happy', then that the situation was affecting them 'terribly'. She had not told them about the farm, as they were 'broken-hearted' whenever the subject came up and she didn't want to spoil their summer. Informing James that he and his family were the only relatives she had, Ray indicated she might move to a smaller apartment in September:

> Gregory, as you might expect, is getting uglier and really vicious. He threatens all sorts of things if I do not get a divorce, and the way I feel the faster I get rid of him the better, but I will not be bullied and threatened any more.

Despite her stated desire to rid herself of her husband, Ray's simultaneous refusal to be 'bullied and threatened' meant digging in her heels and refusing to budge in an effort to preserve some self-respect and autonomy. She and Gregory would continue to be at loggerheads.[23]

Gregory meanwhile went to see his Dominican friends in Montreal in July, a visit that certainly included spiritual reflection as well as intellectual discussion, and he managed a few days with Peg at the Hatchers' in Pennsylvania. Between the bombing of Hiroshima and Nagasaki in early August, Gregory handed the farm over to its new owner, then took a train to Chicago, where he saw his Catholic friend and colleague Leo Bartemeier. Anxiously awaiting the Japanese capitulation that would end the war, Gregory spent a week in self-imposed retreat, albeit in the elegant Ambassador East Hotel and including at least one afternoon of window shopping. He wrote Peg of 'long hours of contemplation' in his room and in church; he skipped a supper he didn't feel inclined to eat and took joy in Bartemeier's faith and hearty optimism. Much of Gregory's reflection concerned his relationship with Peg and their future; he and Bartemeier talked about intellectual matters but mostly about the hoped-for marriage. Still in the humid Midwest when Japan finally surrendered on 15 August, Gregory joined Peg four days later in Nantucket, where she and Nora were waiting for him when the ferry from Woods Hole docked in Sconset. During a halcyon fortnight Peg swam and sailed and basked in the sun; Gregory looked on and read and wrote with Nora at his side. Perhaps there was even time for a set of tennis. In the evenings they had cocktails with acquaintances, dined on bluefish and lobster at seaside restaurants, went to bed early, made love, slept well.[24]

Back in New York Gregory probably saw Eugenia, who stayed briefly with Ray en route to deliver Lydia to Oakwood, but with Ray sorting out the 'much too much' in preparation for the move to a smaller place, it had been decided that young Greg, too, might be better off at boarding school. Before he began at Friends Academy in Locust Valley, Long Island, Peg took him to Rogers Peet and, astonished by his awkwardness, realised he had probably never actually tried on clothes in a shop before much less been fitted for a suit. It would be Peg, too, who sewed in Greg's nametags in preparation for his fresh academic start, while to celebrate the beginning of the school year, Gregory took Peg and both children to dinner at Copacabana, a nightclub whose Brazilian décor and Latin orchestra made for a festive evening.[25]

That September Gregory began his second year at Catholic University and pursued the matter of divorce with renewed energy. Not yet demobilised, Lou wrote from England with hard advice: Gregory should get a 'very tough' lawyer, someone who would 'tell him just what cards he has in this poker game and how many of them he can play'. In Lou's opinion, they could not afford to wait until, as Peg had written, Ray 'cooled down'. Lou further recommended that Gregory transfer to 'some good friend every cent' he had as well as all his insurance, pointing out bluntly that if a woman 'needs dough and wants dough and is willing to bargain and cavil over dough', her position is weak; they should attack 'that poor position' so instead of being 'Lady Bountiful' about whether she would give Gregory a separation, Ray would actually be fighting to see she got what he considered a fair settlement before it was too late. In the end, Lou was convinced, it would all come down to money.[26]

The situation that Peg called 'a gray mess' and Lou termed 'this present cruel impasse' was becoming progressively more difficult for Louise. Her letters to her eldest son now solely concerned Peg and Gregory: She had 'tried so very hard to play their game', but just couldn't do it anymore and saw less of them because of her distress. She confessed, 'Peg is always dear and lovely to me, and more than understanding of all my questions spoken and unspoken.' Indeed, she told Lou, 'I believe Peg and I understand each other better than anyone can understand we do. We respect and love each other deeply, and I am sure she sees why I can't accept this situation as it is.' Before Thanksgiving things had become so difficult that Peg decided Louise and Gregory shouldn't even talk until there was definite progress with the divorce. Helpless to offer more than understanding and sympathy in his letters to his sister from across the Atlantic, Lou was as affirmative as he knew how to be. Peg had shown 'tenderness and patience and faith with all of us', he told her; 'You have found a very exceptional man and you and he together have found a very exceptional love. The man and the love are worth clinging to.' He then added with characteristically jaunty masculine jocularity, 'Gregory Zilboorg is a very lucky guy.'[27]

Gregory and Peg did feel lucky despite their difficulties. In early February they escaped to Baltimore at Sigerist's invitation, a reprise of the many halcyon weekends they had shared with him and Genevieve. Henry wrote that Ilza Veith, one of his graduate students, whose husband was trying Goering and Ribbentrop in Nuremburg, had 'an excellent kitchen', where he sometimes cooked. Genevieve collected Gregory and Peg at the train station and drove them to the apartment on

the outskirts where the two couples enjoyed 'a first-rate dinner', including a bottle
of 'liberated Rhine wine' from Germany.

Henry Sigerist's menu for the dinner he and Gregory prepared together

Amid the wide-ranging conversation there must have been much sampling of
sauces and hearty laughter, glasses filled and refilled, the two men glad of each
other's company, the young women happy in their adoring and intimate roles. It
would, however, take over a month for Gregory to thank Henry for his kindness.
Consulting his files in late March, Gregory discovered he hadn't written except in
his mind – 'the usual fate', he admitted, 'when too much fantasy takes the place
of reality'. The real trouble was that, outside his immediate work with patients,

Gregory's time was crowded with what he simply referred to as 'a number of difficult and painful problems'. He amplified only by alluding to his stressful struggle to settle matters with Ray: 'Lawyers in human relations are not pleasant people to deal with. It is hard to do a thing without them – it is disgusting at times to do certain things with them.'[28]

The post-war euphoria was wearing off and the spring didn't begin well. In March, well aware his son was having a hard time, Gregory addressed the Parent-Teachers Association of Friends Academy on 'Social Pressures in Growing Up'. Greg was unhappy, his reports were abysmal, and he again had no friends, complained all the teachers were against him. Peg felt another change might be the answer – not a Quaker academy but Kent, the Episcopal school in Connecticut both her brothers had attended. Lou would pull out the stops to get Greg with his failing marks a place for September. Meanwhile, at the end of the month, the Theatre Guild revived *He Who Gets Slapped*. Opening at the Garrick Theatre before moving to Broadway, the play ran through April, but the production – with the number of acts reduced from four to two and 'He' renamed as 'Funny' – was a bowdlerised version that reduced the work's symbolism and even its Russianness in an apparent effort to make it more accessible. The programme didn't mention Gregory as translator and it seems unlikely any royalties were paid – not so much a financial slap in the face as a blow to his ego, a marginalising of his role in championing Russian literature and Andreyev in America.

There were lighter and more affirmative moments. Nora 'graduated' from obedience training and received congratulatory letters and telegrams from her 'Grandmother Louise' and her 'Uncle George'. At a late March dinner out with Peg and young Greg, Gregory basked in the affection between his growing son and the woman already standing in as a second mother. Leo Bartemeier passed on a copy of Al Capp's popular 'Li'l Abner', in which one of the comic strip characters declared there would soon be an official government psychiatrist by the name of 'Gregory Spellbound', an allusion to the man who by 1946 was a household name. Bartemeier joked, 'What are you and Al Capp cooking up together?'[29]

Despite his personal problems, Gregory's life remained typically hectic and diverse. He had given his talk in Locust Valley just after returning from Saint Louis, where he had addressed a more august group than parents and teachers on the topic of 'The Psychiatry of a Technological Civilization' at the annual meeting of the American Association for the Advancement of Science. Pointing out that social functioning is reflected in and affected by technological progress, he posed what he considered two fundamental questions: If a machine is a material expression of human adaptation, how does a person adapt to the adaptation? And does the person as a result become psychologically and socially more or less efficient? Machines may give us more leisure and a great sense of ease, but a rapidly advancing technological civilisation creates 'disindividualized anonymity' and an illusory sense of mastery over life and death. Gregory concluded that technology may save people time and energy while generating and preserving

material wealth, but it gives people a 'megalomaniac sense of power' and gener-
ates aggression, hatred, and destruction – in short, it fails to save human beings
themselves.[30]

Indeed, whatever the pressures of his personal life, Gregory was invariably
concerned with values in the larger scheme of things. At the end of April he
attended a dinner in New York to celebrate the first year of the Independent Citi-
zens' Committee of the Arts, Sciences and Professions. Andrei Gromyko, then the
Soviet delegate to the United Nations Security Council, spoke at the event, and
Gregory's fellow diners included friends and acquaintances as well as former and
current patients, among them the playwright Marc Connelly, Moss Hart, Herman
Shumlin, Dash Hammett, and Lillian Hellman. The organisation promoted democracy, world peace, full employment, and a 'decent standard of living for all' –
the latter goal evidence of the group's covert Communist sponsorship and the
Communist sympathies of many of its members, although it was also an element
of Roosevelt's New Deal and Gregory's lifelong socialism.

Throughout the spring, however, Gregory's mood was particularly volatile
and mixed. In May Sigerist thanked him for his heartfelt promotional letter in
support of *The University of the Crossroads*, a forthcoming collection of lectures and essays. Gregory had written that the book 'gives a lesson in how to
become a learned man without becoming a bookworm, in how to be a scholar
without losing the sense of actuality, or of civic responsibility, or of social struggle'. Henry told him how much he valued his judgement and affirming warmth.
Clearly emotional about personal matters as well as America's xenophobic reactions to the post-war world, Gregory was moved. Hinting only obliquely at his
raw state, displacing the personal onto the political, he responded in general
terms. He fully agreed with Henry about 'the sorry picture our civilization presents': 'This is rather a difficult time – very – and one feels the need of contact
with friends, and yet there is so little time and there are so many urgent things
to do.' Writing from Chicago, where he was attending the annual meeting of
the American Psychiatric Association, Gregory then reflected on the future of
medicine. A champion of health reform, Sigerist was a passionate advocate for
national health insurance. Despite his having become an American citizen in
1943, his leftist politics and interest in socialised medicine in the Soviet Union
had finally made him *persona non grata* in the United States, where the Civil
Service Commission had classed him in 1944 as ineligible for government work
because of his perceived 'Communist' sympathies. Gregory now observed that
'Everybody is full of so-called post-war problems, no one understands them,
and what is really sad is that so many keep on fighting "socialized medicine"
without even the faintest understanding of the issues involved.' He concluded
his emotional letter somewhat wistfully, telling Henry he was 'always the most
welcome friend.'[31]

Gregory's personal difficulties and his teaching obligations at Catholic University had from the summer of 1944 meant fewer lectures, after-dinner speeches,

and public addresses; fewer talks had meant less writing, and with the publication of *Mind, Medicine, and Man* in the spring of 1943, he had finished what he had to say about the general history of medical psychology. 'Legal Aspects of Psychiatry' in *One Hundred Years of American Psychiatry* and 'Masculine and Feminine' had occupied his attention in early 1944, and he would continue to think about both topics particularly in the context of the history, treatment, and punishment of criminality, but sideswiped by his struggle to escape his marriage, for the rest of the decade what literary energy he had went primarily into relatively short essays and book reviews; emotionally and spiritually torn, he would be unable to concentrate on another book until the 1950s.

Towards the end of the academic year, Gregory and Peg took Nancy, perhaps in celebration of her May birthday, to collect Greg from the school to which he wouldn't return. Aware of his father's disappointment, Greg must have felt inadequate as well as relieved, both hostile and grateful for the reprieve. Now 13 and 14, the children were awkward teenagers, and neither of them seemed particularly happy as their parents set up separate households. They had another summer of camp ahead of them, but no farm to look forward to, and while Greg's dog, a recently acquired male boxer, was waiting for him in the city, he would have little time to spend with him in the weeks ahead.

Feeling personally constrained and confined to a limited present, in 1945 and 1946 Gregory repeatedly wrote Peg about what he termed 'faith'. Reflecting on their keen 'pain and sorrow and thoughts and strivings', Gregory surmised that 'scores and hundreds and many more people' must be feeling similarly. Some of them would fail, lose each other, and be heartbroken, while others would make their way together 'into life, hope and goodness'. To find their way, people had to have 'faith in one another, faith in living', and they had to live by that faith and not by 'the calendar' since 'If their

Greg and Nancy, late spring 1946

faith – and love – is solid – no calendar will ever prevent them from achiev-
ing their goal.' With his faith in living and in Peg, he offered her 'everything';
without such faith, he reminded her, 'any offering would prove specious'. The
way into 'life, hope and goodness' involved a faith with a spiritual dimension;
it required belief and trust not only in one another but in abstractions (like love,
hope, and goodness) in contrast to ordinary and materialistic life lived by 'the
calendar', by immediate and worldly counting.

A mundane counting of time, however, as well as disgusting dealings with
lawyers would necessarily come into Gregory's finding of his way as finally,
in the last week of June, things began to move ahead quickly. The climactic
turning point Gregory mentioned to Sigerist was vague, but it involved a good
deal of money, as Lou had warned it would. The family story is that Peg woke
up beside Gregory in the middle of the night and told him to ring Ray despite
the hour; her idea was that he propose an amount and just keep raising it until
Ray accepted then and there on the telephone in the wee hours of the morning.
Gregory told Henry that Ray had 'suddenly' become 'amicable' and 'reasonable', but it seems likely a lawyer negotiated the terms that at last persuaded
her to go to Reno for the six weeks of residence the state of Nevada required
for a divorce.[32]

In an effort to avoid unwelcome publicity as Ray prepared for her trip and –
likely on his lawyer's advice – to avoid any accusation of coercion, Gregory went
to a rustic cabin in the Laurentian Woods north of Montreal for a fortnight. Probably also at the lawyer's urging Peg, too, left the city – for ten days with Eddie
and Mary Warburg at Marshall Field's Long Island estate. With matters nearly
settled, the separation was particularly difficult. Alone in the Canadian mountains, Gregory listened to birdsong and – constricted by the calendar life he had
denigrated – he counted the days. On 5 July his lawyer informed him in typically
'lawyerish' fashion that 'the ticket for flight 15 last night was used, apparently for
the person for whom it was bought.' On what seemed to Gregory an 'abnormal'
and 'unnecessary' trip, he felt 'hollow', but devoted at least some of his solitude to
thinking practically about the home he and Peg would soon set up. No longer able
to underwrite both an office and a separate residence, he would combine the two
in a large apartment they had found at 885 Park Avenue. Studying the floorplan,
he now proposed rearranging the library as a waiting room, which would simultaneously accommodate a secretary and serve as an occasional space for a guest,
while one of the four bedrooms would become his treatment room. Architecture,
space, designing something aesthetic and functional – these captured his imagination and consoled him. He looked at Peg 'through the distance and imagination'
and thought about her with 'gratitude': 'Let us live', he wrote her, 'let the cares
of life, the cares about the big as well as the small things, be concerns born out of
love and not burdens and frustrations of two hounded people'. They had been, he
declared dramatically, not only hounded but 'torn apart and asunder many times',
yet their 'faith' in one another had survived. He felt anxious – not about their
material welfare; he had no anxiety about her goodness, their love, or the prospect

of their having children together, but only about living up to what Peg expected and he felt she deserved.[33]

Among the things that Peg had been brought up to expect was a church wedding. Unwilling to marry a divorced man, the rector of Bronxville's Episcopal church refused outright, but ever resourceful, Peg found a Presbyterian pastor who, while he balked at performing the service in his church, was willing to preside at Field's home. Nothing could be definitely arranged, however, until confirmation from Reno, and Peg and Gregory waited on tenterhooks for the news that would, via Ray's lawyer to Gregory's, be communicated privately with 'lawyerish' discretion. The official 'complaint', however, was a public document routinely consulted by reporters eager to spill the dirt about all and sundry. Neither the syndicated journalist Travis Hoke nor the local *Reno Gazette-Journal* hesitated to publish details of the decree finally granted on 14 August 1946: The parents would retain joint custody of the children, while Ray, who had cited the standard 'mental cruelty' as grounds for the divorce, would continue as the beneficiary of Gregory's $75,000 life insurance policy, on which he was obliged to continue to pay the premium. She would in addition receive $11,500 in cash and 50 percent of her husband's net income yearly, the hefty price Gregory had agreed to pay for the new life he and Peg imagined together.

If the lawyers were discrete and Gregory and Peg meticulous in following their instructions to avoid publicity, Ray didn't share their desire for decorum. Neither so amicable nor reasonable as Gregory had claimed to Sigerist, Ray was understandably angry and resentful. Unsympathetic to what she viewed as Gregory's impulsiveness and unable to understand either his work or the feelings underlying what he called 'faith', she was apparently more than willing to discuss their personal lives on the steps of the Reno courthouse where new divorcees were routinely waylaid. However sensationalised, her comments were her chance to disparage her former husband and his new partner and to try to save face. She was quoted as saying, ' "It was a long, happy marriage, but we were simply incompatible in later years. I have no condemnation for him ... People change as the years go by – their hair, their minds. Gregory has changed, that's all." ' Becoming flippant, arch, and boastful, she then added,

> Why not, after all? I'm no glamour girl, though I had hoped to be one before I met Gregory. Instead, in the language of psychoanalysis, I 'sublimated' the urge toward beauty. I studied at the Art Students' League and the National Academy, to learn to create beauty rather than possess it.

Pressed about the possibility that Gregory might marry again, Ray retorted,

> Why shouldn't he? He has the right to, and he's reached the age where other women than wives frequently seem irresistibly attractive. It wouldn't surprise me if he married Margaret Stone, who has been his laboratory assistant for the last six years.

Ray probably didn't explain Peg as Gregory's 'laboratory assistant' – perhaps she said 'research assistant' and the journalist extrapolated – but the rest of her statements sound authentic and she remained dismissive: Gregory's work was ' "the most complicated kind of science, and like any other scientist he is apt to make sudden and inexplicable decisions regarding himself as well as others." ' Defensively romanticising their marriage and attributing Gregory's relationship with Peg to a mid-life crisis, Ray apparently considered him foolish as well as capricious.[34]

K. Avery's sensational illustration, with Peg portrayed as a 'glamour girl', which accompanied the spicy syndicated article by the popular journalist Travis Hoke

By the middle of August, however, Gregory was beyond resenting Ray, beyond being angry with her even for the unwelcome gossip and embarrassment her comments provoked. He simply had too much to look forward to. Immediately after receiving news of the divorce he told Peg with typical humour and joy, 'Look here, dear – if we don't get married pretty soon, I'll bust – and stay busted –'.

On 19 August 1946 Gregory and Peg were married at Caumsett. Eddie Warburg stood up as Gregory's best man and his wife Mary was Peg's matron of honour. The bride did not wear white but a simply tailored beige suit Gregory had ordered as a surprise for the occasion. Marshall and Ruthie Field attended the event, and although Lou and George had yet to be demobilised, Louise and Margo drove down from Bronxville to represent Peg's loving family. After the formalities, champagne would have been served on the estate's elegant terrace where the happy group toasted the happy couple as the sun shone on the magnificent garden whose manicured lawns swept down to the sea. Gregory's heart was filled with unmitigated joy and overwhelming confidence in the future that lay ahead.

Notes

1 GZ to HES, 31 January, 23 March 1944; HES to GZ, 17 January 1944; Hope Trebing for HES to GZ, 8 February 1944.
2 Notes, GZ and MSZ; Gregory Zilboorg Jr to GZ, nd.
3 NM to Donald Pleshette, 23 August 1976, APD.
4 GZ to HES, 19 April 1944; GZ, 'Some Aspects', 'Affects', 'Psychiatric Problems'.
5 GZ to HES, 19, 26 April 1944; HES to MSZ, 5 June 1944.
6 GZ, 'A Play', 3, 6, 11, 22, 25, 31, GZB.
7 Pauline Turkel to JZ, 19 May 1944, JEZB; GZ to JZ, 22 May 1944.
8 HES to GZ, 21 June 1944; GZ to HES, 29 June 1944.
9 MSZ to GZ, July 1944.
10 GZ cited Horney's 'On the Genesis of the Castration Complex', 'The Denial of the Vagina', and 'The Flight from Womanhood', and Helene Deutsch's 'Homosexuality in Women'.
11 GZ, 'Masculine and Feminine', passim.
12 Neenan, 199; GZ to 'Très Saint-Père', 31 January 1953, APD.
13 JZ to GZ, 21 October, 4 December 1944; in the latter, JZ quoted GZ to JZ, 16 November 1944, a letter that hasn't apparently survived.
14 Email from AZ, 31 October 2013.
15 HES to GZ, 11 January 1945; George Stone to MSZ, c. 20 January 1945.
16 Lou Stone to MSZ, 24 April 1945.
17 JZ to Pauline Turkel, 6 March 1945, JEZB.
18 Adele Bernstein, 'Experts Disagree on Sanity: McFarland Denies Any Part in Murder as Case Nears Jury', *Washington Post*, 1 February 1945, np.
19 GZ to MSZ, February 1945; email from Daniel Burston, 12 May 2019; Brennan, *History*, 190.
20 HES to GZ, 13 February 1945; GZ to HES, 15 February 1945.
21 GZ to HES, 1 March 1945; GZ, 'The Psycho-Social Paradoxes', 4, 6.
22 GZ to HES, 15, 23 May 1945.
23 Ray Zilboorg to JZ, 11 July 1945, JEZB.
24 GZ to MSZ, 13 August 1945.

25 Ray Zilboorg to EZ, 16 August 1945, JEZB; MSZ, Dar interview.
26 Lou Stone to MSZ, 20 August 1945.
27 Lou Stone to MSZ, 28 December 1945.
28 HES to GZ, 7, 14 January 1946; GZ to HES, 19 March 1946.
29 'Li'l Abner', note from Leo Bartemeier to GZ.
30 GZ, 'The Psychiatry', 202, 203, 205.
31 GZ, blurb for Sigerist, *The University*; GZ to Henry Schuman, nd; HES to GZ, 14 May 1946; GZ to HES, 20 May 1946; Fee, 1643.
32 GZ to HES, 15 July 1946.
33 GZ to Louise Stone, 3 July 1946, and to MSZ, 5 July 1946.
34 Hoke, 8; 'Granted Divorce from Psychiatrist', *Reno Gazette-Journal*, 15 August 1946, 22.

Chapter 5

Health and happiness
1946–1950

Given the private nature of the wedding, there would be no formal wedding pictures and no immediate honeymoon. Instead, Gregory and Peg moved into a suite at New York's St. Regis Hotel. Gregory continued to see patients at his office on 75th Street, but there was a great deal to pack up in anticipation of the move to the new apartment. The honeymoon wouldn't occur until November, giving Gregory over two months to plan a working holiday in South America to celebrate his new life with Peg and compensate for the loss of his faculty appointment at Catholic University. A divorced psychoanalyst was simply a step too far for the university administration.[1]

In the wake of his divorce and marriage, Gregory's world changed in ways both slight and significant. Most immediately, Louise was at last able to welcome him into the family. Peg's brothers, finally demobilised, could openly affirm their sister's status as Gregory's partner: Lou resumed his job in his New York law firm in September while George began to cast about for his true calling, knowing at least that it would involve nothing explicitly medical. Both men would be frequent visitors in the couple's new home.[2]

Gregory and Peg soon after their wedding on 19 August 1946

DOI: 10.4324/9781003190974-5

Greg and Nancy would also visit. While Greg was technically living with Gregory and Peg, Nancy in the end felt she couldn't leave her bereft mother and was in principle living with Ray. It was decided, however, that the best thing for a girl torn between two parents was boarding school. As Greg headed off to Kent in September, Nancy began at Westtown, a Quaker school near Philadelphia. Fera did not visit. She and Gregory continued to speak regularly on the telephone, so she was probably not surprised by her brother's divorce, but she couldn't approve of his having left Ray nor of his marrying Peg. Fera would keep in polite contact with Ray and remain a link with the family in Mexico, but Fera's social circle and Gregory's were by now far apart. She would inevitably be cool towards her brother's second wife, a woman with whom she had little in common. Gregory's marriage must have struck her as absurd.

James for his part didn't even acknowledge the change in his brother's circumstances, although Fera surely informed him. When he wrote to Gregory in September for the first time in nearly two years, he began by mentioning that the doctor who had treated Moses would be in New York at the end of the month. Boasting that in Mexico he had 'the highest reputation in psychiatry', James felt Gregory should arrange to meet him. As if incidentally, James then went on to the likely reason for his letter: Anna was 'not at all well'; she had had, he explained with his peculiar medical ignorance, 'some kind of stroke which the doctor thought was a cerebral haemorrhage'. He concluded melodramatically, 'Whether this is the end or how near it might be, no one knows. A couple of times last night she asked for you.' Gregory probably responded by speaking with Fera and then telephoning James. Correspondence between the two brothers slowly resumed, but Gregory would maintain a strategic reserve.[3]

Feeling the ground shift under him, aware of how much had changed and predominantly for the better, Gregory realised certain acquaintances and professional associates no longer felt quite or at all the same about him. Having married a Christian half his age, he seemed as alien to them as he did to Fera, someone no longer to be taken seriously. Eddie and Mary Warburg had become not only dear but enabling friends; always admiring, Abe would be supportive of anything Gregory did, but Gregory waited for others to take the initiative in acknowledging the marriage or simply reaffirming their connection to him as a family member, friend, or colleague. Gregory reflected on the problem in a letter to Leon Kroll: He had been 'sort of set adrift for a while without a home', and having found himself 'not entirely acceptable to some people, either because of their loyalties or because of their prejudices', he had taken the only course he felt possible: to wait passively until those who wanted to see him 'made themselves heard'. Despite Gregory's domineering bluster and sudden outbursts of anger, he was capable of discretion, circumspection, and wisdom, although his sharp intellect and rational good sense could be undermined by his emotional sensitivity. Not having heard from Sigerist, who had spent the summer in Europe, Gregory worried. As he and Peg prepared for their trip, he wrote to tell him how sad they were, how much they loved and missed him; they felt a 'keen and painful' sense of loss as a result of what Gregory feared was an 'estrangement'. Before he could post his letter, however, he received a missive with Sigerist's warm congratulations. Gregory sent his revealing 'melancholy letter' anyway, accompanied by an additional note in which he expressed his joy that he and Peg did 'have our good friend, Henry, after all'.[4]

Europe as well as South America was on Gregory's mind. Having been expelled from the German Society for the History of Medicine in 1937 for his anti-Nazi views, he had no intention of ever rejoining and now felt unable to answer the many letters he had received from German colleagues. Convinced those who were anti-fascist had either moved abroad or been 'liquidated', Gregory was relieved to put aside the challenge of dealing with post-war Europe as he packed his bags for the trip to South America.[5]

The honeymoon for the man of many talents was, of course, more than a honeymoon, and when he and Peg left New York by plane on 2 November 1946, Mary Warburg accompanied them. Her work during the war for the Office of Inter-American Affairs meant that she was familiar with Latin American cultural matters, while her support as well as Eddie's during the difficult weeks before the divorce had created a special relationship between Peg and both Warburgs. Mary would enjoy the festive events inevitably part of such a trip, and while Gregory was preparing presentations and speaking with professional colleagues at lunches and dinners in his honour, the two women would keep each other company and confirm an important friendship.

Gregory's schedule in Brazil was hectic and various. In early November Gregory delivered five lectures at the Brazilian Institute for the History of Medicine under the general title of 'The Individual and the Social in Psychological Medicine', 'The Apparent Conflict between Medicine and Psychiatry', 'The Ethical and Religious Conflicts in Relation to Medicine and Psychiatry', 'The Humanists and the Issues of Mental Illness', 'The Discovery of Man and the Impact of Science', and 'The Newer Humanism and Medicine'. Never one to dodge issues, Gregory tackled head on topics popular after the war and significant to him personally.

After less than a fortnight in Rio, the threesome flew to Buenos Aires. Gregory delivered his lectures in English in Brazil; in Argentina he spoke in French during a week as social as it was professional. He lunched with the director of the Association for Argentine Psychoanalysis, went to a cocktail party sponsored by the association, enjoyed lunch at a yacht club followed by a boat tour of the Paraná Delta, and attended a meeting of the city's Psychoanalytic Institute and a dinner in his honour. He addressed conferences at the Medical Association of Argentina, L'Institut Français d'Études Supérieures, the Academy of Medicine, and the prestigious Jockey Club. The social engagements didn't stop when the group flew on to Puerto Rico, where the island's governor Jesús T. Piñero treated them to a private concert at the sixteenth-century Forteleza. Gregory and Peg arrived home – with a signed photograph of the governor inscribed to 'Dr. and Peg Zilboorg with kindest personal regards' – at the end of the month in time to celebrate Thanksgiving in Bronxville, a family affair in which Gregory was warmly included even by Margo.

The return to New York meant resuming the daily round with emotionally demanding patients and settling down with Peg in their new home. The chilly December weather was a sharp contrast to the balmy warmth of the Southern hemisphere, and Gregory developed a debilitating cold. In an effort at continuity he kept the same office phone number and even hired the elderly Swedish cook (Olivia) and maid (Hilda Javert) employed by the apartment's former occupant, but he was conscious of having disrupted the flow of his life. He had missed the opening night of Hellman's *Another Part of the Forest*, the prequel to *The Little Foxes* she directed herself and dedicated to him. The Christmas holiday at 885 Park Avenue must, however, have been particularly precious, the first Christmas of their married life, and there were happy moments spent with Greg and Nancy as well as another festive family dinner in Bronxville.[6]

The new year was replete with speaking engagements. Gregory addressed the St. Elizabeth's Hospital Medical Society in Washington in late January; in early February he in directed three days of seminars at the Topeka Institute of Psychoanalysis in Kansas – occasions that allowed him to see friendly colleagues like Win Overholser and Karl Menninger. In March Gregory spoke at the New York Academy of Medicine's centennial celebration, citing the same anecdote he had trotted out in earlier lectures to illustrate the problem of knowledge and terminology, the 'so much' psychiatrists knew (or thought they knew) that simply wasn't so. Gregory recounted the story of a psychiatrist who defined 'the well-adjusted person' as someone 'in harmony with himself who is not in conflict with his environment'. When asked if he would consider an anti-Nazi working in the underground against Hitler a maladjusted person, the psychiatrist withdrew the latter part of his definition. With sagacious wit, Gregory then withdrew for his audience the first part of the definition, pointing out that many people 'in perfect harmony' with themselves are in fact in 'distinctly pathological states'.[7]

Gregory was keenly aware of disharmonies in post-war American society. Socialist views more or less tolerated in the 1930s were again suspect; virulent anti-communist, anti-Semitic, and Eurosceptic attitudes – put aside when Russia was an American ally and Europe under Nazi siege – resurfaced as the Cold War mentality set in. Because of their shared interest in the Soviet Union's socialist experiments, Gregory had introduced Sigerist to Lillian Hellman, and Lillian – like the Warburgs and the Hatchers – had been particularly kind to Gregory during his divorce. By the spring of 1947 he and Peg had begun looking for the 'simpler' place he had imagined when considering the sale of his farm and often escaped the city for weekends at their friends' country houses, but now Sigerist, too, was in need of escape. Under increasing pressure because of his sympathetic attitude towards Soviet medicine and socialist health care, he had become uncomfortable in America. Giving as an excuse his sincere desire to write more and lecture less, he had taken the difficult decision to give up his post as head of the Johns Hopkins Institute for the History of Medicine. He planned to leave for Switzerland in June.

There would be a farewell dinner, which Gregory with a score of others were organising, but in March Gregory invited his old friend to Lillian's country home in Pleasantville for one of their special home-cooked meals. Arriving with his daughter Nora, Henry donned his tall white chef's hat and took charge of the kitchen with Gregory as his 'kitchen maid', preparing a festive Russian menu of borscht with beef, tomatoes, and beets accompanied by a bowl of sour cream, and sweet blini. Lillian and Dash, Gregory and Peg, Henry and Nora ate and drank, talked and laughed, participating in the good time Gregory and Sigerist always had when they managed to get together.[8]

The formal gala, attended by over 100 guests from throughout the United States and Canada, occurred at the Plaza Hotel on 9 May 1947. The programme with a photograph of Sigerist featured two richly allusive and ironic quotations. The first, entitled 'On Haller's Return to Switzerland', from Sigerist's *The Great Doctors*, attributed the physiologist Albrecht von Haller's decision to leave his university position in Göttingen to overwork, anxiety, and 'colossal' mental strain as well as to the homesickness 'which sooner or later attacks every native of Switzerland who has settled in foreign parts'. The second, without a title, was taken from Sigerist's recent article 'Nationalism and Internationalism in Medicine'. Arguing that civilisation had not kept pace with scientific and technological developments, Sigerist contended that people now were 'in many ways much more savage, brutal and intolerant' than their ancestors. While physicians had a duty to be 'ambassadors of good will', to promote 'understanding between nations' and 'combat nationalistic prejudices', the essay made clear that 'medical personnel' of different countries were struggling to meet on neutral ground. Sigerist like Haller had decided there was 'only one way out': a strategic retreat from America to relative obscurity in Switzerland.

Several luminaries, including the medical historian George Sarton, made speeches as did Sigerist himself, and Gregory's tribute appeared later in the year as 'Henry Sigerist: The Man and His Stature'. Noting that Sigerist's resignation had startled and distressed his friends, students, and 'the scientific world in general', Gregory insisted the decision to devote himself to writing was both wise and courageous. Sigerist, Gregory contended, wasn't fleeing 'the American scene'; it was in America, after all, that he had formulated his medical and social philosophy and grounded himself in English. He would take his generosity of spirit and depth of knowledge back to the Swiss village where, free from academic obligations, he would be able to write the history of medicine that would be the natural product of his admirable 'intellectual and spiritual evolution'.[9]

In spite of the positive cast Gregory put on Sigerist's departure, he knew his friend had become uncomfortable in a country intolerant of his ideas. The lectures Gregory delivered in the late 1940s were shaped by his conviction that the individual's needs must always be prioritised over the expectations of others, that society and its presumptions might be at odds with what was personally significant. Addressing the annual meeting of the American Psychiatric Association in May on 'The Struggle For and Against the Individual in Psychotherapy', he even argued against any imposition of goals by the psychotherapist as a 'denial of that which is individual in each person and which must be clarified, preserved, and duly integrated if neurotic and psychotic patients are to remain human beings'. Over the summer he turned his attention to a series of lectures he had been invited to give in California in October. Endowed by the philanthropist Jack Gimbel to address the issue of 'Sex Psychology', the talks were intended to address contemporary sexual issues, but Gregory interpreted the rubric freely. Unlike some of his colleagues, he was never particularly interested in sexuality per se. George Henry had from the late 1930s focused on 'sex variants'; several of Freud's followers, including the controversial Wilhelm Reich, who had emigrated to the United States in 1939, had devoted their research to sexuality and its expression, while Freud himself was popularised as a champion of 'libido'. Gregory, however, was far more interested in social justice, morality, gender, and history. Choosing as his topic 'The Problem of Sexual Problems', he approached his subject by examining the confusion of sex and love. Drawing various parallels, he pointed out that it is not enough for gifted musicians to be good technicians; they must also have 'a spiritual devotion' to music; while 'in our industrial civilization, we hardly take time out to chew our food, much less contemplate the eternal values of love and forgiveness', people needed to 'take time out for contemplation in order to understand what lies at the roots of a healthy, normal capacity for love'. Gregory's concern with values and his religious language ('spiritual devotion', 'contemplation', 'love and forgiveness') reveal here that larger than merely psychological issues continued to absorb him and now transparently influenced his professional thinking as well as his personal life.[10]

In mid-June, Gregory and Peg travelled to Baltimore for a final visit to Sigerist and Genevieve. Before Sigerist's French coq au vin, they drank quintessentially American mint juleps in the early summer sunshine. Although eager for a vacation, Gregory had patients to see before taking time off, among them formally or informally Field's youngest daughter from his first marriage, Bettine, whose marriage to McChesney Goodall, a professor at the Yale School of Medicine, was on the rocks. While Gregory believed that 'no true psychoanalyst ever advises marriage or divorce as part of the therapy', he had given emotional support to his many patients who had negotiated often complicated divorces or struggled with the challenges posed by the prospect of remarriage. Grateful for Gregory's help, Bettine set out for Reno in early August where, after the obligatory period of residence, she was granted a divorce and joint custody of her three-year-old daughter. Gregory himself finally took a summer holiday with Peg in a rented house in

Bedford, five miles from Pound Ridge. After months of looking about, they had found the country property they wanted to buy: another old farmhouse on seven acres of land with a barn, an apple orchard, copses of fir trees, and a meadow leading down to a brook at the bottom of a hill. Although far smaller than the farm, the property allowed Gregory to imagine a vegetable garden and blackberry bushes, a woodworking shop, and a library. Together they imagined children, and before they returned to the city in September, Peg was pregnant.[11]

The Gimbel lectures were warmly received. Gregory delivered five formal presentations, but he also spoke to student seminars at the University of California at Berkeley and Stanford University and attended cocktail parties and club luncheons in San Francisco and Los Angeles. In Beverly Hills for the annual joint meeting of the San Francisco and Los Angeles Psychoanalytic Societies, featuring a 'banquet' with 'entertainment', Gregory lectured on 'The Clinical and Social Difficulties of a Certain Type of Passivity'. The trip also allowed him to spend time with West Coast friends and colleagues, among them Martin Grotjean, who had emigrated from Germany in 1937, and William G. Barrett, who had founded the San Francisco Society in 1942, as well as Gregory's Berlin colleagues Otto Fenichel and Ernst Simmel, and Sam Hume, Gregory's colleague from his Chautauqua days, and his wife, the psychiatrist Portia Bell Hume. Peg would describe the trip as 'wonderful', filled with 'lectures and eating'.[12]

By the time he returned to New York, Gregory was thinking of a book that might grow out of the rather disparate talks in both South America and California, a volume that could somehow synthesise sexual problems and love, the individual and social responsibility, religious feeling and psychoanalytic health. Resuming his daily round at the office took much of his energy, but he wanted to be writing a book again. The winter, however, was quickly replete with activity of other sorts.

The snow that began to fall in late December did not melt until February and would confine Gregory to the city and often to the apartment, where he celebrated his Christmas birthday with Greg and Nancy, home for the holidays and still wrestling with their divided loyalties. On the first day of the new year Gregory listened to a radio broadcast of Arthur Honegger's operatic oratorio *Jeanne d'Arc*, an American premiere produced by Goddard Lieberson, assistant director (and soon to be president) of Columbia Records, and narrated by his wife Brigitta (an actress and ballerina who performed under her stage name Vera Zorina). Having met the Liebersons through his acquaintances in the performing arts, Gregory had probably come to know them well when, formally or informally, Brigitta sought his counsel during her divorce from the choreographer George? in 1946. Both Liebersons had become friends, and he soon wrote to thank them for 'the beauty, inspiration and lovely simplicity of pain' he found in the performance. Such a response – Gregory's attentive listening, his emotional reaction, and heartfelt expression of thanks – was typical in being personal and sensitive, intense and sincere as well as kind and generous, the very elements of his character often masked by his quick temper. Marriage to Peg, despite her efforts, would do little to restrain his inevitable outbursts of frustration and anger, and happy as they were and appreciative as Gregory could be, it must have been a relief to everyone when the children returned to school.[13]

Meanwhile, the place in the country wasn't yet what he and Peg hoped it would become: Riddled with termites, the farmhouse would need to be razed and a new house built on its foundations. Throughout the winter, the project captured Gregory's imagination and he began designing a contemporary structure, working on plans with Percival Goodman, a New York architect known for his modernist synagogues.

Actual building work couldn't begin until spring, but excited by what would be a stunning country home, Gregory reported his general happiness to Sigerist in January. Noting that 'Civilized man overeats and overworks and never catches up with himself', he was conscious that, as when speaking about Sigerist's experience in the United States, he was describing his own situation: Now in his late fifties, he was not only 'overworking' but becoming overweight and finding it difficult to lose the unnecessary pounds. American politics were also mildly upsetting: The 1948 presidential campaigns were taking shape 'as usual, with the usual and deliberate shifting of the emphasis to insignificant issues designated by misleading catchwords', and he lamented that the appeals 'to the various true issues' made by the Progressive Party candidate Henry Wallace – who advocated universal government health insurance, an end to the nascent Cold War, gender equality, full voting rights for black Americans, and an end to racial segregation – were 'lost in the shuffle and hurly-burly of political avidity'. Yet he was delighted at the prospect of the baby due in May and proud of his teenaged children: Greg – now a husky young man six feet tall and nearly 200 pounds, capable of kindness although still hapless, inattentive, and easily distracted – seemed to his father to be progressing well at school and 'learning to work', while Nancy was 'developing beautifully' and showed 'signs of becoming a good research student'. Even pregnant Peg continued working, an excellent scientific assistant and companion, 'a source of many joys'. Despite the disturbed state of the world, the crass 'social rapacity and avariciousness' that made him feel 'a little ashamed of being happy', a little 'awkward' about his own serenity, he told Sigerist they were all in all 'serenely happy'. Indeed, 'serene' would be a word he would use over and over to describe Peg and their life together as well as – in the face of impinging political, intellectual, and emotional exigencies – the spiritual state he longed for.[14]

As the snow melted, the house plans went out to contractors and Gregory struggled with his book. In late February he cancelled a week of appointments at the office and retreated by himself to the Hatchers' country house in an effort to concentrate. Peg would see her husband's work as a joint enterprise: She was his enabling helpmate, the valiant supporter encouraging him at every turn and reflecting him back to himself – as Virginia Woolf had noted was women's traditional calling – at twice his normal size. His writing now confirmed her unfailing faith in him and the life they were creating together. As he began to put words on paper for the project he strove to imagine, he telephoned her and read aloud what he thought of as its first section. With typical optimism intended both to affirm and inspire, she told him how pleased she was; it had seemed to her he was 'writing in a vacuum', but now, 'on the strength of one passage', she was relieved, delighted, and proud. 'This will be', she wrote, 'a splendid, good book. And you are indeed a splendid, *good* writer.' Confident and full of 'real hope', she even felt that 'Rhadames' (their jocular name, after Aida's faithful lover in Verdi's opera, for the baby they were convinced would be the boy they both hoped for) would be 'a better baby' because of Gregory's writing and the faith and joy she took in it.[15]

With the book still in an amorphous state, Gregory returned to the office at the beginning of March, but the happiness and serenity of family life was shattered before the end of the month by young Greg's expulsion from Kent. The unhappy adolescent had managed in this academic environment for over a year, but he hadn't in fact learned to work and few of the boys had found him likable; he probably didn't even find himself likable. As an ill-judged prank as foolish as it was bizarre, he had urinated publicly in the school chapel. Gregory now realised, as he must have suspected for some time, that Greg needed psychological help and arranged sessions with the child analyst Margaret Mahler. Heavily pregnant, Peg supervised his preparation for the entrance exams for the Lenox School in Massachusetts, an institution willing to accept him on Mahler's recommendation despite his academic deficiencies and emotional immaturity. Greg would live with his father and stepmother throughout the spring. Peg was convinced he had a 'slight touch' of his father's genius, and some of the boy's unpredictability also seemed a family trait, but she and Gregory found him a challenging presence. His departure in June for summer camp in Montana must have been a welcome respite.[16]

While both Greg and her pregnancy kept Peg in New York, nothing barred Gregory from his now regular trips to Canada, where he spent several days in the early spring, or from his participation in professional conferences. He received the news of the baby's birth on 17 May via a telegram delivered to him at a podium in Washington as he introduced a session on 'Faith and Psychopathology' at the annual convention of the American Psychiatric Association. Leaving the two invited speakers (Rabbi Abraham Cronbach of Hebrew Union College in Cincinnati and Noël Mailloux) to address the audience, he hurried back to New York and directly to Lenox Hill Hospital to confer with Abe. The surgeon had been called in to consult with their Columbia classmate Johnny Kilroe, the obstetrician who had overseen the delivery, and Jerome Leopold, the paediatrician who had taken care of Greg and Nancy. Even in Gregory's absence, however, the three doctors had already decided to initiate treatment of the dislocation that affected the baby's knees, a rare and serious situation best corrected by immediate and serial casting. The first time the father and mother held the child they would call Caroline, she was covered in plaster from heels to hips. Their joy was mixed: Rhadames hadn't turned out to be a boy, and the little girl who soon charmed them would provoke worry about her physical well-being that wouldn't be allayed until she walked. Kilroe suggested, even before Peg left hospital, that physical activity should be encouraged: massage as soon as the infant's casts were off, followed by daily exercise in Central Park or the countryside the moment she could toddle. Chatting congenially with Gregory and Peg at her hospital bedside, he also earnestly recommended ballet as soon as Caroline was old enough for lessons.

Ballet classes were a long way off as spring gave way to summer, and Peg and the baby nurse had the onerous job of trying to keep the plaster dry while every ten days there were visits to Lenox Hill to reposition the hyperextended knees. Peg would tell Sigerist that Greg had been expelled from school for smoking rather than urinating in the chapel, but Caroline's upsetting condition was simply not mentioned; there would be no euphemism or white lie to hide the disturbing plaster. The many photos of the sunny baby would instead feature her pretty hats and wide smile while her legs during those difficult early weeks would be carefully obscured by blankets or hidden beyond the photographic frame.[17]

Any disappointment at not having a son quickly faded. Announcing his daughter's birth with evident pride, Gregory told Sigerist in June that 'Caroline Crawford Zilboorg' was 'blue eyed, blonde, weighs now over nine pounds, has a good voice, attempts to smile with increasing frequency.' Peg, too, was 'well, cheerful, robust and serene. She nurses the baby, who accepts this maternal offering with monotonous avidity.' Even the baby's middle name – Peg's maternal grandmother's maiden name had been Crawford – affirmed difference from his previous experience of family. They were, he declared, 'very happy'.

They were also understandably 'a little tired', but with their own house still being 'fixed up', they were preparing to move again to a rented house in Bedford for the summer, and he intended to take off a couple of weeks in July to oversee the building works. He reported specifically to Sigerist on the kitchen: 'I have arranged, in addition to the regular gas range, to have a nice charcoal broiling stove installed. I shall then be broiling all the meats right.' The house Peg had initially described to Sigerist as small and simple, would have clean modernist lines, but it would be neither simple nor small. In fact, the house would be capacious and elegant: four bedrooms, a large study for Gregory, an enormous double living room, a dining room, a big kitchen with two stoves and two refrigerators and freezers, two servants' rooms, five bathrooms, two long terraces, and a rear deck. There would also be an attached two-car garage in addition to the original two-storey barn and a huge basement workshop as well as a guest suite with a separate entrance and a wine cellar. Peg explained the latter to Sigerist: A second small house on the property also had to be destroyed, but underneath was a cellar built 'with good thick walls, wonderfully cool even in summer'. They were putting a strong door on the bulkhead, planned to build shelves and bins. She raved, 'its equal just does not exist for a wine cellar.' Gregory would finally begin to collect his wines from the houses and cellars of various friends who had been good enough to keep them 'all this time'. The Bedford property would in the end more than compensate for the loss of the Pound Ridge farm, and its construction – like his marriage to Peg and the birth of the baby so like her in colouring and sunniness – was an important part of the conscious and unconscious project to recreate and reshape his life, to remake what was lost but to do it differently, to get it right at last.

The house in Bedford showcased in *Architectural Forum*, March 1949[18]

American politics, with the presidential campaign in full swing, continued to irritate him. Wallace, Gregory told Sigerist, seemed to be doing well, but 'the country is inert and labor is fragmented in several political cliques, with little insight – sociological or even pragmatic.' He was also frustrated not to be doing much writing or reading, but insisted he expected 'to be again in my stride in another fortnight' and closed his lengthy letter with characteristic humour and political scepticism: 'Peg sends her love – so do I. None of the conventions, Republican or Democratic, send their love to anyone except themselves.'[19]

Sigerist sent his congratulations and a little dress embroidered with edelweiss for the baby. On the political front, he urged Gregory to take a larger view, explaining, 'you get a totally different picture of the world situation when you see it from the European angle and are not exposed to the daily barrage of propaganda on the part of the American press.' It wasn't only his old friend's political point of view, however, that would bring about a radical shift in Gregory's American lens. His Canadian colleagues also had a more European view of geopolitics and shared his European perspective on history. During their encounters in Montreal and New York, he and Mailloux regularly discussed the work of contemporary French philosophers and psychoanalysts. With post-war Europe once again open to international tourism, Gregory began to reorient himself towards the Western Europe of his youth. Travel abroad would no longer mean trips to Central and South America but to England and the European continent, where he hadn't been since his trip to France, Switzerland, and Italy with Eddie and Bettina Warburg in the summer of 1934. The International Psycho-analytical Association was planning its first meeting since the war, for Zurich in the summer of 1949. Gregory hoped to attend, while an added enticement was the opportunity to visit Sigerist in Pura.[20]

Nancy, Bedford, summer 1948

Gregory managed to take off a few weeks over the summer, but vacations without work were not in his nature and he found it almost impossible to relax and rest. Peg observed that 'for the first week he was away from the office he was busy all day long just getting used to the idea.' During the second week he took a trip to Ontario and Quebec with 15-year-old Nancy, who proved an attentive travelling companion. An excellent and independent student, she would spend much of the summer with her father and Peg, who found her 'wonderfully natural and unspoiled'; unlike her brother, she had, Peg felt, a 'gratifying' approach to learning as well as 'many friends and plenty of plans'.

At home Gregory's attention, like his wife's, focused not only on the building project down the road but on their little girl. Peg told Sigerist that Gregory was crazy about her: 'There's no cry so loud that she won't stop it and smile at him when he asks her what it's all about.' Peg even went so far as to insist that Caroline looked 'wonderfully' like Gregory, 'except that she's as blonde as blonde can be, and has very blue eyes – and, of course, no moustache!' Even if she looked more like her mother than her father, the baby had apparently captured their hearts: She had realised Peg's traditional dream of motherhood and confirmed Gregory's efforts to create another family, a true home.[21]

Caroline and Peg on the lawn of the rented house in Bedford, July 1948

Confirmation also occurred in the form of Caroline's baptism in Bedford at the end of August. The ceremony took place at Saint Matthew's Episcopal Church, a red brick building with a white columned portico dating from 1810, where Peg regularly attended services on country Sundays. If the setting was quintessentially colonial New England and the church completely Peg's, the guest list consisted of her family (Louise, Margo, Lou, and George) and a select number of Gregory's friends from the world to which he had introduced her. The carefully chosen godparents for Caroline – dressed in the Stone family's white lawn and lace christening gown worn previously by Lou, Peg, and George – were the good Catholic Johnny Kilroe, Mary Warburg, and Bettine Goodall. It mustn't have been easy to find Christians among Gregory's friends, most of whom were Jews, however assimilated, or to find two mothers of Peg's generation. Mary and Eddie's son David was a youngster of six; Bettine's daughter had just turned four. Both women were willing to take on the role, while the jovial Irish bachelor was surely flattered to have been asked – and if anyone outside of Gregory's circle of French Dominicans suspected which way his spiritual lens was turning, it would have been Kilroe.

As the summer drew to a close, Peg and Gregory at last moved into the house he had designed. A great deal of landscaping remained to be done, but the property was habitable and they were eager to settle into their sprawling country home. Here they intended to spend nearly all their weekends as well as summers and Christmases; here they would relax, entertain, and embrace rural life. For Peg, Bedford also meant sport: They were already planning a tennis court, and as soon as Caroline was old enough there would be ice skates and snow shoes in the hall closet where Peg would also keep her tall wading boots and the childhood shotgun whose targets were skeet and the crows on the berry bushes in the future vegetable garden. Gregory was meanwhile delighted with his wine cellar and woodworking shop and the library that doubled on occasion as a treatment room whose windowless bathroom would also serve as a darkroom for developing photographs. After the master suite (with its own bathroom, dressing room, fireplace, and private terrace), the largest bedroom (with its own bathroom, dressing room, and screened-in porch) was for Caroline. The other bedrooms were for the other children they hoped to have as well as for Greg and Nancy, who would in the early years be frequent guests.

Caroline and Greg, Bedford, September 1948

En route in September from his camp in Montana to his new school in Massachusetts, Greg spent several days with his father and Peg, cuddling his baby sister for the first time with her legs free. On weekends that autumn Louise and Margo with Lou and George as well as Abe and Mary and Eddie would all come to Bedford to see Gregory and Peg, little Caroline, and their new dog, a standard poodle called Donna Maria, in the home that so

Abe Abeloff, Mary Warburg, Lou Stone, and Caroline, on the south terrace in Bedford, October 1948

delighted its owners. Nancy in her turn would bring friends to the new house during the Thanksgiving holiday in November. Gregory took photos of everyone.

As soon as the work was finished, Gregory arranged a large party on site for everyone involved – the architect, the local surveyor, the carpenters, masons, plumbers, electricians, and stevedores – but the property would be primarily reserved for family and close friends. Gregory's professional life, meanwhile, in New York and elsewhere continued nonstop despite the baby. In early November, still struggling to write his book on the problem of the sex problem, he participated with the cultural anthropologist Margaret Mead and Joseph F. Fletcher, professor of pastoral theology at Episcopal Theological School, in a 'forum' on 'American Sex Standards' at Harvard Law School. Broadcast on the radio, the wideranging discussion touched on everything from biological urges to 'Fear, lust, desire for power and self-assertion'. Unsurprisingly, Gregory came out against broad generalisations based on and about group behaviour and for the individual and particular values. He argued specifically that if children fail to learn love, they won't love their siblings or their parents or their community or state; they won't love themselves or anybody else and they won't love God. The problem of the sex problem for Gregory as a topic and potential book would finally be sexuality and sexual behaviour itself, which interested him far less than love between human beings, and he was beginning to feel that even love between human beings was insufficient without a love of God.[22]

Gregory, who held Truman in part responsible for the Cold War antipathy to Russia, returned to New York to vote not for the Democratic presidential candidate but for Wallace. In the close election, the Progressive candidate didn't stand a chance: Harry Truman narrowly beat the Republican New York governor Thomas Dewey, but even the racist South Carolina Dixiecrat Strom Thurmond came in ahead of Wallace, who garnered a mere 2.37 percent of the popular vote. Perhaps as a consolation, in late November Gregory and Peg left the baby at home and took a brief holiday to San Francisco to visit Bill Barrett and Sam and Portia Hume, a truncated reprise of the good time they had had the previous year. They would be back in New York well before Caroline's first Christmas, which they spent in Bedford, a celebration replete with a decorated tree, piles of presents, and visits from Peg's family. Greg and Nancy were home for the holidays, and select friends and patients would also visit, among them Ruthie Meyer, daughter of the financier and publisher Eugene Isaac Meyer. Gregory and Peg celebrated New Year's Eve with intimate friends at the chic Colony Restaurant in New York. A copy of the menu (featuring caviar, entrecôte, and crêpes Suzettes) suggests the evening's merriness, and everyone was apparently invited to commemorate the occasion. Gregory merely signed his name ('Gregory') and Abe wrote only 'Abeloff', but the others were more effusive. Mary Warburg wrote, 'For Greg and Peg Thank goodness we are together', and even thought of the absent children ('Caroline + David, Happy New Year 1948–49'), while Eddie's doggerel was characteristic: 'I just as leave (unless this trouble you) just sign myself EMMW.' Peg wrote, 'To Mary whom I love and Eddie of whom I am very fond and Abe about whom I am crazy and Grisha – for whom words defy me. But to whom I am devoted MSZ'.

In the new year, with the book stalled and with no academic appointment, Gregory threw himself into lecturing, a mixture of public talks to general audiences, academic addresses to university students and faculty, and professional presentations to his own psychiatric and psychoanalytic colleagues. Despite a devoted wife, adored baby, and his regular round of patients, Gregory's schedule of lectures before a variety of audiences rivalled in breadth and intensity only his Chautauqua summers in the early 1920s. In addition to presentations to American psychoanalytic societies, under the auspices of the Women's Division Society of the Hillside Hospital and the adult education committee of New York's Rodeph Sholom synagogue, he had spoken on 'History of Psychiatry' at the end of October. At the end of January he spoke at the Cooper Union on 'Our Blind Spots about Mental Illness'.

Having lost his appointment at Catholic University, Gregory had also availed himself of other teaching opportunities. In 1948 he had accepted the post of Consultant in Psychotherapy and Research at Butler Hospital in Providence, Rhode Island. Starting in September he spent two days every fortnight working individually with staff physicians to clarify and analyse their evaluations, decisions, and patient treatment plans. The post was a happy one well suited to his gifts and staff needs. David G. Wright, physician-in-chief and superintendent, noted in his annual report that Gregory had worked 'tirelessly', sharing 'his great store of knowledge, warmth, energy, wisdom and humility', and praised his 'rare ability to understand and communicate the valence of the psychological reactions of the physician himself and the effects of these upon the patient'. The bimonthly visits also allowed Gregory to work with old and new colleagues: Arthur Ruggles was the hospital's general consultant, while Louis E. Reik, assistant superintendent and admitting officer, and especially Henry H. Babcock, director of the Out-Patient Department, would become particular friends.[23]

Gregory was also writing articles for mainstream publications, directing his attention to an audience beyond his medical peers. His important article 'Psychoanalysis and Religion' appeared in the *Atlantic Monthly* in January 1949. Reprising and extending much of what he had already written in *Mind, Medicine, and Man*, he contended with typical wit that psychoanalysis, 'with or without Freud', had not discovered 'a single new fact or any new method which would enable it to refute, verify, corroborate, or otherwise assess the existence or nonexistence of God by purely psychoanalytic means'. He also argued that many psychoanalysts, like many other scientists, were subject to a fundamental error: 'they believe that greater intellectual understanding of life and living will make people *better*.' Thus Freud and Einstein were noble and tolerant not because of their intellectual achievements, while 'Neither Göring nor Goebbels lacked great intellectual powers, but these powers did not make them good.' Goodness comes, he insisted, from values and ethics. In a revealing statement Gregory then shifted his focus from values, ethics, and religion in general to the Catholic thinking and practices that were becoming personally more and more important to him:

> Modern Catholic thought has been showing of late both a great interest in and a great understanding of psychoanalysis and its positive relation to religion. This new trend has not yet become properly noticeable in America, but in Europe, particularly among the French-speaking people, it has become rather pronounced both in psychoanalytic and Catholic circles.

He argued specifically that psychoanalysis did not 'take the place of confession and substitute itself for the Sacrament of Penance'. No longer content to call the act merely 'confession', he here capitalised the sacrament and, quoting Maritain, asserted that confession, as an act of reason and will, clearly did not have the power to cure neuroses and psychoses; its object was in no way psychothera-peutic. Penitents confessed voluntarily conscious or preconscious memories to a priest, who responded only as a minister and judge, while psychoanalysis was not moral philosophy but 'a systematized, scientific working hypothesis about human behavior'. Gregory's interest in the Catholic Church's antipathy to psychoanaly-sis had, however, as much to do with personal feelings as with the intellectual understanding he applied to his subject in 'Psychoanalysis and Religion'. Increas-ingly he would turn to Europe and specifically to 'French-speaking people' in an attempt to resolve the problem as he understood and felt it.[24]

Life at home remained deeply fulfilling to Gregory in spite of the tensions between the Catholic Church and psychoanalysis and his own lifelong 'disgust' with social inequalities and abuses of power. He again told Sigerist that he and Peg were personally very happy, but he was more open with Mailloux about his most personal concerns. At the beginning of 1949, he had borrowed from the priest the Swiss psychoanalyst Charles Odier's *Les Deux Sources Consciente et Inconsci-ente de la Vie Morale* ('The Conscious and Unconscious Sources of Moral Life') and the French psychoanalyst Juliette Favez-Boutonier's *Les Défaillances de la Volonté* ('The Failures of Will'). With Mailloux's guidance he was, consciously and unconsciously, working through the moral and intellectual challenges that played a part in his own spiritual anxieties.[25]

More generally, anxiety in and about American society, its defects and fail-ures, was becoming rife. In early February Gregory and Peg were stunned by the Broadway premier of Arthur Miller's *Death of a Salesman*, which would go on to win that year's Pulitzer Prize. Gregory would find the play psychologically perceptive and dramatically moving as well as astute in its sociological obser-vations of American materialism and its pernicious effect on ordinary people; he would make it the subject of several talks he would give later in the year to both general and psychiatric audiences. Arguing that the drama's protagonist lives 'within us 23 out of 24 hours a day', Gregory asserted that Willy Loman's 'tragedy' was his inability to love anything 'for itself alone'; his love depended on a childish and destructive gratification of his desires. Both his sons were similarly 'corrupted' and became unable to love; only Willy's wife Linda, in his opinion the sole character genuinely capable of loving others, remained men-tally healthy.[26]

Morality, however, as much as mental health, was central to Gregory's liter-ary analysis. His very Russian 'spiritual' concerns had always been at once per-sonal and political, a matter of individual commitment, moral vision, and social responsibility, of ethics and action. His principles fostered in the coming decade a particular interest in psychology and the law, while his personal spiritual journey would lead him to Rome as an advocate for psychoanalysis. Yet what might have appeared – to him and his various audiences – an intellectual argument for the compatibility of psychoanalysis and religion would finally emerge as what it had been, however unacknowledged, all along: the result of Gregory's spiritual struggle towards God and the Catholic Church.

As he reflected on Miller's play and American life in early March, Gregory prepared a talk for a meeting of the Pennsylvania Psychiatric Society. Choosing as his topic 'The Reciprocal Responsibilities of Law and Psychiatry', he offered 'a melancholy reflection and protest against the deadly slowness with which the cooperation between psychiatry and the law' had developed 'in this our age of supersonic speed'. Seeing the differences between psychiatry and the law as a moral issue, he declared, 'the psychiatrist in so far as he is a physician can have nothing to do, directly or indirectly, with legal justice'. To force a psychiatrist, who was at best only an amateur lawyer, 'to talk in terms of the ability to distinguish between right and wrong and of legal responsibility' was 'to force him to violate the Hippocratic Oath, even to violate the oath he takes as a witness to tell the truth and nothing but the truth, to force him to perjure himself for the sake of justice'. He argued that using modern psychiatry to convict people in an old-fashioned and time-honoured way was not only unjust but failed to advance psychosociological knowledge of the criminal. Typically concerned with the larger historical and 'psychosociological' state of the world, he contended that the psychiatrist 'has always been forced to combine his career as healer with the job of crusader'. In this crusading spirit Gregory then cleared his desk and packed his bags for his first trip to Europe since 1934.[27]

The trip was a working holiday with a personal agenda. Travelling first class on the luxurious *Queen Mary*, he and Mailloux, who accompanied him on tickets Gregory certainly subsidised, sailed from New York to Southampton in early April. In the days before wheeled suitcases and civilian rucksacks, the baggage of first-class travellers was transported, installed, and even unpacked by porters, bellboys, and ship stewards. Gregory travelled with 14 pieces of luggage, but the only item he expected to carry himself was his bulging briefcase. His many bags contained an overcoat; a selection of ties for day and evening wear; a dinner jacket; several pairs of shoes; numerous starched shirts – and a silver framed photograph of Peg and Caroline that he carefully placed on his shipboard bureau and on writing tables in hotel rooms in London, Rome, Florence, Zurich, Geneva, and Paris.

The immediate reason for the trip was Gregory's desire to see old friends, colleagues, and acquaintances, to reaffirm his European connections, and to re-anchor himself in his professional, intellectual, emotional, and historical past. The future was also on his mind and, as a crusader for psychoanalysis, he had Rome on his itinerary in the hope of addressing the Church's hostility to Freud with the Vatican. Mailloux would accompany him some of the time, but Gregory had his own agenda. The Dominican was neither a psychiatrist nor a psychoanalyst nor a historian of medicine; he was a psychologist, theologian, and priest whose very attire announced his separateness from Gregory's professional, political, and personal world. While Gregory had been warmly welcomed by Mailloux's Catholic community in Montreal, many of those who now encountered Gregory with Mailloux in tow would have been startled by the Dominican, an apparently anomalous interloper.

With his luggage in his room at the Savoy and the photo of Peg and Caroline on his desk, Gregory explored London on foot, observing its inhabitants and admiring its parks, whose trees and flowers were a welcome sight after the days at sea. His only previous experience of England had been his visit to Oxford in 1928, and his focus then had been on the psychoanalytic world just opening to him rather than on nature or the English people themselves. He now encountered Cockneys selling postcards on street corners, salespeople in small shops and hotel staff offering services and local advice. Socialist to the core, he found the British lower classes 'sweet', the middle classes 'nauseatingly indirect and dull and silly', and the upper classes 'tough, disgusting self-delighted baboons and corrupted gorillas'.[28]

Having quickly gotten his bearings in the capital, he set out on his second day in England to see Ernest Jones in his country retreat. Gregory saw spring in Sussex 'in full swing' and thought Jones 'a little too satisfied being far away from everything', but all in all judged this informal afternoon with the president of the International Psycho-analytical Association 'very nice' indeed. Appreciative of Gregory's attempts to nourish connections with international colleagues – especially those who had fled to America or, like Freud, to England – Jones no longer felt the sceptical wariness he had expressed in 1932. Shortly after Freud's death in September 1939, Gregory, as a representative of the American Psychoanalytic Association, had invited Jones to participate in a commemorative session at the 42nd annual meeting in Cincinnati in May 1940. The association had even offered to underwrite expenses, including travel and 'loss of practice'. Jones had initially cabled his acceptance, then detailed his hesitations in a lengthy letter. In the end, his health and anxiety about crossing the Atlantic in wartime had caused him to decline, but he had been honoured by the invitation and the effort Gregory and the association had made on his behalf.[29]

Gregory had also invited Anna Freud, who had impulsively cabled an enthusiastic acceptance quickly followed by another refusing 'with great regrets' for reasons different from Jones's: Her special refugee status as a 'German alien' made it impossible for her to travel directly from England or to get a 'transit visa' through France, where she would have been interned; she had also been concerned about 'the difficulties of return', and understandably hadn't relished the prospect of spending the duration of the war in America. She had, however, been 'genuinely pleased' by the generous offer and regretted being unable 'to share actively in that Memorial Meeting'.[30]

On his third day, Gregory called on Anna Freud in Hampstead, passing en route gutted houses and 'many empty blocks overgrown with grass, weeds and bushes', sober reminders of the war less evident in the city centre. This visit was even more cheering than the afternoon in Sussex: They spent a couple of relaxed hours talking and drinking coffee in the room where the great man had worked. Touched by the warm welcome, Gregory found Anna Freud 'very sweet and kind and keen' and reported to Peg that she seemed to him to have 'mellowed a great deal'. Of course, Gregory had, by 1949, also mellowed quite a bit. Both visits were pilgrimages of homage but turned into friendly moments with colleagues between whom there was now mutual admiration and genuine respect as well as a degree of affection.[31]

Not all of Gregory's English encounters were so heartening. Indeed, Gregory's time abroad was an odd mixture of society, solitude, and longing for Peg. He wrote her perceptive and remarkably revealing letters confessing that he missed her 'more than ever' and loved her 'more and more'. His letters home provide a valuable window on his daily life, his moral values and volatile moodiness, his loving and exacting nature. Having had a drink with Mary Warburg's English brother-in-law Baron Leo d'Erlanger, he confided that he found the titled banker a 'pseudo-modest, charmingly inoffensive and offensively charming money-lender'. After an afternoon in Parliament, Gregory reflected on 'how small the great are: from the House of Commons to the N. Y. Psychoanalytic Society, from Anthony Eden to Sandor Rado – political debate is always the same and it shows up the worst of human nature'. Given his experience of the Russian Duma and Vienna Reichsrat, Gregory had likely already arrived at this conclusion, but still felt, in his surprisingly naïve and hopeful socialist way, that to get to know a country, one should observe its government in action, as if the British Parliament might have revealed to him anything other than the appalling smallness of the supposedly great. He closed this report to Peg with a regular refrain: 'God bless you, dear, and God bless all of us.'[32]

Gregory then flew to Rome. During a layover in Amsterdam, he went into the centre to catch a glimpse of places he had known as a destitute Russian stranded in Holland three decades earlier. Rome during Holy Week would be a completely different experience. Saddened by the conspicuous bomb damage, by 'the ruins of the twentieth-century', he spent much of his time with the American journalist Percy Winner, foreign affairs editor of *New Republic*. On his own and with Mailloux, Gregory was particularly moved by Michelangelo's Moses in San Pietro in Vincoli and St. Peter's Basilica, which he entered just as the Benedictines there were singing the psalms of Tenebrae. At the opera he was touched by Honegger's *Joan of Arc* with Honegger himself conducting. The highlight, however, occurred on Holy Saturday: 'a *private* audience' with Pope Pius XII during which he and the Holy Father spoke, in French, for nearly ten minutes. If Mailloux was present, as he may well have been, Gregory did not mention it in his letters to Peg, nor did he report what he and the Pope discussed, although she would have known about his crusader's agenda. Rather, his letters home record his deeply emotional response to the experience of Catholic Rome itself, how impressed he was when, on Easter Sunday, he witnessed priests in vestments, not only parish priests but priests from local monasteries, blessing every house in the city.[33]

Gregory and Père Noël Mailloux, Saint Peter's Square, Rome, April 1949

His mission in Rome more or less accomplished – or at least the Vatican door opened to psychoanalysis and Gregory himself – he and Mailloux went on to Florence, where again what initially struck him was the devastation of the war: the bridges destroyed and the quarters around the Ponte Vecchio in rubble. 'The German-American ruins of Florence', he wrote Peg, 'make you cry.' His sense of loss was nevertheless tempered by the joy he took in the city's surviving art and architecture. He detailed for Peg the differences between Michelangelo's 'Deposition' in Florence's Duomo and his Pietà in Rome. Waking early, he described the beauty of Florence at dawn and his visits to the cloisters of San Marco and Santa Maria Novella, the city's main Dominican church. Impressed by Fra Angelico's frescos, he treasured a few quiet moments on his own in Savonarola's little study cell and admired the 'glorious' oil portrait of him by Fra Bartolomeo. In contrast to Italy's ruins and art, Geneva seemed to him, as he travelled north, 'like a jewel', both 'peaceful and cheerfully dull'.[34]

Gregory's European odyssey continued to be a hectic mixture of nostalgia and discovery, of solitary, reflective moments and intense social, cultural, and professional activity. Having deposited his luggage at Zurich's grand Hotel Baur au Lac, he set out to explore the city on foot before dining with Manfred Bleuler at the Zimmerleuten, the historic restaurant in the mediaeval guild hall. Back in his room late that evening he wrote Peg of Bleuler's 'considerable friendliness'. His old colleague was 'kind, keen, simple, friendly and very unassuming', conservative and tolerant in a way that seemed to him characteristically Swiss. Despite a persistent loneliness, Gregory felt, now that he was in Zurich, 'almost fully relaxed' for the first time since he had left home. Earlier in the day he had seen three twelfth-century cathedrals with all their crosses removed but realised he couldn't recount everything he had done or analyse fully his emotional responses in the letters he wrote at the beginning and end of his long days. He told Peg he would save the details of his very full weeks until they could again sit together on one of their terraces; then and there, 'I will hold your hand and tell *all* the things I saw and *all* the thoughts I had.' Late on his first night in Zurich, he simply missed home; he missed Donna and Bedford, Peg and Caroline; he felt his wife 'everywhere and nowhere' and Carrie, too, 'everywhere and nowhere'.[35]

The following day Gregory lunched with Manfred and Monica Bleuler on his hotel terrace, then walked around the city again before dining at the Bleulers' home, the same apartment at the Burghölzli Klinik that Manfred's father had occupied when he was a professor at the University of Zurich. There Gregory also met Bleuler's colleagues and found himself giving an extemporaneous lecture in German. Before a group of psychiatric colleagues he was inevitably in his element and rose convivially to the occasion. The real occasion, however, was his formal lecture on Vesalius scheduled for the next evening. Ever the dandy, he reported his attire to Peg (a black cashmere suit and a grey tie) and translated for her the glowing German epithets that his talk elicited ('captivating', 'gripping', 'moving', 'revealing') before humorously pointing out that they were 'about the paper – not me, dear'. All in all, it was wonderful evening: 'Your husband was a great success', he told her, and he had been 'deeply moved by Bleuler's modesty when he in the course of his discussion recalled his days in America and at Bloomingdale and called me his teacher'.[36]

Gregory with Manfred Bleuler in the garden of the Burghölzli Klinik, Zurich, April 1949

With his formal obligation fulfilled, Gregory truly relaxed and spent his last two days in Switzerland with Sigerist, who had travelled from Pura to see him. Gregory would now experience Zurich through his friend's eyes as they talked and walked in the city where Sigerist had been a schoolboy and a university student and finally a professor. The place he repeatedly pointed out was a restaurant, 'Kröne', where he used to eat as a student. He told Gregory that the food there had been 'really good' and they decided to eat lunch there – and indeed the food was really good, so at the end of their day together, they returned to the 'Kröne' for dinner. On his last evening in Zurich, Gregory and Sigerist joined the Bleulers at the city's opulent opera for a performance of Verdi's *Macbeth*.[37]

Gregory then left for a week in Paris. Habitually eager to get on with whatever awaited, he once more left his bags at his hotel and went out walking. His feelings were again mixed. The city felt exactly as it always had, but hollow. He was saddened by the plaques in the Tuileries paying tribute to those killed during the German occupation and repelled at how expensive and commercial Paris had become. 'This glorious city', he informed Peg, 'is depressing and dull and drab in its very display of luxuries.' He had been feeling unwell ('no fever, no cold, just endless dragging "digestive disturbances"'), but Mailloux was waiting for him and he soon began to feel at least physically better. Georges Parcheminey, one of the founders of the French Psychoanalytical Society, seemed to him 'a nice but sad man', while most of his French colleagues were also 'nice' but not sad despite the impact of the war. They were interested in his lectures, 'serious and very detailed' in their responses. Many, including some of Mailloux's fellow Dominicans, had been in concentration camps or German prisons and wore the ribbon of the legion of honour or other decorations received for their wartime services. Gregory still felt lonely, pronounced the long trip 'tough', and continued to miss his wife and daughter very much. He signed his last letter to Peg from Paris 'yours lonesomely'.[38]

Accompanied by Mailloux, Gregory returned to England at the beginning of May. Ever the leftist revolutionary, he judged London marginally better than the French capital, although his spirits weren't lifted by the predicted 'miraculous' tourist season, which he was certain would not help 'the common people'. He now considered his digestive problems an 'intestinal flu' and his current 'draggy depressive state' as influenza's usual aftermath. Confident of recovery but counting the days until his return, he told Peg he would soon be merely *normally depressed* because of missing her and the baby and the dog and Nancy. In spite of his mood, his schedule quickly filled up with stimulating social and professional engagements. The day after his arrival he had dinner with the English Quaker John Rickman, then president of the British Psychoanalytical Society. The following evening he dined with Anna Freud and the English psychoanalyst Sylvia Payne. The next day he was the guest of honour at a lunch at Maudsley Hospital arranged by Aubrey Lewis, professor at the Institute of Psychiatry at the University of London and head of the hospital, where in the afternoon Gregory addressed a large audience of medical students and staff on 'Disease: A Historical Survey of the Concept in General Medicine and Psychiatry'. That evening he attended a meeting of the British Psychoanalytical Society. On his last night in England he dined with Mailloux and two other colleagues at Leoni's famous 'Quo Vadis' in Soho, then packed his bags and hoped for calm seas as he and Mailloux prepared to head for Southampton the following morning. On the birthday Peg shared with Freud, Gregory rang her from a special telephone on board the *Queen Elizabeth*. He simply wanted to hear her voice, he told her, to be reminded of her sweet warmth and honest heart.[39]

Gregory arrived in New York with even more than he had left with: leather gloves for Margo; handbags for Olivia and Hilda; a chess set for George. There were presents for Peg and Carrie, too, of course, while perfume from Paris and the chocolates he had bought with Sigerist in Zurich would arrive in due course by post. Carrie met him on his return in an 'upstanding' way: She had started walking in his absence, a completely normal and natural feat that must nevertheless have relieved the parents who had worried about her dislocated knees. Although he needed to catch up with his patients, at the end of May Gregory went to Montreal for the annual meeting of the American Psychiatric Association. Speaking on 'Clinical Variants of Moral Values', he argued that psychoanalysis is scientific in the best sense of the word, 'the sense of being constantly in search of the truth and fearless as to how much the truth, if and when found, might contradict and refute the truth as it appeared to us theretofore to be'. Such apparently objective statements were consonant with his lifelong attitude towards 'truth', consistent with his voiced scepticism about all that people think they know that may turn out not to be true at all, and compatible with his historical search for knowledge of the external world and of inner, psychological experience, but 'the truth, if and when found' was, by the summer of 1949, also a private and spiritual matter.[40]

It was family, however, that filled Gregory's summer in the two months between his homecoming and his departure in mid-August on his second post-war trip to Europe. Determined to avoid the loneliness that periodically overwhelmed him, he took Peg with him to Canada, and when the family moved to Bedford at the end of May, he decided to commute to the office in order to be with them. On a business trip to the States, James met Peg and the baby for the first time and saw his older brother content in the country house he had helped design, full of joy in his second marriage, and delighted with his second chance at fatherhood.

When Gregory and Peg then drove to Massachusetts for the graduation ceremony at Lenox, they watched Greg march blithely across the stage with his classmates, but he hadn't learned to study after all. His father would have been deeply disappointed to discover in the leather case the headmaster presented to his son not the diploma awarded to the other students but merely a certificate of attendance. Greg himself was likely neither particularly surprised nor disappointed. He seemed simply glad that his father and Peg were there, delighted to be leaving school, happy to be driving away to Bedford through the lush New England countryside.[41]

Greg and Gregory, Lenox, Massachusetts, 13 June 1949

Five days later Gregory and Peg were in Baltimore where Peg was maid of honour at George's wedding to Jodie Pymer at the city's Second Presbyterian Church. Jodie was an only child and the event was very much a Stone family affair with Lou as his brother's best man, but Gregory was a welcome guest and knew why Peg felt nauseous even before she understood she was pregnant. The baby-in-utero would again be denominated Rhadames, and the summer in Bedford would be peaceful, social, hopeful, and happy. Nancy stayed for much of her school holiday and Greg visited often. Gregory spent the festive July fourth weekend at Eddie and Mary's country home in Westport, looking on while Peg swam and Carrie paddled in the shallow water on the swimming pool steps. Lou visited Bedford with his Yale classmate Harold Turner and his wife Virginia and daughter Louise, who was just Carrie's age and named after Peg's mother, who had welcomed Harold and Virginia and their baby into the family as if they were her own. Mary-Alice came up from the city for at least one weekend, and Louise and Margo regularly drove over from Bronxville for Sunday lunches.[42]

Gregory left for Europe in late July to attend various meetings and to give a talk at the 16th congress of the International Psycho-analytical Association. Eddie travelled with him first to Stockholm, where Abe and his colleague Harry Stern joined them, and then to Zurich and Geneva. In the war's immediate aftermath, displaced individuals and populations, destroyed cities, occupying armies, and the judgement of war crimes had taken priority, but by 1949 preventing future wars and creating a just and peaceful world were high on the international agenda. Israel had been declared a state on 14 May 1948, three days before Caroline's birth. In August of the same year the International Red Cross had met in Stockholm, the organisation's first international conference since 1938. Between April and August 1949, the World Health Organization convened in Geneva to set modern standards for humanitarian treatment in war. Both Eddie and Abe were active members of the American Jewish Joint Distribution Committee, working closely with international groups in the post-war period, and Gregory was now a consultant to the World Federation for Mental Health, established in London in August 1948 by the British military psychiatrist John Rawlings Rees, one of the founders of the Tavistock Clinic, and the Canadian psychiatrist George Brock Chisholm, the first director general of the World Health Organization. Although Eddie would seek Gregory's personal council throughout his life, he now accompanied Gregory as a friend and colleague rather than a patient, and he, like Abe and Gregory, would attend meetings of international humanitarian groups in both Sweden and Switzerland.

The International Psycho-analytical Association convened in Zurich in mid-August. Participants included Anna Freud, Melanie Klein, and Jacques Lacan; European psychoanalysts who had settled in the United States (including Klein's daughter Melitta Schmideberg, René Spitz, Ernst Kris, and Raymond de Saussure); Gregory's former Berlin colleague Carl Müller-Braunschweig, who had managed to continue his career under the Nazis; and Arnaldo Rascovsky from Buenos Aires. The association's membership had been diminished by the war – 64 fewer members attended than in Paris 11 years earlier – and the chemistry of the group had changed since Freud's death. After 17 years of service, Ernest Jones stepped down as president, and Leo Bartemeier, the first American, was elected to replace him. On the opening afternoon Gregory addressed the congress on 'Varieties of Passivity – Individual and Social', then snuck away with Eddie and Abe to see Sigerist in Pura.[43]

In the hills above Lugano they had 'a grand time' with much cooking, eating, laughter, and picture taking. Gregory announced that he and Peg were expecting another baby, and everyone likely toasted everyone else with a glass of the local wine. Sigerist photographed the group enjoying American iced tea on his shady terrace, and Gregory, unsurprisingly reluctant to leave after only 'one short day', pronounced the visit 'wonderful'.[44]

Harry Stern, Eddie Warburg (with his camera), Sigerist's secretary Claire Bacher, Abe Abeloff (with his camera), Gregory (with his camera), and Emmy Sigerist in the foreground, photographed by Sigerist at 'Casa Serena', Pura, Switzerland, 17 August 1949

Gregory, Eddie, Abe, and Stern left the following day for Geneva and the ongoing convention. During a busy week Gregory attended formal sessions and diplomatic events, the antithesis of the convivial day in the Swiss countryside. He dined with Brock Chisholm at his home in the hills overlooking the city, met with international representatives in Geneva's lakeside cafés, and discussed the world's health and the health of the world with medical professionals and sophisticated advocates of global peace.

Before the end of the month, however, Gregory left Switzerland for a final few days in Italy. Although not completely devoid of tourists, Rome was cooler and calmer than he had anticipated. Probably travelling on his own and once more missing Peg and home, Gregory had again arranged appointments with influential Vatican prelates, although perhaps not another personal audience with the pope. As an advocate for psychoanalysis, Gregory's status as a Jew and a member of the Society of Friends was at least anomalous, but it was nevertheless apparent, even without Mailloux at his side, that he was addressing the issue from a Catholic as well as a psychoanalytic point of view. If the Church wasn't yet ready to embrace psychoanalysis, however, individual priests were prepared to spend time with him as an individual.[45]

Having accepted an appointment as associate professor of clinical psychiatry at Manhattan's New York Medical College, Gregory returned to the United States in time for the start of the 1949–1950 academic year. There were also, of course, patients to see, papers to write, and talks he had agreed to give. Even family weekends in Bedford were never free of work, but with Peg four months pregnant and no longer feeling ill, there were also dinners out at restaurants and at home both in the city and the country as well as at the homes of friends and colleagues. It was not at all unusual for Peg and Gregory to host 12 or more people – psychiatrists, opera singers, artists, writers, and philanthropists – for dinner at their apartment, congenial occasions requiring three wines and finger bowls, squab and wild rice, Bavarian cream with raspberries – no matter what the season – and postprandial brandy, cognac, or Benedictine. All this meant a great deal of work for Olivia and Hilda, who put on a black taffeta uniform with a small white apron in order to serve, but by the autumn of 1949, they were used to such events when the doctor, as they called him, was home.

Gregory was home much of the time, but invariably peripatetic. At the beginning of October he delivered two of the year's four Sommer Memorial Lectures at St. Vincent's Hospital in Portland, Oregon, addressing an audience of physicians and medical students on 'The Concept of Disease in Medicine and Psychiatry' and 'The Origin and Evolution of Psychosomatic Medicine', expanding on the lecture he had given in London in May. En route back to New York, he stopped off in Detroit to speak to the Michigan Society for Mental Hygiene on 'The Magic of *Death of a Salesman*', a topic that neatly combined his interest in both drama and psychology. Again drawing at least through allusion on the literary world that was a constant frame of reference, he spoke in the middle of the month to the Long Island Psychiatric Society on 'Pride and Prejudice in Psychosomatic Medicine'. These absences seem strategic given the chores he left behind for Peg to oversee: clearing library shelves, filling boxes, and packing suitcases for the move to a larger place that could more easily accommodate not only his office and lavish dinner parties but a second baby.

On November first Gregory and his entourage moved into a 13-room apartment at 33 East 70th Street, a convenient Manhattan address between Park and

Lexington Avenues. There was plenty of space here for his treatment room and waiting room, and two of the four small rooms off the kitchen and pantry would accommodate the live-in servants on whom the household depended; the other two would serve as a photography lab and a nursery. Hilda and Olivia had been considering retirement when Gregory and Peg moved into 885 Park Avenue. The move now was too much for Olivia, but Hilda, in her early sixties, agreed to stay on and recruited Betty Smith, another Swede, as a replacement. There would be daily and weekly help, too, of course (a laundress, a cleaning woman, an office accountant), and further staff in Bedford (another laundress as well as a gardener, and a handyman who assisted when required in the woodworking shop) in addition to Caroline's nurse and Gregory's personal staff (a secretary-receptionist and a research assistant). Needless to say, Peg had a desk in the large master bedroom and continued to work as Gregory's copyeditor, office manager, right-hand woman, and lady of the house responsible for everything from meal planning to solving everyday and cosmic problems, such as noise outside the treatment room door (eventually soundproofed) and her husband's constantly shifting, passionately felt moods. With four bedrooms, six bathrooms, a living room with a grand piano, and a capacious dining room off a hallway long enough for a child to build up steam on a tricycle, Gregory's city home was complete; he could – at least in theory – finally settle into something resembling a normal pattern of work and family life.

The move itself was destabilising, and Gregory was uncomfortable 'among boxes, crates, packages and dust' yet aware that his inability to focus was attributable to something more transcendental. As overcommitted as ever, he felt he hadn't properly recovered from his trip to Europe; constantly fatigued and dealing with the aftermath of a self-diagnosed 'bout of grippe', he felt unable to work well, frustrated that he couldn't do the creative work he felt called to do. Unwilling or unable to be more explicit, he wrote Mailloux in November that he felt the need of his 'companionship' very badly. Torn between work and home on the one hand and a need for spiritual nourishment on the other, Gregory wanted to visit Mailloux in Quebec, but couldn't see leaving his office before mid-December, and he wanted to be with his family during Christmas. Putting personal needs aside to engage in intellectual argument, he responded to a letter from Anna Freud that Mailloux had shared. Gregory contended she simply didn't understand the problem of psychoanalysis and religion. Making the significant point that 'the analysis of the psychological mechanisms of religious belief in no way means to deal with the truth or untruth of the claims of religious faith', he insisted,

> All psychoanalysis ought to demand of religious feelings is a strict differentiation from pathological states. The scientist cannot prove or disprove the existence of God by scientific means, but a scientist has a right to demand of the faithful that they do not confuse magic with science and religions with scientific truth.

In short, he was convinced psychoanalysts had been wrong in taking Freud's thinking in *The Future of an Illusion* and *Moses and Monotheism* as 'the ultimate answer'. The conundrum of what the ultimate spiritual answer would be for him, Gregory sidestepped and couldn't yet solve.[46]

Gregory evidently regained his bearings during a calm Christmas in Bedford that involved neither crates nor dust and where the only packages were the neatly wrapped presents under the tree. Caroline was walking and beginning to talk, and Peg, now seven months pregnant, wasn't yet uncomfortable; she was feeling optimistic about the coming year and confident the baby would this time be a boy. Greg had surprisingly passed his end-of-semester exams at New York University while Nancy, having maintained her stellar academic record at Westtown, had submitted her application for Radcliffe, the prestigious women's college affiliated with Harvard, where Mary Warburg's eldest son, Stephen Currier, was now in his second year. The Warburgs had had a particularly happy Christmas, Mary having just given birth to a little girl, Daphne. The overlapping pregnancies had drawn the two families even closer: Peg and Mary, whom Caroline called 'Mamie', spoke on the phone nearly every evening with the first martini.

In the chill of January, Gregory decided that they needed a little vacation. Leaving Mary at home with Daphne, Eddie joined Gregory and Peg for a week in Puerto Rico. This would be a holiday with sunny mornings on the beach and evening drinks on the hotel terrace, but it seems unlikely that Peg, heavily pregnant, actually went swimming and just as unlikely that Gregory and Eddie left work completely behind; there were certainly colleagues to see, people to meet, a formal or informal talk for Gregory to present if given the occasion.

Family would keep Peg close to home not only for the remaining weeks of her pregnancy but for the next few years, and Gregory, in his turn, was emotionally tied to his wife and children. Anticipating the baby's arrival and fretful about his writing, he hesitated to commit himself to European medical conferences scheduled for the summer of 1950. He explained to Sigerist the pressure he felt to get on with work that was 'lagging behind', his uncomfortable sense that that he 'must catch up – just must', but his letters weren't predominantly anxious. Gregory regularly reported on his domestic contentment and seldom lost his sense of humour. With typical authoritative élan, he shared a recipe he had recently prepared: 'Take a veal cutlet about ¼ inch thick. Beat it with a wooden hammer; beat it to death.' His instructions concluded, 'Serve and report how it tasted.' Sigerist responded in kind with his versions of 'Escalopes Cordon Bleu' and 'Wild Spanish Rice'.[47]

Gregory travelled to New Haven in mid-February to hear George Sarton lecture on Boyle to the Beaumont Club, but this time he was careful not to be at a podium when Peg went into labour. On 4 March she gave birth to 'a nice big little boy' whom they named John – after Kilroe, who delivered him, and after the Evangelist, whose opening chapter was particularly apt for parents who loved language: 'In the beginning was the Word, and the Word was with God, and the Word was God.' With their hopes for a boy fulfilled, Gregory informed Sigerist that they looked forward to a wonderful summer. He added that Peg felt well: Despite a rather long labour, three days after John's arrival she had insisted on walking the length of the hospital corridor; in short, she was 'cheerful, strong, serene'.[48]

American life in general, however, was far from serene. On the day John was born, a young American woman, Judith Coplon, was arrested in Washington, suspected of being a Soviet spy, a case that received worldwide attention and galvanised investigations led by Joseph McCarthy, the senator whose name would come to characterise the xenophobic Cold War era in the United States. Gregory had many left-leaning friends. Some had joined the American Communist Party in the 1930s; some, like Lillian, were outspokenly sympathetic to the Soviet project. Gregory himself was now regarded with fresh suspicion and grew increasingly ill at ease as the political atmosphere in America became vicious. Having been warmly welcomed in both Canada and Europe, he was reminded daily of other than general American attitudes towards those values he cared most about, towards truth and facts, towards intellectual freedom and difference, towards justice as well as mercy.

Mailloux spent several days in New York at the end of the month. Invited to the apartment for dinner, he congratulated Peg and Gregory on their expanding family, greeted the new baby, and smiled benevolently at little Caroline. While the evening was predominantly a social occasion, Gregory and Mailloux had begun work on what they would call the Aquinas Foundation. It would fund scholarships for the study of psychology in Europe and support the expansion of Mailloux's department at the University of Montreal. Gregory had begun to raise money and set the wheels in motion to incorporate in New York and Canada. Developing their plans, the two men talked late into the evening over cognac and Cuban cigars.

Then, on the last Saturday in March, the baby became suddenly ill. His nurse tried to calm Peg's concerns, but as the hours wore on, Miss Tietjen finally agreed that something might not be right with the infant who cried and cried and refused to nurse. The two women waited, however, until Gregory's return from a dinner party to take a decision. Appalled to find his son ashen and pinched, he immediately took charge and shortly after midnight Johnny was operated on for an inguinal hernia. There was talk afterwards of letting Miss Tietjen go, but no one was to blame and the baby quickly recovered. The impact on Gregory, however, was profound. A week after the event he recounted the incident to Sigerist: The baby had suffered an 'acutely developed, strangulated hernia at the great age of twenty-one days' and been rushed 'back where he came from' (Lenox Hill Hospital); he had undergone surgery, recovered, returned home, and rapidly regained his previous weight. 'Thus far', Gregory reported, Johnny was 'gastronomically speaking' a strict specialist, partaking 'only of the cuisine which Peg provides from her own biological laboratory'. Despite his medical objectivity and humour, Gregory had been deeply moved by the experience and would reflect on its personal significance throughout the spring.[49]

Gregory continued to be enthusiastic about the Aquinas Foundation, a project that captured his imagination and demanded considerable attention, but other obligations also pressed upon him and mitigated the happiness he felt when he allowed himself to focus on Peg and their children. He still hoped to turn the Gimbel lectures into a book, but had made little progress, and had meanwhile agreed to contribute a short volume on Freud to a series on great twentieth-century figures. *Sigmund Freud: His Exploration of the Mind of Man* wouldn't be a full biography but a reflective 'historico-sociological' and 'historico-philosophical' appraisal. Personally, he told Sigerist again, he was happy but 'more busy than is good for one', and there seemed to him no way out: 'One just goes on going on and at times one is a little weary.' Taking a larger political or historical view didn't help, for the 'state of the world as seen from here and through the political atmosphere of America' was disheartening. He confessed more revealingly than he probably intended that he wished to turn away from 'this all' – not so much 'by way of escape but by way of not wanting to spend too much energy on the futility of sadistic verbiage'.[50]

Family worries again took priority in April when Nancy was refused admission to Radcliffe despite her strong academic record. However mature and settled she may have appeared to her father and stepmother, she could be socially naïve, maladroit, and imperious. She had been effusively negative about Westtown during her college interview when she was apparently asked to explain her school's less than completely positive recommendation. Gregory's assessment was that Nancy had displaced her distrust of her mother onto Westtown's Dean of Girls, who had in turn disliked her, but the result of Nancy's foolish arrogance in having applied nowhere else was that she had no university place for the autumn. Gregory and Peg spent hopeful but anxious weeks looking at other colleges that might at this late date be willing to accept an academically gifted student. The search coupled with Nancy's distress was wearing.[51]

On his return from the American Psychiatric Association in Detroit in May Gregory and Mailloux signed the official papers incorporating the Aquinas Foundation, everything having been put in order with the help of Howard Seitz, a Catholic lawyer whom the nominally Catholic Marshall Field had recommended. As one of the foundation's first acts, Gregory arranged for Mailloux's student André Lussier to go to London with the hope of studying with Anna Freud. Mailloux had agreed on a provisional year, but Gregory didn't hesitate to tell Lussier, albeit with a wink, that one year wouldn't be enough if he were accepted – as indeed he would be, on Gregory's recommendation – by Anna Freud.[52]

In early June Gregory delivered the commencement address at Westtown. Reflecting on Christ's admonition that we should strive to be like little children if we would attain the kingdom of heaven, he asked Nancy's graduating class, 'What is it that the adult in his spiritual frailty ought to learn from the child's alleged spiritual strength?' Although he related the story of John's hernia impersonally, Gregory declared that the answer had come to him unexpectedly through his son: 'The striking and almost awesome thing about it all was the sweet simplicity and serenity of the baby between the fits of pain and crying.' As a scientifically trained observer in 'medical psychology', Gregory had noticed, 'Here was resignation that was not weakness; here was acceptance with no self-pity'; the 'little boy' had not been 'self-righteous' but 'humble in his very vitality, and strong in his frailty before life and nature', simple, direct, emotionally honest, 'great in his very littleness'. Gregory explained that the 'gigantic yet humble struggle for life in a non-hating human being' had revealed to him Christ's wise intuition as 'a great moral truth, a great religious truth and a great scientific truth' all in one. Consciously or unconsciously, Gregory in this address gave witness of his conversion, his spiritual embrace of the truth 'beyond understanding'.[53]

What to do about this spiritual embrace couldn't be immediately settled in the summer of 1950, which was taken up with other matters large and small. In early July Gregory underwent an operation on his maxillary bone to correct a problem probably connected to earlier dental interventions. While he wasn't incapacitated, the considerable pain didn't make thinking very easy. He had been obliged to fire a secretary he had found noisy, inefficient, and 'mannerless', and despite Peg's continuing serenity, he was anxious about the war on the Korean peninsula, where a United Nations force consisting almost entirely of U.S. military personnel would soon be deployed.

Additionally, Gregory had decided to go to Europe after all, although he would put off his departure until the end of August. He had resisted Sigerist's suggestion that he participate in a medical history symposium Genevieve was organising in Pura as well as in a large conference on the History of Medicine and the Sciences in Amsterdam, but he wanted very much to attend a meeting of the World Federation of Mental Health and had been unable to refuse Père Gabriel-Marie Piprot d'Alleaume's invitation to speak at the World Congress of Criminology in Paris. An activist who had worked with the resistance to save Jews and who was now devoting his energies to international penal reform, the French Dominican was the honorary secretary general of the International Society of Criminology and wanted to involve psychiatrists in improving incarceration and social reintegration. These were matters of genuine interest to Gregory, who knew of Piprot not only through his own professional work but through Mailloux.[54]

Family, however, held Gregory in the United States throughout most of the summer. John was baptised in Bedford at the end of July, a festive event less formal than Caroline's baptism two years earlier. There was another large reception following the ceremony, but this time the godparents included two of Peg's friends who were completely independent of her relationship with Gregory: Mary-Alice Hunter and Harold Turner. The third godparent was Hal Babcock, who came down with his family from Providence. Louise and Margo drove over from Bronxville with Lou and his fiancée Nancy Ritch, and George and Jodie came from Lakeville, Connecticut, where George had begun teaching at the Hotchkiss School. Bettine Goodall with her daughter and Mary and Eddie with Stephen, David, and Daphne were also among the guests at the church service and at the house afterwards, where the party on the terrace spilled out onto the lawn in the summer sunshine.

Much as Gregory was a presence in Bedford over the summer, he was distracted. As the symposium took place in Pura, he sent his warmest regards to all the participants – particularly, he joked to Sigerist, to those he knew personally – but when Mailloux visited New York in early August, Gregory shared his spiritual concerns. He was deeply disturbed by religious feelings with personal as well as professional implications, but he was also upset at the thought of remaining unchurched. Mailloux, who now made plans to accompany him to Europe, felt the time had come to regularise a situation he understood as 'quelque peu difficile', but he was confident that, if Gregory joined the Catholic Church, he would arrive at the 'paix complète' he craved. In mid-August Gregory went to Montreal to continue their discussion of the matter he wanted to keep as private as possible. Both men likely thought they could see a relatively clear path ahead by the time they boarded the plane.[55]

Before Gregory left there were quiet moments in Bedford where, once the children had been trundled off to bed, he could have opened his heart to Peg, but he may not have been fully frank with her or even with himself. His desire for privacy wasn't only a matter of principle, a matter of wanting to keep his religious life, like his divorce and marriage four years earlier, out of gossip columns and the dinner table conversations of sceptical colleagues. Above all he wanted to keep the matter private because he wanted to protect his family, his serene Episcopal wife and the two children so recently baptised into her church. His embracing Catholicism would have an impact on them, and while exactly what that impact might be was vague, he didn't want Peg to worry about it; he himself didn't want to worry about it. Much that might have been said probably wasn't in the flurry of packing that followed his return from Montreal: It was not only Gregory's suitcases that needed to be prepared but bags for Peg and the children, who would in his absence join Louise and Margo, Lou and Nancy, and Harold and Virginia with little Louise for a week on Columbia Lake in the small Connecticut resort where the Stone family had often spent their summer holidays.

Gregory's spiritual concerns coloured his weeks abroad, but he had much else on his mind from worldwide mental health to penal reform. Whatever his future relationship with Catholicism, he would continue to be himself. He wanted to go to Paris concerts, to the opera and the theatre. Much as he abhorred large, crowded meetings, he would enjoy talking with colleagues over drinks in the capital's brasseries; he looked forward to meeting Mailloux's fellow Dominicans. Needless to say, he also wanted to eat at those restaurants he and Sigerist listed in their notebooks, and he wanted to see his old friend.

Having apparently slept well on their first-class flight, Gregory and Mailloux met with Père Piprot soon after landing in Paris on 26 August. What had seemed 'quelque peu difficile' to Mailloux seemed a good deal more difficult to Piprot, and he began to spell out the complicated impediments to Catholic baptism. If Gregory truly wished to pursue the matter, steps would need to be taken to resolve or at least explain a number of specific issues. First, Gregory had been married to a fellow Jew, with whom he had two children, and that marriage had ended in a civil but not a religious divorce. Second, he had married again, in a ceremony at once civil and Protestant, to a woman who was a Christian but not a Catholic. Third, his current wife had no intention of converting. Fourth, together they had two children and hoped to have more. To Piprot, it seemed clear that nothing was clear – not Gregory's current married state or any future married state or the future status of the children so recently baptised in the Episcopal Church or the children he still hoped to have. It wasn't even clear to him that Gregory was committed. Piprot was encouraging – the obstacles seemed to him significant but finally technical matters involving ecclesiastic law – while Gregory's struggle was a matter of the heart, a matter of faith and spiritual longing.

Undaunted by the complications Piprot so carefully enumerated, Gregory flew to Geneva. Mailloux would investigate what exactly Gregory might write to clarify his situation, what he might do to regularise all those elements in his life that, as Piprot pointed out, were manifestly irregular, what documents might be required, and what routes might be taken in New York or Montreal or Paris or Rome. For his part, Gregory put aside Church law, precedent, and practice as well as his own spiritual unease for 24 hours. Sigerist met him at the airport with his daughter Erica, now working for the World Health Organization, who drove them around the city and lent them her flat for the day. In her small kitchen the friends prepared an elegant *canard aux olives noires*, which they ate with a delicious red Neuchâtel, but it seems unlikely Gregory bared his soul over the duck or even over the wine.[56]

On returning to the French capital, Gregory, as a representative of the American Psychoanalytic Association and consultant to the United Nations, addressed the plenary session of the annual meeting of the World Federation for Mental Health on 'Authority and Leadership'. He didn't feel well, diagnosed mild flu, and spent at least one afternoon in bed, but there were people to see and speeches to listen to as well as evenings out and about – Paris was, after all, still Paris. Despite being under the weather and not the director of the ballet that now swirled around him, Gregory was at least an active participant in the rich cultural life of the city of lights. He attended a Bach concert at the Église Saint-François-Xavier and saw Mussorgsky's *Boris Godunov* at the Théatre National de l'Opéra and Paul Claudel's *L'Otage* at the Comédie Française, and when the international meeting concluded, Gregory joined Mailloux in Versailles at a conference on 'L'Ascèse Chrétienne et L'Homme Contemporain' ('Christian Asceticism and Modern Man') organised by the French Dominican Père Albert Plé. Sympathetic to psychoanalysis, Plé would be an important ally in the work that lay ahead, for at some point during their days together in Paris, Gregory told Mailloux that he wanted to join the Catholic Church.[57]

The moment of decision is impossible to pinpoint. His conversations with Mailloux and other Catholics, both priests and laymen, had contributed substantially to his understanding. Indeed, by the summer of 1950 he was well read and advanced in his study of Roman Catholic thought, but faith was not a matter of study and no one would have taken on the challenges Piprot had anticipated without spiritual commitment. The path towards Christianity in general had had its roots in Gregory's 'spiritual' convictions in Russia, while his approach to Catholicism in particular is evident, at least in retrospect, in his rejection of the flaccid American Protestantism of Link's *Return to Religion*. The warm welcome Gregory received in Montreal in 1946 was pivotal in his conversion as was his friendship with Mailloux, but Thomas Verner Moore's informal catechism had begun even before the short-lived appointment at Catholic University, and Gregory's openness to Catholicism had preceded those conversations. It is tempting to see Gregory's decision to join Jesse Holmes' Society of Friends in 1922 as an early step towards a church, but becoming a Quaker never meant to Gregory conversion to Christianity. Gregory had begun reading the New Testament soon after arriving in the United States, yet acquaintance with the Gospels had made him neither a believer nor a churchgoer. Until he could join the Catholic Church, he would be a Jew outside the Christian fold.[58]

Whatever the journey's beginning and however convoluted it had been, the decisive moment occurred during those late summer days in Paris. Gregory walked with Mailloux in Versailles' public gardens and talked at length over coffee in local brasseries and over wine at dinner. In the shadow of the Eiffel Tower Gregory met several times with Mailloux's fellow Dominicans at the monastery at Latour-Maubourg and at the Dominican seminary and library at Saulchoir south of the Luxembourg Gardens. When it became clear that Gregory had decided to go ahead, the wheels were set in motion for his conversion. Mailloux would manage the ecclesiastical side of the process. As soon as Gregory returned home in mid-September, he would need to tell Peg.[59]

Notes

1 GZ to HES, 30 October 1946; Neenan, 199.
2 'Wed This Week', *Bronxville Reporter*, 22 August 1946, np.
3 JZ to GZ, 10 September 1946.
4 GZ to Leon Kroll, 21 November 1947, Leon Kroll papers, Archives of American Art, Smithsonian Institution; GZ to HES, 30, 31 October 1946.
5 GZ to HES, 1, 21 November 1946.
6 GZ to HES, 16 December 1946.
7 GZ, 'Psychiatric Perspectives', 581.
8 GZ to HES, 3 March 1947; HES to GZ, 2 April 1947.
9 GZ, 'Henry Sigerist', 521, 527.
10 GZ, 'The Struggle', 526; GZ quoted in 'Love and Sex Confusion Cited', *Oakland Tribune*, 3 October 1947, 16.
11 HES to GZ, 11 August 1947; GZ, 'Ignorance', 208; MSZ to HES, 13 February 1948; NM to GZ, 26 September 1951.
12 MSZ to HES, 13 February 1948.
13 GZ to Goddard and Brigitta Lieberson, 5 January 1948, Vera Zorina Papers, Houghton Library, Harvard University; email from AZ, 25 July 2019.
14 GZ to HES, 20 January 1948.
15 MSZ to HES, 13 February 1948; MSZ to GZ, nd; Woolf, 36.

16 GZ to JZ, 1 March 1948, and to HES, 18 June 1948; MSZ to HES, 24 July 1948; MSZ, Dar interview.
17 GZ to HES, 18 June 1948; MSZ to HES, 24 July 1948.
18 'Weldwood Panelling', *Architectural Forum*, March 1949, 56.
19 GZ to HES, 18 June 1948; MSZ to HES, 13 February 1948.
20 HES to GZ and MSZ, 15 May, 24 June 1948; GZ to HES, 18 June 1948.
21 MSZ to HES, 24 July 1948.
22 GZ, 'American Sex Standards', 306, 307.
23 David G. Wright, 'Report of the Physician-in-Chief and Superintendent for the Year 1948', 20, 21.
24 GZ, 'Psychoanalysis and Religion', 49, 50.
25 GZ to HES, 19 January 1949; NM to unidentified friend, 6 February 1949, APD.
26 Sydney J. Harris, 'There Is Real Magic in *Death of a Salesman*', *Chicago Daily News*, 22 October 1949, np.
27 GZ, 'The Reciprocal Responsibilities', 80, 84, 86, 93; GZ to HES, 29 March 1949.
28 GZ to MSZ, 8 April 1949.
29 GZ to MSZ, 10 April 1949; Ernest Jones to GZ, 15 January 1940.
30 Anna Freud to GZ, 26 January 1940.
31 GZ to MSZ, 10 April 1949.
32 GZ to MSZ, 12 April 1949.
33 GZ to MSZ, 12, 20 April 1949.
34 GZ to MSZ, 20 April 1949.
35 GZ to MSZ, 20 April 1949.
36 GZ to MSZ, 21, 22 April 1949.
37 GZ, 'His Own Cook', 159.
38 GZ to MSZ, 25, 30 April 1949.
39 GZ to MSZ, 10 April, 2, 6 May 1949.
40 GZ to HES, 7 June 1949; GZ, 'Clinical Variants', 744.
41 GZ to HES, 7 June 1949; MSZ, Dar interview.
42 GZ to HES, 7, 23 June 1949.
43 Conference programme; Maddox, 258.
44 HES to MSZ, 31 August 1949; GZ to HES, c. August 1949.
45 GZ to HES, c. August 1949.
46 GZ to NM, 20 November 1949.
47 GZ to HES, 14 February 1950; HES to GZ, 15 March 1950.
48 GZ to HES, 7 March 1950; NM to GZ, 13 March 1950.
49 GZ to HES, 31 March 1950; GZ to JZ and EZ, 21 January 1952.
50 GZ to HES, 31 March 1950.
51 GZ to HES, 7 July 1950.
52 Lussier, np.
53 GZ, 'Commencement Address', 8, 9.
54 HES to GZ, 21 January, 15 March 1950; GZ to NM, 6 July 1950; GZ to HES, 14 February, 7, 31 March, 7 July 1950.
55 GZ to HES, 1 August 1950; NM to GZ, 9 August 1950.
56 HES to GZ, 27 July, 7 August 1950; GZ to HES, 11 August 1950; GZ, 'His Own Cook', 158.
57 GZ to HES, 29 December 1950; André Godin to NM, 19 November 1950, APD.
58 Mailloux, 3.
59 André Godin to NM, 19 November 1950, APD.

Chapter 6

Peace and prosperity
1950–1953

Peg would not have been completely surprised by her husband's decision. They had, after all, discussed God together from the start, and she was aware of his friendship with Mailloux and his high regard for the Dominican order, but Gregory's personal and professional relationships with Catholic prelates hadn't involved her. She apparently wasn't jealous of these significant others in Gregory's life and respected Gregory's choice although she didn't share it. With her vague and unreflective understanding of the finer points of Christian dogma and practice, she was merely glad he had made a decision and pleased his search was over: He would have his church and she would have hers. The important thing for her seems to have been simply that his God was the same tripartite deity who was love and wanted everyone to be good and kind, who was forgiving when people weren't good, and sad when they didn't at least appear kind. Gregory must have confided in her, but he also probably shielded her from the difficulties that would follow. He would keep her informed, but his spiritual life was ultimately deeply personal, and the woman he loved and admired, who was serene as he had never been able to be, would be unable to share it intellectually or emotionally.[1]

Gregory's homecoming in mid-September was joyful: He was amazed by the children's charm and health, and found Peg thriving, working hard to make family life rich and calm. In his office, however, he was overwhelmed by 'a maze of papers' and reported wistfully to Sigerist that he was drowning in work 'without any hope of having a little chat with a friend'. Until the cooler weather set in, the family stayed in the country and Gregory commuted. He wasn't in town to welcome Mailloux, who had remained in Paris for an additional week, but arranged for Bettine Goodall and Eldridge Bruce to dine with him before his onward flight to Montreal.

Sensing she would benefit from the kind Dominican's Catholic affirmation, Gregory had apparently mentioned to Mailloux the difficulties Bettine was facing. Her relationship with Bruce was complicated and challenged conventional boundaries of class and race as well as posing several practical problems. She had met him when he visited his mother, her daughter's nurse. A psychology student at Howard University, Bruce was the son of a man newspapers described as 'a negro elevator operator' from a background completely different from Bettine's, whom

DOI: 10.4324/9781003190974-6

tabloids denominated an 'heiress', the 'brunette daughter of Financier-Publisher Marshall Field III'. Uncomfortable in America, the high-profile interracial couple was considering going abroad, but Bettine's ex-husband was now contesting her custody of their daughter. Like Gregory, Bettine and Eldridge's personal problems set the heart against public perceptions as well as legal exigencies, and although their labyrinth was less complex, it was no less emotionally difficult. Dinner with the Canadian priest must have been an encouraging experience.[2]

Mailloux had missed Gregory after his departure, and as both men resumed their separate lives, they communicated frequently. With sincere admiration, Mailloux thanked Gregory for having introduced him to Bettine, whom he liked very much, and felt she already owed Gregory a great deal for all he had done for her as a psychoanalyst and friend. As Mailloux set to work behind the scenes to sort out the complexities of Gregory's entry into the Church, he thought of Gregory in his daily prayers as his 'meilleur ami'.[3]

On the practical front, Mailloux contacted the Belgian-born Jesuit theologian André Godin who, while studying for an advanced degree in psychology at Fordham University, soon began a training analysis with Gregory. As Mailloux's 'man on the ground', Godin would look into how best to tackle the complexities that lay ahead. Because Gregory lived in New York, he should have gone through local channels, beginning with his parish priest. Mailloux's strategy was to ask Godin to recommend a fellow Jesuit with some connection to the chancery of New York – and thus a connection with the archbishop of New York – to ask for the application of the Pauline privilege. This special dispensation allows the dissolution of a marriage between two unbaptised people when one of the partners wishes to be baptised while the other does not and leaves the marriage because of religious differences. Although Ray's failure to understand Gregory's broad spiritual concerns was certainly one of many disparities that separated them, even if he could have convinced her to help him, he hesitated to ask her to sign a document attesting to such a patent untruth. Mailloux may actually have failed to understand the dynamics of both Gregory's marriage to Ray and subsequent marriage to Peg, but his formal representation of Gregory's first marriage was at least politically expedient in the petition he set about preparing.[4]

As trustees of the Aquinas Fund – which in October offered Louis Reik at Butler Hospital an annual stipend for two years of $2,500 ($24,000 today) to continue his research and his own psychoanalysis – Gregory and Mailloux had in addition to the ecclesiastical machinations a good deal of business to discuss, but their correspondence was rooted in Gregory's spiritual life. Acknowledging that many people saw him as incapable of the humility he sincerely felt, Gregory recognised he often didn't appear to others as the man he felt he really was. Conscious of his foibles, he felt undeserving of the high regard Mailloux had for him yet eager to accomplish what he saw as his duty and his aspiration. Despite burdensome responsibilities throughout the autumn, he was doing 'a little studying' of Catholic thought and hoped to do more.[5]

Family was part of what made Gregory so busy in the autumn of 1950. When Nancy, who had begun at the University of Minnesota, came down with chicken pox, Gregory and Peg dropped everything and went out to see her. She would manage to catch up with her studies, but she wasn't happy and hoped to transfer to Radcliffe at the end of the year. Both her father and stepmother would continue to worry about her. Commitments beyond New York also claimed Gregory's attention and he was frequently away from home, lecturing occasionally and travelling twice a month to Butler Hospital. His teaching and supervision there involved hard work, but he thoroughly enjoyed the stimulating community. Staying with Babcock and his young family was a particular pleasure, and in November Peg accompanied him to Providence for a formal dinner for the hospital staff. On the elegant menu reflecting the festive spirit of the occasion Gregory was listed as 'Chef de Cuisine'. A world away from the pressures of his office and hectic city life, Gregory was once more in his element, 'chef' in all senses, master of the ballet corps.

He was not, however, in charge of the increasingly complicated ecclesiastical matters. Godin, who doubted Gregory's conversion could be kept secret, suggested to Mailloux that the Jesuit priest Thomas E. Henneberry, the provincial of New York, might be an appropriate intermediary, but if Henneberry couldn't be sure of complete confidentiality, Godin proposed taking up the question in Rome, where he planned to be early in 1951. In December Henneberry discussed the problem with Monsignor James Kelly, an official in the New York City archdiocese and an expert in canon law. They felt it would be very difficult to maintain secrecy because of the testimonials required to annul Gregory's first marriage and allow a second (that is, to Peg) within the Church. Sworn depositions were required from Gregory's and Ray's families as well as from Ray herself to confirm that neither he nor she was baptised at the time of their marriage in 1919. Further, Gregory would need to appear personally at the chancery to request the Pauline privilege. To complicate matters, the Church would be unable to consider the case until after Gregory had been baptised.[6]

Gregory faced a sort of Catch-22: Until he was received into the Church, his first marriage couldn't be dissolved. The entire question of the validity of his marriage to Peg and the status of their children thus hung in the balance: Since baptism had to occur before his petition could go to Rome, he would need to abide by the Church's rules and refrain from sexual relations with Peg during the period between baptism and his receiving the Pauline privilege – and possibly, in the case of Rome's refusal, for the rest of his life. In good conscience, Gregory obviously felt that this was not something that he could do. If Peg had been Catholic, the privilege would almost certainly have been granted, but since she was Episcopalian, an 'Anglican', one simply couldn't know what Rome might decide. Confidentiality remained a concern as well, although by mid-December Henneberry felt that if Ray and her family attested to her unbaptised state, then Gregory might be able to avoid seeking testimonials from his family; it might be sufficient to get attestations merely from Mailloux and Bartemeier, whom Gregory had taken into his confidence.[7]

Before Christmas, Gregory went to Montreal to discuss the problem face to face with Mailloux for the first time since Paris. He couldn't see involving Ray much less her family in his conversion, and news from Mexico only confirmed his desire to keep his private life private. Fera, who had recently visited James, reported that Anna had become hard of hearing, a debility that made things even more difficult for Basia. Gregory tried to be sympathetic: He found their mother's 'condition and manner of living' at once sad and natural, since the 'business of leaving this world peacefully and graciously' simply wasn't something her generation had prepared for. He also pitied Basia who, like Anna, seemed 'unable to accept the end without endless protests', and even in its least attractive aspects, he found the situation 'heart-breaking'. Reading between the lines of letters from James, Gregory pressed Fera only to discover she was sending Anna as much as $20 a month, an amount that staggered him as he considered the economical life Fera was compelled to lead. He let off steam to James, who in the relatively stable economy of post-war Mexico had finally begun to build a house in Cuernavaca. Although Fera hadn't complained, Gregory had no doubt that her contribution strained her limited finances. Even though he was now supporting two families, Gregory was still sending their mother over $100 every month. When Fera admitted that James was contributing less than $10 a month, Gregory had been puzzled and embarrassed. He told his brother, 'This is something that should hurt our respective consciences, yours and mine.' It must have been a relief to Gregory to spend a calm Christmas and his 60th birthday with Peg and the children in Bedford.

Gregory Zilboorg by Ivan Opffer

At the beginning of 1951, looking forward rather than back, Gregory put aside the idea of writing up the Gimbel lectures and focused on finishing the book on Freud. A sketch in February, sent to Gregory as an affectionate gesture from the Danish-born artist Ivan Opffer, shows a pensive, even contemplative man, sceptical, reflective, absorbed in whatever he is reading or writing out of the portrait frame – a far cry from the engaged performer or sharp-witted teacher, not the charismatic conversationalist or even the family man caught or posing in family snapshots.[8]

In late February Gregory took time off and, with Peg, made a brief trip to California to see Sam and Portia Hume and Bill Barrett. The milder weather was also an attraction, but he simply needed a break that had nothing to do with weighty professional and spiritual matters. The Gimbel lectures had offered him a West Coast network less internecine than the closed world of the New York Psychoanalytic Society from whose history and practice Gregory had resolved to disengage himself. The academic post he had imagined as his calling would never materialise, but year after year he had cobbled together teaching appointments and one-off lectures that kept him travelling at an exhausting pace with itineraries that now included not only Montreal but London, Paris, Geneva, and Milan. The California sojourn was, like the quiet Christmas, a halcyon moment away from the fray that was Gregory's daily life.

Back in New York he addressed the Group Forum on 'Crime and Punishment in Present Day Society' and spoke at the New York Academy of Medicine against 'dianetics', the psychological theory proposed by the science-fiction writer L. Ron Hubbard, the founder of Scientology, whose book of that name had just appeared, but Gregory's attention was distracted by larger issues. In Korea in March, United Nations troops recaptured Seoul for a second time, while at the end of the month *The King and I*, Rodgers and Hammerstein's romantic musical set in colonial Siam, opened on Broadway apparently without any sense of irony. On 29 March Ethel and Julius Rosenberg were convicted of espionage in a sensational case that dominated the headlines and intensified both anti-socialist and anti-Semitic feelings throughout the country. The spring of 1951 wasn't a comfortable time for the former revolutionary whose views of war and art and history as well as justice and mercy gave him a perspective different from that of most Americans. Gregory told Sigerist that the winter had been 'very hard and busy', filled with 'many anxieties', but he had nevertheless succeeded in completing a draft of his monograph on Freud.[9]

In *Sigmund Freud: His Exploration of the Mind of Man*, Gregory set out to historicise the founder of psychoanalysis while explaining his theories and practices for interested non-specialists. Since conventional biographies and accounts of the development of his theories had already been offered 'many times by Freud himself, his pupils, friends and enemies', Gregory declared he wouldn't review either in detail or chronologically Freud's major works; he would instead clarify psychoanalytic concepts (the unconscious, life and death instincts, libido theory, narcissism, fixation, and the return of the repressed) and the psychoanalytic method (whose intuitive 'special means', he admitted, were difficult to define but which were nevertheless scientific, 'definable, usable, teachable and verifiable'). Perhaps unsurprisingly, however, at this point in his life Gregory would struggle to focus on the task he set for himself and to limit his explanations to the id, ego, and superego and the workings of the psychoanalyst's trained intuition.

The resulting book of 132 pages is at once erudite and wide-ranging, historical and contemporary, idiosyncratic and revealing. In seven untitled chapters, Gregory digressed freely. Occasionally he seemed conscious of having a difficult time staying on message. Chapter 2, a scant five pages in length, began 'Let us remember'. Chapter 3, 27 pages long, concluded, 'Let us now return to Freud himself.' Chapter 5, a relatively short nine pages, concentrated primarily on artists, intellectuals, and especially writers (from Dostoyevsky and Guy de Maupassant through Proust, Joyce, and D.H. Lawrence to Thomas Mann and Stefan Zweig) who used Freudian ideas 'intuitively and unconsciously'. Gregory devoted seven pages in the third chapter to a discussion of the English polymath Francis Galton's self-examination in 'Psychometric Experiments', an 1879 article he acknowledged Freud probably never read, in order to make the significant point that, although only Freud developed psychoanalytic theories and methods, late nineteenth-century scientists, among whom Gregory placed Freud, were methodically examining the mind. In the same chapter Gregory argued against a number of those who rejected or diverged from Freud (including Pierre Janet, Alfred Adler, and Carl Jung), contending they had misunderstood the great man, while much of what might have gone into the book about the problem of sex – had Gregory ever written it – ended up in Chapter 4 in his discussion of the psychoanalytic understanding of sexuality.

Although many readers might have expected a short biography and precise explanations of popularised Freudian concepts, Gregory not only digressed but abbreviated, declaring it wasn't necessary, for example, 'to dwell on the details of Freud's conception of the Oedipus complex'; what mattered was 'Freud's discovery that the psychosexual development of man (and woman) was diphasic'. Readers might have been confused as well as frustrated by the time, midway through the book, Gregory stated that what 'Freud actually pleaded for' was 'tolerance and charity', that 'loving a child means to allow him to live his child's life fully and honestly in an atmosphere of the special security that only true human love can offer', and that 'love of one's neighbour, as well as true adult parental love, is impossible' without having attained the 'genital level' of psychosexual development and thus the capacity for 'the love which Christ preached'.

In the book's second half Gregory's attention shifted to where it had been drifting from the start: the issue of psychoanalysis and religious faith. Freud had erred when he equated the superego and conscience. In fact, Freud's scientific theories supported Christian doctrine 'without injury or injustice'. Citing many 'truly religious people' who were also scientists and even psychoanalysts, Gregory concluded by quoting from Karl Stern's autobiography, whose page proofs the author had sent him in January. Taking a long-range view of 'the history of the human spirit', Stern had asserted that psychoanalysis reaffirmed and enriched 'the Christian idea of Man' because it had 'rediscovered the primary position of love'.[10]

Reviewers would be, in the main, generous. Calling Gregory 'one of the country's most famous psychoanalysts' and praising the book as 'lucid and unhampered by jargon', the anonymous critic in the *Kirkus Review* nevertheless noted the author's failure to organise his material into 'well-defined sections' and conceded that, even as the book succeeded as 'a study of a man of genius in relation to his era', a 'certain amount of prior knowledge of the subject on the part of the reader is assumed'. While praising the author's common sense and erudition, David

Goldknopf in the *New Republic* similarly noted that the book seemed in places to be organised 'along free-associational lines'. Patrick Mullahy in the *Saturday Review of Literature* was unconvinced of the genuine rapprochement between psychoanalysis and religion and sceptical about squaring Freud with Christianity, arguing that the author resorted to 'vague metaphor and unverifiable analogy' on crucial points, although he remained impressed with Gregory's 'rhetorical skill' and 'comprehensive knowledge of classical psychoanalytic theory and practice'.

Reviewers who knew Gregory well were kinder. Barrett asserted that because the book's 'approach' was 'from the level of meaning rather than content', it would be of real interest to psychoanalysts since 'the historical perspectives are developed with fine scholarship' while 'the author's gift for reaching to the core of significance in Freud's discoveries' gave the book 'great vigor'. Barrett made clear, however, that Gregory's treatment of his subject led inevitably to his consideration of 'the relationship between psychoanalysis and the problems of value, faith and religion'. Bartemeier was kinder still. In his review in the *New York Herald Tribune* he recommended the book as 'a successful condensation of what Freud and psychoanalysis are all about' whose 'fresh' perspective was particularly 'valuable and inspiring' since it was written with 'both knowledge and faith'.[11]

Yet knowledge and faith were at loggerheads in the book not because psychoanalysis and religion were incompatible but because Gregory was struggling to come out as a Catholic psychoanalyst at the same time that he was struggling to enter the Church. As the book's flaws illustrated what Gregory himself must have recognised as his confused sense of purpose, both matters weighed heavily on his mind and heart.

Home life continued to offer him affirmation and comfort. As he prepared a talk on 'Love and Hate in Health and Disease' for the Rhode Island Society for Mental Hygiene at the end of April, Donna Maria gave birth to seven poodle puppies, an unmitigated joy in the New York apartment. A wooden board at the master bathroom doorsill kept them from invading the bedroom while newspaper on the tiled floor addressed the inevitable mess. Gregory and Peg simply needed to tread carefully. Three would be sold, three would be given away, and one of the females would be kept. Bill Barrett took 'Martini', a name likely chosen in consultation with Peg, while Lillian Hellman took an assertive male she denominated 'Gregory'. With her parents' permission Caroline selected the quietest female as the one the family should keep and named her simply and conventionally 'Sally'. If it had been completely up to Gregory and his heart, he would have kept them all.

But it was not Gregory's heart that dictated his life in the spring of 1951. His professional responsibilities took him hither and yon, and he wouldn't even be able to celebrate Peg's birthday with her and the children in New York. In early May he was in Cincinnati for the annual joint meetings of the American Psychoanalytic and American Psychiatric Associations, where he participated in a panel addressing 'Problems of Etiology'. Among the 12 discussants was Franz Alexander, but the psychoanalysts on the podium were seated from left to right in alphabetical order, so Gregory neatly avoided proximity to the man he still held responsible for the confrontation with the New York Psychoanalytic Society a decade earlier. With Frieda Fromm-Reichmann, Gregory was also a discussant for Florence Powdermaker's 'Considerations in the Psychotherapy of the Schizoid Patient', but he left the conference early to fly to Montreal. Meeting with Howard Seitz, Gregory and Mailloux wanted to set up an institute for the study of human relations in Paris to involve lay people and Dominicans. As they began to tackle the legal and financial details, the complicated project seemed costly; despite reservations, however, the three men still hoped the project, particularly dear to Mailloux, might be realised.[12]

Gregory did manage to be in New York for Caroline's third birthday, then took the family with him for a celebratory weekend in Providence where, following Wright's resignation, Babcock had been appointed acting superintendent of Butler Hospital. The men were eager to discuss Gregory's newest idea: the establishment at Butler of a research library. Peg and Hal's wife Fran, who had become good friends, looked after Johnny and baby Kent as the two older Babcock children took Caroline in tow, romping upstairs and down in the family's large house. Although Gregory had the galleys of his book in his briefcase, he managed to put work aside on Saturday night and took over the Babcocks' kitchen. The general joy continued even as he waited with Peg and the children for the Sunday train back to New York.

Josie Babcock, Hal Babcock, Caroline, and Gregory, holding his own overcoat and Peg's fur stole so she could take the picture at the Providence train station, 20 May 1951

At the end of the month Gregory and Peg attended the Broadway opening of Hellman's new play. More a Chekhovian drama of dysfunctionality than social commentary, *The Autumn Garden* received mixed reviews, and neither the author nor the audience seemed to care much for any of its unhappy characters. Indeed, Lillian's feelings were elsewhere as spring turned to summer. Her interest in the Soviet Union had made her generally suspect, but it was Hammett who was now drawing the attention of various government committees and agencies. Gregory would visit Mailloux in Montreal before setting off for seven weeks in Europe in mid-July, but by then Dash was in jail. Summoned before a New York judge to testify about his work with the Civil Rights Congress, he had repeatedly pled the Fifth Amendment, neither incriminating nor exonerating himself and refusing to 'name names'. Found in contempt of court, he was sentenced to six months in a federal penitentiary.

Gregory's summer would be a heady combination of business and pleasure. Having missed her so much on previous trips, Gregory had persuaded Peg to accompany him and, knowing how busy he would often be, in an act of typical magnanimity he had invited her mother to join them. This would be the first time he would travel to Europe with Peg, the first time he would be able to share with her the European experiences too vivid even for his vivid letters. For Louise, who had never been abroad, the trip was a dream realised, and her unsophisticated enthusiasm would make her a charming and often amusing traveller. As soon as they boarded the sumptuous *Île de France*, however, Gregory and Peg missed Caroline and John, sequestered in Bedford with Betty and Hilda (now known by Caroline's diminutive 'Lala') as well as Gregory's kind research secretary Valerie Reich and visited serially by Margo and Lou's wife Nancy, all of whom, in their different voices, would report on the children's good health and country activities.

Gregory wouldn't, however, miss the bitter xenophobia of the United States, and he had left Mailloux the unenviable chore of drafting the official account of his spiritual journey, a personal and political document sincere in its purpose and ostensibly correct in its details but whose careful wording would present the best possible case for Gregory's baptism. Having witnessed the evolution of Gregory's religious life, Mailloux began by stating that Gregory had wanted to become a Catholic for a long time and now wanted to be baptised as soon as possible. They had hesitated to take the necessary official steps because of the extreme complexity of the situation, but well-known church leaders and several prudent men had advised them to take the case directly to Rome, and this they were now proposing to do.

Mailloux explained in terms as simple and straightforward as he could manage: Gregory was a Jew. He had married a Jew and had two children. The wife had asked for and obtained a divorce in a U.S. court. Gregory had subsequently married a devout and practicing High Anglican. They had two children. Mailloux's impression was that his present wife would soon follow Gregory into the Catholic Church; in any case she didn't object to his conversion and would put no obstacle in his way. Specifically, Mailloux hoped the Pauline privilege could be applied to the first marriage, 'thus opening the possibility to obtain the necessary dispensation for the validation of the second'. The first wife was never baptised and in fact had very hostile feelings towards the Catholic Church. Mailloux 'personally' remembered that when Gregory first began to show sympathy towards the Church, Ray thought he was going crazy:

> I am practically certain that these divergences of opinion between the partners towards religion and morality was the principal reason which led to their separation. This profoundly materialistic woman didn't want to accept a husband whom she judged to be very idealistic because he was spending his time doing something other than earning money.

Mailloux next moved on to describing Gregory's 'true' and exemplary character. Gregory had shown unflagging 'charité' towards the mentally ill. He had given unstintingly of his time and care, especially when their mental condition had provoked crises of a moral or religious nature. He was a doctor very sought after by a rich clientele, but Mailloux was 'personally' aware he had also conscientiously extended his help to those without means. He often faced complex moral problems in his work, but each time he had felt a spiritual doubt, he had consulted Mailloux. Gregory had even helped young Catholic students reconcile their faith with their pursuit of science. Mailloux declared that Gregory's *History of Medical Psychology* was a classic used in all medical schools and that *Mind, Medicine, and Man* was in part an effort to reconcile the thinking of Thomas Aquinas with psychoanalysis. Since 1944 Gregory had given himself to the serious study of Christian and specifically Thomistic thought and to incorporating these principles into his psychoanalytic thinking. He had courageously defended Catholic ideas in his professional life in the face of criticism. Indeed, his Catholic convictions had compromised his professional life. Mailloux (again 'personally') had witnessed Gregory's particularly courageous acts in various circumstances.

Convinced that premature publicity would provoke an angry reaction, Mailloux finally came to the matter of discretion. In his opinion it would be best if Gregory's conversion and baptism could be accomplished privately. Gregory had already attracted criticism on account of his Catholic sympathies, attacks on his prestige often rooted, Mailloux contended, in professional jealousy. Gregory's contemporaries realised he was Catholic in his thought and in his heart. If they learned by gossip and hearsay that he had become a Catholic in fact, they would be further provoked.

Calling him 'mon ami très cher', Mailloux declared Gregory was very sincere and really hoped to serve the Church to the degree he was able in both speech and writing. He was seeking with great humility to become a child of the Church, which he already loved with all the force of which he was capable. Mailloux knew Gregory had suffered because of the difficulties that had slowed his conversion; he had prayed for the conversion and would continue to do so. By the time

Gregory and his entourage reached Rome, Mailloux's heartfelt statement would be in the hands of Emmanuel Suarez, master general of the Dominican Order.[13]

There was, however, a great deal on Gregory's agenda before the group made it to Italy. Their 'grand tour' began in Paris. Peg and Louise visited the Champs de Mars for a view of the Tour Eiffel and admired the rose windows in Notre Dame and the views from Montmartre's Sacre Coeur, but Gregory, who may have accompanied them on some of their sightseeing, had more serious matters on his mind. He saw Jean Pinatel, the secretary general of the International Society for Criminology, and spent time with both Plé and Piprot, with whom he certainly discussed the document Mailloux was preparing on his behalf but also business. Specifically, the Aquinas Fund was considering underwriting the purchase of a five-room apartment at 34 Avenue des Champs-Elysées to accommodate the new Institut d'Études des Relations Humaines and hoped to provide salaries for Piprot as director and a secretary, and additional funds for scholarships, a library, and colloquia. There were a great many details still to be worked out.[14]

At the beginning of August the group spent three days in Copenhagen, where Louise marvelled at how little the Little Mermaid was, before going on to Stockholm and then Amsterdam for a meeting of the International Psycho-analytical Association. Gregory and Peg attended a welcoming reception at the Rijksmuseum hosted by the city of Amsterdam, and the following day Gregory was the third speaker in the opening session, addressing his international colleagues on 'Clinical and Technical Aspects of Free Association in the Light of Five Decades of Psychoanalysis'. The conference was a social as well as professional event, but while Gregory probably didn't take the dawn excursion to the Aalsmeer Flower Auction (where 'millions of flowers' were 'sold by a special electric device'), he may well have gone with Peg and Louise on the cruise along the Amstel or on the bus trip to The Hague, where he had spent so many difficult months after leaving Russia.[15]

As soon as the congress concluded, Gregory and his wife and mother-in-law headed south to Zurich, where they saw Bleuler and his family, before going on to Pura to visit Sigerist. Whatever the many reasons for Gregory's European trips, seeing old friends ranked high among them. Leaving their bags at the Albergo Paladina, the threesome spent a relaxing Saturday evening with Henry and Emmy. The basement of 'Casa Serena' featured a rather primitive stove and, by American standards, a rather primitive refrigerator and primitive sinks, but none of these physical difficulties dulled Henry's joy in his kitchen. On Sunday he cooked a copious breakfast for his guests, chatting all the while, then walked with them among the flowers in his garden before starting to make lunch. Indefatigable, he creamed the chicken with gusto and explained the virtues of various vinegars, olive oils, and butters. After the meal there was more good conversation in the living room about history, social issues, care of the ill, public health, music, theatre, photography ... and, of course, good cooking and good wine. Gregory and Henry then returned to the kitchen to begin the preparation for the main event: dinner.[16]

Emmy Sigerist, Gregory, Louise, and Peg, photographed by Sigerist at Lake Lugano, August 1951

Gregory must have been sad to leave, but on Monday morning in a car with a chauffeur, the group was driven through the mountains to Como, where they caught a train to Milan. Gregory had thoroughly enjoyed the cooking and the eating and all the talking, admired Henry's plate warmer that had kept the dishes at just the right temperature, and appreciated the local white wine. His spirits buoyed, when he wrote to thank him he asked if Henry could get him exactly such a plate warmer and, while he was at it, could he also get a case of the Merlot Bianco and ship both to the United States – requests a bit more onerous than the attractive paper clips he had asked Henry to ask his secretary to send him from Baltimore nearly 20 years earlier. For his part, Gregory wanted to buy Henry and Emmy tickets to the Russian ballet 'Les Sylphides' at Como's Teatro Sociale, but arriving just after noon, he found the box office closed, so he asked the chauffeur to get the tickets and post them along with 'an especially good automobile clock' like the 'Swiss beauty' he had discovered in the hire car. Trusting the man with a sum he expected would cover the tickets and the clock as well as the driver's time and effort, he hoped Henry would ask one of his friends going to New York to do him the favour of bringing the clock or, if no one Henry knew was planning on going to America in the near future, Henry could simply post the clock with duty payable in dollars on receipt. Such financial impulsivity, brazen directness, and cavalier presumption were typical of the man who was more sensitive, considerate, humble, and naïve than others thought. As often happens to God's fools, however, all turned out well: Henry received the tickets in time to see the ballet and, after several weeks, the clock, which had to be ordered, made its way to Gregory in time for Christmas. The good chauffeur turned out to be as trustworthy as Gregory had assumed and apparently no one involved felt insulted or put upon or even surprised.[17]

After several days of sightseeing in Milan, Florence, and Siena, the group pushed on to Rome. After more than a month abroad, they were beginning to feel a bit travel-worn, but Gregory wanted to share the splendours of this Catholic city that had so impressed him on previous visits, and he had arranged to see both Suarez and Pedro Maria Abellán, rector of the Pontifican Gregorian University. Mailloux's statement was by now in Suarez's hands and both priests would consider Gregory's situation carefully. Indeed, the case was so delicate and complicated they could offer no immediate advice but would communicate their opinions to Mailloux after due reflection. The days in Rome were inconclusive and unsettling. They all became ill with something 'digestive', and Peg was particularly uncomfortable in the 'merciless' heat. Conceding that Rome was a 'splendid city', she decided with uncharacteristic negativity that she had never liked it very much; if she ever returned, she would visit in December. Gregory surely understood that Peg's antipathy to the seat of Catholicism wasn't simply due to the weather, that her discomfort was not only physical but emotional.[18]

The last stop on their grand tour was London, where the summer was milder and Peg a good deal happier. They visited the National Gallery, observed the pigeons in Trafalgar Square so like those in Central Park, and marvelled at the grand façade of Saint-Martin's-in-the-Fields where there were no longer any fields. They saw Lillian, who had left for Europe immediately after Dash was sentenced, and went at least once to the theatre. Peg and Louise attended an Anglican church service, where they were gratified by the familiar prayers although disappointed that the hymns whose words they knew were sung to tunes they didn't recognise. Gregory went to mass on his own, as yet unbaptised but Catholic in his mind and heart as Mailloux had reported to Suarez. On the last day of August Gregory, Peg and Louise sailed from Southampton on the elegant *Liberté*.[19]

The respite of the transatlantic crossing was all too brief. The academic year that increasingly defined the rhythms of Gregory's life began in earnest almost as soon as he stepped off the boat. His autumn included a course of 15 lectures on social problems, values, morality, and will at the New School for Social Research in lower Manhattan and, as a visiting lecturer at the Washington-Baltimore Psychoanalytic Institute, ten two-hour Saturday sessions on 'Applied Psychoanalysis: The Spheres of Psychoanalytic Influence'. There would be few full weekends to spend with the family in Bedford, while in New York there were patients who had eagerly awaited his return. Although Gregory often mentioned to his correspondents that he was worn out by all the work he was doing, he was becoming aware that his fatigue had not only physical but psychological and spiritual roots. He had always taken on more work than was reasonable or healthy, had invariably felt the solution to any of his problems lay in working harder, but such a pattern of living wasn't only exhausting; it was ultimately insufficient and unsustainable. In a rare instance of raw confession, he told Mailloux, 'All I want is not to be tired. I am so weary, Father. I don't know what it is that is lacking, but there is an anxious weariness which disquiets me.'[20]

By October Mailloux had heard from Suarez, whose view of the situation was worrying. Doctrinally, Gregory's first marriage as a civil marriage between two Jews was a 'naturally valid marriage'. Despite the civil divorce, the first marriage hadn't been annulled by a competent religious authority, so the second marriage was, according to canon law, invalid. One possible way forward would be for the pope to annul the first marriage, a judgement that would open the way for the regularisation of the second. However, Gregory would need to be baptised before he could ask the pope to intercede. Furthermore, although Gregory might then ask for and be granted an annulment of his first marriage, Suarez thought it would be difficult to get permission to regularise his second marriage – that is, to remarry Peg within the Church – because Peg wasn't Catholic.[21]

Gregory made time in his busy life for a trip to Montreal. While conversion was the primary topic of his conversations with Mailloux, there were other matters they also needed to discuss. On his return from Europe Gregory had spoken at length with Seitz about various legal issues and practicalities. With so much money going towards Piprot's project, it would simply be impossible at this point for the Aquinas Fund to support the physical expansion of Mailloux's institute in Montreal. Gregory was deeply apologetic and Mailloux was disappointed, but no disagreement over the fund's management would separate the two men with more important things on their mind. Gregory trusted in their friendship, knew he could rely on what he called Mailloux's 'charitable understanding and generosity of spirit'. Expressing his frustration with the French psychoanalyst Henri Ey's apparent satisfaction with 'disindividualized generalities' in the recently published *Le Problème de la Psychogenèse des Névroses et des Psychoses*, Gregory made clear to the kind Dominican that it was always the particularity of the individual that mattered. Whatever their differences, Gregory would count on Mailloux as 'a wonderful friend, a wonderful priest, and a man of wisdom'.[22]

Gregory continued, however, to feel overburdened. He declared to Henry in November that at the 'terrific pace' things were going, he was again finding it difficult to keep up. While he and the family were all well, he bewailed that there was 'no time to be fully alive – to read – to think'. Despite his real distress, he retained his capacity for humour: Looking far ahead, he told Henry that he was planning to devote the entire summer of 1952 to his report on suicide 'which (report – not suicide)' was 'several years overdue'. Knowing he needed a break, when the opportunity arose to attend the congress of the World Federation for Mental Health in Mexico City in early December, Gregory jumped at the chance. Invariably extremely discreet about his Russian family, whom he would also see, he merely told Mailloux he would be going to Mexico 'more for a rest than to attend any meetings'.[23]

Gregory would attend the opening reception and speak at one morning session on 'Mental Health and Race Relations', and he must at least have had coffee or a drink with colleagues, but the week in Mexico was mostly taken up with family. James and Eugenia hosted a dinner to celebrate Gregory's arrival, and a luncheon at a restaurant included not only the two brothers and Eugenia but Eugenia's sister Vera Saitcevsky and Olga, now a vivacious young woman of 18 studying at the National Conservatory of Music. Less happy were the visits to see Anna and Basia. Gregory managed to sustain a degree of sympathy for his ailing mother, but as always he found the two women 'intractable, rigid, deeply sunk and set in their platitudinous devotion to food, sleep and complaints'. In the end, the congress was dull and the week not very restful nor even soothing. With the prospect of a relatively calm Christmas in Bedford, Gregory was happy to return to New York and his immediate family.[24]

The Christmas period turned out to be less calm than Gregory had hoped. While Nancy had indeed transferred to Radcliffe, where she seemed to be happy and thriving, Greg remained unsettled. Having left Lenox without having made friends or discovered anything he was particularly good at or enjoyed, he been living with Ray for the last two years and had yet to find consistent or gainful employment. The war in Korea, meanwhile, had become a stalemate on the 38th parallel where American military personnel made up 90 percent of the United Nations force attempting to hold the line. Rather than risk conscription into the army, many young Americans voluntarily enlisted in one of the military's other branches. As Nancy headed back to Radcliffe, Greg joined the Marines. By mid-January he was a private in basic training in Parris, South Carolina. A lifelong pacifist Gregory had mixed feelings about the military, but service during the Second World War had done Ingersoll good; Abe had flourished as a military surgeon. Greg would at least be getting up in the morning and following rules, doing what those in charge expected him to do, probably losing a bit of weight, perhaps even making friends.

The news from Mexico wasn't calming either. Eugenia's sister had gone into hospital for a hysterectomy, during which the surgeon had discovered an intestinal cancer. Six weeks earlier Vera and Gregory had chatted amiably; she had helped her sister at the dinner party, told him how impressed she was with Olga. Vera's sudden death two weeks into the new year shocked everyone. James informed Gregory melodramatically that they had suffered 'a tragedy' from which they would be unable to recover 'for some time' and wondered why the doctor had decided to operate, why he hadn't pursued radium treatment or some other course of action a medical man must have known about even if James did not.

Gregory was quick to respond. He, too, was surprised by Vera's death but more sanguine. He surely shared the news with Peg, and the letter he wrote suggests she once more did her editorial best to temper Gregory's response. His perspective, so at odds with his brother's worldview, was realistic, psychological, and philosophic, but rather than begin with intellectual or even exasperated explanation, his disquisition this time began with over-the-top commiseration: 'Peg and I are deeply grieved and share with you your sense of loss and desolation.'

Peg had never met Vera, and Gregory had only renewed his acquaintance with his brother's sister-in-law on his infrequent visits to Mexico, but Peg recognised condolence was what was called for and so condolence was what Gregory duly expressed.

The letter that followed wasn't insensitive, although it concerned not what James might have wanted to hear but what Gregory wanted to say as a medical man. He pointed out that physicians 'seldom get a word of true sympathy and an expression of true understanding of what we feel, and what we experience in our failures'. But after the 'need and effort to heal', a major part of doctors' human functioning was the understanding of the human weaknesses with which some of their failures were met. Gregory wrote on behalf of those called to the profession:

> we understand that anguish comes with bitterness on the part of those who are bereaved and do not understand. We don't reject that bitterness, we don't resent it: we accept it and by our acceptance we hope to teach a little to those who are bitter how to take life and death as they come with serenity – no matter how melancholy – and forbearance, no matter how pained.

As at Westtown, he then drew on his personal experience of Johnny's hernia, an incident that continued to carry great significance for him. He bared his soul to James with characteristic eloquence:

> when our little boy almost died at the age of twenty-one days and my dearest friend [Abe] operated on him at four o'clock in the morning, Peg knew, I knew, and the paediatrician knew, and the dear friend, the surgeon, knew that that might be the end – and if the end it was to be, we were ready to stand at respectful attention before the mystery of death as we stand at joyful attention at the miracles of living.

Gregory insisted that no doctor looks at a patient as a case;

> what really drives us, what sustains us in our work, what keeps us alive, is… *the person* behind the case, behind the operation. No one of us ever fails in that – if one did, one would drop out of the profession automatically. There is so much less work and more money in so many other things than medicine.

He reflected,

> No one in the outside world sees our grief or even our tears which we preserve and reserve to ourselves, and which we treat as our human weakness. We don't get angry or suspicious of the forces of nature. We just persevere and keep on keeping on without bitterness or reproach. And even one hour after we are hit in our professional faces by our patients who die and by their

relatives who live to reproach us, we go on to the next case which just as often as not might prove more difficult with even a more tragic outcome.

He concluded philosophically: 'We did not create the nature of man, and we will not change his mortal destiny.' To Olga, particularly upset by her aunt's death, he wrote more succinctly but also sincerely and generously in early February. Hoping she had recovered from the shock and could again look at the world 'with serenity and without anxiety', he once more made a philosophic point: 'Life is not what death makes it.'[25]

With his semesters finally over in both New York and Washington, Gregory spent the last weekend in January fulfilling his duties at Butler Hospital. In early February, for the first time since September, he spent a full weekend with his family in Bedford. He desperately needed a break and now planned a weeklong holiday in Cuba at the end of the month. Unlike his visits to Puerto Rico, this would be, to the degree it was possible for Gregory, a real vacation. He would take Peg and the children with him and, perhaps to make sure he didn't work, Eddie and Mary and little Daphne as well as Abe and Gertrude Kopsch, the nurse-receptionist in Abe's office who would soon become his wife. Daphne's nurse Maggie and Lala completed the entourage and took care of the children, especially during the balmy evenings when the adults relaxed on the hotel veranda as the moon rose over the pristine sea.

The holiday at Varadero Beach was a halcyon moment in a hectic and emotional year, but as soon as Gregory returned to the United States, he resumed his highly pressured life. In frequent contact with his brother who was struggling to regain his equilibrium, Gregory recounted a typical week: After a full day at the office on Monday 10 March, he flew to Providence for the dedication of the new library, then took a night train back to New York to start seeing patients at 8:15 am. On Tuesday night, after a 'tough' day's work, he flew to Detroit for two medical meetings, which didn't conclude until 11:30 pm on Wednesday. There was no transport back to New York at that hour, and much as he would have enjoyed a good night's sleep, he couldn't afford to lose 'a half day's or even a whole day's earnings', so he returned to the airport and caught a plane at 4:20 am on Thursday. He was home by 7:00 am, took his first patient at 8:15 am. Sleepy all day, he nevertheless worked until 11:30 pm. 'This is work, life, death', he told James in an attempt at consolation; 'It is fatiguing, exhausting at times, irritating – but there is nothing tragic in it.'[26]

In Mexico, however, one family 'tragedy' followed another. The gruelling week Gregory described culminated in a telephone call from Fera with the sad news that Anna's recent shortness of breath was due not to a heart condition but to lung cancer. Panicking, Basia had rung Fera and asked her to come to help. As irritating as Gregory could be, his siblings sought him out when they needed money, advice, emotional support, or – as now – intercession. Gregory immediately wrote to James. He insisted Fera wasn't in a position to leave home; she was 'a serious and hardworking person' who took her many obligations seriously. Sincerely sympathising with everyone, Gregory realised the situation was harder on his brother, who was present, than on him at a distance, but he also understood that it was especially hard on Basia 'with her life-long and chronic addiction to desperation'. The current situation, he told James, would require considerable 'authoritative management'; it would be necessary 'to take the situation as it is and do what is needed': 'Let us have plain, human courage and face the facts with the simplicity and the dignity which true laws of nature deserve.'[27]

While Gregory surmised that his mother would have several painful months ahead of her, Anna seemed relatively comfortable until the end of March, then declined rapidly. Basia nursed her as best she could, administering various drugs and oxygen, and James visited daily. On 5 April 1952, Anna died. Gregory received the news via a chain of phone calls from Basia to James to Fera to Peg, who reached him in Providence. Gregory probably rang Fera for whatever further details she could supply and to express his sympathy, then as soon as he returned to New York, he wrote James with great compassion, acknowledging the distress he knew his brother must be feeling. 'There are not', Gregory told him, 'many or any words to say about it.' He was sorry James had been exposed 'to the intensity of it all and to the gruesome anxiety which is so inevitable in such situations' and regretted being unable to alleviate his brother's 'inner burdens'. He concluded, 'Peg joins me in my thoughts as she always does. She shares with me, and therefore with you, the sadness and weight which burdens your hearts.'

On the same day Gregory wrote to Mailloux. The immediate reason was the receipt of a cheque he enclosed for $8,000 for the Aquinas Fund. He also reported that, as a result of his psychiatric testimony, a 30-year-old Catholic woman on trial for murder had avoided a death sentence. Between the lines in what Gregory didn't say was the impotence he must have felt as he witnessed from afar the decline and death of an 81-year-old Jewish woman whose life he couldn't save or even ameliorate either as a physician or a son. Finally mentioning his mother's death in this revealing letter, Gregory confessed, 'I am fatigued and saddened and my spirits are in mourning.'[28]

Struggling with grief in addition to his chronic melancholy, James was grateful for Gregory's kind words, yet felt their mother's death had 'created more problems than it solved' – that is, he told his brother, 'Basia, of course'. Her life had been 'completely wrecked by more than ten years of extremely trying ministrations to sick parents'; she was now 'entirely at loose ends'. James and Gregory might agree about her 'her lack of spiritual resources', but such concord resolved nothing, and Fera, too, discussed the matter when she visited Mexico in mid-April, but other than trying to comfort her sister, there was little she could do. From his distance, Gregory, too, was impotent. On the psychology of mourning, he counselled James to 'watch out for those ruminations which increase our tendency to indulge in philosophical surliness against fate and metaphysical ... combativeness against the biological lot of man.' On the subject of Basia, in 'a vague and somewhat theoretical way', he was sorry for her, but pointed out that her taking care of their parents was, in his opinion, 'nothing more than the result of her total inability to be or do anything else'. He was aware of how fortunate he was with his immediate family. 'Peg and the children', he told James, 'are happy and so serene. Life is warm and human and decent around them and with them.' Yet Gregory also reiterated what he had written to Mailloux: 'there is so much to do that I wish I had a vacation.'[29]

Neither the Christmas holiday nor the week in Cuba had provided any lasting relief from the pressures that weighed on Gregory, and he began to plan what he hoped would be a restorative trip to Europe at the end of the summer. He would be travelling on his own this time as Peg, who suspected she was pregnant again, didn't want to leave the children. Gregory's own feelings were as a result mixed: He felt 'pangs' about leaving his family, unsure if he lacked the courage to stay home or if he was, in fact, courageous in overcoming his pangs and forging ahead. He explained his predicament to Henry: He wanted to attend medical meetings in Amsterdam and Nice, while London and Copenhagen as well as Geneva and Paris were also on his agenda. He was 'awfully tired' and wanted very much just to 'roam' for a few weeks; there was so much to do and the going was so tough at times that he simply wanted a rest. 'Let us meet anywhere', he told Henry, 'I am quite eager to see you, even more so than always.' With Mailloux he was even more blunt. Frequently discouraged, he felt he was working 'all the time against the stream'. Recognising he was 'really tired' and needed a rest, he neverthe-less didn't know 'how to take it or where to take it or what to do with it', felt there wasn't even time now to consider rest seriously. 'I am', he told him, 'almost crushed by the constant lack of time.'[30]

The spring and summer were particularly stressful, and Mailloux was well aware that the pressures on Gregory were not only physical and psychological but spiritual. After a great deal of effort, Father T.M. Sparks, the master general's North American socius, had spelled out the ecclesiastical problems very clearly: As a 'non-Catholic', Gregory had 'no juridical personality in the Church'. If, after baptism, he wished to annul his first marriage, he could petition the authorities 'normally' on a diocesan level or 'extraordinarily' with the Holy Office. If the Petrine privilege were granted, his first marriage could be dispensed as a '*matri-monium validum inconsummatum*' and no '*interpellationes*' (testimonials) would be necessary. Celibate priests rallying on his behalf didn't quite understand Greg-ory's conflicted feelings, and he simply felt unable to enter the Church until the matter of his marriages had been resolved.[31]

Meanwhile round and round Gregory went at his normal pell-mell pace. In mid-April he attended a conference on 'Ministry and Medicine' on Colum-bia University's upstate campus in Harriman, New York, where he spoke on 'Derivation, Structure, and Function of the Super-Ego'. In mid-May, accom-panied by Peg and the children as well as Lala, he attended the annual meet-ings of the American Psychoanalytic and American Psychiatric Associations in Atlantic City, New Jersey, where he spoke on 'Social Convictions and Clinical

Psychiatry'. With the trees in leaf in Central Park and Peg's pregnancy confirmed, Gregory had increasingly mixed feelings about the upcoming Europe trip and confessed to Henry that he had 'tried to bite off too much as usual'. Obligated by professional commitments 'to go to certain places and do a certain amount of work', he joked half-heartedly that since Peg wasn't coming with him, he felt nostalgic even before starting out. He wasn't optimistic about the general state of the world either. Recognising that America's *soi-disant* world leadership depended on 'the flow of dollars', Henry contended that philosophers would ultimately be 'the driving forces of history', but Gregory was sceptical. Humanity had always succeeded in 'utilizing philosophers for all sorts of ends', he responded, and directed Henry's attention to 'what the Inquisition did with Christ, or Hitler with Nietzsche, or Truman with Jefferson or Thomas Paine'. As for his family, he was pleased that Nancy, having just finished her sophomore year at Radcliffe, was developing an interest in Dostoyevsky and Tolstoy as well as in the social sciences, but was frustrated with Greg, who seemed to him to be doing nothing of his own volition and had even stopped communicating with his father directly. Now in Quantico, Virginia, just south of Washington, where he had attained the ignoble rank of PFC, Greg was 'getting accomplished in the exercises of killing'. Gregory feared he would soon be sent to Korea. As for himself, Gregory doubted that he would ever be able to spend five or six hours a day simply reading and thinking. Although consoled by his younger children, who were 'well, happy and dear', and by Peg, who was as ever 'busy, happy, serene', he felt he was living vicariously 'on the spirit that emanates from them'.[32]

Somewhat depressed as well as overloaded with work, Gregory even had difficulty responding to Olga, with whom, since his visit to Mexico, he had developed a special rapport. Asking for her forgiveness at the beginning of July, he didn't excuse himself but attempted to explain:

> a doctor is never a master of his time … never in full possession of his right to have his own interests and preoccupations. At any moment others may (and they do) call on him to abandon his own interests in favor of some problems others are bothered by or preoccupied with.

He confessed that personally he had been going through a period during which neither his mind nor his body were fully his own. Wisely and patiently he told his anxious niece that things had a way of straightening themselves out, but until they did, things 'play havoc with us and torment us and confuse us'. In the end, 'there is no way of solving the problem unless it is done within one's self, and more or less spontaneously. No-one outside the person involved has a right to claim that he possesses the wisdom of telling exactly what to do.' Gregory was nevertheless sorry not to have written for 'if one has not got the wisdom required one must have the warmth of heart and give the other person that inner support – that awareness that she is understood and has a friend.'[33]

In Bedford on 8 July Peg felt under the weather but rallied to help Caroline clean the hutch by the barn where her pet rabbit was more trouble than the family had anticipated. The pen had been placed on stilts so the little girl might attempt to fulfil the responsibility of cleaning the cage herself, but the job was more than a four-year-old could manage on her own. As Peg pulled out the tray, the hutch tipped; she lost her balance and fell. The accident was always blamed for the haemorrhage that night and the miscarriage that occurred in the car the following day as Gregory drove to the local hospital. The experience upset everyone. Peg was transferred to New York for specialist care and Gregory, recounting the incident in detail to Mailloux on 10 July, reported that the past hours had been 'dark' and their hearts remained heavy.

Gregory would divide the rest of the summer between Bedford, where Peg slowly recuperated, and his responsibilities in the city, but he felt bereft on several counts. Bettine had married Eldridge Bruce in a clandestine ceremony in the Virgin Islands in December 1951, and after six difficult months in America during which they had felt compelled to live apart, the interracial couple had now decided to move to England, where Gregory had arranged for Eldridge to study with Anna Freud. Custody of Bettine's daughter, whose father insisted she remain in the United States, was an unsettled matter, but as the Bruces prepared to leave, Gregory realised he would not see them again for some time. Bettine had continued to seek his counsel after her divorce, and he had a paternal affection for the young woman who had never been strictly or merely a patient. He was also obliged to bid farewell to Raymond Saussure who, after 12 years in the States, had decided to return to Switzerland. It was even difficult to feel enthusiastic about the coming presidential contest. General Dwight D. Eisenhower, with Richard Nixon as his running mate, had been chosen as the Republican candidate in early July, but while Gregory had welcomed Truman's decision not to run again, it seemed unlikely that any nominee from another party would stand a chance. At the Democratic convention, Adlai Stevenson finally won the nomination on the third ballot, a contentious process reported in detail in the newspapers and broadcast live on the radio and, for the first time, on television. Uncomfortable in the summer heat, Gregory struggled to write a paper and pronounced American life in general 'painful and noisy'.[34]

Much as Gregory would have liked to have visited Mailloux in Montreal, there simply wasn't time before he left for Europe in mid-August. After five days in London, where he saw friends and colleagues, he flew to Geneva to see Henry, but both men were too busy for more than a few hours together: Henry was en route to Berne for a meeting of the Swiss Society for the History of Medicine and Natural Sciences, while Gregory was due at a medical meeting in Amsterdam. In early September Gregory spent five days lecturing in Copenhagen before flying to Paris, where he spent a fortnight walking in the city's parks, dining with acquaintances, and conferring with French Dominicans about his spiritual state. Just as there hadn't been time for a summer trip to Montreal, it turned out to be impossible to do the roaming in the south of France that he had imagined in the spring. Once again, as if not only the pace of travel but the frenzy of the entire year had caught up with him, he fell ill and spent most of his last week abroad in bed. Nevertheless, he wrote Mailloux in longhand from Piprot's desk that he felt the European trip had been fruitful. It had helped him get over the fatigue and melancholy he had felt in recent months, while 'the problem in connection with Rome' had 'narrowed itself down to a few simple steps' that he hoped to undertake as soon as he got home.[35]

Gregory still felt unwell on his return to New York in late September, but he couldn't avoid commitments that awaited him. In addition to his teaching at Butler Hospital, he had agreed to teach at both New York Medical College and New York University, where he had accepted an appointment as clinical associate professor. Overwhelmed by responsibilities, Gregory didn't immediately take the steps outlined in Paris. By October Piprot prodded Mailloux for a formal statement indicating, among other things, that Gregory had completed the necessary instruction for baptism and was willing, despite marriage to a non-Catholic, to give his children a Catholic education. Having carefully considered the extenuating circumstances, Piprot now proposed that the baptism occur in Rome.[36]

Throughout the autumn, with much of his attention divided between the Church and his teaching, Gregory was hard pressed to catch up. Having accepted an invitation from the Southern Psychiatric Association, he spoke on 'The Vitiations of the Will to Get Well' in White Sulphur Springs, West Virginia, in early November. He also agreed to speak at the centenary of the Central State Hospital in Nashville, Tennessee, in early December, taking as his topic 'The Enduring and the Ephemeral in Psychiatry during the Past Century'. Despite such commitments, he made time, though frequently not enough, for the individual people in his life: his patients and his family but also his close friends both near and far. His circle in New York now included not only Abe and Gertrude and Eddie and Mary but Dominque and Jean de Menil, avid art collectors and committed Catholics who divided their time between Houston, Texas, and New York City. No matter how busy Gregory was, there was always some social life: evenings with friends at elegant restaurants, large dinners at home organised by Peg, Sunday lunches in Bronxville on the way back to the city from weekends in Bedford. The boxing matches that gave Gregory vicarious pleasure were frequently televised, and the family now had a television, but seeing Sugar Ray Robinson and Rocky Marciano from a ringside seat was an experience that rivalled going to the theatre – and Gregory still, when he could, went to the theatre, regularly attended concerts by the New York Philharmonic at Carnegie Hall and performances of the Metropolitan Opera, whose Saturday afternoon radio broadcasts were, when he managed to listen, a highlight of his week.

He was, in addition, a man with serious hobbies. A good game of chess rewarded his full concentration. He invariably travelled with a camera in anticipation of photographic opportunities, while his city darkroom was well stocked with chemicals and Kodak paper, boxes of specialist clips, and a line on which he could hang his negatives to dry. Underneath his modernist country home, the sprawling basement of the original house held the lathe, circular saws, and power drills that, with the slabs of birch and ebony, the plywood panels and fiberglass and steel rods, made up his shop. There, when he had a free Saturday, he could work all morning with the help of Bill Reich, a local handyman who could fix anything but especially loved wood. And then there was cooking: Never a daily activity for the family but one that required an audience of discerning diners, his recipes typically began, 'Take three quarts of cream.'

The struggle to catch up noted so regularly in correspondence was, however, very real. His brutally long working days meant he was constantly torn. His professional commitments and obligations to particular people were matters of moral responsibility he felt he couldn't shirk. Yet even as he saw hours of reading and 'lounging' as impossible, he also realised he needed rest physically, psychologically, and spiritually. The complaints about his work were evidence of the tension he was under as, torn between what he wanted to do and his obligations, he came up against time.

In mid-November, as Mailloux began to draft the document Plé required, Gregory addressed a joint meeting of the Washington Psychiatric and Psychoanalytic Societies. While the formalities of his baptism hung in the balance, he apparently felt morally compelled to present himself as the believer he already was. He spoke as a psychoanalyst, as an educated man of reason and science in a voice distinctively his own, but that voice was now explicitly also Christian. He told his attentive listeners that the apparent tension between psychoanalysis and religion was just one example of an

> almost eternal, and truly tragic conflict between man's striving to become the engineer of a world in which there would be vast populations but not a single self-conscious individual, and man's yearning to preserve his being in complete unity with the One in whose image he was created.[37]

As the year wound down to Christmas, Gregory's life remained generally unsettled. There was one exception. In the first week of December, Basia and Nadia, who had since her marriage divided her time between her fretful mother in Mexico and her husband in the United States, left their adopted country for California. Basia would no longer be a financial responsibility or a persistent worry for either of her brothers, who were unsurprisingly relieved, although Gregory couldn't help reminding James that, as far as he could tell, the decades of living in Mexico had apparently left Basia unchanged; she might as well still have been living in the Podil district of Kiev.[38]

Throughout December Gregory, writing longhand in English on yellow legal paper, recast his formal petition for baptism. Mailloux meanwhile composed in French an expanded version of his supporting attestation. Both documents told much the same story as those prepared two years earlier. Mailloux stressed that Gregory's instruction had now been completed under his guidance, and added that in his view Ray had thwarted Gregory's efforts to instil Christian values in their children. Gathering the supporting documents, such as they were, in Montreal and New York would continue into the new year. Just before Christmas Louis Lachance, the superior of the Dominican Order in Montreal, wrote a short letter of recommendation, but Gregory was still struggling to provide what was technically required. He reiterated to Mailloux with some irritation that he had no birth certificate nor any other document to indicate he was a Jew and nothing to indicate he and Ray had been married; the divorce certificate, which he did have, would simply have to do as evidence of both the existence and civil dissolution of his first marriage. As to a document to indicate Peg had never been married before her marriage to him, there simply was no such thing.

At the end of January 1953 Gregory finally signed a long document in French petitioning the pope to grant him baptism in Rome in relative secrecy. He declared he did not want to die in a state which was increasingly burdensome and had troubled him for a long time. He also asked specifically for the immediate application of the Petrine privilege to precede the sacrament of baptism. He did not ask for the Pauline privilege because he anticipated that Ray, whom he called 'a passionate atheist', would refuse any attestations he might ask for and create both personal and professional problems. He described Peg as a pious Anglican and declared her full support. He also made clear that celibacy would represent a moral danger to a man of his age accustomed to married life. Adding that he hoped one day to convert Peg to Roman Catholicism, he emphasised he was seeking authorisation for a mixed marriage because it was with Peg and their children that he wanted to live and die.

While the petition was a carefully crafted political document for political purposes, it was in the main truthful. Gregory may have fudged a bit about his first marriage, omitting or exaggerating aspects of his relationship with Ray, but beyond the facts several important things were clear: He was desperate to enter the Church, extremely uneasy and even fearful of the impact his conversion would have on his public and professional life, and saw Ray as a threat to all he had managed to achieve. Longing for spiritual wholeness, he hoped to minimise the publicity he anticipated; such 'vulgarity', he wrote, 'would cast a sad shadow over the serenity and peace' he hoped for. The completed document would be sent in early February to Plé in Paris, who continued to collect recommendations and attestations for the dossier he planned to send to Rome before Easter. There was nothing Gregory could do now but wait.[39]

The new year began well, although the Cold War and American politics had created an uneasy political atmosphere that not only dominated the news but touched many of Gregory's friends, acquaintances, and patients quite personally. Gregory felt the last years of Truman's administration had demoralised, disorganised, and corrupted the whole country, while McCarthy's ongoing 'witch-hunt' for alleged Communists reflected 'a cruel world of generalized suspiciousness and almost complete breakdown of individual honesty'. Gregory observed trenchantly to Henry, 'A cold war kills human minds and destinies as much as a hot war kills bodies. The French Revolution, and the American Revolution, had nothing on us except their tools were less efficient.'[40]

At home, however, 1953 looked like a good year. Peg was pregnant again and they were looking forward 'a new baby'. Going on three, John, 'the old baby', was no longer a baby but a generally sunny little boy, while Carrie quickly recovered from 'an uneventful tonsillectomy', an anticipated medical intervention without the impact of John's hernia and Peg's miscarriage, and was soon again 'her bright and cheerful self'. Home life was such a solace that Gregory hated to leave and resolved to limit his future travelling as much as possible. Happy at Radcliffe and majoring in Russian, Nancy was engaged to Alan Dworsky, a Harvard law student, both of whose parents had been born in Russia. Alan seemed 'a nice chap' and his parents 'nice parents' who loved her, which particularly pleased Gregory, who was well aware of his daughter's rough childhood in a family with unhappy parents. Professionally, however, life was still too hectic. He confessed to Henry that he didn't feel fully recovered from the fatigue of the previous year's trip to Europe and had been unable to catch up on his work; there was simply 'so much to do'. Still rebounding from a bout of flu in early February, he wrote in the same vein to James: So much correspondence and work had piled up that he had become 'an irritated pessimist'.[41]

Throughout the spring Gregory continued to teach in New York and on alternating weekends in Providence and Washington, while he inevitably agreed to take on additional professional responsibilities. In early March he chaired the section on Historical and Cultural Medicine at a meeting of the New York Academy of Medicine. Ilze Veith, Henry's former student and the first to receive a doctorate in the history of medicine, dined with Gregory and Peg in the middle of the month, and the following week Gregory spoke, again on Columbia's upstate campus, on 'Psychology and Medical History' at a conference on 'The Utility and Value of Medical History', where Veith and Owsei Temkin also presented papers. In late March Gregory addressed a multidisciplinary gathering for Columbia University alumni on 'Differences in Mental Attitudes'. These were not occasions he felt able or even wanted to refuse.

With mixed feelings, including hope, Gregory planned to spend the first half of April in Europe. Constrained by his academic schedule and reluctant to leave the family that so cheered him, he arranged a shorter trip than usual, although he must have felt relieved to be escaping, even if briefly, the suspicion and dishonesty he felt was poisoning the American atmosphere. At the end of March Dash Hammett was called to testify before the House Un-American Activities Committee but refused to cooperate. No official action was taken, but he was quickly blacklisted. Lillian was upset; almost everyone Gregory knew who had anything to do with literature or art or testifying before HUAC was upset. In his own cheerful home, however, Peg was now noticeably pregnant and thinking ahead to the summer. The Bedford Golf and Tennis Club was building a pool that would be inaugurated in June. It would be such fun, she thought, if she and Caroline and John could swim. She organised the appropriate recommendations from her country neighbours and submitted the application for membership. The committee's response was predictable: The club would be happy to welcome Peg and the children but only on the condition that Gregory never accompany them; it was the club's policy, they explained, not to accept Jews. Peg was stunned, infuriated, astonished; she bewailed such overt anti-Semitism, vowed never again to set foot on the club's property even if invited. Gregory was neither shocked nor surprised, and his reaction was immediate and characteristic: They already had a tennis court; as soon as the baby was born and Peg was free to supervise, they would build their own pool; it could even have a diving board.

The spring trip to Europe was a truncated version of earlier visits. Gregory arrived in London on Good Friday and spent the day getting his bearings after the overnight flight. His heart was still with Peg in New York, and as soon as he got to the Dorchester Hotel, he telephoned her just to hear her voice, then followed up with a disjointed letter. He was sort of disturbed, he told her, and quite unhappy. To no avail he had rung a number of airlines in an effort to get a sleeper on his return flight. His emotional response was, he realised, 'so damn silly', but he was tired and, as an emotional man who wept easily in private, he sat in his room 'hurt and crying'. Reflective and analytic, Gregory attributed his feelings of dislocation and sadness not only to frustration and longing for Peg and home but to the fact that it was Good Friday. As he regained his equilibrium, he left off writing, then started again. The letter began, 'My very dearest', then later, "Hello, my dearest', and he concluded several times: 'At any rate Sweetheart – I love you', 'Love to everybody'. In the gaps between passages, Gregory probably went to church.[42]

Responding to his phone call in a letter Gregory received several days later, Peg wrote sympathetically to her 'dearest, faraway husband'. She told him the entire household was terribly quiet and forlorn without him; everything and she herself 'ached' for him. She was thinking about him especially as Easter drew closer. Collapsing Gregory's spiritual yearnings, his Good Friday blues and frustration with the airlines, as if they were all matters of equal moment and as easily resolved, she told him cheerily, 'I do hope you are at peace inside, and pretty much so outside, too!' Gregory didn't hold such simplicity against her; he cherished her optimism, depended on her unwavering support, on the serenity that counterbalanced his own volatility, his seriousness that made him at times angry, at times depressed, invariably realistic.[43]

On Saturday afternoon Gregory flew from London to Milan, where he hired a chauffeured car and was driven to Pura to see Henry. Gregory had hoped for a few sunny days of 'plain loafing' during which he could read, take a few photos and talk, but the rain that fell on and off throughout the weekend didn't in the end bother either of them. They spent some time with their cameras, took all their meals at Henry's home, and on Easter prepared a succulent leg of lamb. There was, of course, plenty of good conversation. After less than 48 hours, however, Gregory returned to Milan, where Mailloux joined him, and together the two men pushed on to Rome.[44]

The ostensible purpose of their visit was the fifth Congrès Catholique International de Psychothérapie et Psychologie Clinique, where on 9 April Gregory spoke in French on 'Anthropologie de l'agressivité', but an audience with Pope Pius XII, who personally addressed the congress, had also been arranged. The subject of the meeting was psychoanalysis and the Church, but it seems likely Gregory's baptism was also mentioned. He had hoped to be baptised in Rome before the audience, perhaps by Emmanuel Suarez at the Dominican Basilica Santa Sabina or even discretely in the Vatican by the Holy Father who alone had the power to grant the privileges on which Gregory's baptism depended, but the matter of his entering the Church was moving through channels very slowly and the pope had not yet received his petition.[45]

After an inconclusive three days, Gregory and Mailloux flew to Paris, where they met with Seitz and Plé to discuss the Aquinas Fund's support of Plé's institute. Naturally they also discussed the serious matter of Gregory's dossier, but there must have been time during those two spring days for a good dinner with his Dominican friends, an espresso at a brasserie on the Champs-Elysées, a moment of window shopping on the Rue Saint-Honoré. On 12 April Gregory flew back to New York, where he arrived less refreshed than he had intended, unbaptised, and without having slept well. Indeed, he felt 'a little tired and a little ill'. A week after his return he must have been additionally deflated by Sparks's report from Italy. Having received Gregory's petition and the supporting recommendations from Plé, Sparks had shared the dossier with Suarez who, after careful examination, had decided the documents had 'a solid foundation' and could 'go ahead', although he remained convinced Gregory should first present his dossier in person to the New York curia; in due course it could then be sent on to the Holy Office. Sparks was sending the entire dossier back to Gregory in New York.[46]

Even had he wanted to pursue the matter in the city, Gregory was already overcommitted. He had patients waiting for him in his office every day of the week, while teaching took up many of his evenings and weekends, and there were special events: A meeting of the World Federation for Mental Health and a television interview on Simone de Beauvoir's *The Second Sex* were on his schedule as soon as he returned from Europe; the following week he was the dinner speaker at the Institute of Psychiatry and Neurology in Lyons, New Jersey. In early May he was in Los Angeles for the annual meeting of the American Psychiatric Association, where it was formally announced that he was the recipient of the Isaac Ray Award for 1953. Two years earlier Gregory with several other psychiatrists had organised the prize to recognise an association member for an outstanding contribution to understanding psychology and the law. The honour brought with it the opportunity for a series of lectures and a publication contract. As one of the founders, Gregory wouldn't have been an appropriate recipient in the award's first year; that honour had gone to Win Overholser, whose lectures at Harvard would soon appear as *The Psychiatrist and the Law*. Although Gregory had been notified of the honour earlier in the year, he simply hadn't had time to craft an entertaining acceptance speech. He reported the event to Henry with pride and chagrin: He had made 'the shortest acceptance speech ever', had merely stood up and said, 'Thank you'.[47]

Gregory returned to New York in time to attend Abe's wedding to Gertrude on 15 May and to celebrate Caroline's fifth birthday two days later. As the weather grew warm, Peg and the children wanted to be in the country and Gregory once more began commuting between Bedford and the city. Peg was putting a good deal of energy into Nancy's wedding to Alan, planned for mid-June, an event to which Gregory much looked forward. He was unable to attend another wedding: that of Ralph Ingersoll's stepdaughter Patricia Doolittle. Giving as his reasons Nancy's marriage, Peg's pregnancy, and an overwhelming amount of work, he wrote Ingersoll with genuine warmth, 'I raise my glass to you all and greet the newlyweds with all my heart', and concluded, 'Yours ever, Gregory Zilboorg'. The claim to be overwhelmed with work was no less true for being a constant refrain; his supportive tone and the slightly reserved formality of his valediction were a typically affectionate and professional response to a former patient. Gregory surely raised a glass with heartfelt joy to Nancy and Alan. Acknowledging the announcement of her marriage, the liberal New York politician Stanley M. Isaacs, whose path had crossed Gregory's both professionally and socially, told him he knew how pleased Gregory must be because of his obvious devotion to Nancy.[48]

The summer wasn't an unalloyed joy, however, for it was impossible to avoid news of McCarthy's zealous pursuit of those he branded Communists while the Rosenbergs' approaching fate dominated the headlines. Despite international protest and appeals for clemency going as far as the White House, there would finally be no stay of execution. The tabloids' 'Spy Couple Doomed to Die' and 'Spies Get One More Day' gave way to 'Last Minute Plea to President Fails' and, on 19 June, 'Rosenbergs Go Silently to Electric Chair'. Sylvia Plath would remember the sultry summer of 1953 as 'the summer they electrocuted the Rosenbergs', and for Gregory American anti-socialist feeling became personal at the end of the month when the *New Republic*, in a special feature on 'Book Burning', listed his name on a roll of authors whose books were to be banned.[49]

Much as Gregory might have wanted to stay in Bedford with his family, he had agreed to present a paper on 'Freud's Fundamental Psychiatric Orientation' at the International Psycho-Analytical Congress slated for London in the last week of July. In for a penny, in for a pound, on a programme including Karl Menninger, Leo Bartemeier, and Ernest Jones, he had also agreed to lecture on 'Psychopathology and Religious Issues' at the Royal Society of Medicine at the end of the month, and there were inevitably convivial lunches and dinners with colleagues as well as drinks with friends in the sumptuous bar of the Dorchester Hotel, where he now regularly stayed.[50]

With his dossier stalled, there was no need to go to Rome, but having fulfilled his commitments in London, Gregory was eager for a rest and spent a couple of quiet days in Paris, relaxing to the degree he was able. On the first Sunday in August he took an overnight train to Geneva. There Henry collected him at dawn and drove to Erica's new apartment, where the two friends cooked a hearty breakfast. Presuming that Gregory would want to buy 'a couple of watches', Henry proposed they prepare lunch and have dinner at a lakeside restaurant. Constantly talking, in the end they cooked all three meals of the day at the apartment before, late that evening, Henry delivered Gregory to the station for the overnight train back to the French capital.[51]

After a few additional days in Paris, Gregory returned to London, then flew back to the United States on 8 August. The trip had been hurried, but he was eager to be home before the baby came. As soon as he arrived at the apartment, however, he received an urgent message from Mailloux. The exact problem wasn't clear to Gregory and remains vague, but it probably concerned his dossier, Rome, and the New York curia, and whatever Piprot, Plé, Suarez, and Sparks as well as Mailloux were doing or unable to do on his behalf. Two hours after Gregory's plane landed in New York, he was back at the airport and on a flight to Montreal.

Peg went into labour on 11 August, and Gregory boarded a plane for the third time in four days. He made it to Lenox Hill Hospital shortly before the baby made his appearance. With one son named after an evangelist, they would name this hale and hearty little boy after another: Matthew. His middle name would be 'Stone' – like his sister's and brother's middle names, a name from Peg's family. After five days in hospital, the baby and mother would come home with Gregory to join Caroline and John for the rest of what should have been a restful summer in Bedford.

Unable to take unalloyed joy in his expanded family, unable to relax, unable to work or even to settle, Gregory experienced an emotional crisis. He wasn't actually needed in Bedford, where the new baby nurse, Lala, Betty, George the gardener, and Sarah the laundress kept the household wheels turning, but it certainly wasn't not being essential that upset him. Indeed, the dependable staff reassured the man who didn't participate in childcare, for whom cooking was a hobby and dog walking a task only accepted under duress. Although the weeks abroad had been no more hectic or exigent than usual, they had provided little of the rest he had hoped for. Gratified to have another son and proud of his wife, he was nevertheless 'in a constant state of tension', psychologically and spiritually troubled, deeply disturbed apparently by whatever had transpired in Montreal. Two days after Peg and Matthew came home from hospital, Gregory grabbed a few books and papers and flew to Saint Thomas in the Virgin Islands, where he spent a completely uneventful and solitary week. The sun shone every day and gentle sea breezes mitigated the Caribbean heat. He read and wrote a little and tried as hard as he could to relax.[52]

Gregory's impulsive escape was evidently sufficient to enable him to resume his normal hectic life on his return. He had lectures to write, and before the end of September he would resume teaching in both New York and Providence. He was soon again routinely tired and deluged with work, but as Caroline began kindergarten at the Brearley School, chosen because of its academic excellence and because Bettine had gone there, the autumn assumed a regular rhythm and

Gregory slowly regained his composure. Peg would drive to the country every weekend as soon as Caroline got out of school. Gregory would spend alternate weekends at Butler Hospital. When he could, he joined the family in Bedford on Saturday night. On the weekends he wasn't in Providence, once he had finished with the last patient on Friday, he would drive to the country in the falling dark.[53]

By October Gregory was commuting not only fortnightly to Providence but to New Haven for the six mid-week lectures at Yale, and he wisely began to plan a January cruise with Peg to the West Indies. He looked forward to it throughout the autumn, but one of the things that kept him working so hard was financial necessity. In Bedford the diggers had begun digging for the pool that would please Peg. Gregory's comfortable life was paid for only by what he could keep coming in, and half of what came in went to Ray. His idea was always simply to work harder. His friend Jean de Menil must have sensed as much, recognising both the toll of Gregory's obligations and the significance of the holiday for his psychic wholeness. As Gregory wrote, commuted, lectured, and worked generally harder, Jean sent a cheque for $1,200 ($10,000) directly to the travel agency in charge of the cruise and followed up with a resonant note to Gregory: 'Please accept this as a Christmas gift from your two friends Dominique and Jean: quite a case of Christmas in July, but I had to act now to take the wind out of your sails.'[54]

The autumn proved particularly exhausting, but when the lectures at Yale concluded in early December, Gregory came up for air. Although 'extremely tired', he looked ahead to a summer he anticipated would be both 'hopelessly busy and fascinating' with conferences in Montreal, Toronto, and Rome. He took time now to see friends in New York, among them Bettine and Eldridge Bruce, back in America for the birth of their first child, whom they would name Eldridge Gregory Bruce, news that must have touched Gregory and that he would have shared with Mailloux, who joined him at Butler Hospital during the weekend before Christmas. Despite the exhausting pace of his professional life, the holiday season brought some respite. His life was, he reported to Henry, full of the children's contagious joy. He wrote more specifically to James. Peg had fully recovered from her childbirth, and it was hard for him to realise that she had had a child so recently and was already a mother three times over. He was amused by Johnny's 'Christmas list', which included a thoughtful if fanciful 'new library for Daddy', while Carrie seemed to love school where she was also 'loved a great deal'. In fact, it seemed to him she was becoming more and more like her mother, developing into 'a serene, kind human being'.[55]

Much remained unresolved, however, as the year drew to a close. Gregory would be 63 on Christmas day, but despite the decision taken over three years earlier, he hadn't yet been baptised and the stress – managed but not reduced by holidays taken and anticipated – was taking its toll. Reflecting on their recent meeting in Providence, Mailloux assured Gregory that he 'understood and measured the heavy burden of uncertainty' currently weighing on his heart. 'I hope', Mailloux told him, 'that the year 1954 will bring us a solution to a problem that … will be for you the dawn of an ultimate peace.'[56]

Notes

1 André Godin to NM, 19 November 1950; MSZ to NM, 25 October 1954, both APD.
2 'Milestones', *Time Magazine*, 21 December 1953, np.
3 GZ to HES, 29 December 1950; GZ to NM, 3 October 1950; NM to GZ, 26 September 1950.
4 NM to GZ, 26 September 1951; André Godin to NM, 19 November 1950; Paolo Dezza to GZ, nd, all APD.
5 GZ to David G. Wright, 3 October 1950, APD; GZ to NM, 3, 24 October 1950.
6 André Godin to NM, 19 November 1950; Godin's summary of a conversation between Henneberry and Kelly, 9 December 1950, both APD.
7 Godin, summary of a conversation with Henneberry, 13 December 1950, APD.
8 Ivan Opffer to GZ, 8 February 1951.
9 GZ to HES, 19 April 1951.
10 GZ, *Sigmund Freud*, passim; GZ to Karl Stern, 1 February 1951, quoted in Burston, 89; Stern, 278.
11 '*Sigmund Freud* by Gregory Zilboorg', *Kirkus Reviews*, nd, www.kirkusreviews.com/book-reviews/dr-gregory-zilboorg/sigmund-freud-5/; Goldknopf, 18, 19; Mullahy, 13; Barrett, 617; Leo Bartemeier, 'Fresh Perspective on Freud', *New York Herald Tribune*, 20 January 1952, 5.
12 Virginia Tarbell to NM, 10 October 1951, APD.
13 NM to Emmanuel Suarez, 27 July 1951, APD.
14 Augustin Laffay, 'Piprot d'Alleaume Gabriel-Marie', *Dictionnaire Biographique des Frères Prêcheurs*: http://journals.openedition.org/dominicains/860
15 Programme.
16 GZ, 'His Own Cook', 157–158.
17 GZ to HES, 16 May, 16 August 1951; HES to GZ and MSZ, 25 September 1951; HES to GZ, 12 October, 4, 27 December 1951.
18 NM to Emmanuel Suarez, 27 July 1951, APD; MSZ to HES, 3 September 1951.
19 MSZ to HES, 3 September 1951.
20 GZ to NM, 24 September 1951.
21 Emmanuel Suarez to NM, 5 October 1951, APD.
22 GZ to NM, 10 October, 7 November 1951; Lucien Bonnafé, *et al.*
23 GZ to HES, 7 November 1951; GZ to JZ, 27 November 1951; GZ to NM, 8 December 1951.
24 GZ to EZ, 24 December 1951; GZ to Olga Zilboorg, 28 December 1951, Schaeffer; GZ to HES, 19 December 1951; GZ to JZ, 14 March 1952.
25 JZ to GZ, 16 January 1952; GZ to JZ, 21 January 1952; GZ to Olga Zilboorg, 7 February 1952, Schaeffer.
26 GZ to JZ, 17 March 1952.
27 GZ to JZ, 14, 17 March 1952.
28 JZ to GZ, 25 March, 13 April 1952; GZ to JZ, 7 April 1952; GZ to NM, 7 April 1952.
29 JZ to GZ, 13 April 1952; GZ to JZ, 22 April 1952.
30 GZ to HES, 16 April 1952; GZ to NM, 22 April 1952.
31 T.M. Sparks to NM, 15 March 1952, APD.
32 GZ, 'Social Convictions'; GZ to HES, 10, 13 June 1952; HES to GZ, 10 June 1952.
33 GZ to Olga Zilboorg, 1 July 1952, Schaeffer.
34 GZ to NM, 10, 16 July 1952; GZ to HES, 23 July 1952.
35 GZ to NM, 15 September 1952.
36 Piprot's colleague to NM, 22 October 1952, APD.
37 GZ, 'Scientific Psychopathology', *Theological Studies*, 297. GZ's thinking on this topic was so important to him that he delivered this essay twice as a lecture and published

it three times, with minor variations: in France in April 1953 (as 'Psychopathologie Scientifique'); in America in *Theological Studies* in June 1953; and, after presenting it as a lecture in London in July 1953, in England in 1954 ('Scientific Psychopathology' in *Journal of Mental Science*). His conclusion, quoted here, remained the same.

38 GZ to JZ, 8 December 1952.
39 Louis Lachance, recommendation, 23 December 1952; GZ to NM, 26 January 1953; GZ to 'Très Saint-Père', 31 January 1953, all APD.
40 GZ to HES, 27 January 1953.
41 GZ to HES, 27 January 1953; GZ to JZ, 8 February 1953.
42 GZ to MSZ, 3 April 1953.
43 MSZ to GZ, 5 April 1953.
44 GZ to HES, 10 February, 16 April 1953; HES to GZ, 14 February 1953; NM to GZ, 2 February 1953.
45 NM to GZ, 2 February 1953; GZ to NM, nd; MSZ to GZ, 5 April 1953.
46 GZ to HES, 16 April 1953; T.M. Sparks to GZ, 19 April 1953, APD.
47 GZ to HES, 18 May 1953.
48 GZ to HES, 23 May 1953; GZ to Ralph Ingersoll, 11 June 1953, Ralph Ingersoll Papers, Howard Gotlieb Archival Research Center, Boston University; Stanley M. Isaacs to GZ, 16 June 1953, Stanley M. Isaacs Papers, Manuscripts and Archives Division, New York Public Library.
49 Plath, 1; 'Special Report on Book Burning', *New Republic*, 29 June 1953, 8.
50 GZ, 'Freud's Fundamental Psychiatric Orientation'; GZ to HES, 23 August 1953.
51 GZ to HES, 23 May, 23 July 1953; HES to GZ, 28 July 1953; GZ, 'His Own Cook', 158.
52 GZ to HES, 23 August 1953.
53 GZ to HES, 9 October 1953.
54 Jean de Menil to GZ, 9 October 1953.
55 GZ to HES, 8, 16 December 1953; GZ to JZ, 16 December 1953.
56 NM to GZ, 29 December 1953.

Chapter 7

Faith, hope, and charity
1954–1955

The new year Mailloux was so hopeful about began with two baptisms, but neither of them was Gregory's. The Bruces' son was baptised in January. Bettine and Eldridge were eager to return to London, and the reception, a combined welcome to the baby and send off for his family, was held at 'Caumsett'. Gregory was honoured as the boy's godfather as well as namesake and Peg was his happy godmother, relationships nourished by the photos Bettine would regularly send of 'Greggie' growing up in England. Matthew would be baptised a month later at Saint Matthew's in Bedford; his godparents would be an odd triumvirate that reflected the variety of people Peg and Gregory included in their joint circle: Virginia Turner, Goddard Lieberson, and Bill Barrett.

As for his own baptism, Gregory had resolved with Mailloux's help to take a new tack. With Rome apparently no longer a possible site for the sacrament and still determined not to pursue the matter with the New York curia, they had come up with a new place and advocate: Montreal and the city's Archbishop Paul-Émile Léger. A champion of ecumenism and expert in canon law, Léger had been raised to the cardinalate in late 1952 and given the additional status of papal legate. In early 1954 Mailloux and Gregory began redrafting the required documents in order to plead his case in Francophone Canada – a precise process of months rather than weeks.

During the first weeks of the new year, however, Gregory began revising his Yale lectures for publication and prepared for his long-anticipated trip to the West Indies. A post-Christmas holiday had become his yearly break from the intense routine of lectures and patients, at once an escape from winter and an interlude with Peg during which he could more or less relax in a warm and sunny spot. California had on several occasions served as a destination, but the Caribbean had drawn him from his first visits to Mexico and Cuba in the 1930s, its islands' Spanish, French, and British foreignness an additional attraction, its beaches, sunsets, and elegant accommodation with views over the sea or mountains offering a stark contrast to his daily round.

The Psychology of the Criminal Act and Punishment, the book that grew out the Isaac Ray lectures, would make stimulating, provocative, and occasionally lurid reading – a detailed account of the crimes and punishment of a coprophilic

DOI: 10.4324/9781003190974-7

cannibal executed for murder in 1936 shocked readers unaccustomed to clinical details. Indeed, the material was perhaps better in lectures delivered in Gregory's dynamic style rather than in cold black and white on the page, and its author had, only somewhat wittingly, stepped into a hornets' nest: Psychiatrists were generally laudatory while lawyers felt attacked; penal reformers were sympathetic, while law enforcement officials were uncomfortable with Gregory's emphasis on forgiveness and what he argued was the preventative as well as potentially curative power of love. Law professor Henry Weihoffen had 'trouble' with the book because its author was 'no lawyer'. Despite finding the fourth chapter, 'Aggression and Transgression', particularly valuable, he felt Gregory's 'observations and propositions' – some 'piquant and provocative', others 'shallow, dubious, or clearly wrong' – did little to foster mutual understanding between psychiatrists and lawyers. In a lengthy and trenchant summary, L. Whiting Farinholt Jr. was more sympathetic: The book contained 'a good deal of interesting and provocative material' that might be useful, but failed 'to create an atmosphere conducive to rapprochement of the two fields of endeavor'. Citing as minor deficiencies a 'redundancy of ideas', a topical rather than 'logically progressive' organisation of material, and an 'inadequacy of citations', Farinholt was put off by what he saw as the book's 'exhibitionism, sensationalism, and self-satisfied condescension', yet nevertheless recommended it as 'a thought-provoking work' that might help legal professionals understand not only some of the criminal's motivations but those of the psychiatrist and 'fellow members of the bar'.

In contrast, Jonathan Gould, a Catholic psychiatrist in England, was more positive: The book succeeded in its aim

> to increase the general unease felt regarding the social and juridical response to capital crime, by discussing the plethora of personal (and juridically irrelevant though effective) unconscious factors, which become involved, not only in the crime, but also in the conduct of the Attorneys, the Judge and the Jury.

Praising the author for demonstrating 'the presence of personal, unconscious factors suffusing what is generally taken to be an objective and impersonal or non-subjective system of attitudes and conduct, and thus discrediting the objectivity of the legal procedure', Gould found the third chapter, 'Some Differences in Professional Psychology', especially strong, 'a brilliant essay on the differences and the implications of the differences, in the training of doctors and lawyers'. The American psychiatrist Philip Q. Roche also admired the book and agreed that punishment was not a deterrent to crime and that 'sin' was everybody's battle. Impressed with Gregory's 'vast knowledge of his subject' as well as his 'moral indignation', the British psychoanalyst Walter G. Joffe similarly praised his treatment of the 'eternal struggle between the striving to punish and the yearning to understand and forgive'.[1]

Indeed, that striving and yearning were finally at the core of what were apparently very successful lectures, but as a book *The Psychology of the Criminal Act and Punishment* – inscribed to Peg 'with affection and gratitude' and without any intentional irony – suffered from some of the same difficulties as *Sigmund Freud: His Exploration of the Mind of Man*: Gregory was trying to take on more than one volume, particularly a relatively short one, could do justice to, and he was to a degree working at cross-purposes to his material. In both books he struggled with focus and limits, with organisation and tone, while underlying his struggle was neither lack of knowledge nor hostility towards anyone nor inconsideration for his readers, but a deep desire to bring together Christianity and psychology; his spiritual, personal, and social convictions on the one hand and his professional calling on the other. The personal and the political, the private man and the public persona, emotion and intellect, would never be easy bedfellows, and Gregory would strive throughout his life to get them to lie down comfortably in the same place. His Catholicism would help, as would his experience of love in his relationship with Peg, but they wouldn't solve the problem.

Distracted and overloaded with work, Gregory spent January pushing back against obligations and reshaping commitments. He told Mailloux he now felt the Aquinas Fund should concentrate its support on the study centre in France. To this end, Seitz had agreed to go to Paris in March to liaise with Plé and Piprot. Gregory also hoped Bettine would meet with the French Dominicans as soon as she returned to Europe; she was interested in the cause and it was becoming clear to him that the project would require additional funds.[2]

Reflecting on his own choices and harking back to old themes, he wrote in general but revealing terms to James. A doctor, he told his brother, lives the lives of so many others; it is a life 'of hope and sorrow, complex and urgent'. His vocation created for him an 'atmosphere of appointments, visits and parties' that made it difficult to 'think or talk'. When at times he came to and looked around, he regretted a little having become estranged from so many people except his immediate family, but he was quickly engulfed once more 'in the tense, exciting, deeply stirring existence' of his profession. Life with Peg and their children, however, and the richness of his inner life meant he felt younger now than 20 years earlier. If James could only step aside from the maelstrom of proving himself alive, from the hurly-burly of 'people and things', Gregory felt he would gain 'spiritual perspective'. Gregory recommended a trip somewhere, and imagined meeting in Rome, a moment out of time when the two men could sit down together on a bench in the Piazza Cavour or Trajan's Forum and 'talk a little'. He wished for James what he, in fact, wished for himself: unmitigated and sincere heart-to-heart conversation, confession, absolution, and communion.

Having prepared his lectures for publication, Gregory cleared his desk in anticipation of the holiday to which Jean de Menil had so generously contributed. He had agreed to lecture in San Juan and to participate in a conference in Port-au-Prince, but in between he planned to 'loaf, sleep, read, and sleep again and loaf again'. He felt Peg needed the rest almost as much as he did – she had, in addition to managing the children and the household, continued to be his amanuensis, the in-house editor and proofreader who went through his galleys with an eye even more critical than his own. Gregory inevitably missed her on his solo trips abroad and was delighted she was joining him on the cruise. Indeed, he would not have taken the trip without her.[3]

Peg's reluctance to leave the children meant Gregory frequently travelled alone, but he admired her devotion, regarded her as the ideal mother, a natural font of love, and an excellent disciplinarian. That her higher loyalty was always to him was assumed by both of them, although privileging her husband while managing their children often involved keeping the youngsters at an emotional distance, creating separate physical spaces, and enforcing quiet, politeness, and routine as much for adult convenience as for the children's well-being. According to what Peg saw as universal ethical and psychological principles, she also expected conventional femininity and masculinity. Caroline wore white gloves and a hat in church, curtseyed when greeting adults, and played with dolls. John and Matthew wore Brooks Brothers' suits with short trousers to church and school until the age of seven and played with cap guns while wearing Davy Crocket racoon caps. All three children were allowed to wear dungarees on country weekends and encouraged to build with blocks, ride bicycles, and swim. Carrie from the age of four was enrolled in dancing classes with Isadora Duncan's student Anita Zahn, while Peg spent hours in Central Park teaching her sons to play baseball.

Many of these mid-century American conventions were alien to Gregory, who had no more mastered a bicycle than he had learned to swim, but because Peg authorised them, he felt they couldn't be other than right and good. That some of her expectations were hard on the children was apparently not something they reflected on, and indeed particular rules were not only difficult to follow but potentially unhealthy. Isolation in one's room was a standard punishment followed by what seemed to Peg reasonable interrogation out of her father's book: Had one intended to do it? Was one sorry to have done it? Did one resolve never to do it again? An inevitable final question would conclude the grilling: Had one 'sweetened up'? The correct answer was, of course, 'yes', and only if all the questions were answered correctly would one be allowed to emerge. The children thus learned hypocrisy early. If they were injured or ill or upset, they weren't supposed to mention it, were told other people didn't want to hear about it, to 'put it in their pockets'. Sunshine and sweetness were more important than cut fingers, skinned knees, and anxiety, more important than coughs and colds, sore throats, and tummy aches. The children were inevitably sent to school with fevers and spots, and their mother inevitably called to fetch them – a worry for their teachers but an inconvenience to Peg, who let the children know it.

Yet Peg in her own sweetness and light, in her maternal dedication, her consistency and aspirations, was a stark contrast to Ray. Just as Ray's reluctance to become a mother, her pre- and post-partem depressions and persistent discomfort with maternity had influenced Gregory's early research and writing, so Peg's attitudes and maternal feelings now influenced his thinking about parenthood and family. His view of Ray as a bad mother and Peg as a good one to a degree absolved him of responsibility for the errors he had committed and the difficulties he had posed and continued to pose for all five of his children. Aware of not being an easy or effective father, he nevertheless blamed Ray for most of Greg and Nancy's problems and admired Peg for all she did as a devoted mother. She took the children to the park and read them bedtime stories each night. When Caroline started kindergarten, she took her to the bus stop every weekday morning and waited with the well-trained poodles on leads beside her until her daughter was on her way, school uniform on, coat buttoned, scarf tied, and books and papers in her satchel.

Gregory was less confident than his judgements might have made him seem. Unable to master or mitigate and often even to recognise his specific weaknesses, he realised or at least feared their consequences with chagrin. Confronted with the problems his brash manner created, he often felt both rejected and helpless. When Fera invited him to a dinner party that included her son Mike and his young wife Gloria, Gregory attended without Peg, who might have restrained him, and typically argued with Sol about politics, high-handedly dismissing anyone's point of view but his own. He managed to annoy everyone, and by the end of the evening he knew it, told Fera plaintively he didn't think the children liked him. She responded with characteristic aplomb that they might have done had he behaved 'more like a human being'. Fera herself loved her brother, knew he was capable of behaving like the generous and even humble human being he truly was, but he tried her patience throughout her life. Others, including his own children, were less inured, less tolerant or able to forgive or deal, and Gregory was aware, although at times only dimly and defensively, of the havoc he frequently left in his wake. When he managed to reflect, he would wonder what he had unintentionally done or said that might have ruined a relationship he valued; when he stepped back, he would wonder what had happened and doubt his capacity to make things right.[4]

As soon as Gregory returned from the Caribbean, his hectic life resumed. There were, as always, patients to see, the bread and butter that made the rest of his life possible. Among those requiring his attention now was Marshall Field, who was suffering from a debilitating lassitude. Gregory soon deduced it was not psychological counsel his friend needed and arranged a thorough examination at Johns Hopkins University Hospital, where William Francis Rienhoff, the hospital's renowned surgeon who had studied with the pioneering oncologist William Stewart Halsted, discovered and removed a small lung tumour. Confident the cancer had been completely encapsulated, Field returned home and made a good recovery, grateful for Gregory's sagacity.[5]

Throughout the spring there were also conferences to attend and lectures to give. At the end of February Gregory travelled to Little Rock, Arkansas, for the annual Neuropsychiatric meeting, where he spoke on psychiatry and the law. A month later he spent two days at Butler Hospital for a symposium on 'Religion and Psychiatry'. Chaired and moderated by the Mennonite Norman Loux, now the hospital's assistant superintendent and clinical director, the conference was pointedly ecumenical. In addition to Gregory, who had initiated and organised the meeting, its participants included George Mora, resident in psychiatry at Butler Hospital; Father Albert T. Mollegan, professor of New Testament and ethics at the Episcopal Virginia Theological Seminary; the Jewish educational leader Rabbi Edward Sandrow; and Gregory's Catholic friends Bartemeier and Mailloux.

In early April, as chair of the Consulting Delegation on Criminology to the United Nations, Gregory travelled to Oklahoma City to address 1,000 members of the public invited to the first meeting of the Oklahoma governor's crime study commission. Speaking on 'Science and Crime', Gregory declared that criminals needed treatment and came out once again against capital punishment. He was also widely reported in the local papers as saying that good family relations and 'mother love' keep youngsters 'straight', a message happily accepted as conventional wisdom in midwestern America but firmly rooted in his personal understanding of his own family dynamics. Gregory then went on to Tulsa for yet another meeting before finally returning to Peg, his three young children, and waiting patients in New York.[6]

Gregory and John, New York, April 1954

At the end of April Gregory was again in the Midwest. He spoke on 'Clinical and Therapeutic Aspects of the "Borderline Case"' at the annual meeting of the American Psychoanalytic Association in St. Louis, where he also spoke at the annual meeting of the American Psychiatric Association, on 'The Changing Concept of Man in Present-Day Psychiatry', arguing that historically psychiatry had its roots in philosophy rather than in medicine. Boundaries and margins, intersections and commonalities were also on his mind when, as its dinner speaker, he addressed the annual convention of the Guild of Catholic Psychiatrists in St. Louis in early May. Choosing as his topic 'Borderlands of Psychiatry and Religion', Gregory clearly considered himself as Mailloux had described him, Catholic in his thought and heart, and by 1954 he was accepted by his Catholic colleagues on those terms. Indeed, many would have presumed he had already formally entered the Church, but even without having been baptised, he identified himself with, sought out, and was celebrated as one of their own by the community of Catholic psychiatrists and psychoanalysts, a group including not only Bartemeier and Mailloux but Karl Stern, Karl M. Bowman, Frances J. Braceland, and Francis J. Gerty, all of whom were active Guild members.[7]

Gregory was unsurprisingly feeling even more than normally tired and stressed during this even more than usually busy spring. In between writing conference papers and trips to the Midwest, he travelled to Montreal for consultations and interviews about ecclesiastical procedure and his particular case. In New York he continued to revise his petition and gather the appropriate supporting documents and testimonials for baptism in Canada. He also continued, despite the repeated rejections, to be hopeful, and was gratified and encouraged by recognition arriving from an unanticipated direction: The National University of Ireland in Dublin, a distinguished Catholic institution, wanted to award him an honorary doctor of science degree during their centenary celebration in July. Such a public accolade touched him both professionally and personally. The international award acknowledging him not only as a psychiatrist and psychoanalyst but as a scientist and a Catholic challenged the aspersions he had struggled to counter throughout his life; it undermined the explicit and implicit accusations he had faced when called before the board of the New York Psychoanalytic Society as well as the hearsay and prejudices that continue to dog him. He immediately accepted the university's homage, and began to plan with Peg a European trip to include the ceremony in Ireland.

The pace and consequent stress of Gregory's life was taking a toll on him physically, but his schedule overflowed with commitments and he put off a medical examination as he struggled to clear his desk for the summer. He was in Montreal for the 15th International Congress of Psychology, where on 9 June he spoke on 'Recurrent Trends in Relation to Psychopathology'. One document after another was sent to Mailloux, and on 15 June the dossier was at last presented to Cardinal Léger. In the carefully phrased petition, Gregory argued that Montreal was his spiritual home: Mailloux was his spiritual advisor and it was through the Dominicans and his work with them in Quebec that he had come to the point of seeking entry to the Church. On 22 June Gregory flew back to Montreal to be examined by the cardinal and his staff. The following day his petition, with Léger's approval, was ready to be sent to Rome. Gregory again could only wait and pray, but the interview had gone well, and he probably drank a celebratory whisky with Mailloux before boarding the plane for New York.[8]

Two days after his return Gregory finally entered Lenox Hill Hospital for a series of tests. He felt generally rather than specifically unwell, but the test results worried his doctors, who wanted to follow up immediately with surgery. Gregory was, however, emphatically unwilling to cancel his trip. He realised the vanity in his decision – he wanted to receive the honorary degree in person – but he was also reluctant to forego the pleasure of travelling with Peg not only in Ireland and England but on the Continent.[9]

In the process of vacuuming the Bedford swimming pool on the day before their departure, however, Peg lost her balance on the diving board, jumped or misstepped, and the result was pain she was unable to put in her pocket. Caroline did what her father would have done had he been there: helped her mother to the side of the pool and put her hurt foot where the water was coolest, got ice in a bathing cap when Peg was able to hobble indoors. When Gregory arrived late that afternoon, he was confused by the lack of swelling, but another visit to Lenox Hill Hospital that evening revealed that the foot was indeed badly broken while the lack of swelling at least meant it could be put in plaster immediately.

They set out for Europe the next morning with Gregory much in need of a holiday and Peg on crutches. They were heartened, however, by Caroline's quick thinking and the news in the morning papers: Federal Appeals Judge David Bazelon's opinion in *Durham vs. the United States* had overturned the M'Naghten Rule. Bazelon had additionally advocated a new and different insanity test:

> The legal and moral traditions of the western world require that those who, of their own free will and with evil intent ... commit acts which violate the law, shall be criminally responsible for those acts. Our traditions also require that where such acts stem from and are the product of a mental disease or defect ... moral blame shall not attach, and hence there will not be criminal responsibility.[10]

The transatlantic crossing on the elegant *Queen Elizabeth* continued to buoy their spirits. They ate well, relaxed with fellow voyagers, drank champagne at the captain's table, slept late, and revised their itinerary: Even the ship's doorsills challenged Peg on crutches. Leaving her on her own in London, Gregory made an abbreviated trip to the Continent, where he wanted to see Henry, but his old friend had an engagement he simply couldn't break on the one night Gregory felt able to spend in Milan. Gregory was deeply disappointed: He had hoped to talk with Henry, wanted to tell him 'a few things'. Gregory would likely have confided his hopes for baptism and his concern about his health, two topics he would naturally have talked about with Peg but would have discussed with Henry differently.[11]

Back in London Gregory and Peg had tea with Bettine and Eldridge and little Gregory and replaced Peg's cumbersome crutches with a stylish walking stick before setting off for Ireland. Gregory and Peg arrived in Dublin in time for the centenary events preceding the ceremony: festive luncheons, garden parties, a celebratory mass on Sunday 18 July followed by a formal dinner that evening and another the next. On 20 July 1954 Gregory received his honorary degree with all the pomp and circumstance the university could muster. Among other notables similarly honoured were the Oxford professor and novelist J.R.R. Tolkien; the botanist Eric Ashby, later Lord Ashby, one of the future founders of Clare Hall, Cambridge; and the Cambridge historian Sir Herbert Butterfield, author of *The Whig Interpretation of History* (1931). Ironically, the list also included the vociferous American critic of psychoanalysis Bishop Fulton J. Sheen, who received his honorary doctorate *in absentia*. Professional commitments likely precluded his attendance, but he would probably have been uncomfortable sharing the limelight with a psychoanalyst whose views on the compatibility of psychoanalysis and Catholicism were so different from his own. The group photograph on the lawn was followed by an open-air concert of traditional Irish music.[12]

Gregory (far left) in academic regalia, the National University of Ireland, Dublin, 20 July 1954

Gregory and Peg returned to Southampton with the plangent sounds of flutes and fiddles ringing in their ears. The voyage home on the *Queen Mary* was as social and relaxing as the crossing on the *Queen Elizabeth*, and Peg's walking stick made strolling on the deck and navigating doorsills a good deal easier. She wouldn't have the plaster removed until a fortnight after their return, but spent the remainder of the summer increasingly mobile and concertedly following a prescribed programme of exercise. Gregory, in contrast, struggled to recover his bearings.

He had, however, a commitment ahead of him he felt he could not cancel: a workshop sponsored by Saint John's University in Collegeville, Minnesota. Established the previous year, the programme for clergy was directed by predominantly Catholic therapists who discussed problems at the interface of psychiatry and religion. Gregory was honoured to have been invited, excited by the opportunity to address issues close to his heart and mind, and obligated not only by his deep sense of personal responsibility but as an aspiring Catholic. Still unbaptised, he must have felt all the more privileged; at the same time, no matter what he had written and Mailloux had affirmed about the state of his thought and heart, he must have realised he would be interacting with his religious students as to some extent a Catholic imposter.[13]

Away from the honour and Celtic harps, he allowed himself a measure of anxiety about his own physical health. He accepted that he needed to submit to the further examination his doctors had urged in June, and he knew they were likely to discover something serious requiring attention. He was, after all, a medical man; he may have been reluctant to admit infirmity and he may have been fearful, but he was no fool. Even if he managed the trip to Collegeville, he couldn't keep deferring the inevitable. Indeed, he must have acknowledged at least to himself both the facts and his feelings before leaving for Europe. As he left Peg for his overnight trip to Milan, he surely realised that, in order to create the necessary window to see to his own health, he would need to renege on autumn engagements, among them participating in the International Congress for the History of Medicine in September in Italy, where he had much looked forward to spending time with Henry.

In short, Gregory felt powerless and fearful not only of the impending hospitalisation but of the Church's rejection of his petition, yet he imputed his lack of control over his life to other people as if they rather than physical frailty, bureaucracy, and the normal vicissitudes of life were depriving him of freedom and fellowship. Before leaving for Minnesota, he wrote Henry of his disappointment at having not seen him in July. Keen to hear from his friend, he said nothing about his spiritual limbo but confided that he was ill. Just as he had doubted their friendship after taking the momentous step of marrying Peg, now on the brink of baptism and surgery, he flailed about emotionally. 'To put it bluntly', he wrote, during the past few months he had sensed a reluctance on Henry's part to keep in touch: Although he might be 'quite wrong', his friend's last letter had given him the impression that he didn't want to see Gregory this year. Gregory wondered if his impression was right but had nothing to do with him. Unsure and confused by his own perceptions, neither he nor Peg had been able even to guess at what could have led to the coolness he now imagined. 'At any rate', Gregory wrote, 'I can't tell you how sad I feel when I think of our friendship of so many years being nicked by something or other. What could be wrong?'[14]

Gregory's distress as he prepared to set off for Collegeville was, however, a fleeting crisis. By 1954 he was approaching a spiritual peace previously inconceivable for such a volatile man. He would continue, of course, to be volatile in both his moods and behaviour, but his secure religious faith and the affirmation he found in marriage and family had enabled a profound inner serenity. He had further resolved for himself in personal as well as intellectual terms any possible tensions between psychoanalysis and religious belief and practice. His life-long concern with the individual and social justice would from now on be contextualised explicitly in terms of human and particularly Christian love.

Gregory's writings in the mid-1950s reveal a man whose voice was subtly but markedly different from that of the writer of *A History of Medical Psychology* and *Mind, Medicine, and Man*. In reviewing Alfred Kinsey's *Sexual Behavior in the Human Female* in March 1954, for example, Gregory criticised the author for an inaccurate presentation of Freudian hypotheses because he had omitted from his studies what Gregory insisted were 'the central points of Freudian considerations – the evolution of the love affects that accompanies the evolution of psycho-sexual development'. Echoing and expanding on points he had made in the Gimbel lectures in 1947, Gregory concluded,

> To omit love and the inner aspiration to become a parent is to omit that which makes the human (male or female) human. Leave love out of consideration and you have no sexual behavior, but only a manifestation of the physiological reaction of the sexual organs and their adnexa.[15]

Gregory now saw human beings not only as having values in themselves but as living units who in addition to their responsibilities to society had 'obligations to God'. Such religious assertions became increasingly common in his writing and often appeared in passing as if his audience shared his beliefs. Many of his more secular colleagues were uncomfortable with his assumptions and felt he was not only presumptuous but also proselytising. Reflecting on what he called 'the changing concept of man', he deplored the lack of fellow feeling in contemporary society, attributing it to human 'disindividualization' in favour of 'the social, or mass machine', a familiar theme he returned to in contemporary terms. He bewailed the fact that even in psychology and psychopathology 'our language has become neologistic and rather mechanistic. We don't live with one another anymore, conveying to one another directly and indirectly our feelings and intuition; we "communicate" instead. We don't talk to one another; we "communicate."' Making a modern point, he emphasised human isolation:

> We no longer establish relationships to and with people; we 'relate' instead – well or badly as the case may be. We don't adjust ourselves to this or that situation; we merely 'adjust' well or poorly as the case may be – but intransitively, as it were.

He lamented that we 'no longer put ourselves in the place of another person, we don't identify ourselves by way of conscious or unconscious psychological processes with this or that person; we omit the word *ourselves* and we plainly "identify" – quite intransitively.' He understood this decline as 'the penalty we pay for the mechanistic and organismic point of view that took possession of us under the influence of world wars and global mass movements.' In brief, to the extent that the individual had been sacrificed in the name of science and objectivity, people were losing their understanding of the meaning and value of human beings.[16]

On the same point, that psychoanalysis is concerned with the individual, Gregory cited as 'the greatest contribution of psychoanalysis to criminological thought' the fact that psychoanalysis focuses 'on the *actor* not on the *act*' and claimed psychoanalysis 'rediscovered the individual among his human acts'. While stressing that Freudian psychanalysis had led 'in the struggle for the recognition of the psychological autonomy and indivisibility of the human person', Gregory hinted again at his own acceptance and understanding of Christianity when he added that the Judeo-Christian tradition had also 'recognized the primacy and the indivisibility of the human individual'. Indeed, in reviewing a book on punishment, he argued that science in general and specifically psychoanalysis were insufficient to make the world a better place; it was an error 'to identify the good with the healthy, good society with mentally healthy society and criminal people with mentally sick people'. In fact, psychiatry couldn't enable goodness and greatness since it 'does not possess the true knowledge of what is good and right and moral'; there is 'something missing in psychiatry as well as in human law, something that is neither scientific nor judicial, but extremely important in the individual and social functioning of man'.[17]

By the mid-1950s, Gregory explicitly tackled the relation between psychoanalysis and religion in Christian terms. In an essay on the derivation, structure, and function of the superego, he confessed he had struggled for a long time with the 'concordistic attitude of taking psychoanalytic mechanisms and pointing out how they "concord" with religious experiences, psychoses, phenomena of social action, and crises' and had finally concluded that such an attitude was 'methodically untenable, clinically unjustifiable, and scientifically unpardonable'. Pointing out that all 'biopsychological' mechanisms were 'neutral' as far as 'true values' were concerned, he insisted that the activity of these mechanisms reflects an individual's psychological life processes which must not be confused with a person's spiritual, moral, and religious life. In fact, 'The spiritual level cannot be taken away from the human being, any more than you can take the human mind away from him and leave him still a human being.' He continued:

> The secret of a possible true cooperation between the religious leader and the psychiatrist will be uncovered not when they come to a verbal compromise as to who will do what and when and in what manner, but when they each come to understand in each given act of man the differential characteristics between superego and conscience; between the psychobiological aspects of man

and the source of morality, which Gregory argued, following the Christian theologian Paul Tillich, was 'fundamentally transcendental'. Pointing out that the superego was 'fundamentally amorphous' and incorporated teachers, parents, even 'the bad servant and the good stranger', Gregory emphasised that it incorporated without choice and almost always 'without pure love': 'There is a lot of hatred in the superego; there is a lot of intolerance; there is little if any charity.'[18]

Gregory now freely used words – like 'charity' – whose connotations were unavoidably biblical and specifically Christian. Addressing a lay audience on the value of books, for example, he described a library as 'the true temple in which the liturgy is silence, the worship is study, the communion is the contemplative unity of the student-reader with the treasury of human thought and tradition.' It should have surprised no one that when his essay 'Love in Freudian Psychoanalysis' appeared in print in 1954, it was published by a Catholic press.[19]

Leaving Peg and the children in Bedford, Gregory set out for Saint John's University in Collegeville, a small town outside Saint Cloud 75 miles north of Minneapolis. There, joined by Mailloux (as a fellow lecturer) and Plé (as a participant), Gregory spent the second week of August lecturing and participating in seminars with priests from the secular clergy and religious orders. Topics included anxiety and mechanisms of defence, personality development, psychiatric classifications, and individual problems such as alcoholism and depression, while Gregory's interactions with students and colleagues were serious but also spontaneous, replete with wit and good fellowship. Peaceful strolls along the paths of the wooded Benedictine campus allowed him to relax, and he must have appreciated some intimate talks with Mailloux. The week also offered opportunities for reflection and prayer. Pretty sure of 'what the matter was', Gregory was naturally apprehensive about the surgery he anticipated and the prognosis. During one of the vesper services, praying to be spared 'for a little while', he perceived his fears dissolving; he felt 'a new sense of oneness with the source of all life' that made him 'serene and humbly grateful for whatever was in store'. Indeed, the week at Saint John's was an altogether positive one, and Gregory regretted being unable to stay longer because of having agreed to speak at the International Congress of the World Federation of Mental Health in Toronto, but he would return home reaffirmed professionally and spiritually.[20]

At the Saint John's Institute for Mental Health, Collegeville, Minnesota, 9–16 August 1954

Standing: Père Noël Mailloux, Father Alexius Portz, director of the Institute; Dr. H. Waldo Bird; Sister Annette Walters, Père Albert Plé; Dr. John R. Cavanagh
Seated: Dr. Louis L. Flynn and Gregory with his ubiquitous camera

Gregory was back in time to celebrate his eighth wedding anniversary with a bottle of Dom Pérignon on the Bedford terrace. He had missed Matthew's first birthday, but he was ready to reorient himself for what lay ahead. His spirits were further boosted by two envelopes from Switzerland waiting for him on his desk. Gregory's confused letter questioning their friendship had crossed Henry's written the same day, an apology in which his friend twice repeated how 'awfully sorry' he was that at such short notice he had been unable to free himself from other commitments. Unaware that Gregory was ill, Henry warmly invited him to spend a few days in Pura before the medical history congress in Rome. In his second letter, written as soon as he received Gregory's letter of distress, Henry told him he was 'a god-damned bloody fool': 'How could you think that anything could interfere with our friendship and how could you misinterpret my letters? That nothing is wrong', he wrote, 'is evidenced by the fact that we both thought of one another on the same day.' Gregory was, Henry insisted, always welcome to visit and, reiterating his apology for having been unable to meet him in Milan, he emphasised that '*absolutely nothing*' had interfered with their friendship; his feelings towards Gregory were the same as they had been for the previous 25 years. Sorry to hear his friend was ill but not realising how serious the situation might be, he tried to comfort him with humour: The doctors would, he wrote, 'give you a thorough examination and will not tell you what is wrong with you'.[21]

Gregory was immeasurably relieved, his heart warmed by Henry's reaffirmation of their friendship. He was typically delighted to be called 'a bloody fool' by his dear friend, and when he shared the letter with Peg, probably on the terrace with the champagne, they both laughed. Less than a week later, on 22 August, he checked into Johns Hopkins Hospital.[22]

Peg accompanied him to Baltimore. The 'thorough examination' Henry expected took several days, and the result was the surgery Gregory and his New York physicians had anticipated in June. Peg shared the diagnosis with Henry: Rienhoff, the same specialist who had operated on Field, had discovered 'a small carcinoma wrapped around the inside of the transverse colon about two inches beyond the hepatic flexure'. Using the terminology Rienhoff had employed with Gregory in explaining what he had found, Peg was passing on to another medical man what she knew he would want to know in terms he would understand. When she went into detail, however, her own perspective coloured her language: The surgeon had done 'a beautiful, complete and very quick job', resecting only 'a very small portion of the intestines'. While the doctors were there, 'they took a peek around and assured themselves that Gregory was in excellent shape in every other way inside.' Just as the physicians had done 'beautiful' work, Gregory had come through the three-hour operation 'beautifully'; on the third day, 'he was already drinking small amounts of water, ginger ale and tea.' Rienhoff had assured him he was 'completely cured and would be better than ever within a few short weeks'. Gregory wouldn't be back in his office until early October, but Peg knew, she wrote, he would want her to get in touch with Henry 'right away'. She stressed that he meant 'a great deal' to Gregory before signing off 'with all my love'.[23]

Throughout this extraordinary letter, Peg was her sunny, optimistic self. She was trying to put a positive cast on a clearly disturbing event, but she was probably nearly as naïve as she sounded. Despite the precise medical language and her own intelligence, she may not have understood Rienhoff's explanation even as she repeated it. Gregory himself, in trying to shield her from the seriousness of the situation, may have tried to minimise the impact and implications of what the surgeon had discovered. In her letter to Henry, Peg reduced her husband's major cancer surgery to something simple and easy and familiar. It was, of course, none of those things.

Carcinoma of the transverse colon is a common colorectal cancer, but the progression of symptoms is frequently insidious and diagnosis is often, as in Gregory's case, delayed. Although transverse annular cancers are generally smaller than other colorectal tumours, their central location and advanced stage at presentation pose difficult surgical choices for lymph node dissection, the extent of resection, and the re-establishment of intestinal continuity. Curative resection is generally possible in only half the cases, and in the mid-1950s there was no targeted follow-up involving chemo- or radiotherapy. The prognosis was poor, and no responsible oncologist would have assured anyone that the patient was 'completely cured'. Gregory would have been well aware that he wouldn't soon be 'better than ever' – the thick welted scar that ran from just beneath his left nipple to just above his right hip would be a daily reminder – but the surgery seemed to have been successful. He was sober, relieved, and hopeful.

News of Gregory's hospitalisation spread quickly not only among his friends and colleagues but even among the general public. Addressing him as 'Darling Greg' in a heartfelt letter, Mary Warburg was quick to tell him how 'delighted, happy, pleased and relieved' she was that he was recovering. Reflecting on their friendship and all that he had done for Eddie, she confessed they loved him 'very dearly', felt abiding 'devotion and affection' not only for him but his family. A Baltimore journalist who interviewed him at Johns Hopkins reported Gregory's thoughts from his hospital bed. Gregory admitted he was being treated like a colleague rather than merely a patient, but insisted he was doing his best to conduct himself as 'what every patient should be'. 'I ask no questions', he declared; 'I just do as I'm told. I don't even know quite when I'm going home.' While it seems unlikely Gregory refrained from asking a great many questions, he didn't doubt the necessity for medical intervention and hospitalisation, and accepted the judgements and authority of those tasked with looking after him. Having finally put the rest of his life aside to see to his own physical health, he was deeply appreciative. He took the opportunity of the interview to praise the quality of his care while focusing on the hospital rather than the specifics of his personal experience. At Johns Hopkins, he told the reporter, the human being was 'never lost in the midst of superior medicine'. Indeed, 'the concept that caused this institution to be founded' continued to exist: 'moral values' were preserved and the patient did not 'lose faith in God – or men'.[24]

Having cancelled his autumn lectures at Butler Hospital and his September appointments with patients, after a few days at home, Gregory flew to California to recuperate. He saw his Bay Area friends and did his best to take it easy. In a letter to his friend and colleague the Chicago psychoanalyst Max Gitelson, Gregory reflected on his recent experience. Sitting in the sun near San Francisco, he was recovering from what he merely called 'a serious operation'. He admitted having gone through 'some dark hours', but everything had turned out 'extremely well'; all in all, he felt he had had 'a very easy time' and was grateful.[25]

In Quebec Mailloux was neither sitting in the sun nor taking it easy. During the week in Minnesota Gregory had naturally shared with the good Dominican his concerns about his health and the anticipated surgery, and matters moving slowly through Catholic bureaucracy were finally hastened along. Gregory's 'supplication' along with humble petitions, legal documents, and supporting letters from Dominican, Jesuit, and Carthusian priests and Catholic friends and colleagues were all in order. At the end of September, apparently in response to a request for yet another piece of paper, Mailloux sent the archbishop's office his own attestation indicating Peg's support of Gregory's baptism as well as her understanding that children born of their union were obligated, according to Church law, to be educated as Catholics. Earnest and sincere, Mailloux had no reason to doubt Peg's commitment, yet the important thing now was not the details but the sacrament that would allow Gregory to enter the Church he so longed to join.

On Friday the first of October Gregory arrived in Montreal with a discreet entourage. The following day he was at last baptised '*in nomine Patris, et Filii, et Spiritus Sancti*' by the Archbishop of Montréal Cardinal Paul-Émile Léger in the Basilique, Le Cathédral de Montréal, in the parish of St-Jacques-le-Majeur. Before the mass that followed, Gregory went to confession and was granted absolution of his sins. During the service, he and Peg were then married and he was confirmed at the altar where he took his first communion. The day managed to include five of the seven holy sacraments, and there was surely immeasurable joy in everyone's hearts at the final '*ite, Missa est*'.

Gregory took at his baptism the name 'Gregory Francis Zilboorg', 'Francis' likely for France. The witnesses were Jean de Menil and Leo Bartemeier. The marriage was everything Gregory had hoped for: 'the dispensations from the publication of the three banns of marriage, from the impediment of mixed religion and for greater security from the impediment of disparity of worship were granted by the Ordinary of this diocese'. Jean de Menil is indicated in the marriage register as the witness for the bride and Howard Seitz the witness for the groom. The couple as well as both witnesses signed the official document – as in no necessarily official capacity did Noël Mailloux.

Less than six weeks after his surgery, Gregory resumed work at his desk. He wouldn't feel fully fit until January, but he began to see patients again, slowly resumed his normal, varied, and hectic professional life. He was a bit overwhelmed by how much work he felt obligated to catch up with, had a gnawing sense of being constantly behind with obligations. He didn't mention his conversion when writing Henry, but reported that Peg and the children were as ever a source of great joy and asked his friend to write him again soon. Gregory would be less guarded with Thomas Verner Moore, now Father Pablo Maria, who had returned to the United States from Spain, where after his retirement from Catholic University he had sought a more contemplative life in a Carthusian monastery. Having subsequently founded in Vermont the first Carthusian community in North America, he was briefly in New York, perhaps on business associated with the Charterhouse, but probably expressly to see the man for whom he had been a spiritual confidante and guide. Moore reported to Mailloux that while Gregory openly attended mass at Saint Ignatius Loyola, his parish church on Park Avenue, he had asked Moore not to speak publicly about his conversion since he wanted as long as possible 'to keep it out of the newspapers'. Despite his conversion, Gregory continued to feel vulnerable. His first line of defence would always be pre-emptive action.[26]

Throughout the autumn Gregory was reminded that his days were numbered while events confirmed how ephemeral life could be. Religion as well as science humbled him, and he reflected both intellectually and personally on ruptures and continuities, on the limits of life and those liminal spaces he had called 'borderlands', on time and grace, and on what happens when one's luck runs out.

Gregory's conversion had, however, little evident impact on his wife and children. In September Caroline had been promoted from kindergarten to first grade at the secular Brearley School, where a large portion of her classmates were Jews, and John had started nursery school at the Central Presbyterian Church. Apparently no effort was made to enrol him in a Catholic preschool, although Saint Ignatius Loyola's nursery, founded in 1910, was prestigious at least within the Catholic community. The complexity of borderlands passed Peg by, and she didn't feel any obligation to arrange a specifically Catholic education for their Episcopalian children either through the schools they attended during the week or through Sunday school or private tutelage. Peg recognised how important conversion was for her husband, but she understood neither its process nor its substance. She knew Mailloux had worked hard on Gregory's behalf, and as a proper and grateful wife she wrote him to tell him so. Thanking him for his support, strength, and love over the years leading up to the recent events in Montreal, she typically simplified matters and treated them with remarkable humour: 'I hope you will understand my feeling that Gregory and I are at last children of the same church – just slightly different branches!' It may have seemed to her the same church, but as Gregory and Mailloux well knew, the struggle her husband had gone through was largely predicated on the fundamental differences between the two as opposed to their similarities. Given all that Gregory's conversion had involved, Peg's astonishing equation seems ridiculous, even stupid, but her gratitude was sincere. Insisting on unity rather than division, she told Mailloux he was truly her own priest as well as Gregory's, and closed 'With warmest affection, Peg Zilboorg'. Peg's personal relationship with Mailloux would remain polite and – despite her declared warmth – cool. She simply refused to see that disparities in belief and practice could really matter.[27]

In Switzerland Henry didn't respond to Gregory's last letter, and at the end of October his daughter Erica wrote to explain: Henry had been hospitalised with a cerebral embolism, his right side paralysed and unable to speak. Gregory would miss his friend at the other end of the epistolary conversation that had begun a quarter of a century earlier, would think of him often in the coming weeks, could only hope as well as pray he would recover. Gregory couldn't have avoided feeling the acute irony of Henry's unanticipated illness so fast upon his own, his own recovery from surgery a stark contrast to Henry's sudden limbo.[28]

Still recuperating even while trying to catch up with all he had put aside while away from his desk, Gregory made an apparently conscious effort to affirm friendships he especially valued. He and Peg spent an early November weekend with Harry and Doris Hatcher, and he visited Hal Babcock and his family when he finally resumed his fortnightly lectures at Butler Hospital in early December. As this challenging year drew to a close, Gregory had not only continuities to sustain but matters to wrap up. On 13 December 1954, he formally relinquished his membership in the Society of Friends, resigning from the New York monthly Hicksite meeting he had joined almost to the day 32 years earlier. Christmas in Bedford, however, was much as it had been since 1949. On Christmas eve Peg with the three children in tow attended a service at Saint Matthew's, an early candle-lit occasion especially for families. Gregory meanwhile went to midnight mass at the Church of Saint Francis of Assisi in Mount Kisco, taking communion for the first time on the birthday he shared with Jesus, but he attended the service on his own, drove there alone over the five miles of country road in the December dark.

Gregory did, however, feel welcomed within the very different Catholic church communities in which he took part. Saint Ignatius Loyola was sophisticated and congenial. Its sumptuous marble interior with Tiffany glass mosaics could accommodate over 1,000 people, while its Jesuit rector, Father Robert Ignatius Gannon, had previously served as president of Fordham University. Saint Francis in Mount Kisco was altogether humbler and attracted predominantly working-class Catholics of German and Irish decent, but Gregory felt comfortable there, too. Molly Hanrahan, who helped out in Bedford as a laundress, was a faithful parishioner, as was her jovial husband Tim and Gregory's workshop assistant Bill Reich.

Gregory with Bill Reich, Bedford, 1955

The new year began as if Gregory had never been ill, as if he were indeed cured and dependably strong and healthy. Concerned about the administration of the Aquinas Fund, in January he flew to Europe. In London he navigated the city's legendary winter fog, saw the British psychoanalyst Denis Carroll, the serving president of the International Society for Criminology, had tea with Bettine and Eldridge, and marvelled at little Gregory's beaming smiles. Over the sandwiches and cakes at the Bruces' home, the fund was certainly again a topic of conversation. For a man who never knew where his cash went when it left his pockets, Gregory was as good at raising money as he was at working harder, for he knew it was the way of money to run out. Bettine likely agreed to contribute further to the worthy cause. In Paris there was no fog, but the wind blew down the Champs-Élysée as if it had followed the entire sinuous length of the Seine from the sea. In the sheltered warmth of the Dominican premises he met with Plé but not with Piprot, whose serious illness probably occasioned the trip Gregory considered 'sudden and rather urgent'.[29]

Back in the United States before the end of the month, Gregory resumed his demanding round of lectures. At the end of January he spoke again on a 'border-line' topic, 'Aspects of Some Denials and Assertions of Religious Faith', at the Seton Psychiatric Institute in Baltimore, where Bartemeier was now medical director. He spent the following Saturday teaching at Butler Hospital, then travelled to Newark, Delaware, to address the Delaware Psychiatric Society. He reported to Mailloux that while things in general were going well for him, at times he was still looking for the 'spiritual companionship' he found only when with Mailloux or 'occasionally' with the Jesuit theologian Father John Courtney Murray, a vocal advocate of cooperation between civil and religious institutions and a professor of theology at Woodstock College, a Jesuit seminary west of Baltimore.[30]

Not having had time during his recent European trip to see Henry, still incapacitated in hospital in Lugano, Gregory was elated to receive a letter his friend had managed to dictate in early February. 'Bully for you!' Gregory responded, and declared nothing could have lifted his spirits more than knowing Henry was recovering. Confiding that he had recovered 'from the operation at least', Gregory reiterated what was now a constant refrain: 'I worry all the time about being behind.' It is clear that he was realistically cautious about his health, concerned that the colon cancer, the cancer of his 'behind', would return, that he would never 'catch up' but die with not only his work but much in his life unfinished, his marriage to his much younger wife still in its early years and their children still children. He identified himself with Henry, announcing that 'each in his different way' had been 'at death's door', but both had 'learned the same hard lesson'. In this first letter since his stroke, Henry had sent his love to both Gregory and Peg. Gregory also closed with a simple declaration of special affection: 'We all love you.'[31]

Affirming continuities while he acknowledged inevitable change, Gregory increasingly emphasised in both his life and writing what he saw as lasting truths and shifting realities. In February he addressed a combined meeting of the New

York Neurological Society and the New York Academy of Medicine on 'The Newest Trends in Forensic Psychiatry' as well as the staff of the Seton Institute on 'Morality and Contemporary Psychology'. At the beginning of March he took his annual week in the sunshine, again in California, where he relaxed with friends and delivered two lectures, both of which explored what is given (facts, history, truth) and what unavoidably alters, what is predicated on fallibility, perceptions, time. He thus addressed the San Francisco Psychoanalytic Society on 'The Trends Towards the Evaluation of Freud's Personality' and the San Francisco Mental Health Society on 'The Errors and Truths about Mental Health'.

Gregory continued to speak on old themes – at an early April symposium sponsored by the New York Academy of Medicine he took as his topic 'The Role of the Psychiatrist as an Expert Witness in Criminal Court' – but he was also thinking about the finitude of things, about limits and fixed boundaries. For predominantly financial reasons, the decision had been taken to close Butler Hospital. Babcock had been let go months earlier and there had been changes in the provision of care, both of which Gregory deeply regretted. Emphasising that he was not 'a Pollyanna', but making the sort of grammatical error that, when emotional, he still sometimes made, he told Babcock he thought they should not 'feel despaired'. With great generosity of spirit Gregory didn't blame the administration:

> It occurs to me as a possibility that those responsible felt so weak in the face of what life demanded of them that the only act that might give them some sense of power is to do what they did: to close, to put an end to what they were too weak to sustain.

He didn't exonerate 'their pusillanimous decisions and actions' but tried to understand them to avoid feeding his resentments. Whether or not his explanation consoled Babcock, Gregory told him he left blame and forgiveness to God.[32]

Explicitly taking up the issue of liminality in Saint Louis on the first of May, Gregory addressed the annual meeting of the American Psychoanalytic Association on 'Clinical and Therapeutic Aspects of the Borderline Case'. At the annual meeting of the American Psychiatric Association in Atlantic City nine days later, he elaborated in 'Psychoanalytic Borderlines'. He told his colleagues,

> Freud worked as we do, empirically in a borderline area.... As soon as we make a misstep and make one move beyond our purely empirical domain, we at once touch the vast and sensitive and awe-inspiring area of another domain: that of morality, religion, or at least theology, and ontology.

He argued that 'a psychoanalyst, more than any other professional man, must cultivate a philosophy of values, because the field that he is working in is always on the borderline of ontological and moral issues.' The analyst, he insisted, 'must learn to be aloof yet interested, objective yet charitable.' After pointing out that Freudian psychoanalysis isn't concerned with morality *per se*, Gregory finally contended the only moral foundation in Freud's teaching was his statement that by 'Eros', he meant what Saint Paul termed 'Caritas' in his Epistle to the Corinthians. In contrast, Gregory concluded by calling the Bible 'one of the richest sources of moral philosophy', a statement which made perfect sense to him, a step over the threshold into the 'moral philosophy' of Christianity that – for him if not for all of his colleagues – was the necessary complement to psychoanalysis.[33]

Throughout the spring of 1955 Gregory balanced seeing patients with speaking engagements that stressed the topic of morality broadly considered for a professional audience or more narrowly focused on Christian ethics for an audience of predominantly Catholic clergy. His patients had to be indeed patient and wait while Gregory travelled. However needy and dependent, they were also dedicated and preferred to work with Gregory despite the frequent interruptions. Among them now was Marie Colbert, a confused and unsettled young woman, the daughter of French Catholic parents who knew Gregory well and trusted him unreservedly. The analysis had begun following a disturbing incident when she was found late one night wandering in Central Park in her nightgown. As she emerged from the serious breakdown, session after session was devoted to her uncontrollable anger and her resentment of her mother, her emotional and social immaturity and deep general unhappiness. Gregory felt a particular responsibility for Marie and for her younger sister Agathe, who followed her into analysis. Given his respect and affection for their parents, Gregory was once again in a borderline area, treating members of a family he knew socially, but he had long before accepted that in his world these overlapping allegiances would occur, and he trod carefully, engaged and disengaged, involved and distanced.[34]

Despite the seriousness with which he treated his patients, despite his hectic agenda, demanding lectures and associated travel, his commitments to the Church and to God, Gregory continued to enjoy a vivid social life replete with dinner parties, good food and wine, heady conversation, and much laughter and music. He had season subscriptions to both the New York Philharmonic and the Metropolitan Opera, where Guiseppe Di Stefano and Mario Del Monaco, Risë Stevens and Zinka Milanov were in their prime. Eddie had given Peg and Gregory a Steinway grand piano as a wedding present, had celebrated the completion of their house in Bedford with the gift of a Steinway baby grand for their country home. Whatever her voiced intentions, Peg never seriously resumed the piano lessons of her Bronxville youth, but at their frequent parties someone often played. Goddard Lieberson played like a dream; impromptu, he or someone else would be invited to perform. The cabaret entertainer known only as Hildegarde lived on the third floor just below the Zilboorgs' apartment and didn't need much persuading to sing 'Darling, *Je Vous Aime Beaucoup*', while guests couldn't help but smile when Ezio Pinza reprised 'Some Enchanted Evening', a song that always made Peg cry. Long past his performing prime but still a great raconteur, Giovanni Martinelli's moving rendition of '*Vesti la giubba*' filled the living room as it had filled opera houses decades earlier. Old friends like Eddie and Mary, Johnny Kilroe, and Abe, now with Gertrude, were frequently among the eclectic guests – but so were Jean and Dominique de Menil; Lillian Hellman, with her husky voice and throaty laugh; the illustrator Garth Williams and his Austrian wife Dorothea; and Bob Giroux, Gregory's editor at Farrar, Strauss. Many of Gregory's psychiatric colleagues were often included, and even occasionally compatriots from his revolutionary days: Marc Slonim, now professor of comparative and Russian literature at Sarah Lawrence College, and Alexander Kerensky, who after the war had settled in New York.

Despite their spontaneous elements, such evenings were highly organised events with their own protocol: Place cards indicated Peg's carefully planned seating arrangements and candles in silver holders graced the black lacquer dining table where finger bowls were presented between courses. Betty cooked invisibly deep in the kitchen. Lala in a black taffeta uniform with a sheer white apron would announce that dinner was served, then serve and clear the dishes in efficient silence. The children would be brought in early to say good night while their parents and the guests (whom Lala called 'company') were still drinking drinks. They were not to stay long, but they could greet and be greeted, were allowed to taste the caviar with sour cream Gregory heaped on Carr's water biscuits, the smoked salmon on the dark brown bread. If the music from the living room (that Betty called 'inside') was so mesmerising that Caroline at least was still awake when Peg came to check on her, one of the guests might be permitted to come into her bedroom to say a second good night – her godmother Mary or Mary-Alice or even Brigitta Lieberson with her gentle voice and stylish hair. Once the dishes were cleared, Lala would come back to check again and, if Caroline were not yet asleep, sing to her in Swedish 'Mors Lilla Olle' while the guests in the living room with their cigarettes, cigars, and brandy continued to talk and laugh.

Throughout the spring of 1955 Gregory was every bit as mesmerising as Martinelli and much in demand on the variety of topics that captured his attention. In early May he spoke on 'Today's Fears', a radio programme on mental health, and agreed to be the principal speaker during the centenary celebration of Saint Elizabeth's Hospital, where Ezra Pound had been incarcerated for a decade. Focusing on reforms in the institutional treatment of mental patients, Gregory spoke on 'The Unwritten History of Inspiration'. He was surely aware of the irony of his title, which drew his audience's attention not only to insufficiently acknowledged mental health reformers but to the unbalanced American poet who had inspired a generation and whose supporters were now rallying for his release.

Invited to comment on an article on religion and psychiatry, sin and salvation by William H. Roberts in the May issue of the *New Republic*, Gregory was withering. Taking issue with the author, he contended that Aristotle rather than 'the perverted Plato of Calvin' was 'the true philosopher of Christianity', and dismissed the essay by declaring he was 'certain that Mr. Roberts meant something here which he did not succeed in saying'. Continuing to make fine distinctions,

Gregory was equally compelling in a more positive vein when he spoke at the French Consulate at the end of the month and chose yet another liminal topic, 'Maladies Physiques et Maladies Mentales: Rapprochements et Divergences'. Presenting paradoxes and oppositions with 'magnetic charm' and 'calm clarity', Gregory appeared to the effusive reviewer in *France-Amérique* as 'a great painter of ideas'.[35]

As a fully fledged Catholic, Gregory was once again welcome on Catholic university campuses. In June he was the principal speaker at the first Institute for the Clergy on Problems in Pastoral Psychology at Fordham University. Taking as his topic 'The Sense of Guilt', Gregory now succinctly summarised his view of Freud and religion, arguing for Freud and against Jung and Adler, who he contended mixed their own mystical or sociological thought with their personal psychologies. In contrast, Gregory asserted, 'Freud's great advantage lies in the very disadvantage which he has as compared to Adler and Jung. He was a poor sociologist and a poor philosopher, but somehow neither his sociological nor his metaphysical excursions seem to be really a part of his scientific empirical system' – Freud was thus 'a clinician despite himself'.

In this carefully argued presentation, Gregory came as close to self-revelation as he ever would or could from the podium. He wasn't averse to drawing on his own experiences in lectures and published writings, but he was always careful to present case studies and other professional encounters anonymously while he recounted personal anecdotes with a degree of detachment or humour or so stripped of intimate detail that they could have occurred to anyone in the situations he described. As early as *The Passing of the Old Order in Europe*, he had been circumspect and self-protective; the sensitive reader can only glimpse the autobiography underlying the history and philosophy that dominate his first book. Such discretion was part of Gregory's defensiveness, the complement of his verbal belligerence. At New York's Jesuit university before a clerical audience, he was no less discreet as he set out what he saw as the relationship between Freud and religion, but both consciously and unconsciously he opened a window onto his inner spiritual and psychological life. He might well have been speaking of his own spiritual journey when he told his audience that Freud had pondered at times

> in a rather impersonal way on life, death, and God. But instead of allowing himself to follow his own spiritual trends, he preferred to depersonalize them, and thus deny as illusions many of those things which ... were part and parcel of his spiritual search and struggle.

As a result, making what in his own case was a critical distinction, Gregory pointed out,

> the clinical, empirical system of Freud seems to stand very well the test of time and experience; his metaphysical excursions stand apart from his clinical

findings as something personal which is of Freud … but no more of psychoanalysis than Freud's purely personal and cherished possessions.

Much that was 'of' Gregory – his 'spiritual trends', his 'spiritual search and struggle' stretching as far back as his Kiev youth – remained separate from his clinical, psychoanalytic self, yet as he finally focused specifically on guilt, he approached however obliquely what had brought him to the Catholic Church. Distinguishing between psychoanalysis and religion – between psychoanalysis and specifically Christianity and even more specifically Catholicism – between the superego and conscience, Gregory made his most important point with extraordinary passion:

> Conscience *regrets* while the super-ego is *angry*. Conscience glows with hope when its owner repents and makes amends. The super-ego never says: Go, and sin no more; it merely says: Wait until I get you next time, or: It is all right to be sorry, but you must pay for it time and again until the end of your earthly days. Conscience knows forgiveness, and cedes its position to charity; the super-ego concedes nothing and cedes less.

Guilt was at the heart of the self-doubt and insecurities that dogged Gregory throughout his life, at the heart of his deepest needs and the bullying only his closest friends understood or forgave, at the heart of his search for the serenity he found only in the Catholic Church. Gregory had begun his lecture at Fordham with a revealing case study, a conventional approach in a clinical presentation. He described a deluded man who felt he was a murderer and a cannibal as well as a bad son, a bad friend, a bad husband, and a bad father. Actually, Gregory pointed out, the man had never killed anyone and was never a cannibal; he never even liked meat, and when he did eat it, insisted it had to be 'so well done that it looked and felt like leather'. With and without justification Gregory had been made to feel and felt throughout his life that he had been a bad son, a bad friend, a bad husband, and a bad father. The man who only ate his meat well done was remarkably like himself.[36]

Notes

1 Weihoffen, 289; Farinholt, 91, 92; Gould, 365; Roche, 178; Joffe, 410.
2 GZ to NM, 20 January 1954.
3 GZ to JZ and to HES, both 21 January 1954.
4 Email from Gloria Levitas, 14 October 2013.
5 Becker, 464.
6 For example, J. Nelson Taylor, 'Criminals Are Sick People: Crime Parley Draws 1,000', *Daily Oklahoman*, 10 April 1954, np.
7 GZ, 'The Changing Concept'; NM to Emmanuel Suarez, 27 July 1951, APD.
8 Père Léonard Crowley, summary of interview with GZ, May 1954, APD.
9 GZ to HES, 9 August 1954.

10 GZ, 'A Step Toward', 334.
11 GZ to HES, 7 July, 9 August 1954.
12 MSZ to Caroline Zilboorg, 13 July 1954; programmes and memorabilia.
13 GZ to Alexius Portz, 17 March 1954, SJU.
14 GZ to HES, 9 August 1954.
15 GZ, review, '*Sexual Behavior*', 1045.
16 GZ, 'The Changing Concept', 446, 448.
17 GZ, 'The Contribution of Psycho-Analysis', 322, 324, and review, *The Urge to Punish*, 176–177.
18 GZ, 'Derivation', 103, 116, 117.
19 GZ, *Freud: An Address*, 2.
20 GZ to Alexius Portz, 23 November 1954, SJU.
21 HES to GZ, 9, 14 August 1954.
22 MSZ to HES, 1 September 1954.
23 MSZ to HES, 1 September 1954.
24 Mary Warburg to GZ, 14 September 1954; 'Dr. Zilboorg at Hopkins', *The Sun*, 3 September 1954, 6.
25 GZ to Max Gitelson, 13 October 1954, Max Gitelson Papers, Manuscript Division, Library of Congress, Washington, D.C.
26 GZ to HES, 13 October 1954; Pablo Maria (Thomas Verner Moore) to NM, 18 October 1954, APD.
27 MSZ to NM, 25 October 1954, APD.
28 Erica Sigerist Beeson to GZ, 21 October 1954.
29 GZ to MSZ, 16 January 1955; GZ to NM, 1 February 1955.
30 GZ to NM, 1 February 1955.
31 HES to GZ, 4 February 1955; GZ to HES, 7 February 1955.
32 GZ to Hal Babcock, 28 April 1955.
33 GZ, 'Psychoanalytic Borderlines', 709, 710.
34 For reasons of confidentially I am not using the patients' real names or those of their parents; AZ interview; email from AZ, 28 September 2019.
35 Roberts, 16–17; GZ, 'Scientific Positivism', 18; Lecompte du Noüy, 'Une Conférence de M Gregory Zilboorg', *France-Amérique*, nd, np.
36 GZ, 'The Sense of Guilt', 8, 10, 21.

Chapter 8

'His should be the path of spiritual development'
1955–1957[1]

As soon as school let out, the household decamped to Bedford where Betty and Lala replaced the local weekend staff and Peg turned on the swimming pool filter. The children were allowed, now that it was June, to run barefoot on the lawns, and the three poodles followed them in and out of the screen doors at will. In such relaxed but orderly daily life Gregory found in the bosom of his family much of the serenity he sought.

With plenty of space for guests, friends came from New York, from their Westchester and Connecticut country homes, from all over the country, from Canada and Europe. The Bruces, on a visit to America, came for the weekend. Patients with particular needs arrived for analytic sessions in the library, and clergy in cassocks came for the opportunity of serious conversation with Gregory. In a special drawer in the long corridor Peg kept bathing trunks in various sizes so, should they be inclined, the generally unprepared priests might swim. In bathing trunks, even the monks looked like quite ordinary men.

Peg's family often visited. Louise and Margo drove over from Bronxville once a week and were sometimes joined by George and Jodie, who had embraced life at the Hotchkiss School, where George now taught mathematics, a subject he had surprised everyone including himself by growing to love. Neither he nor Jodie seemed interested in producing offspring, which Louise confided to Peg was probably just as well, given those childhood convulsions. Even now Jodie always drove – which was, as Louise repeated, just as well. Lou, who seemed preoccupied, visited with his family that now included two-year-old Charles and the new baby. Peg and Louise wondered if Nancy's drinking so much was good for the children, wondered if there were something bothering Lou at his new job at the Columbia Broadcasting Corporation. Gregory looked carefully at the tall man with his broad shoulders slumped, his laughter forced at his brother's jokes, and suspected his momentarily vacant eyes indicated something more than trouble at work. It was understood and accepted that Gregory would retreat to his study when everyone else swam. There would be drinks on the terrace afterwards, and the children would play at a distance during the cocktail hour, a moment when in New York they were banned from the living room, a moment in Bedford when they were forbidden to be wherever that hour took place.

DOI: 10.4324/9781003190974-8

Gregory flew to Europe in mid-July. The International Psycho-analytical Association was holding its 19th congress in Geneva at the end of the month, and he was eager to see Henry as well as to meet with both the archbishop of Milan, Monsignor Giovanni Battista Montini, a prelate sympathetic to ecumenism and psychoanalysis, and the Franciscan Agostino Gemelli, a doctor interested in psychology and the founder and first rector of Milan's Catholic University of the Sacred Heart. Gregory hoped to advance the cause of psychoanalysis with the Milanese prelates, but he was less sanguine about this year's pilgrimage to his diminished friend. Six weeks earlier Henry had still been struggling to express himself verbally despite being intellectually alert. Gregory had suggested he not try too hard since 'It is the trying so hard that makes a person with motor aphasia so impatient.' He had also done his philosophical best to be comforting: 'Luckily one afflicted with motor aphasia is able to contemplate and therefore cultivate a considerable amount of tolerance and, consequently, of patience.'

This time Gregory took three days out of his busy schedule to visit Henry in Pura, where he was pleasantly surprised and gratified. The ground floor had been modified to accommodate a man no longer easily able to manage stairs, and Henry was delighted to see him. He still wanted to cook even if he couldn't eat everything he prepared, and they talked at length and as always about recipes and restaurants, wine and photography, history and medicine and all the other topics they always talked about when in each other's company. Henry continued to be impatient with his limited physical capacities, but expressed his frustration with mock irritability, having evidently cultivated a good deal of tolerance in the months since his stoke. Gregory was sorry when he had to push on to Geneva.[2]

During the last week in July Gregory attended the congress, where he spoke on 'The Contribution of Psycho-Analysis to Forensic Psychiatry', dined with psychoanalytic colleagues, and took time out to see friends in Geneva who had nothing to do with psychoanalysis. As soon as the congress concluded, he flew back to the United States. His family was waiting for him in Bedford and he had writing he needed to get on with, although he wrote as usual wherever he went: in his hotel rooms in Lugano and Geneva; in Frankfurt, where he changed planes; and in his room in Collegeville, where this year he headed, after a few comparatively restful days with Peg and the children, for a fortnight of lectures and seminars, convivial conversation, and walks in the woods between the two lakes on the Saint John's campus.

The experience the previous year had been cut short by his lecture in Toronto. This year, his weeks in Minnesota would be even more rewarding. A great deal had happened since the summer of 1954, and he was now free to be more forthright in his views, openly Catholic in his assertions about Freud and religion, psychology and faith. Gregory likely addressed the workshop participants on the substance of what he discussed in an important essay that would appear in the autumn in *Faith, Reason, and Modern Psychiatry*, a collection edited by Frank Braceland, who introduced Gregory's contribution by arguing that attention to 'moral and religious values' – as opposed to 'the purely automatic, unconscious functioning of the human ego by way of its psychological mechanisms' – was an essential part of the synthesis the book envisioned. Psychological thinking needed go beyond the analysis of mental operations to consider 'other determinants in human existence, those borderline activities between the strictly natural and the strictly supernatural – between science and religion – and the relations between them'.[3]

'Some Denials and Affirmations of Religious Faith' was a revised and expanded version of Gregory's talk at the Seton Institute in January, the first lecture he had felt able to give after his surgery and conversion. His thinking on this 'borderline' topic, with its intellectual and moral as well as personal implications, had matured and developed during the year. He was now ready to tackle head on as a Catholic psychoanalyst what was often presented as the struggle between theology and science, between religion and modern psychology, but which he contended was actually the human struggle between respect for God's will and the wish to abolish it in favour of what appeared to be 'the exclusive supremacy of a given scientific discovery'.

Gregory began, however, by quoting the Trappist monk Thomas Merton, who had cited Teresa of Avila's 'example of stupid direction' in *Ascent to Truth*, his exposition of the doctrines of Saint John of the Cross. A priest had advised a married woman attracted to a life of prayer to drop her household work and pray whenever she felt the urge. Prayer thus became an obstacle to the woman's happiness as a wife and to her marriage while simultaneously erecting a barrier between the woman and God. Gregory may well have used this anecdote in Collegeville to point out that the relation between pastoral counselling and the 'so-called realities of life' persisted as a formidable problem. Indeed, Saint Teresa's homely story suggested to him the 'fundamental contradiction between charity and animosity, between moral values and "purely" technological progress, between free obedience to the will of God and to reason … between religious faith and egocentric science, between principles and practical formalism'. Drawing on both George Sarton and Maritain, Gregory argued the conflict wasn't 'between science and religion as it appears to be but between what man wants to do with science, and what he wants to do with religion'. Gregory's logic and faith led him to assert that science and religion were actually one; true knowledge of humankind and God were one.

Gregory then moved on to the familiar topic of love he had approached so often, reiterating that love was central to Freudian thought and that by 'healthy love', Freud meant something close to Saint Paul's conception of charity. Yet, Gregory added, Freud was never able to resolve two fundamental problems: first, a potent gravitation towards the very religious attitude he tried so hard to deny (by wrongly equating faith with ritual and interpreting ritual as neurotic), and second, the relation between reason and faith and fear of death. Freud erroneously equated faith with the rejection of reason, apparently ignorant of Aquinas's respect for reason and intelligence as well as of the emphasis placed by Saint John of the Cross on reason, intellect, and rational knowledge. Freud thus fell into the trap of 'mechanistic concordism' or 'psychomechanistic parallelism': Religion seemed to him an illusion and religious practice, a compulsion neurosis.

In the essay's final section, 'The Psychology of the Sacraments', Gregory elaborated on the difference between conscious guilt and the unconscious workings of the superego, tracing the conscious 'road from the beginning of the act of penance to the act of communion'. The psychological result of the sacrament of penance is, he explained, 'the elimination of one's ambivalence, the reduction or sufficient attenuation of the sense of guilt which was due to sins of which one had taken cognizance, and the establishment of a sense of humble unworthiness' that permits the communicant 'to perform the sacramental act of identification with the Lord'. The sacrament of communion is thus in no way 'an unconscious performance by one's ego in the service of the superego, but an incorporation vouchsafed by God the Father through the authorized priest'.

Aware that his explanation might seem 'self-evident to the initiated' and 'a little irritating to the agnostic or atheistic psychoanalyst', Gregory emphasised what he saw as 'the depth of the psychological understanding which religious faith offers as it leads one from sin through penance and communion to an identification with Christ the Redeemer'. The result of communion is 'gratitude and awareness of one's sense of duty and striving for service', a sense of humility and 'simple serenity'. Conscious guilt for things done and undone weighed heavily on Gregory, but he saw nothing neurotic in such feelings. The Church's sacraments at least 'attenuated' his guilt in what he believed was a psychologically healthy way. He felt as a result grateful, reminded of his responsibilities and his capacity to serve others, humbled and serene. For a man as complicated and passionate as Gregory, who felt called to do more than was perhaps humanly possible and deeply guilty for all his inevitable and inevitably repeated human failings, the Church offered a consolation he needed and was unable to find anywhere else. Shifting his focus from the communicant to the pastoral psychoanalyst he felt called to be, Gregory insisted finally there was no need for the contentious reader to quarrel with Freud: His discoveries were made 'despite his conscious antireligious attitude', perhaps even 'because of his unconscious, intense, positive religious leanings'.[4]

The weeks in Collegeville that grew out of Gregory's current understanding of both Freudian psychoanalysis and Catholic theology were particularly rewarding, but this year they were bracketed between two trips to Europe. Without the commitment in Minnesota, Gregory might have spent the entire summer abroad, although he wouldn't have wanted to be so long without Peg, and Peg didn't want to leave the children for what would have amounted to more than eight weeks away with her itinerant husband. Despite the pre-war tours with her aunts, Peg had never been the world traveller Gregory was, wouldn't have felt comfortable flying with him to Europe and then leaving him, abbreviating the journey to return on her own – nor would she have left the children and travelled alone to join him wherever he might be. The expense was likely a lesser consideration, but two European trips for Gregory in one summer were expensive enough when his lectures hither and yon meant fewer analytic sessions, when it was only his work with patients that contributed to the family coffers.

Gregory boarding the plane for Italy, 23 August 1955

Gregory flew back to Europe in the third week of August. He likely met again with Montini in Milan before setting off by train for Munich via Zurich, but he couldn't pass through Switzerland without seeing Henry. There wouldn't be time this time for a relaxed visit to Pura, but Henry managed to make it to Lugano, where they met at the station with its high arched ceilings and sat together in the restaurant overlooking the lake and mountains. Henry ordered a cup of tea, then described a tea he had once got from a merchant in Boston, asked Gregory, '"Do you know that tea?"' Gregory hated to disappoint him and tell him 'no', so he just nodded silently, as he must have done regularly to acknowledge his patients during treatment sessions. Henry looked at him with a pale, already 'outworldly' smile. Their conversation, such as it then was, was cut short by the announcement of Gregory's train.[5]

In Munich Gregory changed again for Garmisch-Partenkirchen, where Richard Strauss had died at his country home six years earlier, then took a taxi up the steep roads to Ettal Abbey to attend the sixth Congrès Catholique International de Psychothérapie et de Psychologie Clinique. The Benedictine monastery, where Dietrich Bonhoeffer had spent several months during the first years of the war, opened its halls and vast cloister to the participants, its baroque church not only a place of prayer but an architectural marvel in the mountain town where Sergei Prokofiev had lived for a year in the early 1920s.

In this scenic and evocative setting Gregory addressed his sympathetic Catholic audience on 'Diagnostic et Thérapeutique des Scrupuleux', spoke French and German with his colleagues, looked at the stunning views from his hotel window, and missed Peg. Presuming it would be dull, he reluctantly attended a production of Wagner's *Lohengrin*, but moved by the depth and beauty of the performance, he found himself in tears from the middle of the first act. He recounted his experience in a postcard he sent Peg before departing for Paris. He told her he missed her. In fact, he missed her 'very much all the time'.[6]

By the middle of September Gregory was again in London where, as a vice-president of the International Society of Criminology, he addressed its third congress on 'The Psychological and Penological Aspects of Various Types of Recidivism'. Jean Pinatel addressed the audience in French, and the conference was truly an impressive event: Gwilym Lloyd George, then home secretary, gave a welcoming speech, as did the Spanish criminologist Manuel Lopez-Rey, representing the secretary general of the United Nations. The cocktail reception and concluding banquet proved as interesting as the formal programme, and Gregory was both stimulated and tired by the time he returned to New York in late September.

Back in his office for the first time since July, he confronted a mountain of correspondence, much of which remained unanswered for months, and what seemed to him 'an endless string of various commitments for lectures and papers', but felt he had to start seeing patients right away to 'try to earn some bread and butter' for the family. He almost regretted the weeks in Europe and he certainly regretted the closure of Butler Hospital, but liberated from his fortnightly commitments in Providence and now recognised as a practicing Catholic, he could once more take on academic duties at Catholic institutions. He continued as clinical professor of psychiatry at New York State University Medical College in Manhattan, but beginning with the 1955–1956 academic year, he was also a visiting professor at both Fordham University's Graduate School – where he started in the autumn semester with a seminar entitled 'Psychiatric and Ethical Aspects of Psychoanalysis' – and Woodstock College, where his course was listed in the Jesuit seminary's Latin catalogue as 'Psychopathologia Pastoralis' and his name as 'Gregorius Zilboorg'.

The appellation must have amused him: He had not been called 'Gregorius' since his months in Holland after the First World War.

Gregory spent long hours at his desk throughout the autumn of 1955. He reported to Henry that much beyond domestic life was keeping Peg 'intellectually awake', but while his 'string of commitments' was intellectually stimulating as well as draining, he had little leisure. He confessed truthfully but with typical exaggeration that he hadn't seen a movie or a play the entire year. Gregory would, however, manage time out for prizefights to let off the inevitable steam. Sugar Ray Robinson and Floyd Patterson were in their prime, and Gregory would have made sure he had good seats in New York's Yankee Stadium at the end of September, where he saw Rocky Marciano defeat Archie Moore by a knockout in round nine. Late in the evenings he watched boxing matches on television, a medium coming into its own with broadcasts he did not watch: The children were permitted to see *Howdy Doody Time*, but *I Love Lucy*, *Father Knows Best*, and *The $64,000 Question* passed him by, as did *The Honeymooners*, which began broadcasting in October.[7]

The year was in many ways a hiatus before the countercultural storm that gathered momentum in America towards the end of the decade. Gregory was appalled by Levittown, a post-war expanse of identical suburban houses 15 miles south of the Fields' estate, whose restrictive covenant barred occupation 'by any person other than members of the Caucasian race'. Despite the U.S. Supreme Court's 1954 ruling that segregated schools were inherently unequal, the civil rights movement was in its infancy. Emmett Till had been murdered in Mississippi at the end of August, an event even reported in the Italian papers Gregory had read in Milan, and anti-Semitism, as the Bedford swimming pool attested, persisted despite the efforts of the Anti-Defamation League. Members of the 'beat' generation had not yet been labelled 'beatniks'. Elvis Presley's first hit, 'Heartbreak Hotel', wouldn't be released on a seven-inch 45 until January, while Allen Ginsberg's 'Howl' – whose opening line ('I saw the best minds of my generation destroyed by madness, starving hysterical naked') would certainly capture Gregory's attention – didn't appear in print until the following November.[8]

Among the films Gregory might have wanted to see in 1955 would have been *Rebel Without a Cause*, which came out a month after news of James Dean's death hit the headlines shortly after Gregory's return from Europe. He would also have been interested in the off-Broadway revival of Brecht's *Threepenny Opera* – whose star, Lottie Lenya, was receiving rave reviews – and he surely saw Samuel Becket's *Waiting for Godot*, which had been playing in London during the criminology congress and opened in New York in April.

Between September and April, however, Gregory thought about old themes and explored the implications of new ones, spoke to students and colleagues, civic groups, and even parent-teacher associations, to audiences large and small, prestigious and homely. In mid-October he dovetailed a visit to Marshall and Ruthie Field with a lecture to the Long Island Psychiatric Society on 'Growing Conflicts between Clinical and Theoretical Psychiatry'. A week later he spoke on

'Psychiatry, Psychoanalysis, and Education' at the Devereaux School, a boarding school for children with special needs in Glenmoore, Pennsylvania.

Among the string of Gregory's autumn commitments was the commemoration of Kent School's 50th year. As vice-president of the celebration committee, Lou had asked Gregory for help, and he hadn't felt able to refuse. Unlike young Greg, Lou had been happy at Kent, and work on behalf of his old school raised his spirits. As a favour to Lou and Peg, who urged her husband to keep an eye on her brother who had seemed so down in the dumps over the summer, Gregory had agreed to be one of the judges of an essay contest whose winner would be announced during the celebration at the end of November. The topic, 'The Christian Idea of Education', was congenial, as were the other distinguished members of the jury, which included the British poet W.H. Auden, the American socialist pacifist Norman Thomas, and Yale University's chaplain Sidney Lovett.

Work on the celebration committee – which included Lou's Bronxville friend Cyrus Vance and the Democratic senator Stuart Symington – suited Peg's gregarious brother, and the resulting gala weekend, including panel discussions, proved as stimulating as any international congress: Gregory's group was led by Father Edward T. Foote, S.J., associate dean of the School of Medicine at St. Louis University in Missouri, while other distinguished speakers included the South African writer Alan Paton, Jacques Maritain, the theologian Reinhold Niebuhr, and John Courtney Murray. Gregory certainly had no regrets about participating and was pleased to observe Lou in his element, an effective organiser at ease on the familiar campus among school and university friends, apparently reinvigorated and jovial.

Gregory had serious reservations, however, about contributing to a private fund for Sigerist. After a good deal of back and forth with concerned colleagues in medical history as well as Henry himself, who frankly admitted his dire financial situation, Gregory took it upon himself to ' "fix up" the business' and organised donations through the Eda Kuhn Loeb Fund, whose wealth derived from Kuhn, Loeb, the investment bank closely associated with the Warburg family. Gregory contributed, as did many of Henry's friends, colleagues, and former students, among them Genevieve Miller and Ilza Veith, but Eddie Warburg was probably the most substantial financial backer. Gregory's role, as Henry was quick to recognise, was not so much monetary as choreographic.[9]

The Christmas of 1955 was a calm affair, a week with family in Bedford with a live tree that would be planted in the orchard early in the new year. In January Gregory resumed seeing patients, attended a luncheon at the United Nations headquarters as well as a stunning performance of Puccini's *Tosca* at the Metropolitan Opera, and looked forward to his customary post-Christmas holiday. This year he hoped 'just to loaf' for nine days in the Bahamas, but he inevitably had an agenda. He planned to see Bishop Leonard of Nassau, a Benedictine missionary who had been a member of the Saint John's community, as well as several members of Nassau's Benedictine monastery of Saint Martin. He encouraged Peg to invite Mary-Alice to join them: They would swim together in the clear Caribbean water and lie in the sun in their bathing suits; he would, when not meeting with Benedictines, find a shady spot on a terrace, order an iced tea, and write.[10]

The women had a wonderful time. Peg loved the sea and the expanse of beach, imagined the children building sandcastles and playing in the waves. Bedford was lovely, but it didn't have sand except in the children's sandbox; the swimming pool was lovely, but it didn't have waves. She told Gregory about a happy childhood holiday on Cape Cod, recalled the week in Cuba, the days they had spent together near the beach on Nantucket just after the war. Lillian and Dash, she reminded him, loved Martha's Vineyard. Gregory suggested she look for a seaside property to rent for a summer month or two; several restful weeks near a beach sounded fine to him. In Nassau cruise ships filled the harbour; local musicians played for tourists in the streets. While Peg and Mary-Alice enjoyed the boisterous calypso, Gregory imagined a large private house on the Cape whose environs would be peaceful.

The chill of New York in February was a shock after Gregory's week in the sun, but the spring ahead was more settled than usual. Whether because of Peg's planning or his own sense that too much travelling had an impact not only on his psychological health but on his productivity and effectiveness, Gregory focused on his teaching at Fordham and Woodstock, on speaking engagements mostly in New York, and on his patients. Marie Colbert was particularly needy and he saw her daily, while her sister Agathe, who saw him irregularly, was attending an out-of-town college and anxious about every moment away from her books. Marie had dropped out of university, was still unrealistic and at loose ends, casting about for something that captured her whimsical imagination, and emotionally distressed. Neither young woman would ever need to work for a living, and their parents' wealth may have contributed to their difficulties, but Gregory was used to dealing with wealthy patients and concentrated on Marie's unresolved hostilities and psychic conflicts.

Whatever hostility and conflicts may have been bothering Lou weren't apparently affecting his work, for while Gregory and his sister had been in the Bahamas, he was promoted from business manager in the programme department to director of something CBS called 'talent commitments'. Neither Peg nor Louise or Margo was clear what this involved, but Gregory knew the term 'talent' from the Chautauqua circuit and Lou joked that he was cut-throat in negotiating contracts with everyone from Arthur Godfrey to Gale Storm. His promotion didn't put Gregory's mind to rest, but Peg insisted she was less worried now about her older brother who rang their mother every night and took his responsibilities to both Louise and his own family so admirably seriously.

Gregory lectured throughout the spring. Soon after his return from Nassau he addressed the Westchester Medical Society in White Plains on 'Some Manifestations of Homosexuality'. Offering clinical illustrations, he examined 'the various gradations of homosexuality from manifest and conscious to deeply unconscious and psychotic', but whether he was thinking about his brother-in-law or simply about the homosexual gradations observed over the years in his own practice, homosexuality *per se* didn't absorb him as it did George Henry, whose *All the Sexes: A Study of Masculinity and Femininity*, published the previous year, had offered 'general statements' supposedly based on 'observations of more than eight thousand men and one thousand women'. What concerned Gregory was the individual individually considered, and he now took on the issue of the use of drugs and shock treatment in psychotherapy. In mid-February he spoke at the New York Academy of Medicine on 'The Abuse of the Psychological in Present-Day Clinical Psychiatry'. Stressing the primacy of the individual in psychoanalysis, Gregory claimed Freud's pre-eminence resulted from his emphasis on the individual. In contrast, Adler was more concerned with society, while Jung, whom he praised, was increasingly concerned with the collective. 'A common denominator', Gregory insisted,

> no matter how brilliant and even correct, cannot easily survive in clinical psychiatry, because clinical psychiatry, particularly that of today, more than at any time throughout its history is individualistic, and it genuinely respects the individual, the personality of the patient, the indivisibility of the human person.

Gregory thus explicitly questioned the therapeutic value of 'drugs, electrotherapy or psychosurgery', arguing that when such treatments are used as 'an adjuvant' to therapy, 'the full participation' of the available 'ego forces' is diminished.[11]

In the discussion that followed Philip Lehrman supported Gregory's paper, which he found 'brilliant', while Dr. Louis Linn spoke in favour of the therapeutic use of both drugs and shock treatment. Gregory responded in characteristically withering fashion. Just as his method of argument often depended on language, on the exact use of precise terms, he typically accused those objecting to his conclusions of having misunderstood or misinterpreted because of their failure to use words correctly. Here he objected to Linn's use of 'interpersonal', thus dismissing all Linn might have had to say: 'I regret that people use the term "interpersonal relations". I do not know of any relation of any person to anything which is anything but interpersonal.' Gregory continued unequivocally and brutally:

> I do not believe there are 'interpersonal' relationships which are distinguished from other relationships of the individual. I think all psychiatric thought should be centered on the human being as an individual which includes everything in him in relation to himself as well as in relation to the outside world.[12]

At the end of the month Gregory was again in characteristic form when addressing the Grolier Club on the one hundredth anniversary of Freud's birth. He offered his audience at the bibliophile society amusing lists of unusual and provocative groupings. Praising book lovers as people who help to carry on 'the human quest for the continuity of culture', he then chastised his listeners lest they think too highly of themselves: 'I am sure that there are among book lovers as many narrow-minded and selfish and not too well-informed individuals as there are among psychoanalysts, writers, bankers and taxicab drivers.' Gregory might have seemed to be belligerently accusing his audience – that is, until he grouped himself among them. He continued in a similar fashion as he warmed to his subject: 'What I have in mind is the psychosocial function of the collector of books, regardless of what kind of person he happens to be: ogre, ascetic, dreamer, Republican or philosopher.'[13]

While common themes and tendencies abound in Gregory's lectures, their variety and individuality continue to impress. He spoke at the beginning of March to the city's Young Men's and Women's Hebrew Association on 'Psychological Errors in Social Terminology'. A week later at New York's Hotel Delmonico he participated in a symposium sponsored by the Society of Medical Psychoanalysts on 'Schizophrenia as Seen in Psychoanalytic Office Practice'. Taking as his topic 'The Conceptual Vicissitudes of the Idea of Schizophrenia', he again criticised electroshock therapy and specifically the use of tranquilisers: Drugs dulled communication between patient and therapist rather than enhanced it; they were not 'curative', only 'palliative'. In mid-March, again in New York, Gregory chaired the session on 'Theoretical Problems in Juvenile Delinquency' at the annual meeting of the American Orthopsychiatric Association. At the end of the month, he was a discussant with Ernst Kris for Iago Galdston's talk 'Freud and Romantic Medicine' at the Society for Psychotherapy and Psychopathology at the New York Academy of Medicine.

The rest of the spring was only marginally less busy. In April Gregory gave two lectures at the New York Academy: 'Freud in the Perspective of Medical History' and 'The Clinical Issues of Postpartum Psychopathological Reactions'. In early May he was in Chicago for the annual meeting of the American Psychiatric Association, where he spoke on 'The Problem of Ambulatory Schizophrenias', a paper that included a traditional case study, a rather formulaic approach that suggests how pressed he was beginning to feel. As soon as he returned to New York, however, he spoke on 'The Shadow between Freud and God' at a centenary colloquium in Cathedral House of the Episcopal Cathedral of Saint John the Divine.

The meeting in Chicago had tired him, and as he resettled back home, he felt 'a bit foggy as a result of the milling crowds, papers, discussions and most of all, as a result of the mountain of paper work' that had accumulated in his absence. Gregory had, however, already decided to forgo his now regular summer trip to Europe. What he wanted and needed to do was stay home and work, take time off from seeing patients and spend two months at his desk writing.[14]

Factors other than his hectic schedule of lectures had played into his decision. Peg had found a large shingle-clad house on a cliff overlooking a private beach in West Hyannisport, and Gregory had signed a rental agreement for July and August. He would again spend two weeks in Collegeville, but he wanted to watch Peg and the children enjoying the sea and sand, breathing in the ocean air and relaxing in the sunshine. Marie was also a concern and a responsibility. Her parents would be spending much of the summer in France and agreed with Gregory that it wouldn't be good for her to be in New York on her own. The best thing, he felt, would be if she could experience happy family life with a good mother in it. In short, it was decided that Marie would accompany the family to the Cape: Her analysis would continue when Gregory was there while Peg would be there as *mater familias* all the time.

Family matters had also demanded unanticipated attention throughout the spring. Johnny had turned six in March, and Peg had put a good deal of energy into selecting the right private school for the very bright and gregarious but sensitive boy who would miss his nursery friends when he started first grade in the autumn. His acceptance at the Buckley School was an occasion for celebration. John had already had a birthday party; the dinner at Quo Vadis, the *grande dame* of New York's French restaurants, was a more formal event. Caroline – who was just as bright but less gregarious and, if also sensitive, almost too willing to appease and concede and give rather than take at every turn – would also be included as the sister of the guest of honour, although Matthew, who would not turn three until August, wouldn't mind staying home.

The family party was really more for the adults than the children, who tired as the evening wore on. Peg scolded Caroline when she began to recline on the red velvet banquette, told her she wasn't really sleepy or ill but only thought or felt she was because she was jealous of her brother. When Caroline felt even more unwell the following morning, Peg told her to put it in her pocket; she was nearly eight years old, not six, and should get dressed in her school uniform. Gregory was slightly more sympathetic when he brought his mind to bear on the spots she showed him on her tummy. He couldn't identify what he was looking it, thought it was something children didn't get in Russia. Peg looked up spots in Dr. Spock's *Baby and Child Care*. Her verdict was measles, and Gregory couldn't remember ever having had them. There was a bit of discussion and Peg, who vividly remembered having had measles, decided her husband must have had them; all children had them. Caroline was put to bed, her temperature taken, and Jerome Leopold called. Peg pulled down the shades and turned out the light. Light wasn't good for children with measles. When Dr. Leopold arrived at the end of his working day, he said, 'What is this child doing in the dark?' Caroline in fact had a bad case of chicken pox. She had tried to put it in her pocket, so both John and Matthew had been well exposed and came down with it two weeks later. Peg had her hands full through the end of April, and with some of her time spent at the children's bedsides, she had less time to spend at her desk and with Gregory.

It was not only the children who were ill that spring. When Henry wrote at the end of April to thank Gregory for the generous cheque he had just received, he mentioned as if in passing that had been unwell for the previous two months. Although he added that he was now 'better', Gregory knew how to read between the lines and was understandably concerned. By the time the children were out of school at the end of May and the family installed in Bedford, it was also clear that

Lou wasn't well either, although in his case the problem seemed more psychological than physical, a matter of depression that wasn't entirely abnormal, given his obviously alcoholic wife and their two young children, about whom Louise and Margo fretted. Gregory was consulted, could only recommend a psychoanalytic colleague, whom Lou was reluctant to see.

Not everyone, however, was indisposed to psychoanalysis in the spring of 1956. In the Abbey of Our Lady of Gethsemani deep in the woods of rural Kentucky, Thomas Merton had recently become master of novices. With this responsibility he had embraced the idea of psychoanalysis as a useful tool for evaluating the emotional health of the men in his charge and helping them with their vocation. Having rapidly read a little in the field, Merton had been inspired to write 'The Neurotic Personality in Monastic Life', an essay he sent to his literary agent Naomi Burton Stone in April. She in turn sent the essay to Bob Giroux, Merton's editor, who felt uneasy about it. With Merton's permission, in mid-May he sought Gregory's opinion.[15]

The essay is startlingly naïve. Merton used terms such as 'hysterical episodes', 'deep-seated obsessive compulsive neurosis', 'schizophrenic withdrawal', 'paranoid delusions', 'persecution obsessions', and 'neurotic depressive reactions', and even more unfortunately the popular but unpsychoanalytic 'subconscious'. He generalised wildly that 'Anxiety is the center of all psychological problems' before describing the characteristics of what he termed 'neurotic anxiety': 'a complete lack of proportion to any visible cause and a constant similarity of responses to all kinds of different stimuli' that 'sooner or later' produces 'a kind of disintegration of the character'. Further, 'neurotic anxiety … is always connected with some kind of artificiality, either hidden or apparent' and 'leads eventually to the creation of a false self', while 'The self-will of a neurotic mind … creates a smoke screen of confusion and anxiety, and goes about doing what it appears not to want to do with the sentiment of abulia and compulsion.' Merton even had something to say about the complicated psychoanalytic process of transference, contending that just as

> the neurotic 'transfers' to the doctor his subconscious desires and fears and makes him the object of his infantile emotional drives, so too in relations between religious superiors and their subjects the same phenomenon tends to occur. This 'transference' thus becomes the chief obstacle to grace.

Such terminology so freely wielded and tenuous generalisations so blithely asserted would have made any psychiatrist uneasy: Merton's language was not only presumptuous from someone without psychiatric training but patently dangerous. Unsurprisingly the essay set off alarm bells.[16]

Given the many errors of understanding, Gregory felt the best way forward was to be in direct contact with Merton. Gregory naturally thought Merton needed to know more about psychoanalysis before seriously considering publication and wanted to suggest particular texts. He also felt Merton would profit from attending the summer programme at Saint John's, where he would be teaching again this year. Passing the message on, Giroux praised Gregory as 'a scholar, a linguist, a classicist, a wit, an ex-Menshevik, a Freudian, a psychoanalyst, and a Catholic.' Except for never having been a Menshevik, Gregory was indeed all those things, and Giroux was confident that Merton 'couldn't find a better or wiser advisor' in Gregory's profession. In addition to whatever books Gregory might recommend, Giroux thought Merton should read both *A History of Medical Psychology* and *Mind, Medicine, and Man* and sent him copies.[17]

On the basis of Giroux's description, Merton looked forward to contact with Gregory and wrote him within days of receiving Giroux's letter. Both a contemplative monk and a writer with an international reputation, Merton was a man of many enthusiasms and not at all dismayed by Gregory's response to the essay that, he realised, needed 'a lot more work and thought, and study' and was soon thinking of 'new aspects' to pursue. With 'greatest interest', he plunged happily into *Mind, Medicine, and Man*, proclaiming it 'very helpful', 'fine', indeed 'splendid'.[18]

Giroux had indicated that while Merton would likely welcome a visit to Gethsemani, he would probably be unable to go to Collegeville; despite requests of various sorts, he hadn't been allowed to leave the abbey since joining the order in 1941. Gregory decided to write to the summer institute's director Father Alexius Portz, petitioning confidentially for his help. He explained that Merton's interest in psychiatric problems was 'in some respects good and encouraging and in others rather disquieting'; exposure to 'a serious, scientific attitude' towards mental hygiene would do him as well as the novices in his charge a great deal of good. Giroux had apparently described the situation at Gethsemani, and Gregory told Portz he feared Merton might not take the initiative to come to Saint John's, and even if he did, he might not receive permission to attend. As discreetly as he could, and unsure if it were the right course of action or even what the right course might be, Gregory wrote that some of Merton's 'intimate friends' (that is, Giroux and by extension Stone) thought that if the abbot of Saint John's wrote the abbot of Gethsemani to invite Merton to the institute, the desirable 'exposure' might be 'attained'. While he was at it, Gregory also wondered if Portz could invite the historian and theologian Father Ivan Illich, the newly appointed vice-rector of the Catholic University of Puerto Rico.[19]

Try as he might on behalf of all and sundry, Gregory couldn't help everyone. As Peg packed in preparation for the two months on Cape Cod, Field sought Gregory's advice once more. In May 1956 he had begun feeling inordinately tired. In the middle of June he had an attack of vertigo, then another, then a third so severe he lost consciousness. While Gregory was sure that his friend needed rest, he again suspected Field's dizziness might have a physical cause, although the neurologist he recommended found nothing. As Peg loaded the station wagon for the six-hour drive to West Hyannisport, making space between suitcases for the three dogs, Lala, Betty, and the children with their new colouring books and crayons, Field accepted the prospect of a quiet summer at 'Caumsett', where he continued to feel exhausted and Ruthie worried.[20]

The capacious house on the Cape was everything Gregory and Peg had imagined and more. With its two staircases and numerous bedrooms, 'Harbor View' could and would accommodate the immediate and extended family, friends, colleagues, and patients. The attic contained a huge dormitory with ten single beds. On the first floor each child had a room of her or his own, as did Marie, and the large master bedroom looked out over the sea. There were two living rooms, a dining room, a rambling kitchen with servants' rooms off it, and a glassed-in porch that Gregory used as an office and occasional treatment room. A flagstone terrace surrounded by a low stone wall faced south over a bluff covered with beach plums, scrub oak, and brambles. A steep path from the west lawn led to the private beach where Peg and Marie and the children swam every day, built sand castles, ate jam sandwiches, lay on towels in the sun, and sometimes walked as far as the jetty by Halls Creek that separated Craigville Beach from Squaw Island.

As soon as the family was settled, the kitchen stocked, and the children enrolled in Sunday school at Saint-Andrews-by-the-Sea, Peg came up for air and wrote Ruthie. Summer was always a reminder of the Fields' kindness during those desperate days a decade earlier when they were waiting for the divorce and, their fingers crossed and their breath held, rearranging their lives for their marriage. Ruthie wrote back immediately. Acknowledging what now seemed a 'very severe and deeply frightening illness', she still hoped that when Gregory returned to New York at the end of the summer, he could give Marshall 'equanimity'. Thanking Peg for her letter and for their 'wonderful and cherished friendship', she sent all her love to both of them and signed the letter 'devotedly'. Such emotion was touching, but it did not bode well.[21]

After three weeks of relative leisure on the Cape, Gregory left once more for Collegeville. Portz had passed on Gregory's request to Baldwin Wilfred Dworschak, abbot of Saint John's, who had been happy to contact James Fox, abbot of Gethsemani. Before he had a chance to write, however, he had received a letter from Fox, who had heard about the institute from the abbot at Gethsemani's 'daughter abbey' in Georgia and wanted to attend the workshop himself. Baldwin had immediately invited Fox as his guest as well as Father Louis, Thomas Merton. Gregory looked forward to meeting them both.[22]

Gregory and Merton took their time to settle into the fortnight of lectures and seminars. Merton, assiduously following the readings Gregory had suggested, hoped he could spend an hour with him each day, but previous experience had made Gregory well aware of the workshop's constraints. Practically, there would be little time for one-on-one sessions, and personally Gregory needed time on his own. He confessed to Portz that he recoiled from the commitment Merton wanted and saw it as 'a tough assignment'. Gregory also suspected that Fox might want to speak to him about 'some problems'. He would do his best but wanted to tread carefully. He had had plenty of experience with needy patients who demanded more from him than it was wise for him to give for either their sake or his own.[23]

The first week was stimulating to Merton, who had much to learn from the lectures, seminar leaders, and other participants. Gregory and his colleague Howard Rome, a psychiatrist from the Mayo Clinic, spoke, and Merton paid close attention. In the discussions following Rome's lecture, he raised the topic of Zen Buddhism, something he had begun reading about but which had little connection with Rome's presentation; after Gregory's lecture, Merton asked him to define the dysfunctions of a neurotic. Underlining the monk's naïveté and refusing to offer the specifics he sought, Gregory pointed out, 'Science does not start with a definition but ends with it.' Merton quickly sensed he had failed to distinguish between 'a character problem' and what he called in his journal 'a real neurosis'.[24]

On Sunday morning before mass, a week after their arrival, Gregory finally offered Merton the private consultation he wanted. In what amounted to a typical preparatory psychoanalytic session, Gregory would have asked Merton to talk about himself and what he expected from possible treatment, to describe what was troubling him and what he felt needed to change. Merton would have shared with Gregory his struggles to accept authority and particularly his conflicts with his abbot, his desire to write and communicate with the world outside his monastic community, and his opposing desire for solitude, his desire to retreat not only from the world but from life with his fellow monks.

Gregory would have listened, asked probing questions from time to time, and finally, using layman's terms and colloquial language, confirmed that Merton needed help and evaluated his prospects. Ingersoll had recounted in his autobiography how Gregory approached the process of psychoanalysis, and Gregory himself had explained in detail how he worked when testifying before the board of the New York Psychoanalytic Society: There would be one or two or sometimes several psychiatric sessions during which the prospective patient would talk about his or her life and describe the problems that had brought him or her to seek his advice. Gregory would then offer his view of the patient's situation and suggest what sort of treatment might be useful. This was his usual method, and indeed it was and remains standard practice within the profession. Occasionally Gregory recommended hospitalisation; sometimes psychiatric counselling, which might begin or continue with a colleague or with himself; on other occasions, if the patient was a promising candidate, he recommended psychoanalysis. Gregory had told Ingersoll bluntly that he was a very sick man but a good candidate for analysis because of his optimism, curiosity, and energy.

Encouraged by Gregory's penetrating dark eyes and the warmth of his strong personality, Ingersoll was undaunted by Gregory's judgement and excited by the challenge of treatment. Merton, even before meeting Gregory face to face, had been eager to reveal his difficulties to the man Giroux had described in such exalted terms. Indeed he had already thrown himself into a literary engagement through their correspondence and by reading at least one of Gregory's books as well as some of the other works he had recommended.

On that Sunday morning the two men spoke for an hour and a half about what Father Louis would call his 'troubles'. He likely described his responsibilities at

Gethsemani, the interest in psychology that had led him not only to compose the ill-conceived essay but also to administer Rorschach tests to the novices that he had ended up seriously misinterpreting. Merton certainly mentioned his desire to write while continuing to be a contemplative, his desire for a solitude that would serve both ends, a retreat from others that would simultaneously be an engagement with the world, a silence that would foster his Cistercian vocation and the words he felt called to write. Merton sensed the contradictions here and they made him uneasy. He surely mentioned that they made his abbot uneasy and that there had been numerous occasions when what he had proposed and what his superiors had decided was best had been at odds.[25]

On the basis of Merton's notes on their conversation, Gregory revealed it was he who had put the wheels in motion to enable Merton to come to Collegeville not only because of the errors in his essay but because he had sensed its author's difficulties. Gregory told Merton he was 'in somewhat bad shape': He wanted to live as a hermit, but he was also 'a promoter'; if he were not in a monastery, he was the kind of man who would 'clean up on Wall Street one day and lose it all on the horses the next.' He appeared to be a 'gadfly', although he was also stubborn, repeatedly pushing his superiors to get what he wanted, yet he depended on his vows to limit his sometimes wild enthusiasms. It seemed to Gregory that Merton was afraid to be an ordinary monk; he wanted to be famous, 'a big shot' – in psychological terms (which were probably Merton's rather than Gregory's) 'megalomania and narcissism' were his 'big trends'. Rather than engaging with his emotional difficulties, Gregory explained to Merton that he intellectualised. For example, in his essay he had waxed 'verbological', but his psychoanalytic terminology hadn't helped him to understand himself. When bringing up Zen as a topic, Merton had been self-aggrandising instead of thinking of his own 'priesthood, the apostolate, the church, his soul'.

Merton sensed the wisdom in what Gregory was trying to reveal to him, recording in his notes that the session had shown him things he both knew and didn't know. Gregory had explained that Merton didn't lack intelligence but 'affectivity'; he either intellectualised – by putting his emotions into words, harnessing them in writing rather than expressing them – or became depressed. He was capable of saying 'I am a narcissist', but saw that verbally acknowledging his narcissism changed nothing and didn't help him to understand himself. He also felt Gregory was right about his impulsivity, but these things weren't easy to hear or admit. As he listened, Merton had reacted by disengaging himself from Gregory's interpretations – at one point during the session, observing Gregory's distinctive physiognomy, he thought to himself, 'How much he looks like Stalin', which of course was true – but Merton confessed in his journal – where his record of the meeting was another way of distancing himself from the emotions of the encounter – that 'in reality' he was 'tremendously relieved and grateful' for Gregory's insights.

While Merton's behaviour and internal conflicts bothered him, there was no clear or simple solution. When he apparently asked Gregory how to avoid the sort of error he had made in discussing Zen, Gregory pointed out kindly, ' "These are not things you can foresee. They are traps you fall into as you go along and you don't realize it until you are hurt."' Indeed, it would be difficult to address Merton's struggles. Analysis, Gregory intimated, could be a way forward, but given the monk's cloistered situation, it might well not be feasible. Merton apparently wondered if it would help to be 'forbidden' to write, but Gregory told him insightfully that it would do him no good to be forbidden; he certainly needed a degree of silence and separation from the world, but any prohibition against writing would need to come from his heart. If writing were merely forbidden by someone else, it wouldn't seem prohibited to him.

Gregory probably also saw Merton's stubbornness as an additional impediment to psychoanalysis, as was his struggle with 'affectivity', with what Merton records as the 'heart' – a matter of taking something 'to heart', but also of love of others as well as of self, of the patient's doing the difficult psychoanalytic work rather than anything done by a clerical superior or a psychoanalyst for or to the patient on his or her behalf. Gregory had recognised the importance of both worldly and spiritual love in his own life; what Merton recorded as 'affectivity' would finally have been the end towards which Gregory would have wanted to direct any analysis, helping Merton to find a way of putting aside the verbological, a way to make his words 'incarnate'.[26]

Any treatment, however, would need the approval of Merton's abbot, who did not arrive at Saint John's until later on Sunday. During the institute's second week of lectures and seminars there would be little time for another meeting, but at some point Gregory took a moment out from the full schedule of events to see Fox and Merton together. Apparently the only surviving record of what occurred is Fox's brief recollection over three years later when he pleaded with his superiors in Rome to deny Merton's request to leave Gethsemani to become a hermit in another order. Fox remembered that Gregory had pointed out the foolishness of Merton's essay, then quoted him specifically as having said,

> Fr. Louis, you dream of being a hermit. Yes – the kind of hermit you want to be, is to be a hermit in Times Square, New York City (the center of all the traffic) with an electric sign outside, saying: 'Come in and see the hermit'.

Fox added that Merton had not denied the truth in Gregory's words.[27]

At the beginning of the second week Merton had reported to Stone that Gregory, whom he had found 'terrific' both during the lectures and the private session, intended to speak to Fox about the possibility of analysis. The point of the second meeting was surely to prepare the way for work with Merton so that he could come to terms with his competing impulses. The abbot, well aware of the problem, was evidently supportive of whatever help Gregory felt he might offer, and Merton was encouraged. As the second week drew to a close, Merton wrote his agent again and reiterated that everything was going very well; he was particularly looking forward to further contact with Gregory and whatever 'advice' he could give. As Merton prepared to leave Collegeville, he told Giroux the fortnight had been 'immensely profitable' and Gregory had 'many ideas' for him. Once resettled in Gethsemani, Merton wrote his editor at greater length: The institute had been 'splendid'; he and Gregory had had helpful talks which he anticipated might 'develop into something'.[28]

Thomas Merton (far left) with Gregory and James Fox (smiling on the right) during a convivial moment at St. John's College, Collegeville, Minnesota, early August 1956

August on the Cape was a halcyon month. The sun shone, the children gambolled, Marie laughed, and Peg was with Gregory for the cocktail hour every evening before dinner. Visitors came and went. Louise and Margo came for Matthew's third and Louise's 67th birthday followed by Peg and Gregory's tenth wedding anniversary, and a generally merry time was had by all. Although he thought about Merton and the complexities of accepting a cloistered monk as a patient, Gregory wrote and relaxed to the degree he was able. Just as he and Peg were regretting having to leave and deciding they would simply have to return the following year, Delilah – their youngest dog, bred in June – gave birth to a litter of eight healthy puppies. It would have been more convenient had she been able to hold off for a few more days, but there was always somehow room in Peg's car. The family returned to Bedford with the newborn poodles nestled on newspapers in the well between the back and front seats.

From Kentucky, Fox wrote Gregory to thank him for his attention during the weeks in Collegeville: Gregory had been 'the soul of that workshop', and both he and Merton were looking forward to the 'therapy' Gregory had intimated would be helpful. Merton imagined auditing courses at Columbia University in his free time; Fox wanted Gregory to be frank about what analysis would cost. Even before leaving the Cape, however, Gregory began to have reservations. He had learned from Stone that Merton had told her about the prospect of analysis, and his immediate concern was the challenge of keeping any treatment discreet. When Giroux had first spoken to him about Merton, it had been clear that the monk's high profile was part of his personal struggles but also an issue for his superiors. Fox may have thoroughly enjoyed his week at Saint John's, but he had naïve ideas about psychoanalysis and the analyst's role and expected that Gregory could prevent Merton from running around in New York and mixing with other people, that he could do 'a one hundred and ten percent job' on Father Louis so the volatile monk would be 'straightened out'. Fox wrote Gregory in early September that 'the whole success' of the analysis depended on 'utter secrecy'. He additionally reported that Merton, who continued to carry his journal with him everywhere, hoped that after his analysis he would be qualified to administer Rorschach tests.[29]

Gregory had quickly realised that both Merton and Fox had unrealistic expectations both of analysis itself and of him as a psychoanalyst. For numerous reasons he would now need to back off from the role into which he was being cast and out of the therapy which he had intimated would be helpful and which the two monks so thoroughly misunderstood. He explained his 'apprehensions' in a letter to Fox that must have been as difficult to receive as to write. Merton was a gifted and restless person. In Gregory's opinion, his talent was from God while his restlessness was neurotic and sprang not from his ecclesiastic estate or his spiritual calling but from his human, worldly, even 'revengeful personality'. Merton's constant writing in his journal betrayed 'an overestimation of the external' and would be a serious impediment to treatment as would any effort to impose 'obedience' on him 'because the freedom of the patient must always remain his own'. Merton's idea that his prospective analysis might empower him to administer Rorschach tests indicated to Gregory that he didn't really want to be analysed but to use the treatment merely as a 'stepping stone to greater heights and wider fields'; it suggested he was 'not yet stabilized in his spiritual life', not yet 'inwardly real Cistercian'.

Gregory pointed out that his hesitation to accept Merton as a patient had nothing to do with compensation. From the outset he had been disturbed by his sense that Merton might not be 'stable enough to be trusted outside his abbey without direct and authoritative spiritual supervision'. Gregory very much wanted to help him, had even had 'a very crazy day-dream of coming to the Abbey of Gethsemani and staying there for a few months and doing whatever therapy is to be done', but he had to keep his family going and fulfil his teaching commitments. In short, to undertake treatment with Merton outside the abbey would pose a risk to the monk's reputation as well as to Gregory's and might possibly, as Fox feared, create 'a scandalous moment'.

Gregory had been so disturbed by the problem of accepting Merton as a patient that he had become 'quite low-spirited' whenever he thought about it. He very much wanted to help Merton and his abbey, to help the Church, felt honoured to have been presented with the opportunity, but was so deeply concerned that, without betraying any confidences, he had consulted 'a priest, a wise, warmhearted, mature and very learned spiritual director' – likely Mailloux or perhaps Murray – who had told him that it would be dangerous and potentially harmful to the Church unless Merton were treated *in situ*. Gregory simply couldn't as a psychoanalyst impose upon Merton the 'obedience' the abbot felt was necessary. Under the conditions and circumstances Fox envisaged for Merton, Gregory felt 'only sorrow will come on his and also on my head.' While he was scared of the impact on himself and by extension on his family, if he had thought he could succeed for Merton and for the Church, he told Fox he would have disregarded the personal dangers and proceeded without hesitation.

Gregory did, however, have advice to offer. He thought Merton should stop compulsively keeping a journal and instead become a real student, one who studied to learn rather than to teach others before mastering the material. He recommended reading more theology and particularly Thomas Aquinas. Further, Gregory urged, 'Let him be silent and learn in his silence and with his silence to assess his spiritual functioning.' Merton was both too glib and too much at home with the use of concepts of which he knew very little, so Gregory added,

> Let him learn what Charity really is as an experience, not just a concept. In other words, let him spend a couple of years in his monastery with only one perspective – his inner spiritual one, the one he has chosen.

He thought manual labour might help Merton and continued, 'Let him milk the cows and mix their feed, let him work until he is spiritually stabilized.' In short, Gregory was convinced his 'neurosis' would not be 'cured' unless he underwent a spiritual revolution, unless he became 'capable of making a religious commitment to get well in obscurity instead of functioning as a famous neurotic'. Merton had 'to want to be a well man in order to serve God fully'. Gregory insisted Merton 'could write books, and better books, later; he could be a master of novices, and a better one, later.' Rather touchingly, Gregory finally hoped Fox wasn't too disappointed in him.[30]

The letter's word choice and phrasing indicate Peg had no hand in its editing. Gregory wrote of a 'revengeful personality' (as opposed to 'vengeful'); he wrote 'Rorschach "testers" and "testees"' (rather than 'administrators' and 'subjects'); 'inwardly real Cistercian' (instead of 'really Cistercian'); 'warmhearted' (without a hyphen). He fell back on foreign phases ('*Fecit quod potui*', the Latin aphorism he had used since his youth) and orthography (adding a French accent to 'régime'). Gregory's vocabulary was enriched by his multilinguality and his phrasing by his close reading of the Bible ('Let him…'), but his English would never sound completely natural: He told the abbot that Merton 'must stop indulging himself as to writing, as to keeping a journal' (instead of 'in writing', 'in keeping'). Tenses would always be a challenge: Using the simple past – rather than the present perfect 'have spent' – he wrote Fox, 'I spent many sleepless nights ... since Collegeville'. Reflecting the anguished deliberation that had prompted it, Gregory's heartfelt letter was composed and typed in private.

Far from Collegeville and Cape Cod, Gregory's autumn schedule – even without a volatile monk in it – was predictably demanding. Every Friday afternoon Peg drove the children and the dogs to Bedford where, after his last patient, Gregory joined them on Friday night, sometimes driving himself in his black Cadillac with its red leather seats, but often, simply too tired to drive, he hired a chauffeur, who would come back and collect him on Sunday afternoon. In addition to seeing patients, Gregory taught weekly classes at Fordham University in the Bronx and at Woodstock College north of Baltimore. In mid-October he went to Montreal, where he met with Cardinal Léger and lectured in French at the Université de Montréal on 'Les Rééducateurs des Délinquants'. On his return, he addressed the Brooklyn Psychiatric Society on 'The Centenaries in Psychiatry: Kraepelin, Freud, and Bleuler', and in early November he was a discussant on a panel on 'Guilt and Illness' at a conference on 'Religion and Psychiatry' at Columbia's College of Physicians and Surgeons. Among the things he didn't do in the autumn of 1956, however, was make room in his schedule for the consultation Ruthie Field had hoped for in July.

Even before the end of the summer it was clear that Marshall was seriously ill. Gregory and Peg likely made a point of visiting him and Ruthie at 'Caumsett', where in late September his eyes began to fail, and the doctors, who operated to relieve the pressure on his brain, discovered the tumour that by then everyone suspected. The family gathered round, although Bettine, heavily pregnant with her third child, remained in France. On 8 November Field died in hospital, where the Catholic chaplain had administered last rites, but his funeral was held at Peg's New York church, Saint James Episcopal on 71st Street, where Jimmy and Eddie Warburg were among his pall bearers; Gregory and Peg sat not far from Ruthie in the congregation.[31]

Later in the month Gregory's essay 'Psychological Conflict' appeared in the Catholic journal *Jubilee*, a magazine of literature, art, and ideas edited by Thomas Merton's university friend Robert Lax. What Gregory discussed here can be understood as an oblique comment on his view of Merton's conflicts, a rendition for public consumption of what he had written so privately to both Merton and Fox in September. Gregory began by defining his territory theoretically and individually:

> When we psychiatrists speak of a conflict, we mean unconscious conflict. A conscious conflict is not a conflict at all; it is either an embarrassment or a doubt, or in general a state in which a person feels he cannot make a choice because he is offered two mutually conflicting alternatives. A true conflict in the psychological sense is a meeting in the unconscious of two mutually contradictory trends for which a person's unconscious – not his conscious – mind is unable to find a solution.

One can almost hear Gregory's reflections on Merton's conscious conflicts: his desire to remain in the Trappist community but to live alone and apart; his desire to obey the community's rules and to violate them on his own terms; his desire to remain a monk and to engage with the world through writing and travel. Gregory concluded the article with words that might have applied directly to the troubled monk:

> The technique of resolving ... conflicts is very complex. You cannot teach psychotherapy without actually doing it, without actually dealing with living persons. In a general way the technique of the psychotherapist is to encourage the patient and fortify him sufficiently so that he will have the ability and the courage to recognize his unconscious conflicts. Then he does the work himself.[32]

'Psychological Conflict' was characteristic in being rooted in Gregory's personal experience; it was in no way intimate or personally revealing but reflected experiences and issues with particular and timely significance for its deeply reflective author. Gregory's wide knowledge was inevitably brought to bear on a specific topic, while his attitudes and values informed whatever he had to say. Certain subjects, principles, anecdotes, and phrases would come up repeatedly, but his arguments, as he refined them throughout his life, resonated in the context of his evolving convictions and beliefs. All this was no less true of even such an informal talk as he gave in mid-November to Bedford's Parent-Teacher Association on 'The Friend and the Enemy in the School and in the Family'. He stressed that in the contemporary world 'we mistake literacy for education'; we are 'dedicated to mass testing' and 'put people in cubicles'; we are reduced to living on our 'record'. Gregory had as many reservations about Rorschach tests as about Merton's qualifications to administer them. Gregory felt the problem for friends and enemies in whatever community they might find themselves was that

> Nothing is forgiven and no one is given a chance to expiate his sins. A human being is conceived of as a mechanism today instead of as a growing thing. We have a lack of faith in the ability of people to change.

He wished for children – who were, after all, the express subject of his talk in the Bedford school – what he wished for Merton when he advised that he 'learn what Charity really is as an experience, not just a concept'. What Gregory told his audience of parents and teachers was that children needed above all to learn to love one another.[33]

Both Fox and Merton had been disappointed with Gregory's decision but accepted it with grace and some understanding. Neither man was disappointed in Gregory himself. Fox still hoped that analysis might take place in some vague future; Merton was more sanguine and simply hoped Gregory might arrange to visit Gethsemani where, safely secluded from the world, they might talk again, just the two of them. At Merton's request, Fox invited Gregory to the abbey, and before the end of November Gregory made plans. Without confirming anything, Fox merely informed Merton that Gregory had been asked. The emotional monk was delighted. As the snow fell on the Kentucky hills and the year pushed on towards Christmas, Merton became as eager as a child, frequently asking his abbot, ' "Do you suppose Greg is coming down? ... have you heard from Greg yet?" ' For his part, Gregory agreed with Fox that his visit should be a surprise, but while he would happily address the community and speak with Merton and any other monks Fox felt would profit from conversation with him, he also looked forward to some time for 'solitude and contemplation'.[34]

The three days Gregory spent at Gethsemani just after Christmas enabled him to redefine his relationship with both Fox and Merton, to set the terms and confirm the limits of his strategic retreat. There was indeed time for reflection and prayer, and he found his visit 'inspiring' and 'revelatory'. In thanking Fox, he also told him he hoped he had been of use. He had spoken privately with Merton at some length and felt he had come to know him better; now that Gregory wasn't approaching him merely as a psychoanalyst, he naturally came a little closer to Merton's 'purely human side' and discovered he liked him a great deal. In no uncertain terms, however, Gregory repeated to Fox that he had not changed his mind about Merton's being analysed: 'He should not be.'

Gregory continued to feel Merton could be helped by studying and reading, and with the abbot's permission, he was willing to offer occasional guidance through correspondence 'in proper dosage, of course – not too frequently'. The personal details Gregory confided about his own spiritual needs as well as the degree of impersonal formality he now employed in a letter that was nevertheless honest and open helped simultaneously to confirm his authority as a wise doctor and to express his deference to the abbot as a humble Christian on his own challenging spiritual journey. He closed with warm reserve, hoping that they would continue to keep in touch with one another and that he would hear from him again soon. As the year turned and Gregory resumed his demanding life in New York, he repeated to Fox what he had come to feel about Merton during the sleepless nights three months earlier: 'His should be the path of spiritual development'.[35]

Notes

1 GZ to James Fox, 3 January 1956.
2 GZ to HES, 1 June 1955; GZ, 'His Own Cook', 158; Monsignor Giovanni Battista Montini to GZ, 22 July 1955. Pope Pius XII appointed Montini archbishop of Milan in November 1954; he became first cardinal under Pope John XXIII in December 1958, whom he succeeded in 1963 as Pope Paul VI.
3 Frances J. Braceland, preface to GZ, 'Some Denials', 97.
4 TM, *Ascent*, 9; GZ, 'Some Denials', 99, 100, 101, 104, 110, 111, 118, 119, 120.
5 HES to GZ, 10 October 1955; GZ to HES, 20 December 1955; GZ, 'His Own Cook', 159.
6 GZ to MSZ, nd.

7 GZ to HES, 20 December 1955.
8 Daniels, 37.
9 GZ to HES, 23 December 1955, 2 April, 17 May 1956; HES to GZ, 26 April 1956; Bickel, ed., *Correspondence: Sigerist-Fulton*, 458.
10 GZ to HES, 20 December 1955; GZ to Alexius Portz, 16 January 1955, SJU.
11 Flyer for GZ, 'Some Manifestations of Homosexuality'; Henry, xiii.
12 GZ, 'The Abuse', 80; GZ, 'The Abuse … Society Proceedings', 303.
13 GZ, *Freud: An Address*, 2.
14 GZ to HES, 2 April, 9 May 1956.
15 TM to Naomi Burton Stone, 2 May 1956, *Witness*, 134; Robert Giroux to TM, 16 May 1956, Samway, 201–202; GZ to Alexius Portz, 16 May 1956, SJU.
16 TM, 'The Neurotic Personality', 5–19, passim.
17 Robert Giroux to TM, 16 May 1956, Samway, 201–202.
18 TM to Robert Giroux, 26 May 1956, Samway, 202.
19 GZ to Alexius Portz, 16 and 29 May 1956, SJU.
20 Becker, 464, 465, 476.
21 Ruth Field to MSZ, 18 July 1956.
22 Alexius Portz to GZ, 26 May 1956, SJU.
23 GZ to Alexius Portz, 26 June 1956, SJU.
24 TM, *A Search*, 55, 56.
25 TM, *A Search*, 59; GZ to James Fox, 10 September 1956.
26 TM, *A Search*, 59, 60.
27 James Fox, 'Report in Regard Fr. M. Louis (TM), of O.L. of Gethsemani, U.S.A. (Order of the Cistercians S.O.)', 9, Thomas Merton Center, Bellarmine University, Louisville, Kentucky.
28 TM to Naomi Burton Stone, 30 July, 3 August 1956, *Witness*, 139, 140; TM to Robert Giroux, 4, 18 August 1956, Samway, 204, 205–206.
29 James Fox to GZ, 13 August, 3 September 1956; GZ to Alexius Portz, 13 June 1956, SJU.
30 GZ to James Fox, 10 September 1956.
31 Becker, 475–479.
32 GZ, 'Psychological Conflict', 12, 13.
33 PTA newsletter.
34 TM to GZ, 14, 20 September, 9 October 1956; GZ to James Fox, 28 November 1956; Fox to GZ, 18 December 1956.
35 GZ to James Fox, 3 January 1957.

Chapter 9

Time and tide
1957–1959

There would be no post-Christmas trip to warmer climes in 1957. Gregory's three days at Gethsemani would have to suffice as a holiday in a year that was full from the start. Having signed the lease for two months on the Cape for the following summer, Gregory certainly realised that expense in addition to his heavy schedule of commitments meant staying at home, where he saw patients and lectured, was interviewed and delivered talks on the radio, and wrote articles and dealt with correspondence.

Fox had understood Gregory's early January letter and sagely took his time responding. When he did, he was affirmative but accepting of the distance Gregory had created. He gave him permission to write to Father Louis at any time, but added graciously that he knew Gregory was a busy man. Merton also understood, surmised that Gregory would never analyse him. Gregory continued to suggest authors and texts, and when Merton mentioned purchasing a statue of the Virgin for the abbey, Gregory put him in touch with Jean de Menil, who was happy to help him find a sculptor. The help would, as Gregory well knew, involve not only finding a sculptor but generously augmenting the abbey's meagre budget. From time to time Fox sent Gregory ham and cheese and other delicacies made at Gethsemani, and Merton began to feel intellectually enlightened and less emotionally troubled. Fox would look back positively on what he called Gregory's 'influence', would call meeting him 'a real Pentecost', a holy intervention.[1]

Gregory was indeed a busy man. In January he delivered a talk on 'Freud in the Perspective of Medical History' as part of a series of radio programmes sponsored by the New York Academy of Medicine. In mid-February he spoke at a dinner in his honour in Boston. A week later in New York he addressed the Cornell Medical History Society on 'The Revival of Classical Medicine and the Birth of Psychiatry'. In early March he participated in a symposium at the University of Vermont's College of Agriculture, where his talk was entitled 'On Law and Psychiatry'. He confided to Babcock that sometimes he was rather sorry he didn't know how 'not to work so hard', a statement Gregory intended to be humorous but which was nevertheless serious and true. In a lighter vein he recalled their Butler Hospital colleague: 'Whatever happened to Norman Loux? He is consistently mute. I wrote him a couple of times and he failed to answer my letters as

DOI: 10.4324/9781003190974-9

many times – so I stopped my sterile support of the Postmaster General's office.'
Gregory had heard Norman's wife was expecting a baby and joked, 'Well, I don't
know, perhaps Norm too is pregnant, or perhaps it is distocia [sic] that he is having' – in layperson's terms, a difficult or abnormal childbirth. Musing again on his
own life, however, Gregory confided, 'The trouble with the business of reading
and writing a great deal is that there is little time for any kind of social life' – yet
his family offered ample consolation: 'Peg and the kids are such a wonderful substitute', he told Hal, 'if not the essence of it all.'[2]

Family as well as close friends rather than a social life commanded Gregory's
emotional attention throughout the year. Lou's psychic distress was now distress-
ing everyone. He was deeply depressed, yet sometimes volatile, and couldn't be
consistently relied on, a changed man from the glad-handing vice-chairman of
Kent's golden jubilee. Indeed, Lou remained his former self only in so much as
Bronxville and his youth seemed his most meaningful frame of reference. He was
now obviously drinking, and Nancy was drinking more. In August, for the first
time since his father died, he had neglected to give his mother perfume on her
birthday, a gift that had been his father's tradition. Lou didn't even seem physically well, and there was some question about his continuing to work. Peg and
George worried that their brother was going 'to pieces'; Margo worried about his
ability to support his family. Gregory considered that hospitalisation might be
necessary but could only advise.[3]

It was through Henry's daughters in New York and Geneva that Gregory heard
of his friend's death in Lugano in March. Their nearly 30-year correspondence had
trailed off after Henry's first stroke and never quite resumed with the same inti-
macy or the engagement. There had been no diminution of affection and respect,
but Gregory had seen from Henry's 'outworldly' smile in the Lugano station that
their paths had diverged. Where Henry was going was the way of humankind, but
he had already begun surveying the territory ahead while Gregory, with his young
wife and family, had so much work still to do. There would be no pilgrimage to
Pura during his next trip abroad, but Gregory would try to see Erica in Geneva.

Gregory's lecture commitments continued throughout the spring. At the end
of March he spoke on 'Recent Attitudes towards Psychiatry and Psychoanalysis'
at the Central Unitarian Church in Paramus, New Jersey, where the anthropologist Margaret Mead had addressed the same group two weeks earlier. In April he
spoke in Brooklyn on 'Development of the Concept of the Dynamic Process in
Psychiatry' at the Downstate Medical Center of the State University of New York.
Relaxed and speaking rather off-the-cuff and personally, he was in fine form, at
once frank and self-deprecating, sharp and insightful. He began by thanking the
department chairmen with characteristic humour:

> As Dr. Howard Potter was telling you about what are usually called, euphe-
> mistically, my achievements, by way of what is called an introduction but
> which always sounds like a funeral eulogy, I was thinking of a … professor
> of medicine in the University of Basel

– that is, of Paracelsus. His dramatic voice captivated the sophisticated medical students and staff as it had America's 'gopher prairie' farmers decades earlier: 'So that I don't tell you too many stories about persecuted people, I will limit myself to one additional example.' He continued, 'Now just imagine a novice in a monastery – and this actually occurred – in the tenth century, who is beginning to study theology and philosophy.' Gregory not only engaged and amused his audience but confessed his tendency to bully while simultaneously bullying his listeners:

> Today I speak to medical students – I say that I speak to them because when I finish they don't want to talk to me – I speak to medical students. The other day a student asked me a question and I answered him and he said, "Well, all right. Now, doctor, permit me to build up another point," and he started building it up. I said, "Please go ahead, but permit me to tell you in advance that a point has no dimensions." This embarrassed everybody and that was the end of his question.

While laughing, his audience was reminded of Gregory's capacity to cow others even when it embarrassed everyone including himself – it would have been a brave student who would have approached him afterwards to discuss a point or pose a query. The dynamic man who stressed his real humility to Mailloux was inevitably imperious from the lectern where, even when the joke was on him, he couldn't easily relinquish high ground.[4]

In May, with various seasonal meetings scheduled for later than usual, Gregory was home for Peg's 39th birthday but spent the following week in Chicago. There, at the annual meeting of the American Psychiatric Association, he spoke on 'Eugen Bleuler and Present-Day Psychiatry' and served as a discussant for a panel on 'Ministers and Psychiatrists: The Problem of Communication'. He then addressed the Association of Mental Health Chaplains on 'The Mentally Ill and Religious Functioning' before travelling to Rochester, Minnesota, to deliver the Mayo Foundation lecture on 'The Development of Humanism in Medicine from Paracelsus to the Present Time'.

A few early summer days with the family in Bedford, where Peg and the children were occupied being 'the essence of it all', offered Gregory hours at his desk and some leisure. Caroline, now nine, had become an accomplished reader, while John was still struggling with the decoding process, happier running about on the lawn than curling up with a book, but also content playing indoors with tin soldiers. Matthew, not quite four, was a good listener to stories, and Peg still read at least to the boys every evening. Every afternoon the children were banished to their rooms for a postprandial hour: Even Matthew no longer napped, but 'rest time' always followed lunch, a consistently enforced pause during which the children were alone, reading or looking quietly at picture books before being allowed to swim again, a moment the grown-ups could count on for themselves. Peg insisted she always took a nap after lunch. The children weren't so sure, but on weekends and during the summers, unless they had guests, Gregory would join her in their bedroom and close the door.

There were, however, often guests in Bedford. A typical June weekend included Gregory's former Butler student George Mora and Agostino Gemelli's student the Italian psychiatrist Leonardo Angelo Ancona. Already a member of the psychology faculty at the Catholic University of Milan, Ancona had spent the year working with Mailloux in Montreal, where his future studies would be supported by the Aquinas Fund. The visitors swam in the pool with Peg and the children and looked on as Gregory cooked dinner in his shirtsleeves.

Gregory and George Mora, Bedford, June 1957

Both Marie and Agathe joined the family for their second season in West Hyannisport. Except for a week in Collegeville, Gregory would spend the entire summer on the Cape, allocating professional hours to the Colberts in the morning and writing when the women and children went down to the beach in the afternoon. Gregory wasn't a man to walk barefoot on sand, but he enjoyed the sunshine on the terrace, the view from the porch windows, the sound of the sea; there was inestimable pleasure for him in his children's laughter and Peg's sunny happiness. He didn't understand their passion for swimming, Peg's love of the water, but he took joy in it at one remove and this year surprised her with the gift of a simple sailboat. It often tipped over, but as Peg explained, it was meant to tip over. One at a time Peg took the older children out and they learned to duck when the boat tacked. On shore Donna would grow frantic, so Peg sometimes took her along instead of one of the children, sailed out so far with the dog low on the bow that Gregory could see them from the living room picture window.

Peg, Matthew, and Donna, West Hyannisport, summer 1957

Gregory could not, however, avoid going to Europe this year and left for a month in early September. The trip began in Zurich with the second International Congress of Psychiatry. Many American colleagues were there – including Frank Braceland, whose year-long tenure as president of the American Psychiatric Association had ended in May – as well as European friends he had not seen for over two years. However keenly he missed his wife and children back in Bedford and brown as berries, Gregory was in his social and professional element. The first days abroad were always difficult. He milled about sociably and posed penetrating questions of other conference participants with apparent confidence, but he bared his more vulnerable self in his letters home. When he finally received a letter from Peg written the evening of his departure, he reread it, as he usually did, several times, his heart 'beating with joy' for the first time since leaving her.

In response, he gave a detailed view of the congress, a glimpse of himself, his feelings and thoughts. On 6 September he had presided over a symposium on legal aspects of schizophrenias. He had been touched that 'Dear Fredi Bleuler – busy, so busy as he is – came in for a while to listen' and had been happy that people seemed truly pleased with the proceedings. The languages of the symposium were French, German, English, Italian, and Spanish, and he had responded to each speaker with a few introductory words in their own language with English or French added afterwards 'so that all could understand'.

However, pleased as he was, he confessed to having been 'a little anxious' because he was to read his paper, in French, before the plenary session the following day, with the English and German version scheduled for the day after. Gregory recounted the events in charming and revealing detail. 'Well dear', he wrote, 'the great experimental genius Prof Baruk of Paris spoke first before me with the house crowded to the upper rafters to hear him.' The flamboyant neuropsychiatrist Henri Baruk put on quite a performance. He spoke for 20 minutes, then showed a 40-minute film 'illustrating his work on Katatonia', following which he spoke again for an hour and 45 minutes, 'carrying the audience all the way' through 30 more minutes of film illustrations punctuated 'with his not less buoyant and brilliant commentary'. When he finished, everyone was naturally tired and an unscheduled 'five minute surcease was declared'. People left the hall 'in droves'.

Looking out at an empty room and wondering how he could possibly compete with 'that wonderful Parisian and magnificent orator', Gregory admitted to having been 'a little discouraged'. At the end of what had become a 15-minute intermission, he was introduced but couldn't start because of the flow of people coming in. The hall was finally packed 'with a lot of shoulders' while Professor Baruk installed himself in the front row beside Professor Juan José Lopez-Ibor from Madrid and Fredi Bleuler. 'Darling', Gregory wrote, 'how I missed you.' He had caught Mora's eye: 'He looked moved. He later on told me that he was anxious because "it was difficult to speak after Baruk."' Gregory confided to Peg,

Well dear, I spoke, my French flowed – There was a general admixture of the literary French idiom. Twice I was interrupted with applause, then when I finished and when I left (I was the last on the programme) I was surrounded by many people who wanted to shake hands with me.

The first among them had been 'the beaming little Baruk', who gave him 'the French accolade', congratulating him with a kiss on each cheek, followed by 'Spaniards, Italians, Frenchmen, Uruguayans, Brazilians'. Gregory finally 'began to believe in myself again', for what he had presented had been 'scientific stuff not sweet stuff' and had been conveyed 'with all the respect and honorable politeness' appropriate for his sophisticated audience.

When Mora had at last triumphantly extricated him from the crowd, Gregory had celebrated with some shopping. He was almost as pleased with his purchases as with his presentation: 'a dress for Carrie' and two short coats in different colours 'for Johnny and Matthew – reversible ones, warm ones with cowls and one side rainproof to the last button and pockets'. Gregory would always be attentive to how things were made, to shape and colour, to material, construction, and purpose; his wide interests and sensitivities meant he was as attentive to the grand as well as the small experiences of life, the brilliant Baruk, rainproof pockets.

He continued to speak in this letter to Peg as if they were relaxing together during the cocktail hour. Some of the conference participants were going on to Madrid for the seventh International Catholic Congress of Psychotherapy and Clinical Psychology, and he had heard there were no longer seats available on planes from Zurich, 'but like you' he wrote Peg, 'I am a smart cookie. I did not marry you for your Polaroid and I have a seat via Frankfurt'. He was proud of his forethought, but never less than self-analytical. He had 'played around' with the idea of rearranging his itinerary so as to get home sooner, even if only by a day, but reflected that the thought of changing his travel plans 'was sort of upsetting': 'When you make reservations on a flight long before and you plan on it – you sort of feel at home and you become sort of superstitious about any other flight.'

Peg had written him about life without him in Bedford, but also about 'Lou, finances, etc.' The end of the summer had been dreadful for her brother's family, dreadful for Lou, who had finally been hospitalised at the Payne Whitney Psychiatric Clinic in New York. Everyone was fretful. Margo, whose husband's wise investments had given his widow a degree of financial security, wanted to take over, but while Peg was wary of her aunt's tendency to meddle, Gregory thought she should be allowed to, at least as far as money was concerned. He pointed out astutely that Nancy Stone wouldn't care while Lou would never forgive them their alleged superiority if they offered help; 'moreover', he added, 'we have our babies and we owe them all we have and right now we don't have much.' For his part, Gregory would do what he could. He had already asked the Swiss psychiatrist Oskar Diethelm, chair of Payne Whitney's Psychiatry Department, to contact a colleague; Gregory would presently have a report on Lou, would confer with whoever was in charge of the case as soon as he returned.[5]

Gregory found Madrid an unsettling combination of poverty and wealth, a European Mexico City with children in sandals and elegant cafés on the main boulevards where traffic was directed by armed members of Franco's Guardia Civil. He was likely moderately impressed with the English Dominican Victor White, who spoke on 'Dogma and Mental Health', but delighted to speak with Plé and Mailloux as well as with the Capuchin friar Peter Dempsey, professor of applied psychology at University College, Cork, whom he hadn't seen since Ireland. Gregory was, however, ready to leave Europe at the end of the month. Despite convivial professional moments, he had continued to miss Peg, and there were patients waiting for him in New York as well as the consultation with Diethelm's colleague.

The psychiatric report was disconcerting. Agitated and disoriented at admission, Lou had also been in physical distress as a result of priapism, a urological emergency requiring immediate medical attention. Cold baths and medication had proved ineffective, and against Gregory's recommendation, Nancy signed the papers for surgery to relieve the blood flow to the penis and eliminate the persistent erection. What psychological confusion had caused Lou's breakdown wasn't clear to anyone. There was professional concern about latent homosexual tendencies, discussion of depression and anxiety, fugue states and psychosis, yet there were times when his doctors felt hopeful, when Lou seemed balanced and rational – not exactly his able former self, not the charming intelligence officer or the successful lawyer finessing television contracts, but lucid and competent. Gregory saw him several times during the autumn, reported to Peg what progress there was, found the case curious and sad.[6]

Gregory resumed his teaching at both Fordham and Woodstock, where Murray had invited him to prepare a book based on his lectures. In a series edited by Murray and the Jesuit theologian Walter J. Burghardt and published by Woodstock's Newman Press, Gregory's *Freud and Religion: A Restatement of an Old Controversy* would be a more focused book than either *The Psychology of the Criminal Act and Punishment* or the volume on Freud's exploration of the human mind. *Freud and Religion* tackled a particular problem in disciplined chapters, taking as its starting point Jones's treatment of the topic in his biography of Freud, the third and final volume of which had just appeared.

Densely argued and replete with references to and quotations from Jones and Freud himself, *Freud and Religion* was far more than a restatement of Freud's view of religion. Gregory's short book began by engaging with Jones's view of Freud's view, pointing out errors in Jones's understanding of Freud even while sincerely admiring the monumental biography by a psychoanalyst who had known Freud personally for over 30 years. Jones, Gregory felt, had nevertheless misunderstood Freud's attitude towards what he called religion, failing to analyse sufficiently or correctly or even logically or scientifically Freud's understanding and criticism of religious belief as a spiritual and cultural phenomenon and a psychological and personal experience. Gregory questioned Jones's assertion that Freud was ' "simply an unbeliever" ', that he ' "went through his life from beginning to end as *a natural atheist*" ', a point Jones had curiously contended ' "needs no explanation" '. Less substantial were the biographer's misunderstandings of religion in general and Judaism in particular, as when he called the Torah ' "a book of Jewish philosophy rather than of religion" ' or the Menorah a synagogue's most conspicuous object. Jones's real error, however, was his failure to analyse Freud's life-long interest in religion, his anxieties about

248 Time and tide

religious practice, his fascination with Moses, and his opposition if not actual hostility to faith.

By his third chapter Gregory was ready to tackle directly what he called Freud's 'vision' of religion. As a knight in scientific armour, Freud had turned his study of religion into an attack, reasoning,

> Religion is an illusion, a fantasy, because it is not scientific. If it is unscientific, it is against science, and since we are for science, we are against all the enemies of science and therefore against its greatest enemy – religion.

Gregory quoted, in contrast to Freud's reasoning, Pope Pius XII's words to a group of French students on Easter Sunday 1949: ' "rest assured that no contradiction is possible between the certain truth of faith and established scientific facts. Nature, no less than revelation, proceeds from God, and God cannot contradict Himself." ' The students were not to be dismayed even if the contrary were affirmed insistently, ' "even though research may have to wait for centuries to find the solution of the apparent opposition between science and faith" '. Gregory was impressed with the Pope's 'dispassionate certainty and serene security', which he saw as rooted in

> a conviction of the unity of the universe and of the unitary endeavors of man to seek for an explanation, synthesis, and understanding of the mysteries of nature – human, social, material, and spiritual – which have such manifold ways of manifestation before the sensible and intellectual eye of man.

Having reduced religion to 'the concept of the man in the street' and its ceremonial trappings, Freud remained, Gregory argued, unclear about what religion really was. The book went on to examine what Gregory presented as Freud's fundamental, albeit unconscious, ambivalence towards the Judeo-Christian tradition, his androcentric focus on patricide, his 'fear of and desire for death, desire for and fear of immortality', and his struggle against 'spiritual trends within himself'. Psychoanalysis, Gregory contended, necessarily revealed 'the human personality as something much more than a complex labyrinth of psychological mechanisms' and pointed to 'the transcending relationship between man and the unknown'.

Gregory finally suggested that Freud was 'an unconscious potential believer': Ever since human beings had started their so-called conquest of nature', they had tried to fancy themselves the conquerors of the universe; logically they had to feel that the maker of the universe was annihilated or their own fantasied sovereignty would be endangered. This 'trend' was reflected in Freud's unwillingness to accept the 'true meaning' of religious faith. Thus Freud unsurprisingly envisioned a person 'who is always unhappy, helpless, anxious, bitter, looking into nothingness with fright, and turning away from "so-called posterity" in anticipatory, almost snobbish disgust'. 'Such a man', Gregory continued, 'feels pressed by his own civilization, tormented by his own culture, isolated by his own society, always threatened with defeat by the wilfulness and aggressiveness of others or by his own "death instinct".' Yet Gregory understood this aspect of Freud as merely testimony to his human frailty, an incomplete reflection of the man who also sensed 'the transcending truth' about human beings 'when he said that to be normal meant to him *arbeiten und lieben*'. True human greatness, Gregory concluded, lies in the humble recognition that one's task and mission is to follow with neither 'superstitious occultism' nor 'megalomanic scientism' the mysteries of the world of human beings and the world of things.[7]

Throughout the autumn Gregory worked on this insightful examination of Freud's struggle with the problem of religion, a provocative book informed throughout by its author's values and religious convictions. Of course, there were also lectures and interviews on topics that had little or nothing at all to do with Jones's biography or Freud's psychology in addition to the daily round of patients and a busy social life. A previous commitment in mid-December during one of Mailloux's visits to New York meant Gregory and Peg left the Dominican on his own for an evening with the children and the servants. Undeterred, he took nominal charge, thanking Peg for the honour in a gracious note in charming English: 'You cannot imagine what a fun it is to be a baby-sitter when children behave so much better than so many grown-ups – Good bye – Father Noël.' The children may not have behaved in any particularly outstanding way, but they were used to being put to bed by Lala in their parents' absence, were amenable if slightly awed by the formal priest, their father's friend, reading them *Babar* in his French accent, blessing them each in turn from their respective bedroom doors.[8]

Christmas in Bedford was filled with comfort and joy. Betty baked a cake and Caroline helped to ice it, took it into the dining room singing happy birthday to both Jesus and her father. Christmas in Bronxville was less calm. Lou had convinced his doctors that he could leave the hospital at least for the holidays. He wanted to be with his family, to get to know his third child, a second little girl, born in early November; he missed Bronxville and wanted to visit his mother and aunt in his childhood home, to walk the New York City streets unfettered, breathe the air in Central Park, watch birds fly and dogs run. Louise worried, Margo worried, George and Jodie and Peg worried. Gregory, who was consulted and whose advice was then disregarded, wasn't at all certain Lou's release, however conditional, was a good idea, especially at this time of year.

Lou managed Christmas itself fairly well, but seemed a bit depressed on New Year's Day, yet that was to be expected if the days at home were, in fact, merely a reprieve before re-entering the hospital. On 2 January he checked into the Roosevelt Hotel on 45th Street, drank an entire bottle of whisky and shot himself in the head. With some restraint, the *New York Times* ran a brief obituary under the headline 'C.B.S. AIDE FOUND DEAD', and 'Louis T. Stone, Talent Chief, Discovered in Hotel Room'. Nancy told the police that Lou had been under treatment at Payne Whitney, not a detail the family were pleased to see in the papers, but she had at least mentioned an autopsy. The funeral occurred on 4 January in the Kent School chapel and Lou was then buried in the school cemetery, a small plot at the north end of the campus just beyond the baseball field. It all happened so quickly there was scarcely time to grieve.[9]

Peg and George grieved but felt their brother had in many ways left long ago. Margo and especially Louise would grieve for the rest of their lives, and the two women would pick up the pieces, taking on daily and financial responsibility for Lou's wife and children. In response to Jean and Dominique's letter of sympathy, Peg told them such letters were a comfort, but wished they could have known Lou 'as once he was – a big, delightful person'. Gregory took little comfort in having been only peripherally involved in his brother-in-law's psychiatric care. He wished he had done more.[10]

At the end of the month Explorer 1, America's first satellite, was launched from Cape Canaveral in Florida, a rival in the 'space race' to the Soviets' Sputnik 1, which had gone up the previous October. John drew rocket ships, but the space race had little impact on the family. Gregory saw patients, taught students, was pleased when *Freud and Religion* appeared in February, its title page preceded by the standard Catholic '*nihil obstat*' and '*imprimatur*' indicating the book was free of doctrinal and moral error.

There would be lectures and meetings throughout the spring, but for the first time in years, Gregory would have no book on the hob. There would be a few articles for Catholic journals, as many patients as ever, almost as much correspondence, and travel as always to annual conventions, but perhaps in part as a result of Field's death and Henry's death followed by Lou's, Gregory finally decided to step back, to spend more afternoons in his Bedford workshop and developing photographs, more evenings at the opera and concerts, more weekends with Peg and the children. He quizzed Caroline on her multiplication tables, taught her and John to play chess. He agreed to see a few of the musicals Peg so enjoyed, saw *The Music Man* and Leonard Bernstein's *Westside Story*.

At the beginning of March, the family spent a long weekend at the Lake Placid Club, a ski resort a five-hour train journey north of Manhattan. Taking both Marie and Agathe along seemed now as natural as their presence during the summers in West Hyannisport. Peg and the young women took to the slopes while the children had classes with local instructors. Gregory stayed indoors, looked out at the mountains, and wrote Philippe Colbert an important letter about his daughters' mental health. Both frank and discreet, precise and vague, Gregory detailed the progress of analysis, reassuring a worried parent while championing the young women's growing independence.

During the previous August, Gregory told her father that Marie's 'true personality' had finally broken through 'the maze and the fog of her neurosis.' He saw real progress as 'The woman awakened in her for the first time and for the first time too the search for God'. Her progress had continued through the autumn and winter. Marie now seemed 'awake to people, to things'. There were other signs of health: 'The future wife and mother are not only visualized through her behavior, but they glow in her with a beaming inspiration and serenity.' Marie had become 'practical, sensible', 'direct and nobody's fool'. Shadows of her illness lingered in flashes of anger and old antagonisms, but there was also now considerable self-control and understanding. At the age of 25 she was leading an emotional 'double life', living 'at her age level' yet still learning what she had failed to learn since the onset of puberty. The process was hard and painful, but Gregory reported that Marie was continuing to do it 'with good cheer, serenity, joy and élan'. While she loved her father 'dearly' – something Philippe Colbert probably already knew – Marie's 'attitude towards her mother' was 'unfortunately neither even nor positive' – something both Philippe and his wife Hélène also likely knew. Nevertheless, 'the passionate intolerance, even hatred which characterized her past and which punctuated the most dramatic and painful periods of her treatment' had moderated, and Gregory hoped her relationship with her mother would 'even out in time'. Marie's main concerns were her father and sister. If it weren't for Marie's 'past history of a severe neurotic involvement' that had once appeared as 'a chronic mental state', Gregory would have been tempted to give her his blessing and 'let her out to be entirely on her own'. However, many 'features, familial and personal', wouldn't permit him to take the risk, so he would continue to treat her through the summer. He told Philippe he found the work 'productive and revelatory and truly inspiring'.

Although she appeared quiet and well-balanced and had never been so obviously ill as her older sister, Agathe was also making slow progress in dealing with 'chronic depressive states'. Gregory considered it a triumph that he had persuaded her to skip her Friday classes for a weekend of skiing, for she took her university obligations so seriously that she tended to become paralysed with intensity and unable to study at all. He remained concerned about her. They were getting along 'extremely well', but she was definitive and strong-willed, wanted and needed 'to be given a chance to do things her own way'. He felt it was promising that she had, despite 'considerable secretiveness', marked 'affections and hostilities towards the various members of her family' as it was 'easier to work with things which are not hidden'. In sum, Gregory found Agathe 'lovely', 'wonderfully loyal', and 'affectionate'; he was 'not pessimistic' about her and glad she seemed to have 'hit it off with Peg'.

Gregory also reflected on his relationship with Colbert. He specifically tried to see Marie's struggle through her father's eyes. Imagining the 'anguish', the 'doubt and uncertainly' Philippe must have felt, Gregory thanked him for his confidence in him, for having 'vouchsafed' him the privilege of serving as 'the intermediary between her potentialities and God's never-to-be-forgotten good will and miraculous help'. The result of the analysis was a double transformation: Philippe now had in Marie 'a daughter come to life' and in Gregory 'a friend, a warm, devoted and willing servant'. The process moved him deeply. He confessed he had had 'difficult and little promising cases before', his share of failures as well as successes, but he found the 'features and qualities' of Marie's 'rehabilitation' particularly inspiring.[11]

Gregory's letter to Colbert reveals the sensitive and skilful psychoanalyst at work, respectful of his patients' independence, their unique problems and different personalities, the demands and forbearance analysis requires of both therapist and client. Gregory would certainly have written differently had he been making a referral or preparing case notes for a professional presentation. With Colbert he was sincere and encouraging but disclosed nothing specific, no confessions or confidences, nothing Philippe didn't already know or couldn't have observed himself. Although Gregory's understanding was psychoanalytical, his circum-spect language was for the most part simple and conversational, and the entire letter was informed by gratitude – for the opportunities so biblically 'vouchsafed', for the trust placed in him, for the chance to further what he saw as God's will. However quick to anger, however forceful in personality and insistent on his own views, however egoistic he appeared to those who didn't know him well and even at times to his friends and family, he was always and predominantly also the man in this extraordinary letter to Colbert.

Throughout the spring of 1958 Gregory continued to accept invitations to speak, couldn't refuse most requests. He addressed the Fordham College Sodality and Psychology Club on 'God and the Psyche' in mid-March. In early April he spoke on 'The Psychology of the Creative Personality' at a conference on 'Creativity' sponsored by the Art Directors Club of New York. He must have been amused and gratified to be described in the brochure as 'one of the few living examples of a Renaissance man today', a recognised authority on early Church Byzantine art, a photographer who had exhibited in international salons, and 'an original creator in metal and wood'. At the end of May he was a discussant at the 'Henry Siger-ist Memorial Symposium' at the annual meeting of the American Association for the History of Medicine, an event sponsored jointly by the Rockefeller Institute for Medical Research and the New York Academy of Medicine. Chaired by Iago Galdston, the symposium featured papers by Owsei Temkin and the medical his-torian and social advocate George Rosen, and in the evening a dinner included old colleagues as well as younger historians Henry had taught at Johns Hopkins and younger doctors Gregory had taught at Butler Hospital. There must have been an air of nostalgia: Among the newer faces were many who had bid Henry farewell when he left the United States a decade earlier. Gregory didn't exactly feel old at the age of 67, but he was aware of a generation diminished of contemporaries, of a younger generation coming into its own, the guard changing, his relation to the Church settled. He thought it would be a good idea to lose weight, to spend more time with friends.

In the photographs taken that summer, Gregory appears unusually relaxed: characteristically animated and engaged, responsive to the world of human beings and things, but also serene. On a sunny day in June, Gregory celebrated Doris Hatcher's birthday with Peg and the children at the Hatchers' home in rural Penn-sylvania. Everyone, even the adults, wore paper hats and ate cake, then the young-sters played croquet, improvising the rules while the grown-ups talked.

At the end of the month, in heavily laden cars, the family headed to Cape Cod in what now seemed an annual pilgrimage. Gregory had sessions with Marie and Agathe, read books and newspapers, welcomed numerous houseguests – among them Jean and Dominique de Menil – and spent unfettered hours with his wife and children. He interrupted the holiday for a fifth stint at Saint John's but was eager to return. When Donna, who had become quite an old dog, died just after Matthew's fifth birthday, she would be buried in a grave Peg dug herself in the property's northwest corner. 'Harbor View' might have been theirs for only two months each year but it felt like home, one of their homes, a part of their heart.

Dominique de Menil and Gregory, 'Harbor View', July 1958

The day after their wedding anniversary, Gregory flew to Europe. Comfortably installed in the Hotel de la Paix overlooking Lake Geneva, he wrote Peg that he intended to see Erica Sigerist but had heard nothing from Marie and Agathe, who planned to accompany him for a portion of his Continental sojourn. In mock irritation but also celebrating their youthful exuberance and impetuosity, he told Peg he expected 'the girls' would typically 'descend' on him the following day 'without warning'. Meanwhile, he had spent a 'fruitful and pleasant' afternoon with Raymond de Saussure followed by dinner with the criminologist Jean Pinatel. In the Protestant city he found calm and cheerfully dull, he missed Peg and Cape Cod. He vowed the family would spend summers there 'next year and next and next, as long', he joked, as Peg could 'wear shorts with Mary-Alice's approval'. He realised the Cape meant so much to his wife and children, had done so much for all of them that he felt they ought not even to think of not being there. Except the following year, he couldn't help adding, when he wanted 'to steal' Peg away 'for about a month', put her on a boat – with him – to Europe and drive around, just the two of them for a fortnight. 'Now, don't say no dear', he told her, 'I know it sounds improbable – but I have ideas, you know.'[12]

When Marie and Agathe finally showed up, Gregory rented a car and drove with them over the Alps, down the Rhone Valley, through Provence towards Spain. Gregory had toured Italy by car, had driven and been driven from Milan to Florence, Siena, and Rome, but the countryside of southern France was a world away from Paris, and he marvelled at the charming villages and small towns. Travelling with the Colbert girls was also a new experience, by turns disconcerting and amusing, completely different from ordered social and intellectual life with European contemporaries. He sent Peg wry reports. In Carcassonne Marie had knocked on the door of his hotel room at one in the morning. Awake '"writing postal cards"' while her sister slept, she had sensed something in her room. Gregory had dutifully gotten out of bed, gone over, and discovered that the 'something' was a bat. Rising to the challenge, he had chased it about until it 'chose' to go out the window. Agathe, he wrote Peg, had remained 'dead asleep' throughout 'the commotion'.

By the time Gregory got to Barcelona, Marie and Agathe were no longer with him. They had arrived at the Spanish border only to find that those travelling on French passports needed visas. Gregory described what ensued:

> Telephoning all over the world to unknown Spanish Consulates, but it was Saturday. Their excellencies left for the weekend – their assistants left for the weekend, everything and everybody left for the weekend. So back to France to Carcassonne where they got a car to drive to Paris.

It seemed just as well since they would have been otherwise pressed to get to Paris for fittings at Dior's. Gregory had fallen exhausted into his comfortable bed at the Ritz only to be awaked at a quarter past midnight by a phone call from the girls to let him know they had arrived in Toulouse.

The young women continued to charm and entertain him despite the real inconvenience they caused, and the new plan was to rejoin him in Milan. Having slept late on Sunday morning, Gregory told Peg that he wouldn't make it to church until noon for a service his Collegeville colleague Howard Rome called 'the Alka-Seltzer mass'. Rapidly recovering his bearings, however, he was surprised to find his Spanish was readily understood. Indeed, he was soon going 'a mile a minute' and felt silly: He had feared he couldn't say a word. During the busy week in the Catalonian capital, he strolled on the Ramblas and socialised with colleagues, including Mailloux, at the fourth International Congress of Psychotherapy. He hit his stride in his paper on 'Individualism, Personalism and Existentialism', arguing against dehumanising battery tests, categorical classifications, and generalised pharmacological treatments, and insisted again on the importance of the human person as an autonomous individual.[13]

The week in Spain was followed by a week at the Palace Hotel in Milan. Gregory had old friends he wanted to see, among them Father Gemelli and Archbishop Montini. When the Colbert girls turned up more or less as planned, Gregory took them to see Leonardo's 'Last Supper' in the Duomo and to the vaulted Galleria

Vittorio Emanuele II for a bit of shopping. There were surely as well elegant dinners at good restaurants he had discovered years ago on Henry's recommendation, and he had the pleasure of the young women's company when he flew to Zurich and then on to New York. If he had been to a degree a chaperone, he had all in all enjoyed the role of travelling analyst and benevolent family friend.

In Gregory's absence Peg had driven once more with the children and the dogs to Bedford and then to New York in time for the children to start school. The academic year also recommenced at the institutions where Gregory taught, and on his return he immediately began seeing patients and lecturing to medical students and priests. The highlight of the autumn was a trip to Texas in early October. Jean and Dominque, whose primary home was in Houston, invited Gregory and Peg to visit for the dedication of two buildings by the modernist architect Philip Johnson at the University of Saint Thomas. Funded by the de Menils, the Miesian structures, including an auditorium and art gallery, were part of their philanthropic efforts to bring art to the city. James Johnson Sweeney, director of the Guggenheim Museum in New York, was among the other houseguests and he, like Gregory, would speak during the festivities.

Gregory gave the dedicatory lecture, choosing as his topic 'The Ever-unfinished Chain of Learning', a talk that allowed him to explore old themes in a contemporary context. The problem, as he presented it, was that people wanted the 'average' person to be 'averager and averager' – not the average of a hundred or even a million people, but the average of billions, a human reduced to 'two little eyes' and a completely unexceptional 'pigeon-sized brain'. Gregory thus found something profoundly wrong in the demand for 'more scientists', 'more engineers', and 'more technicians' – for 'batches' of people. The true purpose of education wasn't to train human beings in useful skills but to nourish minds and interests, logic and creativity, languages and art, exceptionality and individuality.[14]

Gregory's talk was classic, the sort of speech dutifully given to generations of students and faculty at dedication and graduation ceremonies, but in addressing the dual topic of averageness and technology, it was particularly apt in the mid-century America of *The Lonely Crowd*, David Riesman's groundbreaking sociological study of conformity published eight years earlier. Gregory's address had, in addition, personal resonance for the man who had trained as a doctor in both Russia and the United States and who had been persecuted twice over (not as an individual, an exceptional man, but as a Jew and a revolutionary socialist) by two totalitarian regimes. If the resurrection of old and familiar themes suggests that by 1958 Gregory had nothing particularly new to say, it also indicates the abiding importance to him of the coherent and deeply felt convictions that had informed his life. His passion was clear to his Houston audience, who would certainly have noted the ethical dimensions of what he was rejecting and advocating, but Gregory kept personal history and morality out of the words so carefully crafted for public consumption.

When Peg wrote graciously to thank Dominique and Jean for their hospitality, she didn't mention the death of Pope Pius XII on 9 October, wasn't particularly interested in the politics of the Church into which, as Mailloux had told Cardinal Léger, Gregory had, at least at one point, hoped she might follow him. The funeral was, however, widely reported, as was speculation about a successor, and many bet on Montini. It would take nearly three weeks and 11 ballots to elect an old man of 76, whom the conclave felt would be an interim short-term pope. Before the end of the year, Angelo Giuseppe Roncalli, who had become Pope John XXIII, would make Montini a cardinal, a promotion that surprised no one. Surprising everyone four years later, John XXIII would call the Second Vatican Council that would bring about radical changes in the Catholic Church that even Gregory, championing the cause of psychoanalysis with a sympathetic Pius XII, couldn't possibly have imagined.

Unlike his wife, Gregory did indeed follow the events in the newspapers, but while he hadn't felt tired in Europe and had felt only normally tired on his return in September, it had been harder than he anticipated to resume his ordinarily hectic life after the trip to Texas. Watching boxing matches late in the evening, he drank club soda in an effort to settle his stomach. He took Empirin Compound even while knowing that a painkiller wasn't a solution if the pain only came back again. In real distress one night in early November, he called Abe, who immediately came over in a taxi. The two men talked in the master bedroom as Gregory got dressed in his three-piece suit. Before leaving the apartment he stood briefly in the door of Caroline's bedroom to say goodbye to the ten-year-old who had been awakened by the unusual commotion, then went with Abe to Lenox Hill Hospital.

The next few weeks were difficult for everyone. Gregory again underwent major surgery, this time with Abe in charge at a hospital only a few blocks from home, bringing the crisis much closer to the children now more aware than four years earlier of their father's serious illness and their mother's distress. The school bus passed the hospital every morning and afternoon. When Peg visited, she tied the two dogs to a lamppost near the side entrance. If Caroline got off the bus one stop early, she would know her mother was inside if she saw the dogs, could look up at the windows on the sixth floor and imagine her father with her mother at his bedside in the hospital where no one under the age of 16 was allowed to visit. She sent him messages and he wrote back. By the end of November, a corner seemed to have been turned, concerns allayed, a cancerous tumour again removed from the colon, apparently in its entirety.

Gregory returned home in early December, having lost weight but able two weeks later to travel to Bedford for Christmas. Although he couldn't yet see patients, he managed to drive to church in Mount Kisco on Christmas eve, watched the children open their presents on Christmas morning, and sat at his accustomed place at the head of the table for Christmas dinner. He watched the snow fall from the picture windows and saw the new year in with Peg and a glass of champagne in front of the fire. This time his recovery was slower, and he worried more about getting back to work, earning the money that always seemed to go out as soon as it came in, and without work, nothing was coming in.

Family and friends understood and did what, in their different ways, they could. In early January Philippe Colbert sent Gregory a timely cheque for his daughters' treatment. Peg would now pay bills she had planned to put off until February while Gregory sent the Catholic activist Dorothy Day $200. Perhaps sensing this was a Christmas for which Gregory couldn't go shopping, Dominique gave Peg a stunning Tiffany necklace designed by Jean Schlumberger. Less aesthetic but even more substantial was the fat envelope from Jean containing documents indicating that trusts had been set up for each of the three children and additional shares deposited in a separate account to be drawn on at will. The de Menils' generosity was overwhelming. Peg wrote to thank them for all they had done: Their generosity had added 'years to Gregory's life' and changed her whole picture of the children's future and her own. Peg's gratitude was charmingly sincere, revealing both her naïveté and understanding, her belief that Gregory had years ahead of him and her simultaneous sense that a future without him might be a possibility.[15]

Gregory struggled to regain his health, but he was more or less back on his feet by the end of January. He confessed a bit shakily to Babcock that he had gone through 'the wringer' (he initially typed 'ringer'): At times the struggle hadn't appeared worthwhile; at times it hadn't seemed worth being anxious about. But, he wrote, 'here I am doing a full day's work again and I am happy and there are no aftereffects.' As 'a matter of fact', Gregory insisted, 'I am quite normal as testified by the fact that I am behind in my correspondence, behind in my writing, behind in my reading – as always. Hence', he concluded, 'things are really O.K.' He had indeed been through the wringer, but there were as yet no bells tolling for him, though the slip of his pen suggests he had at least at one point thought so. The triple repetition of the word 'behind' also suggests that unconsciously the return of the colon cancer continued to worry him, to influence everything he did, while his insistence on 'facts', on normality, on his own happiness and the absence of 'aftereffects', suggests things weren't so 'really O.K.' as he wanted others to believe.[16]

As soon as he could, Gregory picked up where he had left off over two months earlier and resumed seeing patients. By February he was teaching as well as reading, writing, and attacking the mountain of correspondence. At the end of the month he lectured on 'Psychopathology of the Criminal Act' at the Law-Medicine Research Institute at Boston University. In March he spoke on 'Religion and Psychiatry' at the School of Religion at Iowa State University in Ames. In April he was in Philadelphia for the American Psychiatric Association's annual meeting, where he presented a paper on 'The Tide of Overlooking the Individual' and served as a commentator for two panel discussions: 'Mass Communication and Mass Motivation' and 'Developments in European Psychiatry with Special Reference to Existentialism'.

In the spring of 1959 the publishers of Gregory's translation of *We* agreed to its reissue. It isn't clear who initiated the project, but the additional income from a book whose copyright Gregory had renewed in 1952 would be very useful. Peter Rudy, chair of the Russian Department at Northwestern University, would write a new introduction; Gregory's friend Marc Slonim in the Russian Department at

Sarah Lawrence College would write a new preface; and Gregory himself would write an additional foreword.

Entitled 'Thirty-five Years Later', Gregory's short essay allowed him not only to reflect on the passage of time which had changed the context of Zamiatin's novel but to argue for its continued timeliness. A generation had passed since Gregory's translation had first appeared: In 1924, the Atlantic had yet to be traversed by aeroplane; the survivors of the First World War had prayed for world peace; and there had still been hope in Russia 'that man would be spared the anguish of being lost'. In the intervening years, a second World War had killed millions and the revolution that had promised so much had produced a Russian 'colossus' under whose authority human beings seemed to have lost their value as individuals – a loss that, Gregory trenchantly pointed out, had 'in some degree' occurred not only in Russia but in 'many other nations'. He found *We* just as pertinent in a present of 'secret persuaders' and 'liminal and subliminal' modes of 'so-called communications', and concluded with a noble and valiant exhortation, hopeful that Zamiatin's 'spiritual vibrancy and insight' would continue to inspire those still 'naïve enough' to love humanity and to 'stand up erect and fearless' in its name.[17]

Having *'fecit quod potuit'*, Gregory submitted his new foreword in mid-May. He would spend the next six working weeks valiantly seeing as many patients as he could in New York and the weekends with the family in Bedford. He wasn't, however, as really O.K. as he had insisted to Babcock at the beginning of the year. He tired easily and suffered from persistent anaemia. Perhaps someone said something about a stomach ulcer or attributed his lethargy to a slow recovery from the surgery. He lost his temper with the children when his stomach wouldn't settle, when his head ached. Peg explained their father was 'in pain', but his angry outbursts upset everyone, including himself.

Gregory worried about his health and he worried about John. By the age of nine John had become a fussy eater and careless at school; he daydreamed in class and his handwriting was messy. At some point during the spring Gregory and Peg decided he should see a psychoanalyst. It seems unlikely that Margaret Mahler suggested sending him to Wyoming with 14-year-old François de Menil for a month of 'wilderness camp', the sort of experience supposed to make men of boys, and the idea may have originated with Jean de Menil or even with Peg herself. John would, in any event, be the youngest camper, miserably homesick, and reluctant to survive on fish and rabbits during four days in the woods on the 'pack trip'. Missing his parents and siblings, his baseball cards, and Delilah's new puppies, he sent postcards, addressed and stamped by Peg in advance: He wasn't enjoying currying horses and tying lassos as much they hoped. When François, happy enough in the mountains, decided to stay on for a second month, John wrote that was scared of flying back alone. None of this made Gregory, who missed him, feel any better.

As Gregory prepared to leave for Europe at the end of June, Peg left the other children in Bedford to join him in the city where he had another in a series of transfusions. She wrote John that his father now looked and felt and acted 'much better'; they thought, she told her homesick son, that he would be fine now, joked that afterwards they had eaten supper in bed 'with Eddie Warburg (*not* on our bed) and we had a good time'. Gregory wrote that Abe had taken one of the female puppies for his son Toby, but the other seven were 'still there, barking, getting fat and happy'. He told John he would be back from England even before John returned from Wyoming, then concluded as if he had simply run out of steam: 'Have a good time, son. I hope everything goes well with you. We all love and miss you.'[18]

On the last Wednesday in June Peg drove to Cape Cod with Caroline and Matthew, Betty, Lala, the two dogs, and seven puppies. Two days later Gregory flew to Europe. Why he was there, whom he saw, and what he did remain vague. At some point weeks or perhaps even months earlier he had apparently given up the idea of attending the 21st congress of the International Psychoanalytic Association in Copenhagen at the end of July. Soon after he arrived in London he rang Peg to let her know he was safe but tired, content to be looking out at the trees in Hyde Park from his room at the Dorchester. On Sunday 5 July he reported to Peg that all was not going exactly as planned. If he had left England for Paris or Geneva or Milan, he was now back again in his Park Lane Hotel. Exhausted, he had taken a long nap, gotten up only because he felt he had to eat. Marie, who had come over from Paris, joined him in the evening, but he didn't feel like going out so they dined in the hotel restaurant. Afterwards he went to bed and slept for 13 hours. Gregory didn't feel exactly unwell or in pain, only indolent and 'sort of draggy'; nothing specifically seemed to be wrong and he 'functioned' well, but he felt 'hollow' psychologically and, when he looked in the mirror, he saw he was physically quite pale. He had various obligations in London and reassured Peg he was 'so so'; she shouldn't worry. If things didn't go very well, he would be home on a jet. He sent his love to everybody.[19]

Gregory returned to New York on 9 July. The plan was to drive up to the Cape with Mary-Alice the following morning, but John Waller, his colleague at New York University School of Medicine who had been overseeing his transfusions, insisted on tests at Lenox Hill. This time the size and location of the cancer discovered in the colon made it inoperable. There was a brief moment of reprieve while Abe looked into treating the tumour with radiotherapy, but when he learned that such a new treatment would be ineffective at this late stage, Gregory and his physicians accepted the inevitable and, after two weeks in hospital, he went to the Cape to be with his family.

The news spread quickly. Hélène Colbert wrote to tell him he was 'wonderful.' She recalled his psychoanalytic work with Marie, 'the miracle' Gregory had performed 'in giving us back a beloved child, now an exceptional woman'. She wrote, 'I know what a sacrifice it is for you to have to interrupt your work and remain idle. But I know, you know, that God starts working when we don't have the strength to keep on.' Addressing him as 'Dearest Gregory', Dominique told him, 'I feel so close to you and feel like telling you.' She felt there was no need for

many words because he must already know 'how much we love you; how much
I love you'. She imagined visiting him, told him it would be wonderful to chat
with him: 'It has always been wonderful, but now I feel more prepared to receive
all what you have to give.' She closed her eloquent letter 'With more love than
I can tell'.[20]

Murray, who had visited Gregory in hospital, had found him 'full of faith, and
free of anxiety in his submission to God's will'. Indeed, Gregory was as prepared
as anyone could be for impending death. As a doctor and a deeply spiritual man,
he had reflected a good deal on mortality. Three years earlier, on the centenary
of Freud's birth, he had contributed a commemorative article to *Psychoanalytic
Quarterly* in which he had written that the mind knows that 'the passing of man
is the inevitable course and curse of that which the individualistic libertarian has
always cherished most: the individual, the person.' He had reflected more specifically on the experience of dying from cancer in his recent review of the final
volume of Jones's biography. Freud had been diagnosed in 1923 at the age of 67,
and Gregory had drawn attention to the physical and psychological suffering that
being 'a victim of cancer' had caused for Freud between the first diagnosis and
surgery and his death 16 years later at the age of 83.[21]

In contrast, from his earliest experiences of violent pogroms in Kiev's streets
and treatment of shell-shocked soldiers, Gregory's long spiritual journey and
medical training had reconciled him both to the death of others and to his own
inevitable demise. Reflecting on his father's death in 1942, Gregory had expressed
an astonishing equanimity, not an absence of feeling, but – to use his own words –
an 'outworldly' serenity. His words to his brother had easily assumed biblical
cadences: One could not actually understand death – to 'penetrate its mystery is
beyond our ken, to combat it beyond our sinew'; although most people 'know
not the greatness of death any more than the depth of life' and 'don't know how
to make peace with death', it was possible to accept it. Concern about one's own
life coming to an end had 'nothing to do with the actual facts of life and death':
such anxiety was 'like the natural, silent and anxious gasp when one reaches a
great height' and didn't prevent one 'from climbing high mountains or buildings'.
Death was 'the most natural and simple thing'.

There are no photographs of Gregory from the summer of 1959. Moses, who
had 'found his way in life despite so many odds', had 'found his way out of life
with considerable dignity'. Gregory hoped to do as well. He wanted to see very
few people and, especially as the summer wore on, he didn't want anyone beyond
the family and his closest friends to see him. The man who had always been a bit
of a dandy wanted no one to remember him tended by a nurse with a drip in his
left arm and increasingly debilitated. There would be myriad practical details to
deal with, and some he would address to the degree he was able; the rest would
perforce fall to Peg, who took over as his amanuensis, answering letters, paying
bills, and filtering phone calls and visitors.[22]

Settled in the master bedroom with its view of the sea, Gregory wanted Mailloux to know he had been cheered and sustained by the Dominican's last two

letters. He asked Peg to tell Mailloux that he could write himself but felt it would tire him too much. He wanted Mailloux to know what was wrong with him, so Peg explained and added that the surgeons had no idea how long Gregory might be able to hold on; they thought 'probably several months', although she wondered about that. Much of the time Gregory was in considerable pain only somewhat controlled by Demerol. When he ate solid food, the pain increased. Much on his mind were three papers he wanted to write, and he now had a small Dictaphone. Peg wrote that he counted on seeing Mailloux before the end.[23]

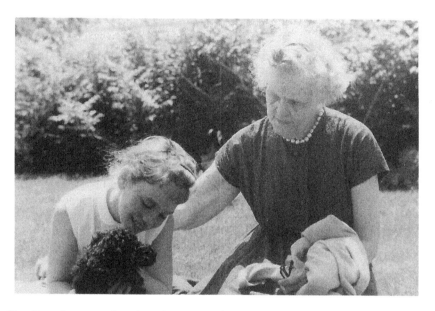

Caroline, her grandmother Louise, and Amanda the puppy, 'Harbor View', August 1959

Mailloux was one of the few people Gregory was willing to see. Peg would later tell James an old friend had driven up from New York, but 'Grisha would not let him come to the house, much less to his bedroom': '"He only wants to see how badly I look."' Peg was sure, of course, that that wasn't what the friend wanted to see, but 'persuasion was to no avail', and beyond persuasion she wouldn't go. Even his dearest friends didn't see him, Peg explained, 'but that was the way he wanted it', and whatever he wanted she strove to see he got – 'it was very little.' Fera was told that she shouldn't come. Leaving Alan in charge of their three-year-old son in Boston, Nancy visited several times. Young Greg was no longer so young but showed no inclination to leave his wife and children in New York and make the summer journey to Cape Cod. Agathe came to help at the end of August.

There were good days and bad days. On three occasions Gregory made it down-stairs to join the family, sat at the head of the table and watched the children have their breakfast, sat on the terrace, felt the sea breeze and looked out at the water. Early one evening Peg took the children into Matthew's bedroom and explained that their father was going to die. It wasn't really a surprise, at least to Caroline, and Peg was glad they knew, felt that, because they knew, they would appreciate their father's 'calm and courage and humor' all the more as they grew older.

Throughout that long summer Peg found her husband 'truly magnificent'. At the end of August, however, the idea of his making the trip by car from West Hyannisport to Bedford and a few days or weeks later by car to New York was simply unimaginable. It was likely the Warburgs who sent a private plane for him. When it was time to go, to say goodbye to the children, Gregory insisted on dress-ing himself. It took him a little over two hours, but he wouldn't even let Peg put his cufflinks in his shirt. He walked very slowly down the stairs of 'Harbor View' and out to the car, then from the car to the waiting plane, and in New York from the plane to a car, and from the car into the hospital and up to his room. He would not even accept a wheelchair.[24]

In early September it was Natalie who informed James how very ill his brother was. Nancy followed up with a letter telling him not even to consider coming to the hospital, emphasising that Gregory was unable to write himself and would be distressed to see his brother, could 'really see no one in his condition'. On 5 September Fera spoke with Gregory on the phone, and although he was quite weak and wanted absolutely no visitors, she thought he sounded cheerful. Peg and Nancy were at the hospital most of the time, but while Ray knew, of course she didn't visit, and neither did Greg. Eddie was one of the very few friends allowed to see Gregory and visited him for the last time on 10 September. Gregory wanted him to tell Mailloux he hoped he would include him in his prayers at Christ-mas. He specifically wanted Eddie to order from Switzerland a wrist stopwatch for Mailloux and dictated its inscription: 'In memory of Gregory to whom you showed the way.'[25]

Peg spent most of 17 September at the hospital. A lamp Gregory had bought while abroad had arrived that morning but without a plug at the end of its wire. At his request, early that evening, she had brought it to him along with a plug, pliers, and a screwdriver. When she left for the night with the functioning lamp, he told her, 'Good. Good. You know, dear – *lieben und arbeiten*', so it was Abe who was with him at the very end. Just as Peg was getting ready for bed, he rang to tell her, his voice breaking, that it 'was all over'; Gregory had died.[26]

The funeral at his request was held at Saint Ignatius Loyola. Bishop John Wright of Pittsburgh presided but didn't officiate; that was left to Murray. Peg invited Marie and Agathe to sit with her and the children in the front row. Fera would find a seat somewhere in the back of the packed church, perhaps near Dorothy Day, who also attended. Mailloux would find a place for himself in one of the small side chapels. Afterwards, just the immediate family went out to the cemetery in the country. According to the records of the Church of Saint Francis of Assisi, in return for a substantial financial contribution, Gregory had purchased two graves in Mount Kisco's Catholic cemetery for which he had arranged what is euphemistically termed 'perpetual care'. He lies in one. The other is empty.[27]

Notes

1   James Fox to GZ, 28 January, 11 June 1957; GZ to Fox, 26 February, 25 March 1957; Jean de Menil to TM, 16 March 1957; TM to GZ, 21 March 1957 – all in the Thomas Merton Center, Bellarmine University, Louisville, Kentucky.
2   GZ to Hal Babcock, 25 January, 16 February 1957.
3   GZ to Jean de Menil, 17 September 1958; George Stone to MSZ, 1 December 1958.
4   GZ, 'Development', passim.
5   GZ to MSZ, 7 September 1957.
6   In a letter to MSZ, 1 December 1958, George noted only the 'hideous, unbelievable things' that had happened. Given Lou's military experience, career in law, period in Hollywood and at CBS, it seems possible his psychological and physical difficulties were precipitated by psychoactive drugs. His profile would have made him a prime candidate for the CIA's Cold War mind control experiments; he may have been formally or informally working for the CIA and an unwitting victim of their LSD experiments.
7   GZ, *Freud and Religion*, 12, 13, 15–16, 23, 24–25, 27, 32, 48, 49, 59–60.
8   NM to MSZ, 15 December 1957.
9   'C.B.S. AIDE FOUND DEAD', *New York Times*, 3 January 1958, 44.
10 MSZ to Jean and Dominque de Menil, c. January 1958.
11 GZ to 'Philippe Colbert', 7 March 1958.
12 GZ to MSZ, 21 August 1958.
13 GZ to MSZ, 31 August 1958.
14 Marguerite Johnston, ' "Satanic Era of Statistics" Condemned by a Scholar', *Houston Post*, 9 October 1958, np.
15 MSZ to 'Philippe Colbert' and to Jean de Menil, both 12 January 1959.
16 GZ to Hal Babcock, 26 January 1959.
17 GZ, 'Thirty-Five Years', xix, xx.
18 MSZ to John Zilboorg, 18 June 1959; GZ to John Zilboorg, 22 June 1959.
19 GZ to MSZ, 5 July 1959.
20 'Hélène Colbert' and Dominique de Menil to GZ, late July 1959.
21 John Courtney Murray to NM, 30 July 1959, APD; GZ, 'Freud's One Hundredth', 146; GZ, review, *The Life and Work of Sigmund Freud: The Last Phase*, 257.
22 GZ to JZ, 16 November 1942.
23 MSZ to NM, 25 July 1959, APD.
24 MSZ to JZ, 4 February 1960.
25 Natalie Zilboorg Fiess to JZ, EZ and Olga Zilboorg, 7 September 1959; Nancy Zilboorg to JZ, c. 15 September 1959, both Schaeffer; Edward M.M. Warburg to NM, 18 September 1959, APD.
26 MSZ, 'Introduction', xi.
27 Email from 'Agathe Colbert', 23 September 2013; MSZ to JZ, 22 September 1959, Schaeffer; telephone conversation with the parish secretary, Saint Francis of Assisi Catholic Church, Mount Kisco, New York, 5 September 2013.

Chapter 10

Aftermath

Coda

After the funeral Peg finally wrote to James directly. She told him kindly that she had thought of him often during the previous few days and felt he would want to know that at the end Gregory did not suffer. She concluded,

> It is still a shock to me to realize that Gregory is gone, and I know it must be in a way even more of one for you when you didn't know that he had been so sick for really so long. He didn't want me to be sad, although I am; I keep thinking that he wouldn't want it. And I know you must be and remember, he wouldn't want that either.

Before the end of the year, Peg would write 484 responses to the hundreds of letters of condolence she received, some of which of course didn't require an answer. She told James in February that she and the children had somehow gotten through Christmas and Gregory's birthday 'quite well'; they would be 'all right'.[1]

James would be all right, too, but he would struggle to come to terms with his brother's death just as he had struggled to come to terms with everything Gregory had been and done. He wrote Pauline about his sadness and regret. She did her best to be reassuring. In her view it was Gregory's fault that the two brothers hadn't been friends; James had, as far as she could see, done everything possible to meet him more than half way. Pauline's letter was finally bitter and snide. She couldn't understand Gregory's conversion, saw it as ostentatious, even foolish. She apparently resented his second marriage and the obvious happiness it brought to both him and Peg. She told James that he needn't feel sorry for his brother. Gregory had had a full life and, in her opinion, had denied himself nothing. He had had the *soi-disant* 'comfort' of the Church and a big funeral at which his 'former wife' had 'wept (perhaps for the years she spent with him)'. Despite having been 'very brilliant, especially in his earlier years', as his own worst enemy Gregory had, Pauline asserted, antagonised everyone. The idea that James was only one among the many Gregory had alienated would be cold comfort.[2]

Ray, to whom James also wrote, was more romantic. She remembered Gregory's 'big vision and great generosity'. His death had brought her 'a sharp sorrow', she told James wistfully, and 'a feeling of such great waste', regret for what might

DOI: 10.4324/9781003190974-10

have been had Gregory lived longer. Through her rose-tinted glasses Ray was grateful 'for many happy memories', for the years she insisted they had spent 'so fruitfully together'. If Gregory had eluded his brother, she felt he had eluded 'all who loved him'. Full of admiration for the man who had eluded them both, Ray reminded James that while most people don't realise their dreams, Gregory's 'drive for accomplishment' had allowed him to overcome all sorts of obstacles: 'There are not many of his stature.'[3]

Unable to understand or accept his brother, James would belittle his brother's achievements. 'So many letters arrived from most unexpected places and various parts of the world!' he wrote with apparent astonishment in response to one letter of sympathy. He conceded, 'Gregory was well and widely known and certainly has made significant contributions in a field which seems to me hardly touched.' Answering another condolence letter, James wrote, 'Gregory worked intensely and, I believe, fruitfully in an area in which so much still continues to be mysterious.' Like other psychiatrists, he had 'tried to probe deeply into the subject', but James nevertheless wondered if much progress had been made beyond 'highly hypothetical conclusions'. A year after Gregory's death, James was still struggling. In a pathetic but well-intentioned letter, he wrote Peg that the past 12 months had been 'rather horrid': 'Gregory seems to have started a whole string of sadness around us. All we are accumulating now is memories and regrets. And there is no escape from either.'[4]

Gregory's legacy comes, of course, to much more than the regrets and memories of those who knew him. Indeed, many who knew him didn't have any regrets, and their memories of him, however initially vivid or eventually fragmentary, would be distorted – positively or negatively – over time. Many of his patients would feel a natural sense of abandonment, a confused mixture of guilt and resentment. Lillian Hellman wasn't alone in trying to understand her own experience in the context of the rumours that abounded particularly after Gregory's death. It would take her a long time to believe what she referred to vaguely as 'the ugliness', the accusations of what she called 'veniality'. She had respected him, had been grateful for her analysis, which she would come to think of as having taken place during Gregory's 'good years' before his purportedly 'odd' end, and would be unable to determine whether the turn against him came because he really had been 'kind of crazy' or simply because the 'magic' of his presence had died with him.[5]

When as a young man John told the gentle giant who was his half-brother that he wished their father were still alive so he could get to know him, Greg retorted in a raw moment that he, too, wished their father were still alive – but only so he could get cancer again and die all over again in great pain. John later sought out Dominique de Menil and received a softer answer:

> Yes, your father was difficult and he deserves some harsh criticism. Among all the people he met, I am one who retained for him love and gratefulness and admiration. He was very self-centered. Great people are also great sinners. He died with faith and I cannot talk about him in the past. He is very present.[6]

There would be many who would argue that, in addition to or even instead of his differently recollected personality, Gregory's legacy lies in his work, in what he achieved as separate from – if separation is indeed desirable or even possible – his individual person. There was little argument in his own time and in the years immediately after his death that his great achievement was his *History of Medical Psychology*. In 1960, Franz Alexander would praise the book in the *Psychoanalytic Quarterly* as Gregory's 'most outstanding contribution', 'the most authentic and comprehensive, and at the same time the most interestingly written history of psychiatry':

> Zilboorg was the first to recognize clearly the significance for modern psychiatry of the contributions of the sixteenth-century Spanish religious philosopher, Vives. His historical analysis of the anachronism which the *Malleus Mallificarum* represented on the European cultural scene, and of the role of Weyer in combatting its sinister influence in introducing into the backward field of psychiatry the spirit of Renaissance enlightenment and humanism, are singular contributions to the history of psychiatric thought. In his book, unlike most historians of psychiatry, he succeeded in presenting the development of psychiatric concepts in the context of cultural history.[7]

As late as 1979 Daniel Blain and Michael Barton in *The History of American Psychiatry: A Teaching and Research Guide* called *A History of Medical Psychology* a 'classic' that was 'still cited in nearly every subsequent history of psychiatry', and praised Gregory's narrative of 'two great psychiatric revolutions, the first one in the sixteenth century, when superstition began to succumb to Johann Weyer's medical reasoning, and the second one at the end of the nineteenth century, when Freud began to work and publish'. Although Gregory's history purposely included very little material on the twentieth century, the authors pointed out that it was justifiably one of the 'most popular books in use now in courses for residents in the history of psychiatry'.[8]

In the mid-1990s, however, George Mora would emphasise that, although 'historiographically' *A History of Medical Psychology* was 'immensely important', half a century after its publication it was 'by consensus, outdated. Its concentration on single personalities' – Gregory would have said 'on individuals' – 'has been replaced by a new concern with social, political, economic and cultural determinants.' The medical historian Gerald Grob recently agreed, criticising Gregory's book because it presented 'the subject in terms of the history of progress'. In an effort to justify his profession, Gregory had emphasised witchcraft and the gradual evolution away from barbarism toward medicine and psychiatry. This was, Grob felt, a common error, a failure on the part of a physician to understand the nature of history as understood by academic historians. Notwithstanding such theoretical arguments, in 2018 the British psychoanalyst Brett Kahr recommended *A History of Medical Psychology* to aspiring therapists interested in the historical and cultural context of psychoanalysis. In short, Gregory's book remains 'the very best written history of psychiatry to date'.[9]

Gregory's legacy rests on more than a single book. Kahr also admired Gregory's early work on schizophrenia. Gregory's extraordinary essay 'Masculine and Feminine' is certainly as provocative in an age informed by twenty-first-century feminism as it was when Gregory published it in 1944. His late essays on psychoanalysis and religion continue to be cited, while it seems impossible that, without his efforts and those of other Catholic psychoanalysts, Pope Francis could have consulted a psychoanalyst in the late 1970s and admitted having done so in 2018. Gregory's name crops up repeatedly in work on those he knew from Andreyev to Merton. Even Gregory's photography has an uncannily enduring life: In the Blue House in Mexico City, now the Frida Kahlo Museum, where Kahlo lived with Diego Rivera, one of Gregory's wonderful photographic portraits of Rivera was at least at one time displayed on a small table, while Tim Street Porter's photograph of this photograph appeared in *Ms. Magazine* in 1991.

Although this biography is by no means a family history, Gregory's family has played a large part in the narrative of his life. For readers curious about what happened to everyone, it seems only fair to offer some account.

James and Eugenia finally left Mexico in 1961 and settled on Long Island, near their daughters Natalie and Olga. James died at the age of 76 in 1968 and Eugenia in 1973. Natalie and her husband Ed Fiess retired to North Carolina, where Natalie died in 2007 at the age of 86. James and Eugenia's middle daughter Lydia married Bob Cato and settled in Kansas, where she died at the age of 69 in 1998. Olga, who became a professional cellist, married Thomas Irvine and died at the age of 83 in 2017.

Basia, who settled in California, would never master English. On the streets of Pasadena, she and her daughter would converse in Spanish; at home, where she lived out her life with Nadia and her husband Bob Hynds and their children, she and Nadia spoke Russian. She died two years after Gregory, at the age of 67 in 1961. Her grandchildren Paul and Cassandra adored her.[10]

Sol Levitas also died in 1961. When Peg, who attributed her alienation from Fera to her failure to invite her husband's youngest sister to sit with the family at his funeral, attended Sol's funeral, she sat strategically at the back and left without speaking to anyone. Outliving Gregory by nearly 40 years, Fera died in 1997 at the age of 99. Her daughter Nora would go on to receive the advanced degree in biology Fera never achieved. Misha changed his name to Mitchel and would always be known outside his parents' family as 'Mike'. He, like his father, would become a journalist.[11]

Nancy taught Russian for many years at the Massachusetts Institute of Technology. When her two children were grown, she left Alan Dworsky and moved to the Blue Ridge Mountains in Virginia, where she become an Episcopal solitary, taking the name Anna Zilboorg. An accomplished and highly regarded knitter, she has written several books, including *Knitting for Anarchists*. She now lives in Maine near her son Jeff, a photographer and retired lobsterman. Her daughter Arianne is a sculptor and lives in California.

Greg married twice, had three children (Gregory, Laura, and Catherine) with his first wife who, when she left him, took the children to California, where they now live. Despite the animosity towards his father that he expressed to John, Anna would remember Greg as 'a deeply sweet person', very much like both John and his father. Greg died in 1993 at the age of 62.[12]

Ray would finally seem to her daughter just as she appeared in her consolation letter to James: 'a simple, essentially kind, intuitively sharp, unimaginative, uneducated and not very bright woman', not the right life-long partner for Gregory, but by no means a bad person. Anna would feel her mother 'spent the last twenty years of her life doing nothing'. Not entirely without affection, Greg would refer to her as 'the potato' and generally called her 'Spuds'. Ray died at the age of 89 in 1979.[13]

John became a teacher of history and Spanish at state and private high schools in the United States and abroad. He now lives in Italy.

Matthew became a licensed psychologist and alcohol and drug abuse counsellor, practicing in Vermont near his wife's family. They have two children. On his retirement to Florida, he became a serious amateur photographer.

I became a university lecturer in English, first at an American college, then at Cambridge University. My husband and I have four children and seven grandchildren. Having retired from teaching, I live in France, where I continue to write.

My mother never remarried. A widow at 41, she remained a widow until her death at the age of 91 in 2009. Her relationship with my father was the pinnacle of her emotional life and she never felt ready or willing or able to enter into another partnership. She moved slowly and steadily away from the world to which he had introduced her; within a decade of his death, few of their mutual friends would be included in her circle, which was increasingly made up of people she had known before she met him or completely new people. In that smaller and duller circle, she was a star.

Within two years of my father's death, we had moved apartments twice and sold the property in Bedford. One of the last things my father did in the summer of 1959 was to rent 'Harbor View' for the following year, our fifth and final summer on Cape Cod. After editing my father's last book, a collection of previously published essays entitled *Psychoanalysis and Religion*, my mother trained as a primary school teacher and taught for nearly 20 years in a New York City private school. She retired first to Wainscott, a village on Long Island where from 1961 we spent our summers, and then to South Carolina, where her home had a swimming pool in which she swam from April to October. She was a regular communicant at her local Episcopal Church, whose kind and dutiful members confessed rather disconcertedly to visiting family that they 'just loved her to death'. She always had a dog. Clementine, her last standard poodle, died not long before she did, and was cremated, as was my mother. According to her wishes, their ashes were mixed together, then divided among her three children, to be scattered in 'living water' – meaning in a river or a lake or the sea (not down a drain).

It was my mother who, from the time she began working for my father in June 1940, meticulously preserved much of the archival material that has made this biography possible. Even she, however, didn't organise everything in purely chronological order. Interrupting the sequence in a family album from 1961 is a page she entitled 'Recollections'. The photographs there show my father in various outfits on various occasions beginning with sepia snapshots from the 1920s, years before she met him, to a cropped enlargement of the photograph taken in the Burghölzli Klinik garden in 1949. Slightly blurred, in a focus that might pass for soft, the edited photograph is the man she knew: Caught off-guard, his hair neatly combed, his ubiquitous camera slung over his shoulder and a pen in the pocket of his cashmere suit, he beams at the camera.

Notes

1 MSZ to JZ, 22 September 1959, 4 February 1960, Schaeffer.
2 Pauline Turkel to JZ and EZ, 5 October 1959, Schaeffer.
3 Ray Zilboorg to JZ and EZ, 2 October 1959, Schaeffer.
4 JZ to Drs. Martin Schreiber and Rex D. Hopper, both 5 November 1959, JEZB; JZ to MSZ, 17 September 1960, Schaeffer.
5 Hellman, 167.
6 Dominique de Menil to John Zilboorg, 29 January 1995.
7 Alexander, 380–381.
8 Blain and Barton, 7.
9 Mora, 59, 66; email from Gerald Grob, 26 March 2014; Kahr, 26; email from Brett Kahr, 25 November 2017.
10 Email from Cassandra Hynds Bullock, 2 January 2018.
11 MSZ to JZ, 9 May 1961, Schaeffer.
12 Email from AZ, 25 June 2019.
13 Emails from AZ, 8 February, 16 June 2018.

Works cited

NB. A full bibliography of Gregory Zilboorg's work is available at https://sites.google.com/view/gregory-zilboorg/bibliography

Alexander, Franz. 'Gregory Zilboorg', *Journal of the American Psychoanalytic Association*, vol. VIII, 1960, 380–381.

Barrett, William G. '*Sigmund Freud: His Exploration of the Mind of Man*, by Gregory Zilboorg', *Psychoanalytic Quarterly*, vol. 20, no. 4, October 1951, 617–618.

Becker, Stephen. *Marshall Field III: A Biography*. New York: Simon & Schuster, 1964.

Bickel, Marcel H., ed. *Correspondence: Henry E. Sigerist – Chauncey D. Leake, 1930–1955*. Bern: online Publication, Institute of the History of Medicine, University of Bern, 2012.

————. *Correspondence: Henry E. Sigerist – Gregory Zilboorg, 1931–1956*. Bern: online Publication, Institute of the History of Medicine, University of Bern, 2012.

————. *Correspondence: Henry E. Sigerist – John F. Fulton: 1930–1956*. Bern: online Publication, Institute of the History of Medicine, University of Bern, 2012.

Blain, Daniel, and Michael Barton. *The History of American Psychiatry: A Teaching and Research Guide*. Washington, DC: American Psychiatric Association, 1979.

Bonnafé, Lucien, Henri Ey, Sven Follin, Jacques Lacan, and Julien Rouart. *Le Problème de la Psychogenèse des Névroses et des Psychoses*. Paris: Desclée de Brouwer, 1950.

Brennan, Robert Edward. *History of Psychology*. New York: Macmillan, 1945.

Brill, A.A. 'Anatomy of Psychoanalysis', *New York Times Book Review*, 16 May 1943, 12.

Burston, Daniel. *A Forgotten Freudian: The Passion of Karl Stern*. London: Karnac, 2016.

Daniels, Edgar. *Mass Producing the American Dream: Levittown, Long Island, as the Fulfillment of the American Dream of Single-Family Home Ownership, 1947–1951*. Chicago: privately published, 2017.

Day, Franklin. 'The Future of Psychoanalysis and Religion', *Psychoanalytic Quarterly*, vol. 13, no. 1, January 1944, 84–92.

Deutsch, Helene. 'Homosexuality in Women', *International Journal of Psycho-Analysis*, vol. 14, 1933, 34–70.

Farinholt, L. Whiting, Jr. 'Book Review: *The Psychology of the Criminal Act and Punishment*', *Maryland Law Review*, vol. 15, no. 1, 1955, 91–92.

Favez-Boutonier, Juliette. *Les Défaillances de la Volonté*. Paris: Presses Universitaires de France, 1945.

Feder, Leah. Untitled review of *Mind, Medicine, and Man*, *The Family: Journal of Social Case Work*, February 1945, 393–394.

Fee, Elizabeth. 'The Pleasures and Perils of Prophetic Advocacy: Henry E. Sigerist and the Politics of Medical Reform', *American Journal of Public Health*, vol. 86, no. 11, December 1996, 1637–1647.

Friedman, Paul. Untitled review of *Mind, Medicine, and Man*, *Psychoanalytic Quarterly*, vol. 13, no. 4, 1943, 566–571.

Galton, Francis. 'Psychometric Experiments', *Brain*, vol. 2, no. 2, July 1879, 149–162.

Goldknopf, David. 'Freud Re-Examined', *New Republic*, 19 November 1951, 18–19.

Gould, Jonathan. '*The Psychology of the Criminal Act and Punishment*', *Journal of Mental Science*, vol. 102, no. 427, April 1956, 365.

Hayakawa, S.I. 'Mind of Man and World Peace', *Chicago Sun Book Week*, 9 May 1943, np., reprinted as 'Parricide and Peace', *Etc.: A Review of General Semantics*, vol. 1, no. 1, August 1943, 60–61.

Hellman, Lillian. *An Unfinished Woman: A Memoir*. Boston: Little, Brown, 1969.

Henry, George W. *All the Sexes: A Study of Masculinity and Femininity*. New York: Rinehart, 1955.

Hoke, Travis. 'Dr. Zilboorg's Brief Freedom', *American Weekly*, 15 December 1946, 8.

Horney, Karen. 'On the Genesis of the Castration Complex in Women', *International Journal of Psycho-Analysis*, vol. 5, 1924, 50–65.

———. 'The Denial of the Vagina: A Contribution to the Problem of the Genital Anxieties Specific to Women', *International Journal of Psycho-Analysis*, vol. 14, 1933, 57–70.

———. 'The Flight from Womanhood: The Masculinity Complex in Women as Viewed by Men and by Women', *International Journal of Psycho-Analysis*, vol. 7, 1926, 324–339.

Joffe, Walter G. '*The Psychology of the Criminal Act and Punishment*: By Gregory Zilboorg', *International Journal of Psycho-Analysis*, vol. 36, 1955, 410.

Kahr, Brett. *How to Flourish as a Psychotherapist*. London: Phoenix, 2018.

Kutash, Samuel B. Untitled review of *Mind, Medicine, and Man*, *Journal of Criminal Psychopathology*, vol. 5, no. 1, July 1943, 201–203.

Lussier, André. 'Rencontre avec … André Lussier', Interview with Pierre Michaud, Montréal, 28 November 2001, *Revue Québécoise de Psychologie*, vol. 24, no. 3, 2003, np.

Maddox, Brenda. *Freud's Wizard: The Enigma of Ernest Jones*. London: John Murray, 2006.

Mailloux, Noël. 'Rencontre avec … Noël Mailloux', interview with Josette Garon, Jacques Mauger, François Péraldi, Gabrielle Clerk, and André Lussier, Montréal, 5 February 1987, *Revue Québécoise de Psychologie*, vol. 20, no. 1, 1999, 1–14.

Menninger, Karl. 'Books on Health', *Hygeia*, July 1943, 536.

Merton, Thomas. *A Search for Solitude*, ed. Lawrence Cunningham. *The Journals of Thomas Merton, Volume 3: 1952–1960*. San Francisco: HarperSanFrancisco, 1997.

———. *Ascent to Truth*. New York: Harcourt, Brace, 1951.

———. 'The Neurotic Personality in Monastic Life', *Merton Annual: Studies in Culture, Spirituality and Social Concerns*, vol. 4. New York: AMS Press, 1991, 5–19.

———. *Witness to Freedom: The Letters of Thomas Merton in Times of Crisis*, ed. William H. Shannon. San Diego: Harcourt, Brace, 1994.

Millis, Walter. 'Impact of Freudian Psychology: An Exposition of its Contribution to Current Problems', *New York Herald Tribune Weekly Book Review*, 30 May 1943, 6.

Moore, Thomas Verner. Untitled review of *Mind, Medicine, and Man*, *New Scholasticism*, vol. XVII, no. 3, July 1943, 285–288.

Mora, George. 'Early American Historians of Psychiatry: 1910–1960', *Discovering the History of Psychiatry*, ed. Mark S. Micale and Roy Porter. New York: Oxford UP, 1994, 53–80.

Mullahy, Patrick. 'Mental Problems', *Saturday Review*, 10 November 1951, 13.

Mulvey, Laura. 'Visual Pleasure and Narrative Cinema', *Screen*, vol. 16, no. 3, Autumn 1975, 6–18.

Neenan, Benedict. *Thomas Verner Moore: Psychiatrist, Educator and Monk*. Mahwah, NJ: Paulist Press, 2000.

Negovsky, Vladimir A. 'Some Physiopathologic Regularities in the Process of Dying and Resuscitation', *Circulation*, vol. 23, March 1961, 452–457.

Odier, Charles. *Les Deux Sources Consciente et Inconsciente de la Vie Morale*. Neuchatel: Editions de la Baconnière, 1943.

Overholser, Winfred. 'Man's Behavior', *Scientific Monthly*, vol. LVII, no. 3, September 1943, 275.

Plath, Sylvia. *The Bell Jar* [1963]. New York: Bantam, 1971.

Quinn, Susan. *A Mind of Her Own: The Life of Karen Horney*. Reading, MA: Addison Wesley, 1987.

Riesman, David. *The Lonely Crowd*. New Haven: Yale UP, 1950.

Roberts, William H. 'How Close are Religion and Psychiatry in their Approaches to Sin and Salvation?', *New Republic*, 16 May 1955, 16–18.

Roche, Philip Q. Untitled review of *The Psychology of the Criminal Act and Punishment*, *National Probation and Parole Association Journal*, vol. 1, no. 2, October 1955, 178.

Samway, Patrick, ed. *The Letters of Robert Giroux and Thomas Merton*. Notre Dame, IN: Notre Dame UP, 2015.

Sigerist, Henry, ed. *Four Treatises of Theophrastus van Hohenheim Called Paracelsus*. Baltimore: Johns Hopkins UP, 1941.

———. 'Nationalism and Internationalism in Medicine', *Bulletin of the History of Medicine*, January–February 1947, 5–16.

———. *The Great Doctors: A Biographical History of Medicine* (1931), transl. Eden Paul and Cedar Paul. New York: W.W. Norton, 1933.

———. *The University at the Crossroads: Addresses and Essays*. New York: Henry Schuman, 1946.

Stern, Karl. *The Pillar of Fire*. New York: Harcourt, Brace, 1951.

Sumner, Francis Cecil. Untitled review of *Mind, Medicine, and Man*, *Psychological Bulletin*, vol. 41, no. 2, February 1944, 134.

Weihoffen, Henry. 'Book Review: *The Psychology of the Criminal Act and Punishment*', *Indiana Law Journal*, vol. 30, no. 2, Winter 1955, 289.

Wertham, Frederic. 'While Rome Burns', *New Republic*, 24 May 1943, 707–708.

White, Victor. 'Dogma and Mental Health', *Life of the Spirit*, vol. 12, no. 142, April 1958, 436–442.

Wickware, Francis Sill. 'Marshall Field III: He Tries to Atone for His Many Millions by Good Works and Profitless Journalism', *Life*, 18 October 1943, 102–118.

Woolf, Virginia. *A Room of One's Own*. New York: Harcourt, Brace, 1929.

Zamiatin, Eugene. *We*, transl. Gregory Zilboorg. New York: Dutton, 1924.

Zilboorg, Gregory. *A History of Medical Psychology* (with two final chapters, 'Organic Mental Diseases' and 'Mental Hospitals' by George W. Henry). New York: W.W. Norton, 1941.

————. 'A Step Toward Enlightened Justice', *University of Chicago Law Review*, vol. 22, no. 2, Winter 1955, 331–335.

————. 'Affects, Personal and Social', *Psychoanalytic Quarterly*, vol. 14, no. 1, January 1945, 28–45.

————. 'Clinical Variants of Moral Values', *American Journal of Psychiatry*, vol. 106, no. 10, April 1950, 744–747.

————. 'Commencement Address', *Westonian*, vol. LVI, no. 4, Autumn 1950, 3–9.

————. 'Derivation, Structure, and Function of the Superego', *Ministry and Medicine in Human Relations*, ed. Iago Galdston. Madison, CT: International UP, 1955, 100–118.

————. 'Development of the Concept of the Dynamic Process in Psychiatry', *The Historical Development of Physiological Thought*, ed. Chandler McC. Brooks and Paul F. Cranefield. New York: Hafner, 1959, 137–147.

————. 'Eugen Bleuler and Present-Day Psychiatry', *American Journal of Psychiatry*, vol. 114, no. 4, October 1957, 289–298.

————. 'Fear of Death', *Psychoanalytic Quarterly*, vol. 12, October 1943, 465–475.

————. *Freud: An Address Delivered at the Grolier Club*. Mount Vernon, NY: Peter Pauper, 1956.

————. *Freud and Religion: A Restatement of an Old Controversy*. Westminster, MD: Newman, 1958.

————. 'Freud's Fundamental Psychiatric Orientation', *International Journal of Psycho-Analysis*, vol. XXXV, Part II, 1954, 1–5.

————. 'Freud's One Hundredth Anniversary', *Psychoanalytic Quarterly*, vol. 25, no. 2, 1956, 139–146.

————. 'His Own Cook', *Journal of the History of Medicine and Allied Sciences*, vol. VIII, no. 2, 1958, 155–159.

————. 'Historical Sidelights on the Problem of Delinquency', *American Journal of Psychiatry*, vol. 100, no. 7, May 1944, 757–761.

————. 'Ignorance – Amateur and Professional', *The Nation*, 2 September 1950, 207–208.

————. 'Legal Aspects of Psychiatry', *One Hundred Years of American Psychiatry: 1844–1944*, ed. J. K. Hall, Gregory Zilboorg, and Henry Alden Bunker. New York: Columbia UP, 1944, 507–584.

————. 'Love in Freudian Psychoanalysis', *Selection II: A Second Yearbook of Contemporary Thought*, ed. Cecily Hastings and Donald Nicholl. London and New York: Sheed and Ward, 1954, 159–179.

————. 'Masculine and Feminine: Some Biological and Cultural Aspects', *Psychiatry: Journal of the Biology and Pathology of Interpersonal Relations*, vol. 7, no. 3, August 1944, 257–296.

————. 'Medical History as a Force in Medical Functioning', *Victor Robinson Memorial Volume: Essays on Historical Medicine*, ed. Solomon R. Kagan. New York: Froben, 1948, 3–8.

————. *Mind, Medicine, and Man*. New York: Harcourt, Brace, 1943.

————. 'Murder and Justice', *Journal of Criminal Psychopathology*, vol. V, no. 1, July 1943, 1–25.

————. ed. (with J. K. Hall and Henry Alden Bunker) *One Hundred Years of American Psychiatry: 1844–1944*. New York: Columbia UP, 1944.

———. 'Present Trends in Psychoanalytic Theory and Practice', *Bulletin of the Menninger Clinic*, vol. 8, no. 1, January 1944, 3–8.

———. 'Psychiatric Problems in the Wake of the War', *Rhode Island Medical Journal*, vol. XXVII, August 1944, 385–386, 413–415, 417.

———. 'Psychiatry as a Social Science', *American Journal of Psychiatry*, vol. 99, no. 4, January 1943, 585–588.

———. *Psychoanalysis and Religion*, ed. Margaret Stone Zilboorg. New York: Farrar, Straus and Cudahy, 1962.

———. 'Psychoanalytic Borderlines', *American Journal of Psychiatry*, vol. 112, no. 9, March 1956, 706–710.

———. 'Psychological Conflict', a section of 'Psychosis & Neurosis: St. John's Mental Health Institute Examines the Problems of Mental Illness', *Jubilee: A Magazine of the Church and Her People*, vol. 4, no. 7, November 1956, 12–13.

———. 'Psychopathologie Scientifique et Questions Religieuses', *Sciences de l'Homme*, no. 2, 1953, 29–40.

———. 'Psychosomatic Medicine: A Historical Perspective', *Psychosomatic Medicine*, vol. VI, no. 1, January 1944, 3–6.

———. 'Rediscovery of the Patient', *Progress in Psychotherapy*, ed. Frieda Fromm-Reichmann and J. L. Moreno. New York: Grune and Stratton, 1956, 108–110.

———. Review, 'Bypaths on the Road to Vienna: The Author' (a profile of Erich Fromm), *Saturday Review*, 11 April 1959, 40.

———. Review, *The Life and Work of Sigmund Freud: The Last Phase, 1919–1939* (vol. III) by Ernest Jones, *Psychoanalytic Quarterly*, vol. 27, 1958, 253–262.

———. Review, '*Sexual Behavior in the Human Female*' by Alfred C. Kinsey et al., *Journal of the American Medical Association*, vol. 154, no. 12, 20 March 1954, 1045.

———. Review, '*The Urge to Punish*' by Henry Weihofen, *Brooklyn Law Review*, vol. 23, no. 1, December 1956, 175–177.

———. 'Scientific Positivism Cannot Be Identified with Calvinistic Theory', *New Republic*, 16 May 1955, 18.

———. 'Scientific Psychopathology and Religious Issues', *Journal of Mental Science*, vol. 100, no. 419, April 1954, 402–410.

———. 'Scientific Psychopathology and Religious Issues', *Theological Studies*, vol. XIV, no. 2, June 1953, 288–297.

———. *Sigmund Freud: His Exploration of the Mind of Man*. New York: Scribner, 1951.

———. 'Sigmund Freud in the Perspective of Medical History', *Bulletin of the New York Academy of Medicine*, vol. 32, no. 12, December 1956, 894–902.

———. 'Social Convictions and Clinical Psychiatry', *Bulletin of the New York Academy of Medicine*, vol. 29, no. 5, May 1953, 411–419.

———. 'Some Aspects of Psychiatry in the U.S.S.R.', *American Review of Soviet Medicine*, vol. 1, no. 6, August 1944, 562–575.

———. 'Some Denials and Affirmations of Religious Faith', *Faith, Reason, and Modern Psychiatry: Sources for a Synthesis*, ed. Francis J. Braceland. New York: P.J. Kenedy, 1955, 99–121.

———. 'Some Primitive Trends in Civilized Justice', *Journal of Criminal Psychopathology*, vol. IV, no. 4, April 1943, 599–604.

———. 'The Abuse of the Psychological in Present-Day Clinical Psychiatry', *Bulletin of the New York Academy of Medicine*, vol. 33, no. 2, February 1957, 89–97.

———. 'The Abuse of the Psychological in Present-Day Clinical Psychiatry: Society Proceedings', *Journal of Nervous and Mental Diseases*, vol. 123, no. 3, March 1956, 302–303.

———. 'The Changing Concept of Man in Present-Day Psychiatry', *American Journal of Psychiatry*, vol. III, no. 6, December 1954, 445–448; reprinted in *Freud and the 20th Century*, ed. Benjamin Nelson. New York: Meridian, 1957, 22–31.

———. 'The Clinical Issues of Postpartum Psychopathological Reactions', *American Journal of Obstetrics and Gynecology*, vol. 73, no. 2, February 1957, 305–312.

———. 'The Conceptual Vicissitudes of the Idea of Schizophrenia', *Schizophrenia in Psychoanalytic Office Practice*, ed. Alfred H. Rifkin. New York and London: Grune and Stratton, 1957, 30–39.

———. 'The Contribution of Psycho-Analysis to Forensic Psychiatry', *International Journal of Psycho-Analysis*, vol. 37, 1956, 318–324.

———. (transl.). 'The Diseases That Deprive Man of His Reason, by Paracelsus, with an Introductory Essay', *Four Treatises of Theophrastus van Hohenheim Called Paracelsus*, ed. Henry E. Sigerist. Baltimore: Johns Hopkins, 1941, 135–212.

———. 'The Doctor and Tomorrow', *Virginia Medical Monthly*, vol. 69, October 1942, 533–534.

———. *The Medical Man and the Witch during the Renaissance*. Baltimore: Johns Hopkins, 1935.

———. *The Passing of the Old Order in Europe*. New York: Thomas Seltzer, 1920.

———. 'The Problem of Ambulatory Schizophrenias', *American Journal of Psychiatry*, vol. 113, no. 6, December 1956, 519–525.

———. 'The Psychiatry of a Technological Civilization', *Social Science*, vol. 21, no. 3, July 1946, 201–205.

———. 'The Psychology of the Creative Personality', *Creativity: An Examination of the Creative Process*, ed. Paul Smith. New York: Communication Arts Books, 1959, 21–32.

———. *The Psychology of the Criminal Act and Punishment*. New York: Harcourt, Brace, 1954.

———. 'The Psycho-Social Paradoxes of Returning from the War', *Mental Health Bulletin* (of the Illinois Society for Mental Health), vol. XXIII, no. 2, March–April 1945, 1, 4–8.

———. 'The Reciprocal Responsibilities of Law and Psychiatry', *The Shingle*, April 1949, 79–96.

———. 'The Role of the Psychiatrist as an Expert Witness in Criminal Court', *Bulletin of the New York Academy of Medicine*, vol. 32, no. 3, March 1956, 196–201.

———. 'The Sense of Guilt', *Proceedings of the Institute for the Clergy on Problems in Pastoral Psychology*. New York: Fordham UP, 1956, 5–22.

———. 'The Struggle for and Against the Individual in Psychotherapy', *American Journal of Psychiatry*, vol. 104, no. 8, February 1948, 524–527.

———. 'Thirty-Five Years Later', *We*, Eugene Zamiatin. New York: Dutton, 1959, xix–xx.

———. (transl.). *We*, Eugene Zamiatin, 2nd edn. New York: Dutton, 1959.

———, et al. 'American Sex Standards: A Law School Forum Discussion', *Harvard Alumni Bulletin*, 15 January 1949, 306–309.

Zilboorg, Margaret Stone. 'Introduction', *Psychoanalysis and Religion*, Gregory Zilboorg, ed. Margaret Stone Zilboorg. New York: Farrar, Straus and Cudahy, 1962, vii–xi.

Abbreviations and notes

APD	Noël Mailloux Papers, Les Archives Provinciales Dominicaines, Montréal, Québec, Canada
AZ	Anna (formerly Nancy) Zilboorg
BIO	GZ, biographical statement, 4 January 1925, Archives and Special Collections, A.C. Long Health Sciences Library, Columbia University
DL	David Levy Papers, Oskar Diethelm Library, Weill Cornell Medical College
EZ	Eugenia Zilboorg
GWH	George W. Henry
GZ	Gregory Zilboorg
GZB	Gregory Zilboorg Papers, Yale Collection of American Literature, Beinecke Rare Book and Manuscript Library
HES	Henry E. Sigerist
HMP	*A History of Medical Psychology*
JEZB	James and Eugenia Zilboorg Papers, Yale Collection of American Literature, Beinecke Rare Book and Manuscript Library
JZ	James Zilboorg
MMM	*Mind, Medicine, and Man*
MSZ	Margaret Stone Zilboorg
NM	Noël Mailloux
NYPS	New York Psychoanalytic Society
NYPSB	Minutes, special meetings of NYPS Board of Directors
NYPSI	Archives and Special Collections of the NYPS and Institute
SJU	Saint John's University Archives, Collegeville, Minnesota
TM	Thomas Merton

In Britain 'psychoanalysis' often appears as 'psycho-analysis' until the mid-twentieth century; I have preserved the orthography without the use of *sic*.

Surviving notes from Gregory Zilboorg to Margaret Stone Zilboorg are in my possession; few are dated, although it is sometimes possible to date them from envelopes or internal evidence; many are similar in wording and spirit. I have used them freely without notes where they elucidate the narrative and offer a view of his life and personality otherwise undocumented.

Gregory Zilboorg's writing in English generally followed American conventions for spelling and punctuation. I have followed the conventions of the originals when quoting while following in English translations of his letters the same British conventions I myself follow.

I have generally chosen to refer to my father as 'Gregory'. Similarly, I refer to my mother as 'Peg' and to my grandparents as 'Moses' and 'Anna', 'Louis' and 'Louise'. Other family members and friends, whom I knew or who were spoken of throughout my childhood, I also refer to by their first names. Edward Mortimer Morris Warburg and his wife Mary Prue Currier Warburg appear as 'Eddie' and 'Mary' and Abram Abeloff as 'Abe'; Henry Sigerist sometimes appears as 'Henry' and Lillian Hellman and Dashiell Hammett as 'Lillian' and 'Dash'. I seldom refer to myself, but appear occasionally in the narrative after 1948 as 'Caroline' or 'Carrie', my childhood nickname.

Index

Chapter titles are accompanied by dates and are generally descriptive; many events can be easily found and do not appear here. For similar reasons, the entry for Gregory Zilboorg is brief and does not attempt to recapitulate the trajectory of his life. Since the biography draws throughout on Henry Sigerist's correspondence, the entry for Sigerist is also brief as is the entry for Noël Mailloux, who played an important role in Gregory Zilboorg's life from the time of their first meeting in 1943. Most Zilboorg family members, mentioned throughout the text, are listed here only to indicate specific images. The entry under Sigmund Freud's name directs readers to references to Freud as a person and not to the many references to Freudian psychoanalysis.

Made in the USA
Middletown, DE
16 October 2021

50412692R00170